Praise for
The Unanswered Letter

"*The Unanswered Letter* combines journalistic precision, compelling narrative, and deeply personal reflection in a profound human story—one with no easy answers, but many crucial questions and important insights. It's a story which we need now, perhaps more than ever. This is twenty-first-century Holocaust literature at its haunting best, inviting us all to consider the unanswered letters that call to each of us, in our lives and in today's world."

— Rabbi Brad Hirschfield, president of the National Jewish Center for Learning and Leadership

"I began reading Faris Cassell's *The Unanswered Letter* as a courtesy, but I soon became absorbed in a fascinating story of her uncovering multiple stories behind a desperate plea for help, reuniting a family in search of its roots, and the grandparents they never knew, and soon discovering the essence of the Holocaust; it is not the story of six million anonymous victims but of one person, six million times. Her writing is powerful, her research prodigious, her human instinct for uniting people admirable, and her encounter with the Bergers and their descendants on three continents memorable. The result is a work of power and passion, depth and determination."

— Michael Berenbaum, former project director at the U.S. Holocaust Memorial Museum and professor of Jewish Studies at American Jewish University

"Farris Cassell's *The Unanswered Letter* is a wonderful book about a terrible subject. I found it hard to put down. Its tender human moments of both desperation and loving care illuminate dark pages of the world's history."

— Larry McMurtry, Pulitzer Prize–winning author of *Lonesome Dove*

"Like Daniel Mendelsohn's magisterial *The Lost*, Faris Cassell's *The Unanswered Letter* beautifully answers the question that plagues the study of the Holocaust: How can we possibly begin to comprehend the loss of six million European Jews? Beginning with a seventy-year-old plea for help, Cassell is able to reconstruct an entire world, centered on a family that loved, lost, and persevered bravely in the face of unimaginable terror. Through her painstaking research and engaging writing, Cassell's readers will feel as if they know the Berger family, will comprehend the near-impossibility of escape, and will keep Alfred and Hedwig Berger, just two of six million, in their hearts. A dramatic, heartbreaking, and poignant book, a study in the power of remembrance."

—Rebecca Erbelding, historian and author of *Rescue Board*

"A journalist's quest, a family's struggle against all odds, a unique perspective on the Holocaust. Faris Cassell's *The Unanswered Letter* weaves history and memory together in her beautifully written and well-researched book. She also tells the story of the living members of the diasporic Berger clan, who through her work came to a greater understanding of their own past, a past marked not only by tragedy, but also by courage, determination, and survival."

—Barbara Corrado Pope, author of *The Blood of Lorraine*, a novel of the Dreyfus era

"Faris Cassell has done a masterful piece of research and writing; tracking a story as a journalist, she finds people and places with important stories to tell that will shed light on an evil past that can only make us better as we navigate the future. A MUST-READ!"

—Steven Ungerleider, psychologist, writer, and coproducer of HBO documentary *At the Heart of Gold*

"This inspiring book, based on an entreaty for aid written by a Viennese Jewish couple in 1939, shares a moving personal foray into the complexities and horrors of twentieth-century Jewish life and the ongoing intricacies of Jewish–Christian relations. Cassell's enthralling account of her search for the fates of Alfred and Hedwig Berger and their families during the Shoah details a remarkable journey that transformed everyone who took part in it."

—Judith R. Baskin, Philip H. Knight Professor of Humanities Emerita, University of Oregon

"As a book editor of thirty years, I can count on one hand the books I knew would be important, not just because they were well written, but because they could transform the reader and change the world. *The Unanswered Letter: One Holocaust Family's Desperate Plea for Help*, written by a Gentile journalist married to a Jewish doctor, traces an extended family's life, love, and attempted escapes based on the author's research after reading one Austrian couple's desperate plea for sponsorship, and wondering what happened. The book's message could not be more relevant to today's readers. It asks us to consider, 'Am I my brother's keeper? How can I help?'"

—Elizabeth Lyon, independent book editor and bestselling author

"In a master stroke of painstaking research, Cassell reveals in harrowing detail the history of the Anschluss and its devastating effects on a Viennese family desperate to survive—a poignant and unforgettable journey of determination and discovery."

—Georgia Hunter, bestselling author of *We Were the Lucky Ones*

"What's most striking about Faris Cassell's *The Unanswered Letter* is this writer's unwavering perseverance. It's as if she's set herself down to untangle a knot of precious gold chains, determined not to break a single one. We are in the hands of a dedicated researcher who comes at her subject with exquisite care and compassion, excavating one family's complex Holocaust legacy and allowing them, at last, to heal."

—Debra Gwartney, author of *Live Through This* and professor of writing at Pacific University

The Unanswered Letter

The
UNANSWERED
LETTER

One Holocaust Family's
Desperate Plea for Help

★

Faris Cassell

REGNERY
HISTORY

Regnery History™ is a trademark of Salem Communications Holding
Corporation
Regnery® is a registered trademark of Salem Communications Holding
Corporation

ISBN: 978-1-68451-190-7

Library of Congress Control Number: 2020006043

Published in the United States by
Regnery History
An imprint of Regnery Publishing
A Division of Salem Media Group
Washington, D.C.
www.RegneryHistory.com

Manufactured in the United States of America

10 9 8 7 6 5 4 3 2 1

Books are available in quantity for promotional or premium use.
For information on discounts and terms, please visit our website:
www.RegneryHistory.com.

To Sidney, wing to wing

And to Sarah, Daniel, Jonathan, Mark, and Sam,
who made lots of noise, asked questions like "what's for dinner?"
made me laugh when I was working, and never lost faith

CONTENTS

Alfred B E R G E R,
Schmalzhofgasse 19, W i e n VI, Germany,   August 9 th 1939

        Dear Madam,
                You are surely informed about the situation of
all jews in Central-Europe and this letter will not astonish you.
                By pure chance I got your address and as our
names are the same I hope that we belong to the same family of
Moravia.
                My daughter and her husband will go in themext
future to America. An aunt of my son in law has given them an
affidavit, but she, unfortunately, is unable to give one also to us.
                We are seized with fright thinking of the moment
when our children will leave us and we shall be left here wlone.
                The only possibility to join our children, the
dearest we have in this world, is the way to America and I beg you
instantly to send us /for me and my wife / an affidavit. - Should it
be impossible for you to procure us this affidavit of support, I am
sure that you have good friends who have this possibility to help us.
                Our children are young and laborious with a good
profession /my daughter is a music teacher and her husband is a
tailor/ and surely they will soon earn their living in order to take
care of us too. Besides we have enough energy to earn our living
ourthelves. Therefore you would not have the least trouble with us.
                I beg you once more : help us to follow our
children, it is our last and only hope.
                Thanking you in advance for your great kindness,
                        I remain, Dear Madam,
                        Yours faithfully,

Includ. Personal statem.   Alfred Berger

Personal Statement

Alfred Berger   born 2 nd July 1877 at Vienna,

    native of   : Vienna
    subject of : Germany
    native lang.: German
    religion   : jewish
    profession : merchandman

    father/dead/ : Salomon Berger

        of Třešt near Jglau /Moravia/

    mother/dead/ : Flora Berger born Brüll,

        of Pressburg, ČSR

        and his wife :

Hedwig Berger   born Grünberger,

    born 5 th August 1889 at Třešt
                near Jglau,

    native of : Vienna
    subject of : Germany
    native lang.: German
    religion   : jewish
    profession : dressmaker,seamstress,
            all householdworks,
            cooking.

    father/dead/: Bernard Grünberger

        of Pišely near Třebíč /Moravi

    mother/dead/ : Mathilde Grünberger
            born B E R G E R,

        of Třešt near Jglau /Moravia/

ALFRED AND HEDWIG BERGER FAMILY

Alfred Berger *(1877–1942) m.1909*   *Hedwig Grünberger Berger (1889–1942)*

Leo Cizes(b.1904) m. **Martha***(b.1911)*   **Gretl***(b.1920) m. Moshe*

Celia Cizes(b.1943)   *Micha(b.1942)* | *Judith(b.1948) Ofra(b.1953)*

ALFRED BERGER FAMILY

Salomon Berger (b.1840)   m. Flora Brüll (b.1848)

*Hermann(b.1873)   Mathilde(b.1874)   **Alfred***(b.1877)*   *Arnold(b.1879)   Richard(b.1883)*

m. | *m.* | *m.* | *m.* | *m.*
Magda(Mitzi)   *Alois*   **Hedwig**   *Mitzi*   *Olga(Hedwig's sister)*

Lisl(b.1906)   Willi(b.1912)   Ernst(b.1916)   Trudi(b.1913)   Loli(b.1914)   Anita(Ani)(b.1919)

m. | *m.*
Fritz Wulkan   *Herta*

Peter(b.1948)   *Amnon*

HEDWIG GRÜNBERGER BERGER FAMILY

Bernard Grünberger (b.1860) m. Mathilde Berger (b.ca.1869)

Hedwig*(b.1889)*   *Olga(b.1891)*   *Hugo(b.1897)   Otto~twins(b.1900)~Julius*

m. | *m.* | *m.* | *m.*
Alfred   *Richard(Alfred's brother)*   *Hella*   *Edith*

Trudi | *Loli   Anita(Ani)*   *Eva Ruth(b.1938)*

Berger and Grünberger family trees.

Foreword

This is a work of nonfiction. It is the story of a journey, mine and others', into the world of a letter dated August 5, 1939, and sent to strangers in America. I was given this letter in early 2000. All the events in these pages are true. Since Alfred Berger and his wife Hedwig lived and died well over a half-century ago, I have relied on survivors, witnesses, scholars and scholarly works, libraries, archives, original documents and archival photos, and the Berger family to bring their story into focus. This book grew out of years of research, countless interviews, and thousands of miles of travel. I have changed the name of just one interview subject, "Frau Huber," for her privacy.

In telling this true story of the Holocaust, I have used a relatively new convention that I first encountered in the writings of James Carroll. In his award-winning book *Constantine's Sword*, Carroll delegitimizes the pseudo-scientific, racist term "Semitic" by writing the "s" in lower case and eliminating the hyphen in "anti-Semitic" and "anti-Semitism." I have also extended this convention to delegitimize the equally ignorant Nazi-embraced term "Aryan," laden as it is with eugenic racism, by decapitalizing that bit of pseudo-science as well.

Introduction
The Letter

January 2000

The letter that so affected our lives came to us, it seemed, by chance. It wasn't addressed to us. We weren't the first to receive it. It had traveled more than seven thousand miles and some sixty years to arrive at our door. But I wonder, is that chance?

My husband arrived home from his office one blustery evening, his arms loaded as usual with files, phone notes, and medical journals. I was stirring soup while plotting the week's writing deadlines—my weekly newspaper column and a complicated feature story—and carpools. Our golden retriever circled, cruising for dropped food. Our teenage son called from the family room, "When is dinner?" A day like many others.

But then it wasn't. Sidney set his coat and papers on the kitchen bench and began rummaging through them, mumbling. "Letter... patient..." Unearthing a wrinkled envelope from the tumbling stack, he turned it over, examining it. I dropped vegetables into the bubbling pot and waited, curious.

He explained that a patient named Margaret had given him this letter. Her now-deceased aunt and uncle had received it just before World War II. After they died in the mid-1970s, Margaret found it among their keepsakes, and she, too saved it.

"Her health is declining," he continued. "She's putting her papers and her life in order. She feels that this letter is important and thought I might know what to do with it."

He frowned, rubbing his forehead, then held the letter out to me.

"Why you?" I took the envelope. How could someone's old family letter be connected to my husband?

An ironic half-smile spread across his face. "I'm probably the only Jew she knows."

✦

I scrutinized the envelope. It felt like a stranger entering my home, unknown, intrusive but somehow important. I doubted it would hold much connection to me. The envelope looked ready to fall apart. It was brittle in my hand. Two sides were slit open, and the third, ragged, clung by a finger's breadth at one corner. The stamp and postmark had been cut off, like medals stripped from a uniform, but the typed address was intact: Mrs. Clarence Berger, 155 52nd Street, Los Angeles, California.

On the back, a return name and address: Berger.

Probably family.

Schmalzhofgasse 19. A street in Wien, Germany.

Vienna, *Germany?*

My background in history kicked in. Pieces began to fit together… Vienna under the Nazis…

I slid two typed folded sheets from the frayed envelope. Tissue-thin pages, fragile as butterfly wings, unfolded in my hand with a rustle that seemed almost a sigh. I realized I was holding my breath.

The letter was dated August 7, 1939—a time when the United States was emerging from the Depression, but a portentous time in Europe. Menaced by Germany's increasing belligerence, nations across Europe had moved to high alert. Desperate Jews scoured the world for refuge from deadly Nazi persecution. I began to read.

"Dear Madam…."

I was the third "Madam" to read this letter, miles and decades away from the world of the writer and the intended recipient. I skipped to the signature: "Yours Faithfully, Alfred Berger." Feeling the crinkled, yellowed sheets, I thought how improbable this was. Alfred Berger could not have imagined that his missive would find its way into my hands more than a half century after he had written it.

"You are surely informed about the situation of all Jews in Central Europe and this letter will not astonish you.... By pure chance I got your address.... I beg you instantly to send us/ for me and my wife/ an affidavit...."

The California Bergers were *not* family, yet the writer had not bothered with any prelude here; there was no polite dance of greetings. He began with a quick explanation, then leapt to a brazen request: he hoped to immigrate to America and needed an affidavit of support from an American citizen—so he had approached a complete stranger.

Despite his urgency, Alfred Berger was purposely vague about his "situation." I reasoned that he was avoiding censors and the dire repercussions for anyone careless enough to criticize Nazis. In reality, Mrs. Clarence Berger may not have been informed about the crisis for Jews in Germany and Austria. Accounts of Nazi persecution had appeared in newspapers, on the radio, and in movie newsreels around the world for several years, but that news vied for Americans' attention with issues closer to home: still dire economic problems and the threat of a new war that Americans—remembering the horror of World War I's carnage—were reluctant to face.

Today Alfred Berger's "situation" is clear. His cautious term referred to the Nazi terror that marked the beginning of the Holocaust.

Germany had overrun Austria in March 1938, the year before Alfred wrote his letter. In one astonishing day, Austria, rich in history and culture, was transformed into a subservient district of the German Third Reich. Even now, nearly a century later, neither historians nor Austrians can agree on an adequate term for that event. Invasion, territorial grab, coup, revolution—it was all of these, but the emotionally debated history is still known by the name Hitler gave it: *Anschluss*, union. On that day, Alfred Berger and his wife lost all their rights and freedom as Vienna descended into a nightmare of hatred, greed, and cruelty.

The late summer sun was probably shining brightly in Los Angeles when Mrs. Clarence Berger reached into her front porch mailbox and pulled out this letter, just days before Nazi Germany stormed into Poland and ignited World War II.

In his letter, Alfred carefully explained to Mrs. Berger that he was writing on the chance they were related. He promised that even if they were not, he and his wife did not need financial support. They wished only to follow their daughter, a piano teacher, and her husband, a tailor, who would immigrate to the United States soon. Near the end of the letter, his restraint crumbled: "We are seized with fright.... I beg you... help us...it is our last and only hope."

Like most people, I knew a little about the Holocaust, its cruelty, and the millions of Jews and other people lost. Here was a piece of that event, a plea from one human being to another: "Help us."

The soup was boiling. I turned it to simmer and returned to the letter. I asked Sidney if Margaret had told him anything more. Did her family help those besieged Jews? Did they know what happened to the Viennese Bergers? He shook his head.

I picked up Alfred's second sheet, a brief family chronology showing that he was sixty-two years old, born in Vienna, and a "merchandman." His wife Hedwig was twelve years younger—quite a difference. He had listed her skills—"dressmaker, seamstress, all householdworks, cooking"—emphasizing her willingness to work also. The Viennese Bergers had been ordinary folks. I noticed that they could not list any citizenship: they were *subjects* of Germany. The term was chilling. Reich laws had robbed Alfred and Hedwig of their very nationality—and the protections of citizenship. In advance of any clear plan for a "final solution," Germany had already begun paving the road to death.

I read on. Their parents had been born in the former Austro-Hungarian Empire in Pišely, Třešt, Jglau. This plea must have felt distant and otherworldly to the Los Angeles Bergers. Would most

Americans have heard of those places? I had not. How is Jglau even pronounced? Alfred Berger's letter probably astonished Mrs. Clarence Berger. It astonished me.

Sidney and I looked at each other without speaking, at a loss for what to say. The thin paper crackled between my fingers. Despite the decades that had passed since the letter was written, I felt that I held lives in my hands, suspended in these lines: the couple carefully identified, the terror palpable. Now, more than a half century later, with hindsight, the danger and the terror that Alfred Berger avoided describing is crystal clear. But what had happened to him and his family? The letter offered no resolution. Had there been an answer to the plea that reached across the years? I reflected that I regularly tossed out emotional requests for help, from scammers around the world and legitimate charitable organizations. But this letter had come directly from the hands of a man fighting for his life and his family. What would I have done if I had received it? I wasn't sure. Alfred Berger's request was large. I did grasp that if Sidney and I had lived at that time in Vienna, our family, too, would have been running for our lives.

I pressed Sidney once more: Did Margaret say anything else? Had he thought what to do with the letter? He shrugged, his half-smile gone.

It was late. I set the letter on the kitchen desk and returned to the stove, but the letter had already taken hold of my heart. I was transfixed, wanting to know more. What had happened to Alfred Berger's family those many years ago?

Part I

CHAPTER 1
Ordinary People

February 2000

The letter begging for lifesaving help lay untouched for weeks. Yet it stayed in our thoughts and disturbed us. We walked past it daily, unsure what to do with it. We felt its grim horror. It seemed that Margaret's family had felt that also; the letter had lived in shadowy corners of their lives for decades.

The letter's unanswered questions tugged at us. What should we do with it? Who were these Viennese Jews? Did the family escape? In 1939, the Nazi noose was tightening around Jews under the control of the Reich, but my natural skepticism poked at me: Could this letter have been some kind of hoax? Did Mrs. Clarence Berger answer the letter?

Our busy lives pulled us in other directions. After several weeks, Sidney seemed ready to put the letter behind us, maybe find a museum that would want it.

Inexplicably, the letter struck me harder than it hit him, jolting my sense of stability. Our family histories are vastly different. My husband's family had lived for centuries in western Russia, now Belarus, but his grandparents immigrated to America around 1900, leaving Russian repression for a better life. All of his family who remained there—aunts, uncles, cousins, great-grandparents—disappeared in the Holocaust. When Sidney was growing up, his parents experienced and occasionally talked about antisemitism in their own lives, but they rarely mentioned their murdered family. When he asked about those missing family members, all that anyone would say was, "They were lost in the war."

Ancestors of mine, in contrast, had come to America with the Pilgrims. Others fought in the Revolution. One distant relative, Hugh Hall, had explored the West with Lewis and Clark. Later generations, including my parents, spoke angrily about the influx of immigrants into "our country." No one mentioned the Holocaust. When Sidney and I first discussed marrying, his family welcomed me, but my parents objected, and the discord, laden with long-held antisemitism, was painful. I hadn't been raised with antisemitic talk, but the animus was there, only gradually to be replaced by a warm, loving bond between Sidney and my parents.

Over the years, Sidney and I built a bridge between our two worlds, Jewish and Christian, but it was shaky. We had experienced both the beautiful and the frigid, clannish, excluding aspects of each religion. Insiders and outsiders, we flinched at hurtful remarks that flew in both directions: "Kike." "Goy." "Chosen people." "You have to choose."

Did we have to choose? We didn't think so, and we couldn't. We loved the common core of both religions, as we loved each other. In recent years, I had thought we'd resolved our distress around this conflicted part of our lives. We participated in both religions and taught both to our children. But Alfred Berger's letter churned up those dormant emotions. In 1930s Vienna there had been no safe, accepting, middle ground like we found in America. The letter stirred my old worries that division and hatred among different groups could flare anywhere, anytime.

I wanted to interview Margaret, and Sidney agreed to tell her about my interest. I hoped to find and write an inspiring, reassuring "Greatest Generation" story of a family that had risked helping a desperate stranger. But I understood that the Los Angeles Bergers might have questioned the letter's authenticity, worried about financial entanglements, and ignored the plea—as my own family probably would have.

I met twice with Margaret and her daughter Lynn, a nurse. White-haired and in her mid-eighties, Margaret repeated to me the brief account she had given Sidney. She knew almost nothing about the letter. She explained several times that her uncle had shown it to her only once, in the mid-1950s, at the time when Clarence had sponsored Margaret herself for immigration to the U.S. He had said very little about the letter, then put it away. When I asked whether her aunt and uncle had sent a reply, Margaret equivocated. She said that they did not; later she said that they did but had not received a reply. Margaret was certain there had been no family connection. Her uncle's family had emigrated from Germany in the mid-1800s and Anglicized their name from Bereger. Her Aunt Bea had emigrated from Canada. Her family was not Jewish, she said several times, as if that explained everything.

We chatted for several hours about her aunt and uncle. They'd had no children. He and Bea had endured lean years during the Depression but managed to build a secure working-class life. Bea had been a home-maker. Clarence owned a car repair shop in the Watts neighborhood of South Los Angeles, then worked for a company that repossessed cars, mostly from the black ghetto emerging around his home. He had developed strong racial prejudices, Margaret admitted.

The fact that both Bea and her niece Margaret were immigrants to the United States added an intriguing angle to the story. But I had come to a dead end in our conversation. I backed up and asked Margaret and Lynn why they thought their family had kept this letter for so long.

Lynn answered that when her mother cut off the envelope's stamps and gave them to a church fundraising project, Lynn had urged Margaret to save the letter.

Margaret's tone was soft as she answered, slowly and thoughtfully. She couldn't speak for her aunt and uncle, she said, but for herself, she would take the letter from its various storage places to read from time to time. "I've always wanted to know what happened to them. Each time

I read the letter, I felt the plea. We have no idea what those people went through, how desperate they were. The letter should be some place where it will bring to mind what happened back then."

Lynn listened quietly during most of the conversation, but when her mother spoke so openly, she burst out, "I knew my aunt and uncle well. I do not believe they would have tried to help those people. I hope they made it. I'm ashamed that our family did not help them."

Here, from both of them, was the solid ground I'd sought, the connection that bound Margaret, Lynn, possibly their aunt and uncle, and me to the letter. More powerful than curiosity or a sense of responsibility for preserving history was the pull of the human heart: we cared what had happened to these terrified strangers in Wien, Germany.

As I gathered my recorder and notes preparing to leave, Margaret suggested that others might know more. She handed me contact information, decades old, for Clarence's and Bea's families. Surprisingly, she then went to a back room and emerged, her arms full of rolled-up papers. If I could find Clarence's relatives, she wanted me to give them these family documents—marriage certificates from the 1800s, newspaper clippings of births and deaths, military records of Clarence's army service in Europe during World War I.

Leaving their home, I accepted that I would not find a straightforward, inspirational tale. This family's emotions were tangled. More than half a century after Clarence and Bea Berger had folded this letter and put it aside, I had set off a defensive reaction from Margaret and an apology from Lynn. I felt that I stood at the edge of a dark world that I wasn't sure I wanted to enter.

Over the next week as I rethought that interview, unresolved questions loomed in my mind and drove me back to the story. I began investigating the slim possibility that the California Bergers had responded to Alfred and Hedwig. Within a few weeks I had contacted four of Clarence and Bea Berger's relatives in California and Canada, but they had never heard of the letter. Disappointed, I accepted the likelihood that the Los

Angeles Bergers had not responded, and I filed the letter away with other intriguing dangling story ideas.

★

Life's currents drew Sidney and me into in our busy routines—his rheumatology practice, my journalism, our family. But even as years passed, I remained deeply unsettled by the plea to strangers in America. Sidney and I sometimes talked about the uncomfortable feelings it provoked. He began telling me stories I'd never heard—about growing up in a small Mississippi town where his was the only Jewish family, owners of a small store and motel. Antisemitism was as pervasive there as the cotton fields that stretched to the horizon. Other children made him pay a nickel to play with them. In school, in that conservative community, religion came up often. When a student or teacher talked about the Jews killing Jesus, he would wait for the inevitable "Sidney is Jewish!" as everyone turned to stare at him. Later, dating had been a problem; some parents refused to let him see their daughter. I had known something about his struggles, but even now, these stories came out reluctantly.

My own suburban Seattle childhood had been so different: upper middle class and Protestant; my father an attorney, my mother a homemaker. I was aware of only two or three Jewish students in my high school of sixteen hundred students. Sidney's ability to manage the obstacles of his youth impressed me. Over the years, he had made close, lifelong friends in that town, but the imprint that he was different had cut deeply. Later he had been accepted at Washington University's highly regarded medical school, but he had been careful also to apply to Thomas Jefferson University's medical school, known to accept Jews. We speculated about whether antisemitism had played a role in the Los Angeles Bergers' apparent decision not to answer the letter.

A level of unease that Sidney did not seem to experience about the letter jarred my carefully balanced world. The letter's recipients could have been my family as I grew up—and its senders could have been my current family. I understood the gaping chasm between them. My parents had belonged to clubs that admitted only WASPs, White Anglo-Saxon Protestants. When I talked about the letter with my parents, my father—who had by now grown close to Sidney, his Jewish son-in-law—made a startling admission. He revealed that before my grandparents married, my grandfather had researched my grandmother's family, the Mangolds, to confirm that she had no Jewish heritage. I learned, too, that my mother's father, a bank president, had decided not to nominate a respected businessman to a corporate board that he chaired simply because that person's family were Italian immigrants. My mother had grown up near New York City, where, she informed me, Jews were "very clannish." It was extremely unlikely that, in 1939, my family would have welcomed any immigrant.

A friend asked me if I felt guilty about this family background. She compared my discomfort to "white guilt." I'd had to think about her question, but then I laughed and said I knew that guilt was significant for some religions and some people, but I didn't find it useful. I believed guilt turns a person inward. It seems a detached, often debilitating response. For me, concepts of personal responsibility and justice are more powerful. This might seem a fuzzy distinction, but I thought not, and, yes, I felt a responsibility.

Others' reactions to the letter also surprised me. Most people who read it expressed pity for Alfred and Hedwig and scorned "those Nazis." Not one considered Americans' unrealized potential for rescuing trapped Jews—perhaps by identifying a church or synagogue that might help even one family. The message I heard was this: ordinary Americans had no connection to the Holocaust.

Sidney and I continued to talk about the letter. We admitted that an affidavit of support was a significant responsibility. We doubted whether we would have made such a commitment for a stranger. I had thought of myself as a compassionate person, but never delved into *why* I assumed so. Fissures developed in my self-image.

On the other end of the letter were the Jewish Bergers and their "situation." Extreme antisemitism had never affected me, but the message of this letter rang out loud and clear: If Sidney and I had lived in Vienna in 1939, we too would have been running for our lives. We too would have been writing letters: "I beg you...help us."

CHAPTER 2

The Search Begins

March 2004

A dding to my warring emotions about Alfred Berger's letter, I was a journalist, and I was curious. A writer writes in large part as self-discovery, and there was much in this letter that disturbed and compelled me. After wrestling with my priorities for several years, I left my work for the *Register-Guard* to begin sleuthing seriously. I didn't know, then, where I was heading, but I was moving. Alfred and Hedwig might have sent multiple letters pleading for help. Did anyone answer? Did they escape?

The first steps in my quest for answers began with Clarence Berger. Could he have met members of Alfred Berger's family during his World War I military service? Looking over his army record, I saw that Private Clarence Berger had served in northeast France, across the Belgian border from the battlefield where young Corporal Adolf Hitler had fought and been injured. In that war Jews were not banned from military service. In fact they had a significant presence in the German army. I was disappointed to learn that Berger had been assigned to an American base hospital for his very brief military stint during the war's final days. I could see no obvious connection to any Jews in Europe.

I found no common thread between Clarence and the Viennese Bergers during that time, but as I read about the period, I realized that for both of those two young soldiers—Clarence Berger and Adolf Hitler—that time had been formative. As Private Berger sailed home to victorious, prospering America, Corporal Hitler restarted civilian life in a decimated, humiliated nation. Hitler dismissed the harsh reality that Germany's economic collapse, long string of defeats, and disintegrating morale had forced its surrender. Despite the service of thousands of Jews in the German and Austrian militaries, he blamed Jews for accepting, and thereby causing, Germany's defeat. He adopted the German generals' face-saving, stab-in-the-back rhetoric, blaming their surrender on a lack of popular support. For Hitler, Jews became the scapegoat vindicating the *Volk,* the German people. He made it his mission, his *Kampf,* to take revenge on Jews. For Hitler, defeat had thwarted Germany's imperial dreams but not destroyed them.

I was appalled to realize that Hitler's vision of a self-proclaimed superior race had been, in different forms, commonly accepted worldwide. Hitler and Clarence Berger both lived in cultures of hardening racial and ethnic stereotypes and prejudice, cloaked in the widely accepted pseudo-science of eugenics. Scientists and leaders from Churchill and Roosevelt in the West to Emperor Hirohito in Japan espoused eugenic policies that promoted ranking and "purifying" races. Religious leaders preached eugenics from their pulpits and on national radio. Thousands of Americans deemed deficient or of inferior racial mix were sterilized. The Ku Klux Klan, targeting Jews, blacks, and Catholics as enemies of the "white race," swelled to record size. Lynching, sometimes as a public spectacle, increased across the country. Hitler admired the racial violence in the United States and used it to defend his own warped and brutal vision.

That racially charged understanding of the world undoubtedly filtered into the homes of the Los Angeles Bergers—and also of my family. Most citizens supported the restrictive immigration laws passed in the 1920s. Those new laws put numbers to the vision of a racial hierarchy, slashing total immigration and setting quotas restricting immigrants from Southern and Eastern Europe, Asia, and Africa. The world kept its "huddled masses"—words inscribed on the Statue of Liberty's base—as Lady Liberty turned her cold copper back on lines of hopeful immigrants.

I learned, too, how Holocaust study had evolved. Immediately after World War II no one knew the magnitude of the loss of Jewish life or comprehended the barbarity of the atrocities. Most Americans and people worldwide—including even Jews—did not have many facts at that time, or even the language to describe such a horror. The genocide was not yet known by the then relatively obscure term *Holocaust*, which originates in the ancient Hebrew word *olah*, "completely burnt offering to God." Even today many Jews prefer the more specific term *Shoah*, the Hebrew word for catastrophe.

Facts about the Holocaust emerged slowly. Now, after decades spent documenting its existence, much historical writing addresses the conundrum of how the Holocaust could have happened and how a recurrence can be prevented. Researchers of all stripes, philosophers, religious leaders...many thoughtful people have proposed explanations, but none account for the cold-blooded murder of millions.

Investigating further, I learned of several Holocaust survivors and former Reich citizens in Eugene. I met an Oregon woman born and raised in an impoverished family in Vienna; she had rushed to eat in Nazi soup kitchens set up briefly after the Anschluss to woo Austrians' support for the German soldiers suddenly in their midst. A neighbor told me about her Protestant German mother who fled the Gestapo after carrying Jews out of the country on her motorbike. Her family had been part of an assassination attempt on Hitler's life. I wrote an article about an Oregon man's experience as Hitler's last courier in Berlin. I had never noticed the footprints of the Holocaust all around me.

✦

Shifting my attention to the fate of Alfred Berger's family, I wrote to the U.S. Holocaust Memorial Museum. An archivist there responded quickly by email: Alfred disappeared from their records in 1942. And that same year Hedwig was deported to Maly Trostenets, a German work camp near Minsk in the Soviet Union, now in Belarus.

"Well," Sidney told me, "that finishes your story. Alfred died in the Holocaust. Hedwig was deported, like so many others." We debated again what to do with the letter. Donate it to an archive? A museum? We hesitated, concerned that no matter where it went it would be filed and forgotten in some dark, dusty corner. It was, after all, a random document—a puzzle, not a story. Questions seemed to fly off the page. Alfred and Hedwig had survived in Vienna for three years after writing the letter. What trapped them there? What had those years been like? What had happened to Alfred? I could find little information about Maly Trostenets. For years records about events behind the Soviet Union's "Iron Curtain" had remained inaccessible to the outside world, and research had not caught up. I wasn't at all convinced that this story was finished.

Considering what to do next, I called the *New York Times* because a journalist there had recently written about his Austrian family's Holocaust story. I asked the operator how to contact him, expecting to be sent to his voice mail. Instead, the hubbub of the newsroom crackled through my phone, and the journalist's voice came on the line, brusque and harried, "Newsroom here." I explained about Alfred Berger's letter and my quest to investigate it. I had intended to ask the journalist about his research, but he jumped ahead, asking bluntly, "Were they important?"

I fumbled for an answer. He pressed on, "You know, were they famous?" Alfred Berger, a self-described *merchandman* and Hedwig, a homemaker and seamstress? I mumbled, "No." He wished me good luck.

I felt terrible. Of all the issues that I had considered, celebrity was not among them. This story was about compassion, moral courage, and survival. I had answered the journalist's question inadequately. Who was not important? Who decides? The question repelled me. He had asked a professional question, but for me that brief, confounding conversation pierced through a wall of indecision I had built around myself.

Alfred and Hedwig Berger had been ordinary people, like most of humanity—like me. They were important because they were human. But

Hitler, the Nazis, and the antisemites who helped carry out "the Final Solution"—or simply turned a blind eye and let it happen—saw them differently: "Jews." "Jewish Problem." "Vermin."

That abrupt conversation between the journalist and me—two people sailing past each other with no real communication—put a sharp edge to my thinking about Alfred and Hedwig's plea. A deep inner drive pushed me to learn how the Holocaust had happened to this ordinary family which could have been my own.

CHAPTER 3
Who Are You?

March 2004

I did not grasp, in the beginning, how complicated and tangled my path on this quest would be. I did know that I would need significant support. Eventually Sidney would join me, but writing, at its core, is a solitary pursuit.

Three times already I had heard that the Bergers were not important. Clarence Berger of Los Angeles had expressed a few words of sympathy about the Bergers' plight, but no compelling concern. The journalist I had contacted about the letter framed his interest solely in terms of the Bergers' public stature. Nor was Sidney impelled to learn who these people were or how that epic storm of hatred had engulfed them, though he supported my efforts to find out. Like his patient Margaret, he felt that the letter was important, but he seemed to need to keep this horrible history at a distance. Through his own family, he had heard enough. I wondered how many times during the Bergers' battle for survival they had been made to feel unimportant, expendable.

Delving into the relevant records, I was struck by the punctilious German-Austrian practice of documenting life down to the last detail. It seemed that a thing not documented was a thing neither understood nor controlled, its value in doubt. And the Nazis carried the practice of exhaustive record-keeping to a bizarre extreme. Archives of that era record staggering amounts of data from the mundane—what tree was planted along what street—to the gruesome—meeting minutes revealing intricate discussions of extermination methods and lists of which Jews were taken where, on what transport, and when they were murdered. The Reich produced astonishing records illuminating the depth and fury of their assault on Jews. This excess of precision seems to reflect pride of accomplishment. Perhaps it created an illusion of sanity in a world gone mad.

The Vienna City Archive maintains a trove of data. In 2004, its website proclaimed that city records extend from "time out of mind." Over centuries of mandatory registration, the city has collected the addresses of every citizen since birth; every move or change of household members, occupations, and marital status; the names and ages of children with their birthplaces and parents' names—and until recently, each resident's religion.

Vienna's Jewish Community Organization records also proved essential for my research. Jews in the Austro-Hungarian Empire had fought for centuries to gain the right to form a community organization like that of the Catholics who dominated Austria's culture and government. In the early 1800s, after centuries of repressing, murdering, and periodically expelling Jews, the Empire finally both permitted and required Jews to record their births, deaths, and marriages. The Community, as Jews came to call their organization, proved a blessing, drawing Vienna's Jews together in a new way, providing not only accurate records but also a range of other services and activities.

The Community thrived for a century, but then became a tool of the German occupation. Immediately after the Anschluss, the Gestapo invaded its offices. On pain of death for themselves and harsher treatment of Jews, Community leaders were forced to cede control of their office to the Reich. Unlike city records, Community files identified all Vienna's Jews separate from the general population. The carefully collected information was a boon for the Nazis and a catastrophe for the

Jews. The forced collaboration remains painfully controversial. It was this difficult history, I understood, that had determined the fate of Alfred and Hedwig under the Nazis.

I mailed, emailed, and phoned requests for information to a wide range of organizations and archives. Months passed with false starts and little progress, but my determination was sustained by the knowledge that the letter had come as if by fate to us—Sidney, Jewish, and me, Christian. A Jewish man had written this letter, two generations of Christians had saved it, and now it resided with us. We were both religious, but the differences between our religions also created a fracture line in our lives. Neither of us could immerse ourselves totally in the other religion, which left a piece of each of us separate—sometimes that was a lonely feeling for us both. For reasons that I didn't at first understand, for many months Sidney followed my progress but kept the letter at a distance. During that time, more keenly each day, I felt impelled to tell this story, though I still didn't know what the story would be.

When the first packet from the Vienna City Archives arrived, it contained photocopies of three household registration forms, *Meldezettel,* for Alfred and Hedwig. The earliest was dated 1909, the next 1929, and the last 1941. The Viennese Bergers had entered periodic updates until that year. These blurry black-and-white images offered a direct, tangible link to the past. Solid primary sources I could trust, they had been filled in by the hands of Alfred and Hedwig Berger.

I laid the cards side by side and pored over them. In December 1909, Alfred and Hedwig had registered at the district police office on Mariahilferstrasse, Mary Our Helper Street, a busy shopping street that ran one block parallel to tiny, three-block-long Schmalzhofgasse. This card also showed that as a bachelor Alfred had lived downtown on the Graben, one of Vienna's oldest, most venerable streets in the bustling heart of the city. After they married, he and Hedwig had moved into their first home at Schmalzhofgasse 19 in a more residential neighborhood. He was thirty-two; she was twenty. By the time Alfred wrote his letter, they had lived in that apartment for thirty years.

Under "Employment" he listed *beamter*—civil servant or office manager. Alfred was born in Vienna, Hedwig in Triesch, later renamed Třešt, a small town south of Prague in Moravia, a region then in the Austro-Hungarian Empire, later part of Czechoslovakia, and now in the Czech Republic. Their citizenship then was Moravian. Their religion "Mosaish," the religion of Moses.

The cards were concise and dense with information, brimming with implications about the Bergers. I was drawn to the sheer physicality of the cards. Unlike today's computer-generated data, the handwriting held its own information. Both Alfred and Hedwig wrote in an older Germanic writing style called Sütterlin, prevalent until Germany mandated a more modern script. Sütterlin includes forms and ornamentation that few German speakers today can read, creating an extra layer of translation difficulty for me.

Nevertheless, looking at the cards, I learned to distinguish Hedwig's handwriting from Alfred's. Her thin delicate writing stretched forward with a regular rhythm. Neat and easily legible, her words floated over the lines, straight as a ruler, with a few small curlicues and flourishes. On the first card, from 1909, Hedwig had filled in most of the information, while Alfred entered only his own birthdate, in thicker, darker, and irregular characters, some numbers splotched and difficult to decipher. Perhaps this was why completing the form had fallen mostly to her.

Two years later, on the same card, with the biggest and seemingly proudest writing on any card, Alfred had added the birth of Martha, the daughter he had referred to in his letter. This was a real breakthrough. With her name and birthdate, I could at last begin to trace her.

A thunderbolt of information appeared on their second card. In 1929 Martha, then eighteen, had dropped off this card, but in 1920 a second daughter, Gretl, had been born. Alfred's letter had not mentioned her. Was she still alive? Where? Did she have descendants?

His profession had changed. In an apparent improvement in his career, he was now a *kaufmann*, a merchant.

As quickly as the cards answered questions, they raised new ones. Alfred had filled in and almost entirely updated this card himself. His thick pen strokes ran light and dark within words, his later updates sometimes so heavy and scribbled they were practically illegible.

A new property owner had signed the third card, begun in 1940. This card bore a large scrawled "J," identifying the Bergers as Jewish.

Alfred and Hedwig's lives, their joys and traumas, were hidden in small spaces on these three cards. The little documents took me from the Bergers' young married life to their growing family, and then to disastrous upheavals. As I followed those once vibrant lives, starkly and impersonally compressed into a few words of happiness and decline, I found the journey of discovery exhilarating, intriguing, and upsetting.

More inquiries to Vienna's archives brought other packets that included a registration card for Martha Berger, *lehrerin*, teacher, age twenty-five, married in December 1936 to Leib Cizes, Polish citizen. Another milestone! This would be essential information for tracing Martha Cizes in America. A June 1938 card for Gretl showed that she had turned eighteen a few weeks before the Anschluss, when she had been an unemployed office worker. The day before Alfred had filled out her card, she had *ausgezogen*—moved out, emigrated. Gretl Berger had registered once as an adult, and then she was gone. I feared that tracking Gretl with only this card would be difficult.

Vienna's Jewish Community Organization sent me a helpful, lengthy email. I saw that Hedwig had been the eldest of six Grünberger children, all born in Moravia: Hedwig, Olga, Albina, Hugo, and twins Julius and Otto. Albina had died in the 1920s. Alfred was the third of five Berger siblings: Hermann, Mathilde, Alfred, Arnold, and Richard. I noted immediately that these two families had considered themselves part of Imperial Austrian culture and named their children accordingly. No Abraham or Israel, Esther or Sarah appeared on that list, which was filled instead with popular Austrian names.

I had imagined Alfred and Hedwig as living in a sort of vacuum, isolated from other people as they contended with the German occupation and increasing Nazi menace. In reality they were part of a large extended family. The new information deepened my knowledge but also expanded my search. My head spun with names and details. I confronted the reality that this story would not be as simple as I'd envisioned. Once again it had jumped the neat boundaries that I had set. New questions arose. Was the family close? Had any of them escaped?

Near the end of her email, the Community's archivist noted that Alfred had died on April 30, 1942, three weeks before Hedwig was deported. "He got an accidental death," the archivist wrote, determined to reach me across the language barrier. I stared at the screen. This ending to Alfred's life under iron-fisted Nazi rule was unexpected. This was why Alfred had disappeared from the records. But how had he died?

One evening Sidney and I sat in my study talking, again, about whether I had hit a dead end. Possibly, he thought. I looked at the piles of papers around me and felt confused. Notes, books, transcripts…and my laptop held countless emails. Despite all of this, Alfred and Hedwig remained unreal, embalmed in the past. I had a bare outline of their lives—a few basic facts—but I didn't know the people. Had they been happy? Outgoing? Solitary? Ambitious? Who were they, and how did they respond to the growing Nazi menace? Had anyone attempted to help them? I was pleased to have come this far, but doubts welled up about what else I could find. The farther I traveled down this path, the more numerous and daunting the tasks seemed to be. I laughed to myself—the devil really is in the details. I admitted, to myself and to Sidney, that I had not found answers to my questions. Following this story would mean diverting attention from other potential writing projects. I was tempted to quit.

At that point Sidney surprised me by encouraging me to continue, at least to check out the leads I'd found. "You've gone this far. I'd like to know more too." Until then, his responses to the progress I'd made had been subdued, sometimes lacking interest, which was unusual for him. Now it seemed that his wall of silence surrounding the Holocaust had developed some gaps. In those small spaces, he and I had found ground we both wanted to explore.

Invigorated, we planned a spring trip to New York's Center for Jewish History, an archive strong in Austrian history. We also set dates for a fall trip to Vienna. There, perhaps, Alfred and Hedwig Berger would emerge from the shadows.

★

Armed with the names and birthdates of Alfred and Hedwig Berger's older daughter and her husband, I began looking for them. Martha had been twenty-eight and her husband Leib Cizes thirty-five when Alfred wrote his letter; they would be quite elderly if still alive.

Decades after the Berger parents had sought sanctuary in the United States, I discovered how dramatically politics still disrupted immigration processes, and it roiled my work. A conservative Congress had slashed funding for the National Archives and Records Administration, so that access to its files was backed up more than a year. I turned to Ellis Island files, but they were being digitized. A search of Social Security records brought the news that Martha and Leo Cizes, U.S. citizens, had lived in Queens, New York. Leo—an Anglicized form of Leib, I felt sure. Martha had died in 1984, Leo in 1993. I was chagrined to learn that they had died but elated to find the information. The Bergers' older daughter and her husband had successfully immigrated to America, as Alfred had hoped.

Years too late to connect with Martha and Leo, I looked for any possible children, beginning with a simple Internet search for Cizes. I was afraid of retrieving a list too long to be useful. Instead, the unusual name brought only a few results and I saw it right away: R. Cizes, in Queens, with a phone number. It seemed that I had found a descendant of Alfred and Hedwig in America.

I held my breath and dialed, but I reached only a digital voice that instructed me to leave a message. I did. The next day, I called again. And again the next day. After days with no answer, I wrote to R. Cizes, explaining that I had come across a letter written in 1939 by Alfred Berger of Vienna seeking a sponsor for immigration to America. I was a journalist interested in learning more. Was this the correct family? Did they want the letter?

Weeks passed. A month. I called every day, left messages, and wrote again. I reasoned that an explanation for why no one answered this phone would emerge, but I grew increasingly worried that my persistence had become harassment. Perhaps R. Cizes would report me to the police.

Five weeks. I was ready to give up.

One evening in late February, I came home from the library to find Sidney eager to tell me, "You have a message you'll want to hear."

I pressed the button, and a woman's low, gravelly voice rose from my answering machine: "Hello. This is Celia Cizes. You've been trying to reach me."

CHAPTER 4
We Meet

March 2004

I returned Celia's call the next day. She was obviously suspicious. Her tone was curt, her words businesslike. She did apologize for not responding sooner: she was in Florida where she had spent the winter, the post office hadn't forwarded her mail, and her answering machine was broken.

I knew that I was a stranger with a strange, intrusive story. I apologized for my barrage of calls and letters and proceeded warily. I repeated the information that I had sent her: I was a journalist who had come across a letter from 1939 that I believed had been written by her grandfather, Alfred Berger, married to Hedwig, living on Schmalzhofgasse in Vienna. In the letter Alfred had asked strangers in Los Angeles with the same last name to sponsor his and Hedwig's immigration to America. I told her that the letter had moved me, and I wanted to find out what happened and write about it.

"How did you get the letter?"

With that question, Celia took a step toward me. I was encouraged. She hadn't hung up.

I explained again, this time in more detail. Having told this story many times, I knew it to be confusing. Celia naturally had questions for me:

"Your husband is a doctor?"

"The patient's great-aunt received it?"

"Where did his patient get the letter?"

"Why did she give it to your husband?"

I backtracked again, telling Celia about my husband, his longtime patient, and her relatives in Los Angeles. I retraced the steps that had led me to call Celia. It was a convoluted tale, and as I told it she cross-examined me, interrupting, probing, and questioning. Periodic silences suggested that she was evaluating, maybe even taking notes. I proceeded slowly, answering what she asked and introducing myself: I wrote for the Eugene daily newspaper, Sidney was Jewish, I was not, we had three children, I had a graduate degree in journalism—anything that might help her to understand my intentions and, more important, to trust me.

What I didn't tell her was the larger truth. That was hard enough for me to see. This dramatic letter had drawn me irresistibly and haunted me with questions that reverberated through my life. Might deadly hatred explode in my own world? I hoped to understand, at least a little, how divisions that separate people could grow to Holocaust dimensions. How could apathy and greed derail the human impulse for compassion? My own feelings were drawn both to the letter's author and to its apparently conflicted receiver. The letter held a story that connected directly to me. But I couldn't express such ambiguous personal emotions and expect to be taken seriously. I maintained a professional facade.

I could imagine how suspicious I would feel in Celia's situation, but I also saw that the letter was magnetic for her. I had invaded her privacy, researched her family in Europe, tracked her down, and still she persisted with her questions.

As her interrogation subsided, I began to ask questions. The first was crucial.

"Do you believe this is your grandfather's letter?"

Silence stretched across the three thousand miles between us. Slowly, quietly, she answered, "That is my grandfather."

My only connection to Celia was the letter. "Shall I read it to you?"

"Yes," she said, "please."

The letter opens with a controlled, factual tone, not unlike Celia's conversation, but even so I started slowly, carefully, knowing that, for her, land mines lay below, and that more difficult terrain would follow. "You are surely informed about the situation of all Jews...."

No response. I went on, "We are seized with fright...." A foreigner's English. The sentence sounds like a Victorian novel, but it reflects real terror. "Our daughter...affidavit...the only possibility...alone.... I beg you once more: help us to follow our children. It is our last and only hope."

Her grandfather was saying that he was helpless, trapped. Up to that point, heavy silences and terse phrases had telegraphed Celia's skeptical stance towards me, but suddenly her emotions overflowed. She said that no one in the family had ever talked about this letter. Rapid-fire, she reviewed what I'd told her about the letter's more than seventy-year trajectory. She asked again about my husband, his patient, and the Los Angeles Bergers.

"This brings up so many feelings," she admitted. "It's very painful. I haven't spoken about these things for a long time, since my father died. Some families never talk about the Holocaust. They think a wall of silence will protect them, but my parents didn't believe that. For as long as I can remember, they talked openly about my grandparents. My mother missed her parents terribly. She often cried."

As Celia spoke, I couldn't help but think about Sidney's family and their "wall of silence." Was one approach better? It was an unhappy question, and I knew that I had no answer. Perhaps there was none.

Changing course again, she said sharply, "Before we talk more, I'd like to see a copy of the letter." She asked me to scan and email it to her. She repeated, "No one in the family has heard about this letter."

This was the second time that Celia had mentioned her family's not knowing about the letter. The first had passed me by, but now the implications registered: during the past month while I awaited her response, Celia had been conferring with family.

Some had survived, and they were in touch.

Who? Where?

I had no information about the fate of Alfred and Hedwig's younger daughter, Gretl. She could be alive and have children. Understandably, Celia was telling me only what was necessary. I saw that she would continue to test me and move forward cautiously.

I had concerns too. When the war ended, its horror did not stop. For many, perhaps for all survivors and their descendants, the Holocaust did not recede into a manageable bad dream, but stalked them all their lives. They grieved and battled demons, built walls, or lived with broken hearts. After surviving the worst that life could mete out, many committed suicide. I had read about the emotional toll of forever wrestling with this dreadful past—trying to forget while vowing to remember. What imprint had one of the worst displays of inhumanity in human history left on Celia?

Two decisions that I had made along my bumpy research path guided me in that moment. First, the story mattered to me and, I believed, to the world. I was committed to this quest. Whether or not I found Berger descendants and enlisted their help, I would learn all that I could, and write about Alfred and Hedwig. That path was set. I wasn't seeking Celia's permission. Second, I would be transparent. I needed help that depended on trust. Celia and I were strangers, living in different worlds and three thousand miles apart. But sitting in my quiet study that spring morning, thinking about what lay ahead, I hoped that Celia and I could travel a distance together.

★

The first scans I sent came through as gibberish, Celia informed me by email. Would I like her computer-savvy partner, Mark, to advise me? "I'll manage," I grumbled. After several hours of grappling with my balky machine, the scans went through. Two days later, Celia called again, her voice animated. We were less guarded with each other, but she warned me, "You must understand. This is difficult." I knew that it was. I was a stranger, asking her to exhume horrible memories.

She told me that she had spoken again with family about the letter, and I asked about them. She said that she was an only child, unmarried, and had no children, but was close to her extended family in Israel. Hedwig's only sister Olga and Olga's three daughters also had lived in Vienna, and they had fled to what was then the Palestine Mandate, the British-controlled region created after World War I in the former Ottoman Empire, now Israel. One of Olga's daughters, Ani, then in her eighties, had told Celia unequivocally not to talk to me, suspecting that my intrusion was an antisemitic ruse, or worse.

It struck me that Ani's defensiveness had similarities to the Los Angeles Bergers' response to Alfred's letter: when strangers knock, keep the door shut. I was thankful that Celia was still open to talking.

Next Celia told me that she had also phoned a younger Israeli cousin, Judith—Alfred and Hedwig's granddaughter by their younger daughter Gretl. I hadn't known Gretl's fate and was pleased to learn that she had escaped. Celia told me that Gretl Berger had fled Vienna on an illegal ship to Palestine. "Do you know about the famous *Exodus?* But a *pirate* ship." Gretl had married, lived on a farm, and raised three children, but died of cancer in 1967.

Again, time was not on my side. I wasn't surprised that the Bergers' daughters had both died by this time, but I was disappointed. Still, my journalist's antennae flew up. I was thankful that Celia was such a generous, knowledgeable source. She drew me in with her colorful descriptions, and I saw that she had a romantic, poetic spirit. I would need to verify all family information.

Celia explained that when she told Judith about the letter, her cousin had dropped the phone and collapsed to the floor, sobbing. They had both wept, and Judith had urged Celia to call Judith's two siblings and contact me again. When they hung up, Judith called her brother Micha, reaching him as he was leaving for a formal dinner. "Stay home," she told him, speaking almost incoherently. "Celia will call you. She has news about our grandfather." When Celia reached Micha, he too wept and urged her to talk with me again. Their younger sister was also astonished, but more controlled. She wished very much to learn about her grandparents but not to become involved.

These cousins hadn't known their grandparents, and they hadn't known what happened to them. They had never heard Alfred and Hedwig's voices, never had the chance to grieve or find closure with their deaths, but now they wept. I was witnessing the lengthy reach of the Holocaust, as it continued to inflict trauma and loss on a third generation.

But Celia's emotional account did more than raise the specter of the Holocaust before me. It also created an unexpected contrasting rush of happiness. This family had survived and grown. I hadn't realized how oppressed I had felt by Alfred and Hedwig's deaths—just one example of Hitler's successful extermination of so many people. The love that this family demonstrated for each other and for grandparents they had never known was like sunlight over a dark landscape, a sign that their close bonds had endured despite the evil unleashed on their family.

Celia and I talked for nearly an hour. I wanted to hear more, but I had to tell her that I was rushing to prepare for a New York research trip in two days. Could we talk again later? Silence. Then, with a catch in her voice, Celia told me that, coincidentally, she would be in New York then too. She was flying out tomorrow for a hectic week of personal business.

An amazing coincidence! Could we meet, I asked? She answered that she would be busy and didn't know her schedule.

Her guard was back up. I couldn't blame her.

Doing my best to contain my zeal, I proposed that she contact me if she found time. Celia said that, well, she could set a tentative meeting time. Her partner, Mark, would be with her, and if my husband was coming, he could join us. Still uneasy, she set and rejected a number of times and places before proposing that we meet mid-week in the lobby bar of my hotel.

★

Five days later, on a chilly March afternoon, Sidney and I watched for Celia and Mark in our New York hotel lobby. "There she is," I said, spotting a short, slim blond woman, about sixty years old, and her taller dark-haired partner hesitating at the door. "But she doesn't look Jewish."

"Bigot. Antisemite," Sidney laughed.

This member of Hitler's stereotyped and despised race had short, straight straw-blond hair, delicate fair skin, and large blue eyes. Her nose was small and straight, and she was fine-boned. She wore a grey velour athletic suit and silky red T-shirt; she had small earrings and light makeup. She pulled a wheeled briefcase, as if it would be difficult for her to carry one. Her partner, Mark, with his dark eyes and olive skin, better fit Hitler's so-called Jewish genetic type.

We greeted each other formally and headed into the bar, which was nearly deserted at that early hour—perfect for a quiet conversation. We ordered coffee and tea. The four of us chatted awkwardly about weather and air travel. Our drinks arrived. How to begin? I thanked Celia for meeting us and took out a thick folder of documents I had copied for her—letters from archives, articles about Viennese Jewish life. Then I took out the large translucent glassine stamp collector's envelope containing her grandfather's letter and laid it on the folder.

I asked how she wanted to begin.

Celia didn't hesitate. "I'd like to see the letter."

"Of course. It's more yours than mine," I told her, "but I hope to keep it until I've finished with my research and writing." Her eyes fixed on the letter.

I slid it towards her.

Sidney and Mark sat silent, watching. Mark's presence was essential, offering support for Celia. She began reading.

"Yeah, wow, oh..." She read a few words aloud in a soft voice, to no one in particular. "See they wrote *Germany* because it was after the Anschluss...Vienna, Germany...mmmm." Celia seemed to have traveled elsewhere, far from us, into the world of the letter. The table next to us filled with a noisy foursome, but she didn't look up. For her, there was only the letter, her hands holding it, her whole being devoted to examining the pages her grandfather had once held and sent with hope, or maybe resignation. She whispered softly to herself, perhaps to her grandparents, her mother. Then she was silent, head bent, her body still, and no one spoke as we waited for her to come back. When she looked up, tears rolled down her cheeks.

She held up the letter, pointing to Alfred's name at the bottom. She looked into my eyes and said, "This is not his signature."

CHAPTER 5
Different Worlds

April 2004

Waiters glided among the tables, and several people filtered from the lobby into the bar. China clinked. Seconds ticked by.

"Not his signature?" I was dumbfounded. How would she know? What was true here?

"No, it's not...to my knowledge...not compared to samples of his handwriting which I have."

"Are you sure?" I managed. *Samples?*

"It might be, and it might not be. He was legally blind. He might have dictated the letter and asked someone to sign it."

Blind?

I waited for Celia to proceed, but she was quiet, mulling over the signature. "What confused me was...it reminded me of my mother's signature, from a letter that my father received from my grandparents, my mother, and an aunt.... I'm not sure."

What was Celia talking about? My heart was still racing when she moved on, flipping through the folder I had given her. I was mystified. There was so much going on here that wasn't clear. I reminded myself that my goal then was not to ask all my questions immediately. Celia and

I needed to understand each other and develop a good working relationship. For now, I would follow where Celia led.

She set the letter down and looked across the table at Mark. She said in a low, hesitant voice, "Mark was there when I first heard about the letter. I was hysterical." Her voice caught, and again tears flowed.

I was only beginning to comprehend the raging emotions the letter had raised in Celia. Again, she seemed to be seeking a safe way forward.

"I'm sorry this is so painful." I offered her a tissue.

"I'm not sorry," she said, turning to me and then Sidney. "But it's sad. It's really sad. It's hard to go back."

"I know," he said quietly. "It isn't easy."

I was grateful Sidney was there. He is a sensitive listener, and more important, he was the one who had been entrusted with this letter.

Celia set the crumpled tissue on the table and turned to her briefcase. Her Israeli cousin Micha, the son of Alfred and Hedwig's younger daughter, Gretl, had sent Celia an email to give to me. I skimmed it quickly: Micha had a strong interest in the letter and my research. He wanted to talk with me. His sister Judith was eager too.

A promising network of contacts that I hadn't known existed was opening up. Celia still didn't fully trust me, and I didn't want to set off alarms that she had introduced her family to a crazy person, so I calmly assured her that I would contact them soon.

I had begun to grasp that this would be Celia's meeting, not mine. Typically people take a passive role in interviews, waiting for questions, then shaping their responses. That was not happening here. Celia spoke quickly, asking her own questions, interrupting me frequently and forcefully. She was lively and emotional and interesting. She would direct this meeting in a way that worked for her, which was appropriate. I had come to her for help. When she handed me Micha's email, I knew that I had passed a first test.

Celia circled back to Alfred and his handwriting, explaining that he had macular degeneration, like her mother, several cousins, and an uncle. She knew that her grandfather's vision had gradually deteriorated until he became legally blind and used a white cane.

This could account for the differences I had seen in his handwriting on various documents, I told her. Alfred's writing ranged from tolerably neat to a weaving, blurred scribble.

I saw, too, that in his letter Alfred had not disclosed his entire situation, which was even more fragile than that of many Jews. Three times damned, he was legally fighting to survive Nazi Vienna, struggling to immigrate—and legally blind. America could turn away an arriving immigrant for something as small as an eye infection.

Sipping her coffee and no longer focused on the signature, Celia began to talk about Alfred, the grandfather she knew only through stories. A wholesale merchant, he had sold dry goods—basically, apparel and fabric—to small shops and market stalls in Vienna and beyond, and also to Vienna's famous large department stores. Martha—Celia's mother, Alfred's daughter—had told Celia that before his vision worsened Alfred had traveled frequently; as his sight deteriorated, so did his business. Though Hedwig began helping with his work, they had struggled financially.

Celia explained that Alfred's father, Salomon, had been a merchant traveling from his hometown of Třešt, in Moravia, across the Austro-Hungarian Empire. The widespread empire, like today's European Union, had facilitated travel around Central Europe; its mail system had also enabled their extended family to remain close.

I saw that these weren't provincial people. The empire's broad reach and their hard work enabled them to become familiar with other areas around Central Europe and make contacts throughout the region. It would be Alfred's misfortune that his connections didn't reach beyond the eventual borders of the German Reich.

Sidney surprised me by telling Celia that, except for the travel, he could identify with Alfred's work. He told her about working from a young age after school and during vacations in his parents' small dry goods store, helping in every aspect of the business. I had visited his parents' store in Tunica, Mississippi, but I hadn't thought about the parallels. The distance between our lives and the Bergers' began to shrink.

Celia continued telling us about her great-grandfather Salomon. He had loved his family and been energetic, hardworking, and determined that his children would be educated and successful. Three generations removed from Salomon, she was proud of him.

She said that Alfred had left school around age fifteen, after his mother's death. As his father traveled, he had worked and helped care for his younger siblings, probably missing or delaying the extensive trade education in textiles that his older brother, Hermann, had completed and his younger brothers, Arnold and Richard, would later pursue. Again I saw how extensive Celia's family knowledge was, and how important it was to her own identity.

Talking easily about her family in those times, Celia at last seemed engaged and comfortable. She said that Alfred's older brother, Hermann, had worked for a textile factory some distance from Vienna. After their mother's death, Alfred's older sister, Mathilde, managed the household, but she soon married a Viennese man, a baker whose marzipan petit fours were a favorite at the Imperial court.

I began to feel overwhelmed by the relationships and stories. Celia knew far more about her family than I knew about mine, and I saw how tightly interwoven this large extended family had been and still seemed to be. Through her stories, those earlier times began to seem close, even for me. I checked my recorder. It, at least, was keeping up with her whirlwind conversation, and I could let the stories flow. They were a treasure for me.

Glancing at Sidney, who was intent on Celia, I was grateful he was there. Later he and I would share impressions of this dense meeting. Mark was quiet, but I noted that besides focusing on Celia, he was watching me. Curious? Thoughtful? Wary? Probably all of those.

✶

A smile lit Celia's face as she began talking about her grandmother. Hedwig loved children, she said. This was an interesting place to start her description. I guessed that Celia, an only child, had longed to be close to such a warm, loving grandma. She went on. Hedwig had a beautiful voice and loved to sing light opera around her home as she worked. She had been a skilled dressmaker and Czech-Viennese cook. "We still use her recipes. Her strudel with lemon peel in the dough is memorable! And I serve cucumbers her way—cold, sliced very thin, sprinkled with salt, and pressed under a heavy plate. Finally, you drizzle them with lemon."

"Mmmmmm," I said, "I'm coming to visit."

I told Celia that I'd once tried to make strudel with a friend. It was a two-person job that required stretching paper-thin dough across my entire kitchen table. Flour was everywhere, the dough had to be patched together. Celia laughed. I imagined Hedwig working on it with a friend or her daughters.

Celia's family tales helped to relax both of us, and she proceeded with enthusiasm. She said that Hedwig's father, Bernard Grünberger, had been a merchant, and might have owned a textile factory near Jglau. Her three brothers—Hugo, Julius, and Otto—lived in Prague, but the siblings phoned, wrote, and frequently rode the train a half day's journey to visit each other, even after the Anschluss. They remained devoted to each other all their lives.

Hedwig's parents had also owned a small farm outside the village of Ranzern, south of Prague. Growing up, Martha loved visiting there with her mother, her Aunt Olga (her mother's sister), and Olga's three daughters—Trudi, Ani, and Loli. The cousins rode on horse-drawn wagons piled high with hay, walked through fields of fragrant purple flowers, and helped to cook big pots of *sterz* (corn meal cereal) for the farm workers' breakfast. I later learned that their farm had been a short distance across a regional border from Hitler's grandmother's hometown. Who knows whether those grandparents' paths may have crossed?

Jglau, the name that had sounded so foreign to me, rolled comfortably off Celia's tongue: Ih-glau. This city, southeast of Prague, is now called Jihlava, but I noted again how extensively her parents had talked about their life in Europe. Celia seemed to dwell in two worlds, one in the present and another in the past with her family. She was preserving that past, keeping faith with those who had been lost. For her, they were as real as I was. Perhaps more.

★

As I mused about Celia's stories, she moved on. Again, I was glad for the recorder. I would not need to pull information from her; she spoke quickly, and her stories flowed with the force of a just-thawed mountain stream.

"Hedwig's family, the Grünbergers, intermarried with the Bergers for so many generations, it isn't simple to define the relationships. My mother's great-aunt…Alfred's grandfather's brother…uh…Alfred and Hedwig were some sort of cousins." We talked about this being not uncommon in many places well into the twentieth century. Celia laughed, "There was so much intermarriage in our family, it's a wonder we're not all retarded, though we don't seem to be."

Sidney broke in to add that his grandparents, born in Russia in the late 1800s, had been first cousins.

Celia smiled again. "Genetically, cousins in these families are close, almost like siblings. For instance, Hedwig's sister Olga, married Alfred's youngest brother Richard," she continued. "My mother's cousins in Vienna were like sisters and brothers. They did everything together."

The lilt left Celia's voice. "But that world is gone."

I had known that Celia's stories would take us to the Holocaust. Yet, even there, we would find joy, family, courage, and the sustaining power of love.

★

The waiter who had been circling our table interrupted to tell us that we should place an order or let others have our place. We were surprised to see that the bar was packed and evening was upon us. We had been talking for nearly two hours. We ordered beer and a cheese plate, then Celia turned again to her grandmother. Once more, her family's world enveloped our table.

Celia's mother Martha had told her that Hedwig and her sister Olga had expressed resentment and frustration at their truncated education and limited career choices. Girls of that era typically attended school until about eighth grade; family resources were mostly spent on boys' education. But Hedwig had grown up at the dawn of a new age and rejected those restrictions for her daughters.

With obvious pride, Celia said that her mother Martha had graduated from Vienna's prestigious Hochschule für Musik Und Darstellende Kunst, the University of Music and Performing Arts. An accomplished pianist, she had once performed in Vienna's internationally famous music venue the gilded Musikverein. Celia explained bitterly how the Anschluss had abruptly terminated her mother's budding career as teacher, performer, and accompanist. It was difficult for Celia to accept, even now. She could feel, even these decades later, her mother's deep disappointment.

I asked Celia about her own education. She said she'd studied viola and voice at the elite New York High School for Music and Art (now the Fiorello H. LaGuardia High School of Music & Art and the Performing Arts) and earned a bachelor's degree in psychology and two master's degrees in special needs education and counseling. Recently retired from her career as a school counselor, she said, "I don't have children of my own, but I've always had a school full of children."

Sidney and Mark, ready for a break, left to stroll outside. But Celia and I were not interested in a diversion. The information we had shared with each other raised a stream of new questions. How had her parents—Martha and Leo—and Gretl managed to escape? And why hadn't Alfred and Hedwig been able to follow their daughters?

I knew that Celia was anxious to learn more, so I spread copies of the Vienna city registration cards on the table. Fascinated, she traced each line on the cards with her finger as she read, as if making contact

Martha and Gretl Berger in Vienna, 1938. *Courtesy of the Berger Family*

with her family. I showed her Alfred's signature and the address of the neighborhood police station where he had gone to report changes in his household situation: Gretl's departure, Leo's and Martha's moves and departures, Alfred and Hedwig's own upheavals.... Celia's mood turned from fascination to grief. "My grandparents moved how many times?"...Look how the handwriting changes.

"When the Nazis took over Austria, Jews understood immediately that they had no choice," Celia said, her voice growing more forceful. "This was not the antisemitism they'd lived with all their lives. They had to leave. They put their resources into getting their children out first. Once they were safe, parents, too, tried to escape." She held up her grandfather's letter, as if to corroborate her words.

"The cruelty after the Nazi uprising—it was more than an invasion—was so vicious, it shocked even Germans. Germans had planned to institute antisemitic policies like those in Germany, but Austrians beat them to it. Germany had to contain the violence.

"I'm always thinking about what happened. Growing up, I lived with a Holocaust mentality. I think I was born with it. I dream about family I haven't met. It feels so real, often I can't tell whether I've been there or just heard about those times. I remember, as far back as two years old, in 1947, my mother crying all the time."

★

Sidney and Mark rejoined us, slipping quietly into their chairs as Celia explained about her mother's unfulfilled need for information. After the war Martha learned through the Red Cross that her father had died in Vienna but heard nothing about her mother. In about 1960 Martha, Leo, and Celia had traveled to Vienna, their first return, seeking answers. "We talked to my mother's distant relative there, Bernard Toch, and his wife Pauline. My mother had known them all her life. Bernard survived the war in Vienna because he was married to a Catholic. They had been able to send their children out, to America.

"They didn't know what happened to my grandmother. They knew she was deported. They knew she didn't come back. It was like that. When the war ended, Bernard searched concentration camps throughout Europe searching for his sister, my grandmother, and others. Bernard was an amateur photographer and took pictures at the camps he visited but he never found his family. They were just gone with no trace."

Bernard's photos would have been horrifying and practically unbelievable; they also would be incredible documentary history. I wondered whether they had survived, and if I could find them.

Celia took a swallow of her then-warm beer. "The Tochs told us that my grandfather died in an accident in Vienna. There seemed a mystery about it. I could tell Bernard was angry, but I was a teenager, and they were speaking sort of carefully." She paused, looking at the papers spread out before us.

"I haven't thought about that visit in a while. We were all upset and tense."

Again, I was witnessing the hardship that survivors and their descendants face in keeping the Holocaust contained in one chamber of their hearts. Important facts had been lost. Celia knew fragments, and for much of her life that had been enough; her family had found a way to move forward.

Several years after her trip to Vienna, she and her parents had visited her aunt Gretl and Gretl's family in Israel. That first reunion of sisters Martha and Gretl since they had both fled their home some thirty years before had overflowed with love and tears, Celia told me, but again, no one knew about their parents' fate. "My cousin Judith and I decided to look for information about our grandmother through Yad Vashem, the Israeli Holocaust Museum. We received conflicting answers. One record showed that Hedwig had been deported to Theresienstadt, another that she was sent to Minsk. We told our parents, but my mother said, 'It's enough! Why push and push? We already know.'"

But Celia didn't know what had happened, and now she wished that she did.

✦

Our waiter intervened. He had been watching our table and had finally had enough and brought the check. We wandered up the lobby stairs to the mezzanine, chatting about random easier topics—Celia's missing the warmth of Florida, Sidney and Mark's interest in jazz, my love of New York, where I'd lived after college.

In a vacant meeting room we slid four chairs into a close circle, and Celia dropped another bombshell. "I think what hurt my mother most was that she couldn't get an affidavit from her father's brother. Hermann immigrated with his wife and daughter fairly soon after the Anschluss. They lived in New York."

"Alfred's *brother* escaped to America and didn't help?"

✦

Celia continued slowly. "In Vienna, Hermann was an executive in the large company that manufactured products that Alfred sold. He helped my grandfather get his job, but at some point, I think there weren't the best feelings between them." She was tiptoeing around this obviously sensitive issue.

At the beginning of this quest, I had hoped to find an American hero who had braved difficult obstacles to help a stranger. I'd been looking for courage and compassion—light in the endlessly bleak Holocaust when Jews stood almost alone in the world. Now, I doubted if I even knew what that light would look like. Alfred's letter to the Los Angeles Bergers had been a plea for exceptional help. Finding a sponsor and place of refuge had been difficult even for well-connected Jews—but if a brother wouldn't help, who would?

I told myself that I was just learning this story, and much of it remained dubious ground. Celia lived with pieces of information and, possibly, misinformation. Whatever the truth about Hermann, all of the Berger family had suffered.

I asked her to tell me more. Celia began by assuring me that she had loved her Uncle Hermann, who had been helpful to her parents. She said that he'd escaped because prosperous American relatives of his wife Magda—whom everyone called Mitzi—had provided an affidavit for him, Mitzi, and their daughter Lisl.

Celia believed that Hermann had tried to help his wife's relatives immigrate. Her deep voice dropped even lower. "That was the situation. Jews who escaped had to choose." She opened her two empty hands. "Who should they help? A brother? A brother-in-law? They had to weigh one life against another. I think he also tried to help Mathilde, his sister, but when my parents asked him to sponsor my grandfather, he said, 'I can't. He's better off where he is.'"

Celia was silent. Again, we waited.

"My parents didn't tell me this until after Hermann died, and I was an adult. I don't know what he meant. Maybe he believed that my grandfather was too old to make the trip, or that America wouldn't admit a blind man."

The relentless cruelty of the Holocaust surfaced again, pitting victims against each other, burdening generations of survivors with guilt and suspicion. We explored possible rationales for Hermann's failure to help his siblings.

"In the 1930s and 40s, immigrants were not welcome in the United States. To arrive and then bring in more family aroused public anger toward immigrant communities."

"Discrimination against Jews, and…actually, anyone who wasn't a white Protestant, was blatant. It wasn't easy to sponsor a Jewish refugee.

"All minorities tried to blend in. Jews feared that if they demanded increased immigration, they might trigger violent antisemitism in America.

"No one knew how bad it was in Europe.

"Hermann didn't work in America. He wouldn't have been approved as a sponsor."

We suggested many reasons why even a brother might not have helped, but our words sounded hollow. The conversation was disheartening.

Sidney raised a related issue. "It seems that the Bergers in Los Angeles also didn't try to help your grandparents. But if they didn't, the question is, why did they save the letter?" He and I had talked about this paradox. Why safeguard a letter that reminds you of what you did not do?

Celia and Mark both nodded, as if they had wrestled with the same puzzling issue. We'd come a long way in our conversation. It had started awkwardly, nerves on edge, but we had grown comfortable enough to probe together for insights to uncomfortable questions.

Celia offered, "We don't know what happened. They could have tried to answer, but mail wasn't always reliable. And it was censored. We can't know whether they tried." Alfred's letter had no censor's mark, but she was correct. Germany invaded Poland less than a month after Alfred mailed his letter, and the Reich was fanatical about controlling mail during major military events.

She massaged her temples. "Maybe they just didn't have the heart to throw it away, you know, because it deserved better?"

"It's almost like—" Sidney began.

"Superstition," Celia interrupted.

"A command not followed, a sin not erased," he persisted.

I looked at Sidney. He'd never used phrases like this in my hearing. They sounded ancient, Biblical. Instead of psychology or human needs, he was looking to religion for answers.

"Maybe it was just the appreciation of a document in history," Mark suggested.

His pragmatism brought us back to the present. It was dark outside. We had been talking for more than three hours. Time had crept up on us, and we all were tired.

Walking slowly down the stairs, Mark and Sidney chatted about fishing together some day. I told Celia that I had more information to send her, and a timeline I hoped she could help with. She smiled broadly and said that she would. Risking overreaching our tentative new partnership, I proposed that she join Sidney and me on our September trip to Vienna. She said that it might be too arduous, her health might prevent such travel, but she would consider it.

She seemed fragile. She had been coughing and complained several times about the seats. The prospect of the trip might also have felt threatening. As she had told us, she bore the emotional scars and had the dreams that wouldn't end. Even so, in that moment she seemed as energized as she was worn out.

In the small lobby, noisy then with arriving travelers, Sidney and I watched Mark and Celia move through the commotion pulling her briefcase, then push through the hotel's revolving doors into the New York night.

★

Later, looking back at that first meeting, I saw that I had been wrong to believe I was prepared for all it would reveal. It did proceed smoothly, the start of a lasting friendship. But from the moment I suggested that we meet, it had been Celia, not me, who had understood how it would go. She would hear family history that she had been aching to learn, and only after appraising me would she share information that I needed. Our encounter would distress her, and I couldn't really understand all that she said and what it meant. She knew too well that the Holocaust cannot be explained.

CHAPTER 6
Home

April–May 2004

In Oregon, flowering plum and cherry trees had burst into bloom under bright April skies. The signs of spring were a welcome contrast to the dark world inhabiting my thoughts. The pace of my research quickened as my inquiries brought answers—and more questions. Back in February, when we had set the September date for our Vienna trip, six months had seemed ample time to prepare, but now I saw that I would need to run hard to stay abreast of the fast-evolving information. That was exhilarating, as research often can be, but also a tremendous weight of responsibility. The quest now also involved other people, with their own significant hopes and expectations, which depended on me.

By May, I had contacted sources across the country and on four continents. Inquiries typically provided fragments of information that led me in new directions and triggered more questions. I felt I was working my way through a maze. Still, I went to my computer each day with the hope that I might eventually find some answers. What had happened to the Bergers during the Holocaust? Whatever I learned, what would that mean to me?

✦

Celia and I were now talking by phone and email sometimes several times a day, chatting about her family, new information I'd uncovered, and our own lives. We had begun to rely on each other, a large step from her early skepticism.

Once again I encouraged Celia to join Sidney and me in Vienna. This time, she paused only to take a breath before saying she would come. Her support would be invaluable, and I was delighted. She expressed a new concern: she had been in Vienna as a young teenager with her parents, but she was worried now about facing, as an adult, the city whose cruelty had ravaged her family.

Several weeks after I had returned from New York, my cell phone rang as I drove to an appointment and an animated voice called my name.

"Allo? Allo, Fareess?"

"Yes, this is Faris. Who is this?"

"Yudit!" I heard, followed by a stream of excited conversation.

"I'm sorry. I couldn't hear. Who is this?"

Another burst of talking. I heard Celia's name several times and deduced that this was Celia's Israeli cousin, Gretl's daughter Judith. I wanted to talk, but I was late for a meeting, I apologized.

Judith didn't understand. She kept talking.

"I cannot talk now," I interrupted, speaking loudly, over-enunciating. "May I call you later?" She didn't understand this either. I collected my thoughts. "Please write to Celia," I offered. "She will connect us by email."

Another flurry of enthusiasm. "Yes…to Celia…email…bye bye."

Not for the first time, I wished that I had better language skills.

✦

Two weeks later, Judith emailed both Sidney and me. "First of all, and for all my letters in the future, I must apologize about my English. I will do my best. I am Judith, and I talked with you by phone, and after that I needed time to relax."

Relax. An unexpected word. Then I remembered that this was the cousin who had fallen to the floor weeping when she heard about Alfred's letter. I understood that she meant she needed time to *recover*.

"It's so difficult to tell you," she continued, "what painful thoughts are passing in my mind since we got my grandfather's letter. It's taken me back to my poor mother that surely left her parents there in Vienna with broken heart."

Judith said that she was a nurse midwife, married, and had four children and four grandchildren. "That's our answer to HITLER," she wrote with passion, "all this big family of Alfred and Hedwig Berger." She was tired, she said. She ended there, promising to write again.

★

Judith's brother Micha also emailed me from Israel. "I was in France and five places in the U.S. and very busy.... I am very interested in the important issue of my grandfather's letter and will find the needed time to respond enthusiastically to your questions." Micha explained that while his letters might not always be prompt, he was committed to helping with my work. Below his signature, his title told me that he chaired a graduate research program at Hebrew University.

I wrote him immediately, explaining that many questions remained about Alfred and Hedwig, the life of their daughter Gretl (his mother) in Vienna, and her escape. We scheduled a phone call for the next week.

Emails flowed between the cousins in New York and Israel and me in Oregon, asking and answering questions, exchanging ideas and plans. I recognized how different Micha's and Judith's Holocaust knowledge was from Celia's. Celia couldn't remember a time when her parents hadn't talked about their family's life in Europe. Micha and Judith knew almost nothing. When they were young, they had asked their mother about her life in Vienna, her escape, and about their grandparents, but she had just wept, and they had learned not to ask. For them, family history was dangerous territory, a book of tears. When Judith was nineteen and Micha twenty-six, Gretl had died of cancer, and the knowledge that she'd held inside had been lost too.

Micha and Judith responded to my questions with the same few facts about Alfred and Hedwig. They said that their mother had left Vienna

soon after the Anschluss. Gretl and her cousin Ernst had sailed with other members of their Vienna Jewish Youth Group aboard a "pirate ship" to Palestine.

Those had been Celia's words, almost exactly, about a ship she had called *The Exodus*. Neither she nor Micha or Judith knew anything about the timing, the ship, or how a youthful group of Jews managed to depart Austria, transit through countries whose militaries were on high alert, and board an illegal ship. If it were true, the journey would have been a miracle at a time when

Gretl Berger, circa 1933. *Courtesy of the Berger family*

the Nazis were tracking every Jew and guarding every border.

Celia's words rang in my mind. "They sent their children out first."

★

The time difference between Oregon and Israel in summer is ten hours. At five o'clock on the appointed morning I called Micha, hoping I could elicit more details in conversation than I had by email.

After we had talked for an hour, I accepted the reality that there were no more stories for him to tell. Every question about his mother's life before Palestine had brought the identical response: "I'm sorry, I don't know." For each inquiry of mine, Micha had several of his own. If Celia was the poet among these cousins, often speaking in colorful images, and Judith was social, holding people and their emotions paramount, Micha was the scientist. He wanted to know what archives I'd searched, what information I'd found, and the source of each record. He challenged my facts until assured that they were solid.

But for all three, the bottom line was the same. They were hungry for information. Their grandparents' lives and deaths had been entombed in a few vague stories, and they yearned for more. For them, Alfred and Hedwig weren't history. They were family.

Micha began to tell me about other family members who had escaped Vienna. He was in touch with all of them who were still living. The three elderly sisters Trudi, Ani, and Loli—the daughters of Hedwig's sister Olga—lived in Israel, though Trudi was very ill. Celia had alerted me, and Micha confirmed, that communication with them could be difficult, but not impossible. Hedwig's nephew Wilhelm (Willi), the son of Alfred's brother Arnold, had escaped to South America and lived in Brazil. All four of them had been young adults when they'd fled Vienna, and they had known their aunt and uncle well. Promising news.

As interviews approach an end, it's not unusual that the conversation will wander more freely and unexpected information will emerge, and that proved true again. As Micha chatted, he told me that Peter, the only grandchild of Alfred's older brother Hermann, had recently moved to Massachusetts after living for several years in Latin America. Celia had lost contact with this cousin, so I was elated to hear that he was now closer.

"His grandparents, Hermann and Mitzi, and his parents, Lisl and Fritz, died some years ago, but even in Vienna they'd collected a lot of family documents. Hermann's family emigrated legally soon after the invasion. At that time, they could take most of their belongings. I believe they've kept everything...papers, letters, pictures. Peter may still have a lot of that."

Pictures…letters. I was stunned. It seemed an unimagined treasure. Micha agreed to contact Peter for me.

I proposed to Micha that he join Celia, Sidney, and me in Vienna. He said that he would be in France then, but, "It's possible."

After we hung up, I reflected on what had transpired. There had been awkward moments. "I don't know," Micha had said repeatedly. "I just don't know." His mother's grief had erected a barrier to his heritage, but now, in his sixties, he wanted to know what had happened those many years ago.

I had gained another ally, but we made an unusual team, like travelers from separate galaxies. Our backgrounds could hardly be more different: Micha was an Israeli Jew who had avoided facing his close connection with the Holocaust all his life. I was an American with Protestant roots, trying to make a connection with it. Because of his grandfather's letter, I had brought the Holocaust to his door, but why he and others in his family were allowing me to be their guide I wasn't sure. It was their domain far more than mine. But here we were, both exploring the meaning of a single sheet of paper and seeking some sort of peace.

★

Alfred and Hedwig were still distant silhouettes against a backdrop of war. The information I had gleaned from Judith and Micha filled some gaps, but the Berger family's experience in the Holocaust remained a mystery.

By early June I had connected with Peter, Hermann's grandson, who proved unusually open and as supportive as the other family members had been. He told me that his mother, Hermann's only child, had been born in Vienna and been close to her Aunt Hedwig and Uncle Alfred.

When I asked Peter if he had family papers or photos from Vienna, he laughed. "My whole family, especially my mother, were savers." He had grown up with his parents and grandparents sharing the same Upper West Side Manhattan apartment that the family had lived in since immigrating. "The closets were unbelievable. Absolutely full of papers, books, mementoes, photos...from at least the late 1800s."

That would include Alfred's youth. I hoped that this private archive could lead to my understanding both Alfred and Hedwig. Peter explained that after his mother had passed away in 1999, he'd cleaned out her apartment and thrown away large quantities of papers. My stomach knotted. I understood that most people discard family paraphernalia after a death, but I lamented the loss of this family history.

Fortunately, Peter was not most people. "I saved a lot. I literally built a room onto our house to hold papers and furnishings that my family brought from Europe."

I told Peter that I was interested in his collection—an extreme understatement—and he kindly invited me, Sidney, Celia, and Mark to visit his "Vienna Room": "There's so much there that I haven't sorted, and many of the letters were written in the old-style German script. It's tough even for me to translate—and I grew up speaking German." I assured him that I understood. He suggested we come in a few weeks.

Celia was in Florida when I phoned to propose yet another trip. She agreed immediately and invited me to accompany Mark and her back to her New York apartment afterward to see her letters and mementoes.

The thought flashed through my mind that time was impossibly tight for all this travel before the Vienna trip. But I told myself that a windfall of irreplaceable information was waiting to be explored. Just a few months earlier, when I'd begun my serious research, I had had only Alfred's letter. Since then I had made significant discoveries, but even so I felt stuck, frustrated. I had learned the outlines of Alfred and Hedwig's lives, but a life is not the sum of a few facts. Sidney couldn't leave work to join me, and in any case he wasn't interested in this kind of digging. I regretted that he wouldn't be part of this stage of the exploration, but I eagerly confirmed with Peter.

✸

Two weeks later, in late June, Celia, Mark, and I were riding in Peter's car through the familiar green rolling hills and quaint colonial towns of rural Massachusetts. I had earned a degree at Mount Holyoke College, twenty minutes from Peter's town, and during the past two years I had returned regularly as advisor to the college's quarterly magazine. I'd chatted with colleagues there about Alfred's letter and my search for information, never imagining just how close that information could be.

Peter, his wife, and their eleven-year-old daughter welcomed us into their large historic home in a small town graced by quiet streets and towering sugar maple trees. Peter was a self-described former hippie with untamed graying medium-length hair, a short full beard, and a ready smile. His wife Leslie was friendly but reserved. Their daughter, with large blue eyes and blond hair in pigtails, was the picture of a young Austrian girl.

We set down our suitcases, and Peter led us across a broad hallway to a closed door. A lace curtain covering the Vienna Room's glass door created a delicate but definite boundary between it and the rest of Peter's casual home. He paused, pointing to three pressed-glass platters set like windows in the wall above the door, gleaming in the late afternoon sun. "These, and almost everything in the room, came from my grandparents' home in Vienna." His purpose in creating this room still puzzled me. I prepared for an unusual experience.

We passed under the shining portal into a short entry hall where Peter slid open double closet doors to expose floor-to-ceiling shelves bowed under the weight of boxes bulging with papers that tumbled over the sides. There was no order in that muddle. It was chaos, like a boatload of refugees crammed into the last ship out. Peter smiled hesitantly and repeated that he had tried to organize the papers but had given up.

The sheer quantity made me take a step back. How would we handle this? It was late Thursday afternoon. Monday morning Celia, Mark, and I would catch a train to New York. Peter and I had settled on three days to look at his collection. Facing these packed shelves, I saw that that had been unrealistic. I kept my concern to myself. Peter closed the closet doors.

"The Vienna Room," he announced as we stepped from the hallway. His easy, outgoing manner had changed—his voice quiet, almost sheepish. Celia, Mark, and I took in the scene. I was taken aback. Before us was a crowded, fully furnished dining room from a vanished time and place. In the center six matching chairs surrounded a satiny dark walnut dining table, its heavy legs intricately carved, evening shadows beginning to creep across it. A crystal chandelier shimmered above it, reflecting the fading light.

An oil painting, a few photos, and other framed pieces I couldn't identify hung around the room. Small tables stood along three walls and in corners, leaving a narrow space to move around. Furniture filled the usable space, but the room's dominant feature, extending some five feet along the fourth wall was an ornate wooden sideboard topped by a glass display cabinet rising nearly to the ceiling. Perched on top, presiding over this tableau was a small antique clock, its hands stopped. I couldn't have invented a better symbol of the room.

I took a deep breath. Here we seemed out of real time and place. This was early twentieth-century Vienna. All that was missing was Peter's departed family, ushering us inside.

CHAPTER 7

The Vienna Room

June 2004

Fading rays of summer light danced through windows delicately curtained with remnants of Peter's mother's lace tablecloth, but the air was stale. The lace reminded me of those weblike weavings called "dreamcatchers." So many dreams had flourished and foundered around this table.

The waiting chairs saddened me, and the stillness was daunting, but in truth I could hardly wait to explore the Vienna Room. Its bursting closet promised precious information. The furnishings, too, held stories. I could almost hear forks clanking, children chattering, adults talking about events of the day. Hedwig, Alfred, Martha, Leo, and Gretl surely sat at this table with Hermann's family and shared news, hopes, recipes, laughter, and worry.

The Persian-style rug beneath the table completed the room's elegant, traditional atmosphere. The perfect order and richness here felt formal and rigid in contrast to the rest of Peter's home. The imposing sideboard with its glass display case—the vitrine—had been Peter's mother's and grandmother's pride and joy in Vienna and then in New York, he told us. Maybe even more so in their cramped New York apartment, I mused,

The Vienna Room. *Courtesy of the Berger family*

transporting them back to their former life, its excitement, and Vienna's promises not yet broken.

Peter led us around the table to look at the vitrine's crowded shelves. Behind its glass doors gold-trimmed china, crystal glassware, silver utensils, vases, candlesticks, and figurines vied for space and spoke of an affluent household that entertained friends and family in an expensive bygone style. That image contrasted sharply with the way I imagined Alfred and Hedwig's dining room—much more basic.

We continued around the Vienna Room, pausing at a woodcut of a small village with a castle rising behind it. Peter said that he had toured Austria four years ago with his family. About ninety miles north of Vienna, they discovered a textile museum in the village of Heidenreich-stein, where Hermann had worked as a young man. Peter's grandfather had married the niece of a founder of Honig Corporation and lived in Heidenreichstein for ten years before transferring to the company's

Vienna headquarters. In that museum Peter learned that Jews, including his grandfather, had been at the forefront of modernizing the textile industry, a mainstay of the Czech economy. Celia broke in, adding that Alfred might have worked with Honig as a wholesale representative. Again, I saw that she wasn't certain of her grandfather's history. He was an enigma to her, as well as to me.

We came next to a large, framed collage of currencies that Hermann had collected after World War I. Towns near Heidenreichstein had printed the money when the Austro-Hungarian Empire, like these crumbling bills, fell apart, and before victorious Allies formed the First Austrian Republic. "This money was essentially worthless almost as soon as it was printed," Peter explained. "For most Austrians, that period was crushing in every way." Hermann and Alfred had been in their forties then, struggling with the inflation that ravaged Austria and Germany and stoked radical political groups, including the Nazis.

Celia suddenly squeezed past Peter and rushed to an oil painting of a small country cottage. Laying a finger gently on its frame, she said, "I remember this from your family's Manhattan apartment! My father painted it! He gave it to your family in Vienna." Mark added that Leo had painted in a traditional romantic European style—and done museum quality work. Peter nodded. Hermann had brought Leo's gift from Vienna, and Peter had kept it as part of this memorial room. Despite Celia's comments about tensions in this complex family—especially her reference to mother's suspicion that Hermann could have done more to help Alfred escape—there was obviously a long history of caring bonds.

Peter led us next us to a corner niche furnished with a side table and lamp and pointed at a framed photograph on the wall. "Here are the Bergers."

We gathered around an oval, black-and-white formal portrait with a hazy pastoral studio background. Peering at it, I encountered six young people staring back at me. They were nicely though not elegantly dressed, every wisp of hair in place, suits buttoned, facial expressions set. The

Alfred Berger and his siblings, circa 1893. From left to right: Arnold, Mathilde and her husband Alois, Alfred, Hermann, Richard. *Courtesy of the Berger family*

Berger siblings were all there in the flower of youth, suspended in time like the clock on the cupboard.

Lifting the picture off its hook, Peter pointed them out. "This is my grandfather, Hermann, seated in the chair, with his three brothers, his sister, and her husband."

"This is Mathilde, her husband Alois, Arnold, and Richard." He paused at the serious young man in a starched white, high-collared shirt, bow tie, and snug-fitting suit standing behind Hermann. The side of his wrist, not his palm, rested lightly, awkwardly on his brother's shoulder. "This is Alfred."

Peter handed me the photo. Until a few weeks ago I hadn't imagined I'd be holding a photo of Alfred. I still could hardly believe that a Vienna Room existed, and that I was here. I had encountered Alfred as a sixty-two-year-old, fighting for his and Hedwig's lives, but in this photo he was a young man on the verge of making his way in the world.

I studied the picture. Alfred had medium-tone, slightly wavy, moderately short hair combed neatly up an inch or more above his forehead, probably held in place with pomade. Except for the uncomfortable-looking shirt collar, his hairstyle and fitted suit made him look stylishly contemporary. He wore thick frameless glasses and sported a sparse mustache that predated Hitler but was eerily similar to the Nazi dictator's pinched style. Alfred's mustache was that of a youth, tenuous—probably his first attempt.

He seemed about fifteen years old, stood ramrod straight, and stared intently to his left, as he had probably been instructed. Perhaps the group portrait had been taken for his mother, who may have been ill. She would die of a heart condition within about a year.

Behind the formality of Alfred's pose there was softness in his manner—his broad, earnest face occupying that wobbly, hopeful space between youth and manhood. His lower lip receding slightly, Alfred showed no signs of the detachment on the face of his younger brother Arnold. He didn't have the somewhat mischievous, inward look of Richard, either—at about nine years old still in short pants, or the challenging stare of Hermann. Alfred didn't display the vulnerable, tentative look of his older sister Mathilde, or the easy manner of Alois. Alfred had raised his chin as if to meet whatever came. I couldn't know if I was interpreting this portrait accurately. It was only a picture, a beginning of learning who Alfred was.

Called from our distant thoughts by Leslie's voice summoning us for dinner, we four agreed to begin work promptly the next morning and turned to leave. Evidently, we would not be eating in the Vienna Room.

★

The next three days were among the most unusual in my writing life. Peter, Celia, Mark, and I read, thought, and talked continuously about the Berger family in Europe. Hour after hour, in the dining room from old Vienna, we were in a world unto ourselves, absorbed and detached.

We quickly developed an easygoing routine, gathering each morning for breakfast with Peter's family, cleaning up the kitchen together, then convening around the fine Vienna Room table. That first morning, Friday, I asked Peter how he thought we should proceed. He laughed, raising his hands in gesture of futility, and then hefted several random boxes and set them around the table.

Peter appeared eager to begin. It seemed that he had never looked intensively at the boxes' contents or had anyone to share them with. To avoid misunderstandings, I reminded everyone that we were likely to find much that was interesting, but that I needed to concentrate on Alfred and the story of his letter. They agreed, and we set to work. For three hours Peter and then all of us hauled heavy boxes back and forth from the closet, reaching into their contents like children diving for treasure.

As Peter had warned, there was no order there. A 1960s photo of Peter's family lay between letters dating from the 1890s. World War I ration tickets fell from a 1930s cruise ship menu. We began separating the papers into piles. The largest held the many letters that Salomon Berger had written to his children as he traveled through Central Europe in the late 1800s.

Hermann, too, had been an energetic correspondent. We found dozens of his letters and postcards to his and Alfred's sister Mathilde, and to his daughter Lisl, Peter's mother. Lisl had also written prolifically to her family when she was a young woman studying in France, touring Egypt, and sailing on Mediterranean cruises.

A division of labor evolved easily. Peter and Celia, with their German language skills, skimmed the oldest letters, scanning for Alfred's name. Peter taught Mark and me to recognize family names in the differing forms of handwriting so we too could sort old letters and watch for any by or about Alfred, Hedwig, Martha, or Gretl. Progress was slow. Fading ink on some letters, indecipherable handwriting on others, and the changing cursive scripts used across Central Europe hindered our work.

We checked letter after letter, most of them written between 1890—when Alfred was a teenager—and 1905—when he was twenty-eight. Hours passed with no luck.

We had hoped to help Peter by generally organizing his papers, but as they scattered across the table in messy drifts we saw that would be impossible. We put what wasn't useful back into boxes, marked them as finished, and lugged them to the closet. We had reserved a place on the table for letters connected to Alfred, but other piles multiplied, and Alfred's space disappeared. I began to worry that I wouldn't find Alfred and Hedwig at all in this collection.

As we worked, Celia and Peter were drawn into their family's life in Europe and began translating aloud bits that interested them, telling stories they knew, and commenting on facts they were learning. When any of us came upon papers that piqued our curiosity—What was Salomon doing in Romania in 1891? What happened in the family during World War I? When were these ration coupons issued? —we put them in a pile to talk about later, translate, or copy. As that collection grew, Mark volunteered for the role of tech support and headed off in Peter's car to buy a scanner.

★

Listening to Peter and Celia read these letters, I abandoned my aim of focusing solely on Alfred's life in Vienna. Before coming here, I hadn't understood the significance of this broader history. The Berger family—aunts and uncles, nephews, and cousins—had lived throughout Central Europe—Moravia, Slovakia, Hungary, Austria, Romania—for centuries and yet the extended family had remained close to an extent I hadn't thought possible without modern technology. Through their letters Hermann and Salomon discussed business, relaying what they had sold and where. Aunt Risie asked for help making a will. The family wrote about ailing relatives, celebrated births and weddings, arranged visits, and advised each other on everything from housekeeping to health. Those were the sounds and situations of Alfred's young life. Family is always significant in a person's life, but I hadn't guessed how significant Alfred's extended family had been for Hedwig and him.

My attempts to sketch a Berger family tree that morning looked like tracks left by the White Rabbit in *Alice in Wonderland*. Having encountered an Arthur, two Alberts, and an Arnold, I was dizzy trying to keep up with the sprawling family relationships. Celia and Peter entertained themselves by trying to identify double relationships—a cousin who might also be an uncle because of the many intermarriages in the tightly knit Berger clan.

As I worked I watched Celia and Peter, who had seemed formal with each other the day before, puzzle out translations together, ask each other questions, and erupt in laughter as they tried to fit their own fragments of family information into coherent stories. Had Celia known that their great-grandfather Salomon was a peddler who may have carried a pack from one house or store to another and from one small town to the next? Did Peter know that after Mathilde's husband died of a heart attack her four brothers lovingly arranged for her to visit each of them every week? I found myself taking as many notes from their spontaneous conversation as from the letters. Watching those cousins driven to fill gaps in the old family stories, I began to see that I couldn't understand Alfred's life as distinct from his family. He had existed as part of a rich, interdependent, fertile family support system. For the Bergers, there had been no such thing as "separate from family."

I hadn't experienced that kind of dense family network in my own life. I had known none of my mother's East Coast relatives except for my grandmother. Most of my father's family had pioneered from Virginia to Kentucky, then spread west from Illinois to California; most were strangers to me, too. I recognized regretfully how much more Sidney's family life paralleled the Bergers'. His cousins, aunts, and uncles in Mississippi, Vermont, and Texas were as close as siblings. I found myself hungry for that broad reach of family warmth.

By midday Friday, we still hadn't found Alfred in any letters, but Peter came across a two-page "curriculum vitae" that Hermann had written in New York about his own career. Translating, Peter read that his grandfather had studied accounting and business and done book-keeping in Vienna for two years before becoming a *beamter*—probably an office manager— at age twenty-two at M. Honig Corporation, the textile business with the factory in Heidenreichstein. Alfred had used that same title to describe his profession on his earliest registration card. He seems to have begun his career in his brother's footsteps.

In his CV, Hermann traced the changing Honig Company as it grew to a large corporation producing sophisticated knitwear. He described his rise to top management, responsible for four hundred workers and about thirty managers. At the end of his career, as Vienna's Commerce Minister, Hermann had designed a collective bargaining system for textile companies throughout Austria, for which the city had awarded him a medal of commendation. Translating, Peter beamed, and I saw how the Berger family probably had felt well integrated into Austrian culture.

In a single sentence, Hermann recounted his World War I military service beginning in 1917. He didn't talk about his injury, illness, and return to Vienna two years later, limping and so gaunt that his family didn't recognize him. For Hitler to have impugned Jews' loyalty and sacrifice in that war suddenly seemed to me among the most odious of his lies about Jews.

In my searches of Austrian records, I hadn't found any evidence of Alfred serving in the military. Celia surmised that his poor eyesight kept him out of the war but, again, we didn't know. There were no doting grandparents to tell stories in Celia's home when she was growing up.

I was pondering these facts and the Bergers' paradoxical situation between the World Wars—thriving, but threatened in ways they could not have guessed—and was feeling a bit dazed by my immersion in the past when Mark entered the room, clutching a bulky scanner.

"Lunch break," he proposed. "I'm starved."

✳

We bought sandwiches at a nearby café and ate them around Peter's kitchen table, chatting about our efforts, the Berger family, and our own lives, moving seamlessly between past and present, Vienna and Massachusetts. Peter described his grandparents as secular Jews, like himself. Peter's wife Leslie was not Jewish. Celia said that their great-grandparents, like almost all European Jews then, had been Orthodox. Her parents had been liberal, but religious.

Sidney and I were at the liberal end of our own traditions, and we had raised our children to know both, I explained. Intrigued by our situation, the Bergers asked a series of politely worded questions. I had to admit that our compromise was not a simple place to reside. We had no clear, easy, comfortable words to describe our lives.

Celia and Peter turned to simpler topics, reminiscing about family gatherings for Jewish holidays, birthdays, or just to be together. I asked if they had eaten favorite dishes from Vienna. Enthusiastically talking over each other, they remembered wiener schnitzel; *knodel*, dumplings made with fillings, especially custard; *povidel,* prune paste filling in pastries; and *palachinken*, thin, waffle-like Czech cookies layered with jam like tiny, sweet sandwiches. Celia and Peter agreed that his mother had been an exceptional Viennese cook who served the rich meals she had grown up eating. The largest meal was always midday, Peter said. "It was unheard of among Viennese families to eat in restaurants, sort of an insult to the family cook, except for coffee and dessert. *"Liebe geht durch den Magen"* was a Berger family saying, they both remembered, laughing, and reciting together, "Love goes through the stomach."

✳

Settling back into the Vienna Room, Celia found the first letter that mentioned Alfred. It had been written by Hermann to their sister Mathilde in 1895. She had pulled it from the stack because of its Honig letterhead.

"Our grandfathers' company!" she exulted. The business where Hermann and Alfred had worked was Pereles & Lang, Nachfolger, M. Honig & Nehab, four names plus the word Nehab, indicating that the company had a new name. The tagline describing the business: *Mechanisch Strumpf-und Wirkwarenfabrik*: machine-made hosiery and knitwear.

I waited eagerly as Peter worked through the faded pages. In the affectionate letter Hermann, twenty-one, confessed to his sister that he was bored and lonely in tiny Heidenreichtstein. Fortunately, he said, he had spent a "joyful" Sunday visiting Alfred, then eighteen, in Brunn [later called Brno], a town near Třešt, south of Prague, where Hedwig's family lived. She would have been seven years old at the time.

The letter didn't say much about Alfred, but he had finally surfaced in Hermann's papers, a beloved member of the family. I was elated and relieved to find even this brief mention of the younger Alfred.

That letter was also memorable because it departed markedly from the more routine Berger letters. In it Hermann warned his sister about treacherous times. He urged their sister Mathilde to take their ten-year-old brother Richard out of Vienna and move to Třešt to live near relatives. "You should not feel homesick for Vienna," Hermann insisted, "because people there are very antisemitic and that hasn't changed."

Hermann was not entirely correct: the antisemitism of Vienna *had* changed, and the timing of his warning was not random. The oldest family letters we had found had been written at the peak of the Austro-Hungarian Empire. The Berger family had flourished in that Imperial world, if not always in wealth, at least in security. Emperor Franz-Josef's strict laws enforced peaceful relations and tolerance among the Empire's many regional and religious groups. But by the late nineteenth century that world was under threat. Nationalistic movements brought stress to the Empire. In 1895, as Hermann was writing to Mathilde, the reactionary Christian Social political party had taken over Viennese politics and its wildly popular leader, antisemite Karl Lüger, had been elected mayor. He would serve for thirteen years, galvanizing anti-immigrant, antisemitic, and Pan-German groups—and a young artist then living on Vienna's streets, Adolf Hitler.

Shortly after Hermann's first warning letter, he wrote Mathilde again, once again expressing his deep concern, repeating his entreaty to her to move Richard back to Třešt so the boy could avoid sixth grade public school in Vienna: "As you know, that is where they send all the antisemitic *Gesindel*."

"*Gesindel*," Peter explained, were coarse loutish rowdies. Jews had known for centuries that they must tread cautiously in Vienna, where their situation changed with political winds. Hermann harbored no illusions about the Viennese, even though later he himself would move to the city. Did he forget? Feel immune to attack? His warnings were unnerving.

★

We continued to gain insight that afternoon. Alfred's name appeared in an 1897 letter that Salomon—Vati Berger, Father Berger—wrote to his children after their mother died of heart failure. He gave Mathilde directions on housekeeping, voiced worries about Hermann's health, and said he was happy that Richard was behaving and Alfred and Arnold were doing well. None of it was earthshaking news, but it reinforced my sense of a loving family working to stay close.

We found Alfred's name on Salomon's 1907 death certificate. It revealed that Salomon had been living with Mathilde in Vienna when he'd fallen on some stairs and died of skull fractures. The certificate showed that Richard, twenty-two, lived in Vienna with Alfred, who had filled out the form. Again, I saw two generations of Bergers seemingly inseparable—so different from my own scattered family. The tight web of extended family was familiar to Sidney; I had felt lucky to become part of that.

"Oh!" Peter spied five envelopes slit open along the edges and tied together with a ribbon. He spread them on the table. "Look at these!" Over six weeks from October to December 1941, Mathilde had mailed five letters to Hermann in New York. Each envelope bore heavily inked stamps of Ober Command der Wehrmacht, the German Military High Command, and censors' marks including the Nazi emblem of an eagle, wings spread, a swastika clutched in its talons. Four times per envelope, censors had pounded the thin paper: Geoeffnet, Opened. I looked in each one. They were all empty.

Celia slowly shook her head. "I've heard about these," she whispered. She picked up each one, examining the writing and the stamps. "Censors threw these letters out," she observed, gently stacking and tying the envelopes together again. "This way, you know your family said something important. Mathilde is trying to contact Hermann, but she can't. To send the empty envelopes, it's like the twist of a knife."

Peter agreed emphatically, his body hunched. "It was. My grandfather Hermann was desperate to contact his family, but at some point his letters couldn't get through. He never knew what happened to his beloved sister. It was very, very hard for him."

By late Friday afternoon, the random order of the letters had begun to disorient me. I didn't know what would find its way into my hands next. One minute I heard young, married Mathilde invite Hermann and Mitzi to dinner in light playful verse, and then she was in peril, beyond their reach.

That disjointed information was not so different from life, where time and memory live in jumbled confusion, and change rips through everything. Even so, bouncing between extremes of these lives was exhausting. Here there was no progression. In all that we had seen that day, Hermann's two warnings about Vienna's antisemitism provided the only transition between the stability of the Bergers' lives before the Nazis came to power, and the cataclysm that struck them.

There was nothing to do about the information flow but continue combing through the boxes. I was relieved when we all agreed to quit for the day.

Peter cooked dinner that night—his specialty, tender *wiener schnitzel*, boiled potatoes, salad, and crescent-shaped cookies, a recipe that he said—like croissants—had been created centuries ago in Vienna to cele-brate victories turning back invading Turks.

Again that evening, I thanked Celia, Mark, Peter, and his family for their support, so far beyond what I had expected. I felt humbled and fortunate to have found these committed, welcoming relatives and this preserved place. I hoped this was a positive experience for them. It seemed that my connection to their past had brought it out from behind a cloud of half-known stories, repressed tensions, and layers of guilt passed down to them.

★

A sunny, humid Saturday found us at work again early. Re-energized, we opened a window to the fresh morning air. Sorting the first box of the day, we came on two letters written on Guth, Stern & Co. Inc. busi-ness stationery. They showed that the family of Hermann's wife, Mitzi, had operated an import-export company based in New York and Vienna. Mitzi's mother, Chlotilde Guth, ran the company in Vienna. Her brother John Guth managed it from New York. Those two words—*New York, Vienna*—attested to the good fortune that shone on Hermann. A thriv-ing businessman with connections to America, he had no need to write letters to strangers begging for help.

"So many Jews in Europe needed to escape," Celia said. "It was torturous for American families who wanted to help their relatives, but most American Jews only had resources enough to help one person, or one couple, if they could even do that much."

Carrying loose papers from the closet that morning, Peter dropped several. He scooped them up and held out a card. "My mother's dress-making business in Vienna!" He read, "Marlene, Strickmodell, knitwear styles," and explained that his mother Lisl had trained at the Vienna School of Fashion Design and opened an atelier, a designer's studio, on an exclusive shopping street. *Marlene*—it spoke of trouble for Jews, reflecting the need for Vienna's Jews to use Christian names for their businesses: "Marlene" was a combination of Mary and Magdalene. Another card invited guests to a private showing of Marlene's latest styles.

Celia spoke up, "Hedwig didn't have Lisl's credentials, but she hoped she could work with Lisl in New York. She knew she would need to work when she immigrated."

A few minutes later, Mark held up two typed letters sent to Hermann in 1945 by Robert Brull in Teplice, a town now in Slovakia. Celia and Peter seemed electrified and began talking at once. They had heard about these letters. Peter said that his grandfather had made an agonizing effort during and after the war to locate his siblings. Six months after the war ended, Hermann received these letters from a stranger who had known his youngest brother, Richard. Celia and Peter moved their chairs together and began laboriously translating "...moved around Europe...never take me alive...." They said they would send me a translation.

✦

Saturday afternoon, our energy ebbing, Peter suggested a break for *jause*, pronounced "yow-sa": "It's a terrific Viennese custom, like English teatime but with strong black coffee, when you can relax and chat."

We retreated to the kitchen and made coffee and tea, ready for a break. Peter disappeared into the pantry and returned with a wide smile and a cake tin. "I made this last week and froze it for us—my mother's recipe." He plucked off the lid to display a beautiful *sachertorte,* the most famous of Viennese cakes, made with bittersweet chocolate, apricot jam, and a chocolate glaze. No one protested.

My concern about not having enough time at Peter's home proved valid. After dinner Saturday evening, eyeing the untouched boxes in the closet, I worried that we would not finish. I told the others that I would work late, and they should rest. They grinned with relief, released by their strict crew leader.

Without the constant interplay of stories, questions, and translation, working on my own was not as rich, but I could work much faster, and

I sorted through several boxes. I gave in to fatigue about one in the morning, after finding two letters Alfred had written in May 1918 and a third in 1925—that one on his own business letterhead. The seven years in between had been a time of growth, as Alfred evolved from employee to owner of his own business. I was eager to hear the translations. At last, Alfred would speak in his own voice.

★

Sunday morning, Peter and Celia set to work on the two letters Alfred had written as World War I raged in Europe. In the first, Alfred had been responding to a friend's request for help finding work, and that letter settled the lingering questions about Alfred serving in the war. He had been working in Vienna. He advised his friend to specialize within the textile industry and offered to help him. Eventually, the letter had come to Hermann.

In Alfred's second wartime letter, he wrote Hermann, who lay in a Montenegro prison hospital; Alfred hoped for Hermann's continued recovery and relayed a mix of family and business news. He said that Hermann's wife Mitzi had brought his family "milk and other good things hard to get, even butter." Alfred had sold thirty dozen of some item—the word was illegible—for 360 schillings and received delivery of twenty dozen gloves and suspenders. He awaited permission to enter Tyrol, part of the Empire ceded to Italy after the war. The Empire's defeat, and then its demise, shook the Bergers' business, but not the family's close ties.

Seven years later, in 1925, Alfred, age forty-eight, reported a lively mix of work and family news on his own business stationery; his tagline read like Honig's: *Strumpf und Wirkwaren*, Hosiery and Knitwear. His address, Rosinagasse 14, placed his office in Vienna's Fifteenth District, a working-class neighborhood near the large Rossauer Prison. Sometime after war's end, Alfred had become an independent businessman, a *"merchandman,"* as he would write to the Los Angeles Bergers.

Alfred wrote about school plans for his daughter Martha, age fourteen, and described seeing Hermann's wife Mitzi at the bar mitzvah of their nephew Willi, the older son of their brother Arnold and his wife (who was confusingly also called Mitzi). Work was "very busy," but women's jacquard wool stockings were not selling. Alfred seemed a modestly successful man in the prime of life, engaged, caring, and confident. The letter ended with warm wishes from Hedwig and a tiny two-word note—*Herzliche Gruesse*, "Heartfelt Greetings"—from their teenaged daughter Martha.

Now Celia and Peter turned to translating a typed note written thirteen years before the last letter we had found. Arnold's wife had written to Hermann and Mitzi in verse, excusing herself from a family gathering. She explained that their new baby Willi—the one whose bar mitzvah Alfred would attend in 1925—was ill, regretted missing the fun, and joked that since she was the second "Mitzi" in the family, she should be known as "Mitzi Two." The family's levity made us laugh too. Again, I watched the two cousins feeling close to each other—and to their warm, lively family in Vienna.

Later Celia and Peter came across an account Arnold had written of his flight from Vienna by boat. They had heard stories about this narrow escape but were surprised to find this record. Peter said he would translate this for me, too. I was impatient to read it because it touched on the central issue that continued to concern me. Why hadn't Alfred and Hedwig been able to escape? Why hadn't they sailed on that boat with Arnold and Mitzi Two?

Sunday passed in a blur of activity—letters flew more quickly across the table, the scanner hummed as our time at Peter's was rapidly running out. An intriguing candid snapshot turned up, of Alfred and fourteen Berger family members together around a long picnic table under tall overhanging trees. Peter believed it was a picture of the family in Hermann's Vienna garden around 1925, perhaps celebrating Alfred's July birthday. Hedwig sat at one end of the table, Alfred and four of the young cousins clustered at the other. Alfred smiled warmly at the photographer—who, judging from

The Bergers at a family gathering, likely in the garden of Hermann's house in Vienna, circa 1925. *Courtesy of the Berger family*

the blurry image and low angle, was likely a child—but as I held the picture, Alfred also stared happily at me.

I worked into the night again on Sunday. Three boxes remained. Letter after letter—postcards from Peter's mother Lisl from the Austrian Alps, a letter from Salomon—emerged from the boxes, then disappeared back into them again.

In the final box I uncovered some seventy letters, tied together, from Hermann and Mitzi in Vienna to their daughter Lisl in New York. They had been written from the week after Kristallnacht, in November 1938, to March 1939—a tumultuous time. I hoped these letters might shed light on the Bergers' lives amid the major upheavals erupting in Nazi-controlled Vienna.

The sheer quantity of these letters raised translation challenges I didn't know how I would overcome. But this quest often seemed to have a life of its own. Doors had continued to open when I was at a loss, and at times I felt helped by greater forces.

I was alone that night in a small circle of light—the world behind the lace curtains disappeared in darkness. The motionless clock stared down from above me. Boxes bulged with the vestiges of once vibrant lives. My fatigue and this room tethered to the past detached me from a sense of time and place.

I was no longer surprised to come across letters that were more than a century old. Whatever appeared in my hands—1935, 1891, 1917—I was there, experiencing that event. Time had become elastic and slipped its bonds. With scant justification, I felt close to the Berger family in those years. My calls home every evening to talk with Sidney and keep up with my kids had begun to feel like my only connection to the present. How was Sarah doing in her internship in Boston? Did Daniel like his new job in New Orleans? Jonathan had decided to stay in Santa Barbara?

Gradually, darkness eased its grip, and the sky lightened to a dim, tired gray. With heavy eyes, I set newly sorted letters on the table to show Celia and Peter. I shoved the last box onto a shelf and closed the closet doors with the strong feeling that the stories in this room were not finished. Alfred's younger brothers Arnold and Richard had made only brief appearances. His youthful sister Mathilde had been present, but her older life and final days were like her letters from the empty envelopes—absent. Alfred and Hedwig were here mostly by proxy. The outline of Alfred had emerged, but Hedwig remained nearly invisible.

★

Monday morning. Time was short, just enough to gather our copies and our suitcases, and jump into Peter's car to catch the New York–bound train from Hartford. As I collected papers in the Vienna Room, Peter walked in carrying thick files. "Here are my grandfather's financial records that I told you about. I'll make copies for you."

I had asked Peter whether his family had applied for restitution from Germany. He'd said that he had submitted a claim as part of the New York Attorney General's 2002 group appeal and would search for his settlement records.

With only a few moments before we had to leave, we sat down and made a start. Peter opened one thick file folder. I scanned down the columns and gave a small gasp. This was a Holocaust story in itself, laid out in numbers by a skilled businessperson. I saw the continuous payments— entries for assessments, exit taxes, and the infamous Kristallnacht tax forcing Jews to pay for the Nazis' destructive rampage. The Reich's extortion campaign and unbridled greed were spread out before me.

My finger stopped at an entry by Alfred's name, and then at another by Arnold's. The fact that Hermann had given his brothers money several times before he left Vienna reminded me that I was only beginning to fathom the complexities of the situation of this family caught in the Holocaust.

Peter pointed to a large figure, 133,333.33 RM, Reichsmarks. "My grandfather won the national lottery on March 1, 1938, just before the Anschluss."

"Lottery?" If my jaw didn't drop, it was because I was blurting out questions. This family story was proving an epic. "Of course, they didn't let him have it," Peter was quick to explain. The money had sat in an Austrian bank that was nationalized by Germany and later recovered by Austria. The settlement returned only a fraction of the total he was owed.

Time for talk at an end, we closed the files. Celia entered, saying that she and Mark were ready to leave. Peter told her that he'd just shocked me with the story of the lottery.

She was silent, then said, "You know, your mother asked mine more than once what happened to the money Hermann left to help the family in Vienna. My mother told her she thought Alfred and Hedwig had never touched it, or possibly never knew about it." This windfall would have eased Hermann's difficult new life in America and might have saved Alfred and Hedwig. That theft in itself had caused generations of woe.

I wondered why the Nazis hadn't immediately emptied that blocked account after the Anschluss. With the flimsiest of legal excuses, in countless ways, they had robbed, bullied, terrified, and stymied the Bergers. Why hadn't they simply taken the settlement? Perhaps it had been appropriated by the bank or the Reich, and all that remained had been Germany's careful records.

Hermann's ledgers, never intended to be read like a memoir, were a surprising communication from the past. The figures that this former Vienna commerce minister had penned with such care spoke plainly of Reich crimes and, just as powerfully, of the Bergers' extraordinary loyalty to each other. Later, Sidney stoically pointed out the stark contrast with his own family, wiped out in the Holocaust. After the war, they had had no communication from their Russian relatives.

Mark called to us from outside. It was time to go. Celia and Peter headed out. I picked up my now heavy satchel and turned to leave, stillness settling again over the Vienna Room. I was relieved to reenter the present.

CHAPTER 8
Celia's World

July 2004

Our taxi hurtled from Manhattan's Penn Station through the reverberating noise of the Midtown Tunnel and emerged in Queens, New York's easternmost borough. We raced down Broadway, honking and swerving—Celia, Mark, and I swaying in the back seat until we stopped abruptly in front of a well-kept six-story brick building on a quiet side street.

Celia's multi-ethnic neighborhood, Elmhurst, has been a haven for refugees for a century and home to her family for nearly seven decades. The most recent U.S. census identified it as America's most ethnically diverse neighborhood. Celia's parents had moved to this building in 1948, and after graduate school she had moved back to the same building into her own apartment. At that time the area had been solidly Jewish and Italian. Now, Asians were the majority.

Pedestrians filled the sidewalks. People shouted, bumptious and elbowing one another. Languages intersected. Aromas fresh and fetid mingled in the heavy, humid air. I saw that this area was home to people from around the world. They seemed to coexist, living and working side by side—in stark contrast to the racial hatred of the Holocaust. What had happened in post–World War I Europe to turn neighbor so brutally against neighbor? Redrawn national borders that favored ethnic homogeneity? Economic collapse?

A subway screeched under grates in the sidewalk. Even the pavement shook and roared. Her apartment vibrated too, Celia said with a small smile, since the tunnel passed directly under her building. The contrast between these frenetic streets and Peter's rural Massachusetts town was dramatic. It struck me again that the two cousins' situations in some ways paralleled their grandparents' significantly different lifestyles in Vienna.

Looking up, I felt hopeful that here I would find a sanctuary for Alfred and Hedwig's stories and understand more of what had happened to them not so long ago.

★

I trailed Celia and Mark down the echoing fourth-floor hallway. Maneuvering my suitcase through Celia's doorway and around a small glass table in the entry and dining area, I set down my satchel and looked up to see faces that could only be Alfred and Hedwig's.

"Yes, those are my grandparents." Watchful and quick, Celia nodded toward two oil paintings hanging in the hall. She said that her father, Leo, had painted the portraits from memory and the few photos he and Martha had brought from Vienna.

I walked into the hall to look more closely. About ten by twelve inches, the pictures were emotional opposites. Hedwig seemed to be in her mid-forties. Her unlined skin had a rosy glow, and she wore small earrings, possibly pearls, and a pendant necklace. A wave of dark brown hair swept across her forehead and was neatly drawn behind her ears, perhaps in a bun. She had a Mona Lisa smile, and her large brown eyes gazed ahead with an inscrutable, thoughtful expression.

As in Peter's two photos, Alfred was perfectly groomed in a white shirt, tie, and dark jacket. About sixty, his hair showed some gray. He had combed it, sleek and straight, back from a hairline that was beginning to recede.

What startled me was not Alfred's aging, but the change in his eyes. In photos from his youth, he had lifted his chin, his eyes fixed intently ahead, seemingly earnest and engaged. Here his blue eyes were downcast and half closed, staring toward the floor. Behind dark-rimmed glasses, puffy, terraced folds of skin ringed eyes that had seen trouble. I couldn't imagine this picture had brought comfort to Celia or her mother.

"They're fine portraits. You're lucky to have them," I told Celia, "but they're very different."

"Yes," she said, and turned away.

★

Mark pulled my suitcase into the living room, just off the dining area. "Here you are," he grinned. "This is your room." I hadn't known that when Celia said she had a place for me, I would take over their living room. Again, I was grateful for their extraordinary help. Their drive to explore the family's Holocaust experience was both impressive and a bit startling. The Bergers were driven, as I was, to know their lost family and understand what had happened.

I surveyed the room. A modern black-lacquer-and-glass cabinet ranged along one wall, opposite in style and feeling from Peter's heavy carved wooden furniture. Two birdcages held a cockatiel and a pigeon, both eyeing us.

A grand piano filled the far corner. "I play, but not often," Celia said. "My mother taught lessons on this piano. She would often play while my dad painted at his easel. I drew or read. I loved those times." I could visualize her war-ravaged family in this sanctuary, treasuring their freedom and peace.

Behind the piano a large oil painting of an attractive, young blond woman wearing an Eastern European peasant outfit looked out over the room. She had Celia's grey-green eyes. It was Celia, at about age fifteen.

The portrait surprised me. Leo had placed his daughter in the past, in a romanticized, bygone Europe, perhaps his Polish hometown, Trembowla. In this setting I saw how completely the Holocaust and an earlier life wound through this apartment, with no door to close on it as there had been in Peter's home.

"An interesting portrait," I said. "You're in old Europe. Your dad must have missed those days."

"I have quite a lot of his work," she responded obliquely. "But let me show you around."

At her bedroom door, she beckoned. "I want you to see something." Her muffled voice drifted over her shoulder as she rummaged on the floor of her closet. "I have very little from my grandparents, just what my parents could fit in a suitcase. Before my parents left Vienna, they and my grandparents shipped three crates of their belongings—rugs, household goods…things precious to them…things they would need here…nothing arrived. The crates traveled through Germany…stolen.

"Aha!" Eyes bright, Celia backed out of the closet holding a flat box, which she set on the bed. "When my mother came to America, she brought this outfit and a few other things she could carry. My grandmother had made this for my mother's engagement party. That would have been…1936, three years before she left Vienna."

She laid a black jacket on the bed, smoothing the fragile fabric. I felt the soft, pebbled texture, an unusual knit, perhaps produced in Alfred and Hermann's textile factory. The workmanship was lovely. Some parts of the shapely jacket were hand-sewn with tiny, even stitches; others were machine sewn. The beige lace collar, small fabric-covered buttons, crocheted button loops, and tapered sleeve panels gave the jacket a feminine, tailored look and spoke of skilled work.

"Did your grandmother design it?"

"Probably." She held up a matching vest. It, too, was gracefully shaped, falling below the waist, and meticulously detailed. She said that the suit's flared skirt had deteriorated so badly she'd had to throw it away. Her voice was shaky. She admitted it had been difficult to part with.

With these stitches, a mother's love had blessed her daughter's marriage, and accompanied her across a perilous Europe and on to America. Hedwig must have helped her daughter pack, folding each item, thinking about occasions she would miss. Now, the suit reached out to the grand-daughter Hedwig had never known. The beautiful outfit told Celia a great deal about her grandmother and drew her close. In some ways, I thought, women's history has long been woven into such work.

Hedwig's sewing reminded me of quilts Sidney's mother had made for us, and the love we felt as we tucked in our children. My own mother, who could not knit, had labored many months to knit gloves for me. They were too small and full of holes, but I had kept them until moths made the holes even larger. I felt sure that Hedwig had understood: this suit would carry her love where she could not go.

★

I asked Celia if she had anything that belonged to her grandfather. She led me to the living room shelves, loosely arranged with books, glassware, and souvenirs from her various travels. She picked up a silver-plated shaving brush and small box with a straight handle. "These are all I have from my grandfather."

She snapped open the box, explaining that it was an ashtray, and gently placed the brush in my palm. I turned the cool, smooth brush handle in my hand. These were simple and rather sad artifacts of a life, probably Alfred's last possessions. I doubted whether anything I left behind would be as treasured as these humble objects.

I handed her the brush. "How did these come to you?"

She clicked the cabinet shut and we settled onto the couch. Her pigeon, with a soft *oooo-oooo-oooo*, scuttled next to its cage bars to be near Celia. Stroking the cooing pigeon through the bars, she digressed, "I found her with a broken wing about five years ago and nursed her. She can't survive on her own."

Then Celia turned seamlessly to her 1960s travel to Vienna with her parents. "Our trip had several purposes. We wanted to find my grand-father's grave. The Jewish section of the city cemetery had been vandal-ized, and we needed to take care of his site.

Her parents had also wanted to see the Tochs, close family friends of the Bergers. "My mother didn't ask them much about life under the Nazis—maybe because I was there, or she couldn't bear to hear it—but they told us a little. They gave her my grandfather's things.

"I've always wondered whether the Tochs went to my grandparents' vacated apartment after Hedwig was deported and took them. Why not? They'd been close. Someone had to take them."

"That wasn't pleasant to think about," I said as gently as I could, "but it was unlikely. Nazi authorities required Jews being deported to fill out forms listing their belongings. Officials sealed the vacated apartments, sent teams to itemize and take everything, then assigned the apartments to other Jews being deported, or to favored Nazis. "With every move to more cramped, shared apartments, Hedwig and Alfred probably sold belongings for a pittance, or gave them to friends. These were probably among their last possessions."

Celia continued to stroke her bird.

"It must have been dreadful for your mother to be given these two meager remnants of her father's life."

"It was," she nodded.

★

That evening Mark, Celia, and I walked along Broadway debating where to eat. Within a few blocks we had our choice of small, international family restaurants—Malaysian, Afghan, Philippine, Brazilian, Cyprian, Moroccan, Russian, American. We continued our conversation over curry and naan.

Mark expressed surprise that the Tochs had survived in Vienna. He asserted that that wouldn't have been possible in Poland, where his family had lived. "Being a decorated veteran married to an aryan wouldn't have protected him. Germans didn't worry about public outrage in Poland. Maybe they didn't expect any. They murdered all the Jews and many Poles. In some way, the Tochs were lucky."

Celia reminded him that the Tochs had suffered terribly too. They had sent their children to safety in the United States and after the war weren't able to restore their close, loving bonds. The children had become American, and they lived together as a family only for short periods after the war.

I wondered whether the Toch children would have memories of Vienna and the Bergers. Perhaps tomorrow we would find clues to their current location. For the moment, though, I missed my own family, spread across the country. I had heard all that I could handle of Holocaust misery. We were tired and didn't linger in the restaurant. As we walked back to the apartment, the intertwined accents of people on the streets together formed a language, a melody all its own.

★

In the morning, I straightened the living room, Mark brewed coffee, and Celia scurried around the apartment making toast and collecting family papers. She brought a box from under her bed; a thin brown leather suitcase from the hall closet; folders from a desk drawer. Setting the box on the table, the rest on the floor, she said there was more, stashed around the apartment.

Mark headed to his small study to work on his digital music as Celia and I collected dozens of photos from the box and spread them out on the table. Eagerly, we began winnowing the unruly stacks. Most were postwar vintage, but there were about two dozen older black-and-white pictures.

Sorting through the pictures, I reflected on what understanding they might hold for me. Old photos are gifts from the past, opening a frozen moment. Who was present? What did they wear? We found a picture of Alfred's mother Flora holding baby Hermann. Hedwig's parents were there—Bernard Grünberger distinguished looking, wearing what seemed a finely tailored suit, and Mathilde Berger Grünberger, middle-aged, projecting enough energy to handle her five children. More name confusion arose. Celia tried to help me: the maiden name of Hedwig's mother Mathilde was also Hedwig's married name. So Hedwig's mother had the same first and last names as Alfred's sister, Mathilde Berger. Hedwig's father Bernard Berger had the same first name as the Berger family friend Bernard Toch. Hedwig's parents were first cousins, Celia explained, laughing with amusement at my sighs as I attempted to sort out the pictures and the family.

We huddled over a studio portrait of Alfred and Hedwig, guessing it had been taken just before their 1909 wedding. Hedwig had been twenty, Alfred thirty-two. Her dress was flattering, softly pleated, with a lace-trimmed neckline and rows of crocheted flowers appliquéd down the front. Her expression was sweet and thoughtful. Her wide-set eyes held the same serene, watchful expression that Leo would later capture in his portrait.

As in the two youthful pictures we had seen at Peter's house, Alfred wore a suit, but this one looked softer, finer. The collar of his white shirt was high, his hair neat but curly, longer and freer, his handlebar mustache flaring outward like great wide wings. Once

Alfred and Hedwig. Engagement picture, 1909. *Courtesy of the Berger family*

again, he had raised his chin slightly. I could envision a bright future for this attractive couple.

Two group photos taken a few years later at the home of Alfred's brother Richard and Richard's wife Olga, who was also Hedwig's sister, were magnetic for me. They held so much information about the family. After World War I, Olga and Richard had lived in Baden bei Wien, an affluent spa town outside Vienna, Celia said. She wasn't sure whether Richard owned or was an executive at a textile factory south of Vienna, but their house and garden appeared to be elegant.

This was an important moment, it seemed, a large family occasion. It gave me a chance to see Alfred and Hedwig with their young family, surrounded by extended family. I studied the faces intently. Celia estimated that the first group picture was taken around 1924. We counted twelve family members gathered on Richard and Olga's front steps: Alfred, forty-seven, thinner than before, looked relaxed; Hedwig, thirty-five, was heavier; their older daughter Martha, a young teenager with hands on hips, challenged the photographer with her scowl; their younger daughter Gretl, about four, had an arm around her younger cousin Ani. Besides Richard and Olga's three children—Trudi, Loli, and Ani—Celia pointed out Hedwig and Olga's three brothers—Hugo and the twins Otto and Julius, who had come from Prague and Pressburg for this gathering.

Hugo, an engineer, was a manager for Sonal, an international oil company. Julius, also an engineer, worked on some of Prague's famous bridges, and Otto was an *apotheker*, a pharmacist, at the large drug company Merck.

The family was musical, Celia said, especially the Grünbergers. Hedwig and her sister Olga had beautiful voices. Their three brothers were accomplished musicians, playing piano and violin. Celia had heard stories about these occasions. "They were lively, full of laughter and music. Everyone joined in."

That Hedwig and Alfred shared a passion for music wasn't surprising. Both Vienna and the Moravian-Czech region were known for their rich

The Berger family, circa 1924. Top row, from left to right: Hugo and Otto Grünberger (two of Hedwig's brothers), Olga Grünberger Berger (Hedwig's sister, married to Alfred's brother Richard), Julius Grünberger (Hedwig's third brother who was Otto's twin), Richard Berger (Alfred's brother who was the husband of Hedwig's sister). Middle row: Alfred, Trudi, and Loli Berger (daughters of Olga and Richard), Willi Berger (the son of Alfred's brother Arnold). Bottom row: Hedwig, Ani Berger (Olga and Richard's youngest daughter), Gretl Berger (Alfred and Hedwig's younger daughter), Martha Berger (Alfred and Hedwig's elder daughter). *Courtesy of the Berger family*

musical culture. Gustav Mahler had grown up in Jglau. Alfred and Hedwig regularly attended performances in Vienna's famous opera house and concert halls, Celia said, even buying season tickets for the whole family.

For me, this picture was endlessly interesting, happy, and horrifying. Half of these family members would die in the Holocaust. How could Celia manage such conflicting emotions? To me, it seemed impossible.

The second photo, taken about four years later, revealed a different family mix, including Alfred's brother Arnold, his wife "Mitzi Two," and their two sons Willi and Ernst. In this picture Martha, perhaps near twenty with shoulder-length dark, wavy hair, seemed at ease and cheerful. The younger children captured my heart with their bright energy. Gretl and Ernst, about eight and twelve, apparently buddies, stood front and center, each with an arm flung around the other. Their caps were pulled low over their eyes, and they were the only two wearing coats.

They looked ready for adventure. In about ten years, they would sail together on a Greek ship to Palestine.

Most of the older pictures that we culled from the box that morning captured moments with Martha and Leo as a young couple in Vienna: Picnicking in the Vienna Woods. Posing with a large group from their Zionist Betar youth organization. Their wedding portrait.

Arnold — Wilhelm — Gertrude — Martha — Alfred Berger
Hedwig — Olga — Mary (Mitzi) — Lola
Grete — Ernst — Anita

Berger family photograph, circa 1928. Back row, from left to right: Alfred's brother Arnold, Arnold's son Willi, an unidentified man, Richard and Olga's daughter Trudi (Gertrude), Alfred's brother Richard, Hedwig and Alfred's daughter Martha, Alfred. Front row: Hedwig, her sister Olga, Hedwig and Alfred's daughter Gretl, Arnold's wife "Mitzi Two," Arnold and Mitzi's son Ernst, Richard and Olga's daughters Ani and Loli. *Courtesy of the Berger family*

As I scrutinized the pictures, Celia talked about the Berger family before the Holocaust. They had met for Jewish holidays, New Years, and birthdays. They had attended concerts, picnicked, and vacationed together. She believed that everyone sang. Mathilde's husband had once rented a concert hall and performed light opera publicly. At least four of the young cousins played the piano skillfully, some also a second instrument. Loli studied dance at an elite arts school. Trudi had begun an acting career. Gretl was known as a beautiful whistler.

I imagined those family occasions, fleetingly envious of the large, talented, close family—until the dark reality took my breath away. The faces looking out at me radiated love and possibility. "These must have been golden years," I told Celia, "when the future still looked…well, possible."

That vision had been an illusion—obvious now, but not to Austrian Jews at the time. After Austria's devastating World War I defeat, the widespread Berger family no longer lived in an Empire but in separate countries among more homogenous majorities whose interests had altered. Instead of protecting minorities, new governments resented them. The newly formed Austrian Republic, a shrunken nub of a nation, had—overnight, it seemed—become solidly Germanic and Roman Catholic. Its angry, poverty-stricken citizens sought easy targets to blame for their losses.

As Alfred and his siblings navigated adulthood, the tectonic shift in the Jews' situation emerged almost imperceptibly. Like many other Austrian Jews, the Bergers lived comfortably during that interwar period as the drumbeat of antisemitism around them grew louder, closer, and more dangerous. Vienna's Jews had lived with the noise for so long, they didn't hear it change.

Recognizing which of Celia's photos were taken after the Anschluss proved easy; smiling faces had grown serious, intense. A picture of Gretl and Martha wearing practical tailored suits and low heels and standing together on an empty cobbled Vienna street was eerie. Perhaps the picture had been taken in the early morning; businesses were closed; no traffic or other people were visible. Celia thought it had been taken just before Gretl left Vienna. The girls' expressions were solemn, as if the photographer had showed them the future: Much of their family would die within nine years. The sisters wouldn't see each other for twenty-five years, and Gretl would never see her parents again.

✦

Celia and I worked steadily throughout the day with quick breaks for lunch and tea. One picture we found told its own story: Hedwig was reading from a prayer book, two menorahs blazing nearby. Like most Jews of their generation, Celia's great-grandparents had been Orthodox. Alfred and Hedwig attended the more liberal Schmalzhofgasse synagogue one block from their apartment, but Hedwig had taught both daughters to repeat, every day, the mystical, central, ancient Jewish prayer, the *Shema*:

> *Sh'ma Yisrael Adonai Eloheinu Adonai echad…*
> Hear O Israel: The Lord is Our God. The Lord is One…

"My mother took her Jewishness seriously," Celia said, "but she joked about it, too. When I asked her about other religions, she told me that she directed her prayers to Heaven's Jewish Department."

Once again I appreciated the Bergers' humor. At Peter's home, after days surrounded by the Holocaust, a plumbing problem had triggered hilarious laughter. Celia and Peter couldn't resist adding merriment to our research into their harrowing past, teasing me that I shouldn't look so grim. Perhaps the Bergers' sense of humor had helped them while they waited in lines with no end, applying for documents, paying taxes…relying on their wits and their courage to cope with life in Nazi Vienna.

"What about your father and religion?" I asked Celia. She responded by taking me again to the living room cabinet, where she picked up a small book about the size of her two hands. The ivory-colored plastic cover looked like bakelite, which was used in mid-century jewelry, and it displayed a Star of David in the center. Celia opened the prayer book gingerly, and I saw why. Inside the pages were torn and badly scorched. "My father rescued this from a pile of burning books. The Nazis were always burning books, especially after Kristallnacht."

Kristallnacht, that November 1938 night and day of destruction of Jewish property throughout the Reich, had been a turning point in the intensification of shameless Nazi persecution. Celia said that at that point her parents had been trying to find a way to emigrate while the Nazis hunted Polish Jews who had entered the country illegally— including her father Leo. "My parents tried everything. They knew they had to leave, urgently."

Back at the table with its stacks of papers, Celia carefully untied a bundle of her father's sketches, which captured fleeting images of people and places that Leo had encountered as he fled Europe. I was fascinated, imagining Leo stopping to record moments of intense meaning. There were sketches from his time in French prison camps, hiding in a haystack, sailing to Cuba. The pencil drawings reflected his personal journal of flight in historic times.

Like Peter's family papers, Celia's were frustratingly random. We found *laissez-passers*, safe conduct passes, for Leo for different dates and places, tickets for ships and trains, ID cards, cables to Cuba. Family papers and mementoes were scattered in every room, in closets, drawers, under beds. Many stories resided only in Celia's memory.

Her family's European past had permeated Celia's growing up, her apartment, and her relationships, yet she hadn't attempted to fit the pieces together. I witnessed the courage and determination she had called upon, exhuming these buried stories. We packed those four days and nights full of hard work, tired laughter, international food, and long hours talking. I tried to encourage Celia when her spirits sagged; she teased me when I grew too serious.

On the last night of my stay, Celia drove us to her cousin Myra's New Jersey home so that I could hear her story of survival. Myra and her

Leo's sketch of fellow prisoners playing chess, probably in his cell in Les Sables d'Olonne. *Courtesy of Celia Cizes*

mother Sabina, Leo's sister, had shared Celia's family's apartment for several years; Myra and Celia were still close. Over dinner Myra poured out the story of her family and their leather shop in Trembowla, Poland, where the occupying Germans advancing toward Russia in 1941 forced the Jews into a ghetto. She barely remembered her father; German soldiers had abducted him from their home, and she never saw him again.

Myra vividly recalled her mother pulling her out of bed one night as German soldiers were rounding up Trembowla's Jews. She remembers hearing shouting, guns cracking, and the German commander's huge black dog barking and snarling. Myra said she had grabbed a bouquet from the table before they jumped out of a bedroom window. She clutched the flowers as they ran in terror to the countryside. On the road they had been robbed of the layers of sweaters and coats they had thrown on, though Sabina saved the few gold coins she had sewn into the hem of her skirt. A farmer's family who had been customers of the leather shop agreed to hide them at great risk to their own lives. Myra and her mother lived in a hidden room above the farmer's barn for three years. Now a psychologist helping others, Myra seemed a living Anne Frank.

✦

The next morning Celia called a cab. We hugged, promising to talk soon. Several hours later I dropped into my airplane seat, emotionally drained. I had spent the past eight days immersed in Holocaust stories. Those stories had been painful to Peter, to Celia, and to me—each story like a cut from jagged glass.

I felt fortunate that I had become closer to Celia, heard her stories, and looked at her documents, photos, and drawings; but I hadn't learned as much as I'd hoped about Alfred and Hedwig. I had learned a lot about Gretl, Martha, and Leo, though. My picture of the extended Berger family was filling in and becoming more layered. But Alfred and Hedwig remained in the background.

As my plane rose above the city, I gazed out the window, only to see the damaged Manhattan skyline and charred hole of the World Trade Center. Around it, cars still rolled down the streets. I knew that people went to work, ate lunch at favorite restaurants. It felt bizarre. Looking at the mixed collage of life below, I thought about how violence and everyday life have always coexisted—war and some level of peace intertwined—both basic to the human condition.

CHAPTER 9
The Cache of Letters

August 2006

S ometime during my visit to Celia's home, she and I had become a
team. As we labored together to make progress, we had begun to
understand each other. She was more high-strung and quicker to respond
than I was. I was quieter and mulled things over. Still we had grown to
trust and depend on each other and become friends. We spoke by phone,
sometimes several times a day, reviewing what we knew, identifying
what we didn't. It troubled us both that we had found very little directly
about Alfred and Hedwig at her home or Peter's.

Celia had promised to send me information that I hadn't had time
to copy or read. But then, understandably, she was reluctant for her
papers to leave the safety of her apartment. She doggedly scanned the
large stack we had set aside to peruse more slowly, translating some of
it. The work was tedious, her scanner finicky, and her German rusty.
Peter, too, had unsuccessfully tried scanning papers for me—notably
Hermann's ledgers, his letters to his daughter in New York, and Arnold's
journal describing his flight from the Nazis. Celia and Peter both gave
up. The thin airmail paper the Bergers used blurred the handwriting

from both sides of the paper together. Soon Peter decided to send me his documents through ordinary mail. I knew that Arnold and his wife had been the last members of the Berger family to escape Vienna, and I hoped that Arnold's journal would shed light on Alfred and Hedwig's perilous situation.

Ultimately, another trove of papers would emerge from Celia's closets, illuminating Alfred and Hedwig's fates. Because those documents were key to uncovering the Berger family's Holocaust story, and because those records are also essential to understanding the events of our trip to Vienna, I am jumping ahead in my story of discovery to tell how they were brought to light.

In 2006, two years after our trip to Vienna, Celia was still finding occasional papers in her apartment. Then, late one night, she shot me an emotion-charged email: "OH, MY GOD!!! You won't believe what I found. Letters from my grandparents!"

She phoned early the next day. Breathless with excitement, she said that she had found more than a hundred letters, most of them written by Alfred and Hedwig to her parents as they fled Europe and settled in America.

"Mark helped me reach an old suitcase from a high closet. After my father died…that was nine years after my mother's death…I had only a couple days to clean out his apartment. I stuffed all those letters into the suitcase and shoved it into the closet. I haven't seen it since." She ran on. "I'd totally forgotten. I knew I had more from my parents, but I couldn't remember where it was."

Also stuffed in the suitcase were letters that her parents had written to each other as they struggled, separately, to escape; there were letters from Gretl, too, and from Olga and her daughters, as they all sought safe havens. I had been losing hope that I would ever get close to Alfred and Hedwig's lives, hear their authentic voices, or comprehend, from their perspective, what was happening to them. Finally, here was their own account of the Holocaust! Celia had found a treasure.

✶

Celia's attempts to translate her grandparents' letters met with little success. Her limited fluency in German and the older style of handwriting proved to be daunting. Even just looking through letters she had found from her Aunt Olga, she thought her aunt must have suffered a nervous breakdown. Olga's less tidy Sütterlin handwriting looked to her like gibberish.

Still, Celia kept working. She scanned and sent me several partial translations of her grandparents' letters. Their tone was routine, conversational, eerily upbeat. Writing shortly after Martha fled Vienna in August 1939, Alfred and Hedwig mentioned the weather and visiting friends. They reported that Mathilde, Arnold, and Mitzi were well. They said they hoped that Martha and Leo were safe and healthy. Sidney and I thought that these letters could have been written about a holiday in the countryside. The unemotional prose and absence of solid news were frustrating.

But we hadn't understood. Over the phone, Celia explained. "My grandparents knew that my parents were beside themselves with worry. They didn't want to add to their children's misery.

"Also, they knew that censors read every word. Germany had constructed a sophisticated propaganda machine to deceive the world about what they were doing. Censors blacked out or discarded letters that might incite international condemnation. You could be arrested for criticizing Nazis. They looked for mentions of property they could tax or expropriate. My family wrote numbers in code.

"My parents read between the lines and wrote carefully. Their letters to Alfred and Hedwig, too, could be thrown out or worse—create trouble for family trapped in Vienna."

I thought of my own children in three different cities. Especially when their lives were unsettled, I craved news and assurance of their well-being. Reich censorship had forced heartbroken, ripped-apart families to read and write coded pleasantries and innuendoes, instead of the crucial news they longed for. The censorship was designed to serve the needs of the state and Nazi Party and eliminate the potential of a powerful, sympathetic world response to Jews' suffering. That censorship became yet another form of Nazi torment. The family's self-censorship must have required extraordinary restraint and bred gnawing loneliness and fear. Alfred and Hedwig had effectively become prisoners, yet wrote cheerful, supportive letters.

"The heartache must have been excruciating," I said, beginning to grasp what it must have cost Alfred and Hedwig to withhold their pressing, heartfelt questions and remain silent about their own troubles. I saw that while some kinds of courage dazzle and command center stage, the Bergers' bravery, selfless and resolute, played out quietly.

The self-censorship also meant that to understand those carefully crafted letters I would need to place each one within the context of its time.

Celia attempted to organize the several hundred pages of letters by different writers. A few were tucked neatly in envelopes. Most had missing pages or were scattered in complete disorder. In the end, she counted more than eighty letters from Alfred and Hedwig and an even larger number that her parents, Martha and Leo, had written to each other. There were also some from her Aunt Gretl and from Alfred and Hedwig's brother and sister Richard and Olga and their three daughters Trudi, Ani, and Loli. It was an amazing collection.

Celia had never read these letters, and she wasn't able to translate them without great effort. I set to work looking for a translator. Lead after lead evaporated as I sought someone who could decipher the old handwriting and tackle this large project. Even the University of Oregon's German department lacked expertise with old German script. Some older German speakers I contacted had no interest. I located one person who was able, but worked at a plodding pace for a high price.

I was stymied. Still, from the beginning, each time my quest stalled, doors had opened as if ordained. Once again a solution materialized, this time ten minutes from my home. I had interviewed a number of local Holocaust survivors, and I learned of another who had endured four years in Theresienstadt, the infamous concentration camp near Prague. Hilde Geisen was about eighty years old, with alert grey-green eyes, a ready smile, and a sharp memory for both recent and long passed events. Over tea in her modest home she told me about her deportation and harrowing teenage years in the Nazi camp. She hadn't met Hedwig's siblings who had also been imprisoned there, she said, but she had heard of one brother, Hugo, who had been a camp leader and performed in the famous camp orchestra. "You understand, many, many people came there temporarily. Many died of starvation, disease, and the cold. Others were deported again, farther east, we didn't know where. I was lucky. I was assigned an office job."

As I was leaving, I asked Hilde hesitantly if she might be interested in helping to translate the letters.

"Why, yes," she said.

"Yes?" Caught off guard by her quick, clear response, I explained: "There are quite a few. The handwriting is the old Sütterlin style."

"Sure," she smiled. "It will be interesting."

Overwhelmed by her generosity, I danced a mental mazurka. Hilde would translate the letters! She lived near me and insisted that she wouldn't accept payment.

Celia's stash of letters was too large for her to scan even if she had had a reliable computer and internet, which she didn't. Not infrequently I received emails from her late at night filled with #, @, ! symbols expressing her chagrin that her computer had frozen or crashed, but the idea of sending the originals frightened her.

I saw again how closely her papers and artifacts bound her to her missing family and protected their stolen history. She continued to wrestle with her fear that they would be lost or damaged, but when she heard that I had located a translator, she let go of her anxiety and sent them to me by registered mail.

I scanned and printed those irreplaceable letters. Occasionally Alfred and Hedwig had written daily, more often weekly, but sometimes gaps stretched longer than a month. They had economized on stationery and postage by writing on thin, lightweight airmail paper, around bottom corners, and up along edges. I recognized Hedwig's careful script and Alfred's increasingly splotchy handwriting. I saw that often they had placed lined paper behind their thin stationery so that the writing looked regimented, though Alfred still had trouble. Sometimes his guide sheet had shifted, and entire paragraphs slanted down.

I found blurred spots that could have been tears or coffee and censors' marks—codes I didn't understand: "2748-1542. 9N7 1054." Nazi censors had taken time to make their ominous presence known by stamping the top of each letter sent during sensitive times, as for instance during the military buildup preceding Germany's invasion of Poland. To the Reich, every word passing in or out of the country portended a threat. Those stamped numbers sent a warning: "We're watching you.... We know where you live.... We know your family and friends." I imagined self-important low-level bureaucrats reading letter after letter, scanning accounts of afternoon *jause* [coffee time], recipes, and wishes for good health, searching every line for hidden meaning.

I had anticipated that the task of translating these letters would be formidable. It was. After I returned from Vienna, I would meet Hilde weekly for more than a year in her home, where she patiently translated the letters aloud and I transcribed them on my laptop. She asked questions about the people in the letters, and explained nuances to me— "Hansi? That's their canary. Everyone named their canary Hansi."

"You see, first, the Nazis moved Jews from the countryside to cities, then from one apartment to another to collect Jews in certain areas. It was gradual at first, so other people wouldn't notice and raise concern. Ha!" Hilde exclaimed emphatically. "People didn't care. They knew what was happening."

Breaking for tea and conversation, and working until I at least was worn out, Hilde and I became fast friends. With her determined help, these voices from the Holocaust could be heard—revealing the story behind Alfred's pleading letter.

CHAPTER 10

Vienna Bound

August 2004

After the week spent in Peter's Vienna Room and Celia's apartment, I was relieved to be home, where the Holocaust wasn't woven through every family memory. Even so, I was beginning to feel that the Holocaust now had a presence in our own lives.

Sidney and I discussed the Bergers' lives and fate more frequently. He had become familiar with all the Berger family members' names—no small feat—and asked more about my day-to-day research. When we escaped work to hike in the nearby forests, which we loved to do, the quest accompanied us. Sidney asked whether Celia had decided to join us in Vienna. He hoped Micha and Judith would come. Over dinner, he pondered whether the Los Angeles Bergers had remembered Alfred's letter as they tuned their radio to increasingly grim war news. Did they regret not helping?

I began to see that as my husband followed the history of one real family, he had been deeply moved, though in a more manageable way than if it had been his own relatives. I knew that my quest was becoming his as well. We both wanted to know how the Holocaust could have happened to one ordinary family. I wondered whether our talking and learning about the Holocaust was opening a door that made it feel closer—and, frighteningly, more possible today.

We would head to Vienna in six weeks, and many unfinished tasks still confronted me. I attacked papers, interviews, files, and emails—information I'd gathered over the previous eight months—and explored leads uncovered during my East Coast trip. I worked to arrange interviews with Alfred's three now elderly nieces in Israel and began searching for the Toch children. They might remember Alfred and Hedwig, and I hoped they might have the photos that their father had taken of concentration camps after the war.

Friends I talked to about those photos expressed surprise that such photos interested me. They thought the world had enough concentration camp photos. Why bother searching for more? I couldn't comprehend that logic. We search for meaning in pictures. Newly discovered images of Marilyn Monroe, President Trump, or Hitler endlessly fascinate us as we seek that flash of insight that might make the incomprehensible understandable. The Toch photos, if they existed, would add to the record. Every photo of a victim is an act of resistance against the perpetrators' attempts to erase victims' existence and conceal the crime of mass murder. Who knew what those missing photos might reveal, and how they would touch us?

✦

Just three weeks before Sidney and I were scheduled to leave for Vienna, I was anxious. I had encouraged Celia, Micha, Judith, and Peter to join us there in September, but well into August their plans were still not firm. Health problems made Celia hesitate. Micha, working as a consultant in France, wasn't sure of his schedule. Judith and her husband Avraham were discussing the trip with their elderly cousins. Finally, Peter wrote that work would prevent him from joining us, but the rest of the family said they would come. After a lifetime of hearing almost nothing of their mother's and grandparents' history,

Micha and Judith hungered to learn their family story. Celia knew a lot, but in bits and pieces. She very much wanted to be involved in this process, and to be with her cousins. Sidney and I were delighted. Three of Alfred and Hedwig's grandchildren would meet us and help us in the city their family had fled.

As August flew by, Celia took on the role of family organizer, negotiating with others to join us. She urged her elderly Israeli cousins Ani and Loli, daughters of Olga and Richard, to come. Their older sister Trudi was ill, but Loli still communicated with friends in Vienna and wanted to see the city again. And Ani, though deeply bitter towards the Viennese, was intrigued by this family trip and lobbied her children to take her. Celia also spoke to their cousin Willi, Arnold's son in Rio de Janeiro, but in the end the families of these three older Bergers vetoed the trip as too arduous.

Ani and Loli had been twenty and twenty-five when they fled Vienna. Willi had worked in Hermann's textile company and known Alfred and Hedwig well. All three survivors had been close to their Aunt Hedwig and Uncle Alfred, slept at their home, and vacationed with them. As Celia talked about those cousins, their bright faces in Celia's photos popped into my mind. Their families' objection to the trip made sense but was disappointing. Because of translation difficulties and diminished hearing, communicating with them by phone was impossible. Sidney and I talked over their importance to our understanding of Alfred and Hedwig's lives and arranged to fly to Israel to meet Ani and Loli soon after our Vienna trip.

Two weeks before our departure, Celia emailed me with another surprise. She had spoken with Herta, the widow of Arnold's younger son Ernst. Herta had been his girlfriend in Vienna and escaped with him and Gretl. She and Ernst had lived in Israel before moving to Brazil to be near Ernst's brother Willi. Unlike Ani, Herta had retained her love for Vienna and visited friends there every year. Celia had convinced her to plan her annual trip to coincide with ours. Celia, Micha, and Judith were delighted at the growing family reunion. Herta would be a wonderful addition for me also; no one else who was coming had known the Bergers in Vienna in the way that she had.

I was impatient to begin the trip, but still worried. "How will you manage with five people who all have their own different agendas?" Sidney asked me. I admitted that I didn't know. My quest continued to expand as I discovered more family and it became their quest, too. But, as I had done before when uncertain about how to proceed, I decided to trust the story and follow where it led. It seemed to have a life of its own.

That August the Berger family network was throbbing with new-found energy. Family members spread across the globe were talking to each other about the Holocaust, fitting pieces of stories together, asking questions. Family members whose memories stretched back to before the Holocaust were talking with the younger generation, who had never heard the stories, and with siblings who had held their questions inside.

A number of the Bergers, like Sidney's family and many other Jews after the Holocaust, had maintained a dogged silence about their history, concealing a core of pain. Even Peter's Vienna Room, created with tender care, had seemed sealed up and rarely used. Although the Holocaust connected and affected them all, no one, including Celia, had made more than passing efforts to explore it.

Now, secrets were slipping out…Richard had abandoned his family…pieces of stories were falling into place…I was arrested crossing the mountains. The guard told me, "Try again tonight." I waited in Zurich but no word from Ernst…Repressed longings were welling up…I didn't know. I never dared to ask.

The Bergers were shedding tears, forging renewed connections to each other and to the catastrophe that had shaped their lives, telling their own Holocaust history. They were realizing that they had their own Exodus story, their own *Night*—Elie Wiesel's story of love, pain, and horror—their own heroines, heroes, and victims: family who had braved life-threatening obstacles, a sweet child who had survived in hiding, and another who had perished at Auschwitz.

✦

Just weeks before we left for Vienna, I received a packet from the Vienna City Archives including household registration forms for Alfred's brothers and sister, for Bernard and Pauline Toch, and for several of Bernard's siblings. The first card I pulled from the envelope startled me. Bernard Toch's sister and her husband and Alfred and Hedwig had shared the same final address in Vienna, and they had been deported on the same date as Hedwig. Celia had said the families were close, but she hadn't known how connected their fates were.

Other cards documented Bernard Toch's changing addresses, and as I had hoped, his children's names, birthdates, and departure for Los Angeles. A breakthrough. I could begin to trace them. Later I would locate the Toch children in a Los Angeles suburb and find that both of them were willing to talk with me. Herbert's few memories of Vienna were like random faded snapshots, typical for the young age when he had left. He remembered raucous Nazi celebrations, swimming in the Danube Canal, treats of yogurt and strawberries, but nothing of the Bergers.

Trudy, however, had vivid memories and several boxes of Vienna photos. When I met both siblings at Trudy's home, she shared her pictures. They were fascinating, especially the photos of her young playmates, most of them Jewish. They wore dirndls and lederhosen like other Viennese children, but unlike them, Trudy told me, all of these boys and girls would perish in the Holocaust. She also showed me photos of her parents' dry-goods stall in the Naschmarkt, Vienna's celebrated marketplace. I guessed that Alfred had sold the Tochs suspenders and maybe the women's jacquard socks that he'd described in one of his letters, but Trudy had no pictures of Alfred and Hedwig. Trudy validated Celia's story that after the war her father, Bernard, had searched concentration camps for loved ones, and though he had been distraught at finding no one, he had taken pictures as he went. Unfortunately, she said, her mother had decided that his camp photos were too depressing, that no one should see them, and she had stuffed them in the back of a closet, where they remained until she passed away. A hired house-cleaner had then thrown them away. I could empathize with her mother's horror and the urge to put the atrocities of the war behind them, but the loss of the pictures upset me terribly. An important record of dark human history had been lost.

Trudy did remember Alfred and Hedwig. When I pressed her for details, she described visiting their apartment with her parents. Alfred was tall, she said. Hedwig was friendly and very kind, especially to children. Trudy said that her memories were foggy, but one visit stood out because it had frightened her. Alfred and Hedwig had talked about trying to escape Austria illegally. Trudy was the only person I had spoken with who had actually met Alfred and Hedwig, and her impression of a proactive, determined couple heartened me. I didn't want to think of them simply as victims.

★

Two weeks before our departure for Vienna, I turned to crucial sidelined tasks. The eight-page Berger family time line that I had begun for Celia months ago needed updating so that the family could review, add, and correct information when we were together in Vienna. I scoured hundreds of emails, sorting through piles of documents, notes, and interview transcripts, entering events, dates, addresses.

About 1912- Richard Berger and Olga Grünberger marry. Received two Hitler watercolor paintings as wedding gifts.

April 1926- Gretl writes in Martha's yearbook. "There blooms a little flower...all it can say, always the same, "Forget Me Not."

1934- Communist/labor uprising in Vienna. Pitched street battles. Many dead.

Lights burned late into the night in my study as the chronology expanded to twenty-five pages. Some family stories had been incomplete, and consolidating my research with the family stories sometimes corroborated but other times corrected their memories. Dated ship tickets...exit visas...historical events—bits of information from the mundane to life-shattering took on new meaning in the Bergers' story, though some holes still glared.

> 1936- Martha and Leo marry at Schmalzhofgasse Synagogue. Met through matchmaker? Leo: artist, sales rep. Ani describes him, "A lot of 'go' in him."
> August 7, 1939- Alfred writes to stranger in Los Angeles, begging for help.

Thirty-nine pages. I noted questions to pursue in Vienna. Could I find records of Alfred's accident? When had Alfred and Hedwig registered to apply for a visa, which, had it been granted, would have allowed them to immigrate to America?

A nagging issue that had bothered me from the beginning now loomed even larger: How had Alfred and Hedwig become trapped while thousands of Jews escaped Vienna? Was it because of their lack of resources, Alfred's near blindness, or the absence of an American sponsor? Had anyone tried to help? Perhaps fate had played a role, and time simply ran out in the diabolical race for survival, and they were caught with no options.

One night I sat back wearily and stared at my computer screen. The Bergers' story had come into sharper focus as the chronology took shape; the steady progression of births, marriages, and deaths in Central Europe through the 1800s and early 1900s erupted into a sudden explosion of family movement after the Anschluss.

A panorama of the Holocaust spread out before me. In many Jewish families, like in Sidney's, the story is one of either death or escape to a limited number of locations. But the extended Berger family's scramble for survival had carried them to New York, Shanghai, France, Slovakia, Romania, Turkey, Palestine, Kenya, Cuba, Trinidad, and Brazil. Scrolling farther down my time line, I saw words that spelled death—Auschwitz, Theresienstadt, Riga, Minsk. Family members had been robbed, imprisoned, shot, gassed, run down on the street. The Bergers' experience illuminated a broad sweep of the Holocaust.

I had also compiled a Berger genealogy, which lay that night unfolded, four feet long, across my study floor. Gazing at it, I saw this family's place in an even larger picture. Their family tree had been torn from its historic European roots, as the Bergers joined the new Jewish diaspora. I had started this quest to explore how the Holocaust had affected one family, but on that night I also saw their story illuminate the Holocaust's place in Jewish history, a foundational event alongside the exodus from Egypt and the Babylonian exile.

✦

The most difficult planning for our trip turned out to be a decision between Sidney and me, connected to our own family. As I had learned more about the Bergers' fate, I decided that I wanted to add Minsk to our itinerary, intending to trace Hedwig's final journey to its end. Checking maps, I was stunned to see that Radoshkovici, the Belarusian village that had been Sidney's family's historic home, was only twenty miles from Minsk. Again, the story was traveling in directions I could never have invented. Sidney's history and the Bergers' had intersected in Belarus.

When I brought up the importance of Minsk to my quest and the proximity of his family's village, my husband balked at visiting either place. "I'm not interested. My grandfather fled Russian pogroms and military service in the czar's army. He left everything he loved, hid in hay wagons, and then sailed alone to America to escape that place. He wrote a memoir about growing up there. That's enough!" I knew that Sidney's grandmother's family had emigrated legally about that same time, seeking opportunity and security, but except for a few vague sentences, I had never heard him talk about the family left behind. Now he had begun to sound like Micha and Judith, edging closer to talking about his family's Holocaust past.

I asked Sidney's mother about her Russian family. She replied succinctly. "Before World War II, we exchanged letters and handmade gifts, but after the war…you know, the Communists, the Iron Curtain. There was no way to communicate, even through the Red Cross. That was so many years ago. Anyway, all the family in Russia died in the war." Then she changed the subject. When I told her that we might go to that area, color flooded into her face—and my usually deferential mother-in-law forbade us to go.

The subject was not open for discussion with her. The same distancing from the Holocaust that we had seen in Gretl's family was threaded through Sidney's. With no solid information, they simply closed the door on their own past. Now the trip I was proposing had triggered shapeless fears, terrifying my mother-in-law.

But Hedwig's death in Minsk had become a focal point for me, the culminating event of the Bergers' anguishing experience. The Gestapo record of her deportation, on a small typed index card, included her transport number, destination, departure date, and, one week later, her death. Nothing more. With that, the Gestapo had closed the books on one more Jew.

I didn't want to pressure Sidney and his mother, the very suggestion of this trip distressed them so greatly. Still, their thinking seemed irrational, stuck in a painful and frightening but largely unknown past. I attempted again to explain to Sidney. "I need to follow Hedwig's path as closely as possible. No one can understand her experience, but I can watch the landscape change. I can feel the growing weight of time and distance, experience the strangeness of passing countries. How did she die? And, where?"

Eventually he admitted the importance of Minsk to our trip. He suggested flying.

"I can't learn about Hedwig's journey from an airplane." I suggested we should take the slowest local train, where people were jammed together, ate and slept in their seats, the air thick with smells of long travel.

As he had many times these past eight months, my husband listened, sighed, and said he understood—to a point. A local train was one step too far. I talked again with his mother, offering to abandon the idea that was so distressing. Somehow that relaxed her, and she told us to go. I purchased tickets for the Vienna–Moscow Express—my concession to Sidney's wish for an easier journey; even so, it would be a fifteen-hour sojourn with few stops through the Czech Republic and Poland to Minsk.

The Minsk complications did not end with those issues settled. Belarus had declared independence from the Soviet Union in 1991, but the country retained a repressive Communist government. Even as potential casual tourists, we felt its eyes on us. To obtain visas we needed to send our passports to the Belarusian embassy in Washington, D.C., along with a detailed questionnaire demanding our entry and departure dates, the names of people we would talk with, the places we would visit, and an approved guide who would accompany us for our entire stay. As required, we agreed to stay in a government hotel staffed by monitors on every floor. We should not take any photos. Applying for the visa was a daunting process; we were intimidated.

Sidney and I continued to discuss visiting his family's village of Radoshkovici. No one in his close-knit family spoke about their lost family. They treated those people as if they had been distant relatives from a remote past instead of first cousins, aunts, uncles, and grandparents. I persisted in urging my husband to consider making the trip, reminding him that his grandfather had once asked Sidney to take him to Radoshkovici. Sidney, then twenty, had hesitated, and his grandfather had dropped the idea. Finally, the village's proximity to Minsk proved too tempting for Sidney to resist. He had developed his own curiosity and decided we should go.

My parents remained ambivalent about my quest. Their lives were mostly restricted to their own Protestant culture. My father's country club had recently considered admitting Jews, but at that point there still were no Jewish members. Our upcoming trip agitated them, too. Why get involved, they asked—obviously made uncomfortable by the fact that I was becoming immersed in a world they had carefully avoided.

I suspected that the Los Angeles Bergers, reading Alfred's letter, had pondered the same question. It was a good question, and I wasn't sure that I knew the answer.

★

Feeling eager and nervous, Sidney and I drove to Portland and boarded our plane. We watched the ground disappear as we turned east toward Vienna, the city that for centuries had been a haven and a hell for Jews.

Part II

CHAPTER 11
Gilded City

September 2004

In the tiny western Austrian border town of Landek, Sidney and I boarded a sleek train painted with the red and white colors of Austria's flag. We had spent several days hiking and relaxing in Switzerland and looked forward to seeing the scenic Austrian countryside whirl past our window as we rolled the 350 or so miles east to Vienna. I had tensed as I presented my ticket and identification to enter the train, unable to prevent myself from envisioning the documents required for Jews in 1939—not so long ago, really—stamped with a large red "J." Had we lived here then, Sidney's passport would have carried that damning mark. Without the crucial papers to prove we were emigrating, we would have been pulled off the train and arrested.

We left the station and history streamed past our window like a silent film, marring my enjoyment of the spectacular Alpine views. Austria was a major power in Western history for over five hundred years, with Vienna reigning as capital of an empire that at its greatest extent reached from Spain to Romania. Now, after its defeat in two world wars, the shrunken nation looks squashed and distorted in the slim corridor between its former allies, Italy and Germany. Modern Austria is smaller than the state of Maine.

For a time our train followed Austria's border with Bavaria, Germany's southern state, known as the birthplace of the Nazi Party. Hitler had loved this scenic area where few Jews or immigrants resided. He had completed his venomous *Mein Kampf* manifesto in Berchtesgaden, just across this border from here.

And as Führer he had built a luxurious mountaintop retreat on the ridgetops above Berchtesgaden. But this Austrian and German countryside had been antisemitic long before Hitler. During the fifteenth century, Jews were burned here. Few Jews lived in rural Austria in the succeeding centuries. As late as the 1930s many locals had never seen a Jew. Some actually believed the medieval superstition that Jews had tails. Others believed they had horns.

Like many Viennese, the Bergers had loved Austria's mountains. Alfred and Hedwig brought their family to mountain resorts in Austria for holidays and for Martha's recuperation from childhood pneumonia. Both Hermann and Mathilde returned every year to favorite mountain spa hotels. Ani and Loli hiked and skied in Austria's mountains. Loli was a mountaineering guide. In the gathering storm of 1930s antisemitism, Jews were excluded from Austrian outdoor clubs, encountering jeers like "Keep our mountains pure! No Jews!" Jews formed their own clubs in response, but Loli's club discontinued outings when its members were shoved out of mountain huts.

We rode smoothly and almost silently past Salzburg's quaint pointed steeples. Jews were central in creating the celebrated Salzburg Music Festival, and "Max," the impresario character in *The Sound of Music*, was Jewish: the real-life Max Reinhardt had been born to an Austrian Jewish merchant family. A creative genius, Reinhardt was a major force in Berlin and Vienna theater and is credited—along with Richard Strauss and a librettist of Jewish descent—with founding the festival in 1920. After the Anschluss, Reinhardt fled Austria and immigrated to the United States.

Past Salzburg, we stopped at Linz, the Danube port where Hitler's father had been a customs inspector. As Führer, Hitler was determined to remake this city into a major economic and cultural center. Germany dismantled countless factories in conquered Czechoslovakia and re-assembled them here. That may have included the Czech textile factory connected to Hedwig's family. Honig, the Jewish-owned textile company where Hermann, Alfred, Arnold, and Willi once worked, was aryanized after the Anschluss. Because the factory was located in the Reich, it wasn't moved, but the Jewish owners and workers were thrown out. With Hitler obsessed with expanding Linz, inmates of the nearby Mauthausen-Gusen concentration camp were forced to quarry stone for an extravagant new Führermuseum to hold artwork stolen from enemies, especially Jews and conquered peoples. I was thankful our stop there was brief.

We glided over verdant hills, past towns and villages surrounded by expanses of forests and fields. A scattering of modern buildings blended smoothly into the idyllic traditional countryside, but I remained uneasy.

The insistent clacking of wheels quieted to a soft hum as we eased toward Vienna's Westbahnhof, West Rail Station. Window boxes displaying red flowers like those we'd noticed across the countryside passed by our window. I had read that Austrians love their traditions, but this level of uniformity—even in their flowers—was remarkable. Americans are accustomed to wild cacophonies of styles, colors, patterns—and ideas. Austrians did not appear to value diversity—something that I thought might help explain their mass embrace of the Nazi movement.

Through a fringe of trees lining the tracks were tantalizing glimpses of Vienna, including the now familiar red and grey tiled roofs we had seen all across the country. The city has a surprisingly low skyline for a major national capital. Few buildings have more than five or six stories, allowing Vienna's church domes, towers, and spires to rise over the city as if keeping watch.

We jerked to a stop and Sidney and I easily passed from the train through a maze of modern pedestrian tunnels to the Underground, where more tracks and trains awaited. Fifteen minutes later we were climbing a staircase to Mariahilferstrasse, the famous Vienna shopping avenue I

had traced many times with my fingertips on maps, locating landmarks
of the Bergers' lives.

✱

We emerged into a thin, brittle afternoon light that illuminated the
city but did not warm it. Dazzled, we pulled on light jackets as we looked
around.

History surrounded us here. The four- to seven-story thick-walled
plaster buildings were mostly very old, with dormer windows opening
onto steeply pitched roofs. Eggshell colored designs—gargoyles, women's
profiles, faux balustrades—ornamented upper floors. Shops ranged from
pricey to touristy, local to international chains. Signs, old and simple,
neon and blinking, hung above the sidewalk. On one building a cutout
picture of a referee extended from the first floor to the roof, advertising
an American sportswear chain. Churning with mixed feelings, enthralled
to be in this famous city, we made our way to our hotel.

A block from the U-Bahn stop, near the intersection of Kirchengasse,
Church Street, and Mariahilferstrasse, Mary Our Helper Street, we
found the sign for the Continental Hotel-Pension above a single door
along the sidewalk. The modest hotel stood a convenient fifteen-minute
walk from the Ringstrasse, Vienna's famous half-circle ring road around
the city center—and from Alfred and Hedwig's Schmalzhofgasse apartment. I stopped a minute to collect myself. Reaching this place had been
a long journey. I was eager to begin my work, but nervous about how it
would go. What could I learn? Would the eight of us, strangers and family meeting here, work well together? Sidney gave me a reassuring smile
and pushed the doorbell.

Following signs that pointed us higher, we ascended a dark spiral
stairway where lights popped on as we moved upward. On the second
floor, Celia rushed to greet us. She called a cheery welcome to Sidney
and threw her arms around me as if I, too, were her family. It had been

just six weeks since I'd visited her in New York, but this trip stirred heartfelt emotions for her and, I guessed, for all the Bergers.

The rest of the family had already arrived, she told us and then disappeared to alert them that we'd come. Chatting and laughing, Micha and his wife Chava, Judith and her husband Avraham trailed Celia down the short hallway to meet us. We introduced ourselves, and Judith explained that the elderly Herta Berger—widow of Ernst, who was the younger son of Alfred's brother Arnold—had arrived the day before but was staying at a different hotel not far from ours. She would meet us the next day.

Sidney and I registered and dropped our bags, and we all set out for dinner a block away at a three-generation family restaurant our hotel manager had recommended. Servus Café, with its large 1950s-era neon sign, sat at the edge of a plaza dominated by the three-hundred-year-old Mariahilferkirche, Mary Our Helper Church, that gave the plaza and both cross streets their names. From the roof some forty feet above us a large statue of Mary with a spiky golden halo over her head, baby Jesus in her arms, and an enigmatic expression gazed down over a statue of Haydn, a clutch of market stands, hordes of passing shoppers, and us. Coming from Oregon, I was not accustomed to seeing history at every turn; in Vienna, the enveloping arms of history and religion were omnipresent.

The Servus Café itself had seen much history, but dark wooden ceiling fans turning slowly overhead were the only remnants of an earlier decor. Pink upholstered booths had a 1950s feel. I reflected that during the Nazi era even Jewish neighbors who had once been regulars here, were not permitted to walk through the café's doors.

Micha, who spoke fluent German, helped us translate the menu, which featured traditional Viennese cuisine, a mix of influences from across the Empire: wiener schnitzel, Hungarian goulash, Serbian-style pike, Carinthian cheese noodles, roasted pork leg with crackling crust, blood sausage, liver noodle soup, dumplings of many varieties. Hamburgers and apple pie back home seemed provincial by comparison. For dessert, Servus promoted *Mohr im hemd* (Moor in a Shirt). We learned that these were small individual chocolate bundt cakes with chocolate sauce, and a name that held racist overtones.

The waiter described an Austrian fall specialty, *eiswein*, a light sweet "ice wine" made from partially frozen grapes. He explained that this seasonal specialty is served from large barrels at autumn festivals around the city. The café also featured *sturm*, Austria's pale golden wine made from the fermenting, freshly pressed grape juice of the first harvest and served in thick beer glasses. For the Viennese, he told us, smiling, *sturm* marks the beginning of the harvest season. Soon we were clinking mugs with a hearty *Prost*, cheers, like the others around us, and the more serious *l'chaim*: to life.

Over the next ten days, we would meet regularly for dinner at the Servus Café. We adopted our own favorite foods, served by the same waiter who greeted us and led us to "our table." The Viennese have a word for one's own table—*stammtisch*. I began to understand how easily life in this city could become—as the Viennese say—*gemütlich*, charming.

★

In the morning we straggled into the hotel's breakfast room before gathering in Micha and Chava's room. Judith and Celia perched side by side on the bed. Micha and Chava pulled chairs up to a small table. Sidney and Avraham leaned against the back wall. Setting my satchel of documents on the floor, I stood by the door, watching as the family settled in. Micha wasted no time. He turned to me and said, "Well, tell us what you propose."

As the outsider in this family group, I was eager to begin but felt awkward directing their exploration into their family roots. Still, I had done the research and organized this gathering. For the moment, this was my show.

To be certain that everyone had the same information, I reviewed my quest since receiving Alfred's letter—the archival research that had led me to Celia; our meetings in New York; the emails, phone calls, and conversations that had led me to Peter, the Vienna Room, Celia's apartment, and now here.

As I spoke I scanned their faces. Each of them already knew most of what I was saying, but they listened intently, nodding, leaning forward as if I were the finest storyteller they'd heard. I knew this was an extraordinary, curious moment for them—that anyone would make a significant effort to discover their family's hidden story was still somewhat astonishing to them, and now they, too, had become part of the search and the story.

We had a lot of ground to cover, and I needed to propose a framework for our joint effort. I explained the chronology. Whenever I had uncovered information over the past seven months, I told them, I'd added it. I gave each family a copy of the time line, plus the genealogy I had created. They were rapt. I had some experience addressing groups, but never one so intense—or in a small bedroom.

I suggested that we meet each morning to coordinate plans and read the chronology together, a section at a time, filling in voids when possible, identifying discrepancies and mistakes.

"Mistakes?" Micha interrupted.

"It's a work in progress." Celia leapt to my defense.

I explained. "For instance, I've found different birthdates for Mathilde in family records. And we've learned that Hedwig did not go to Theresienstadt, as Judith and Celia once believed. Talking through the information, we can compare different stories we've heard, and sort soft information from what can be verified."

Micha gave a single definitive nod.

I proposed interviewing each family member during the week and invited everyone to join me at my appointments at various archives. I suggested, too, that we go together to places in the timeline, starting that morning with Alfred and Hedwig's Schmalzhofgasse apartment. "Later, we can go to their second and third apartments, and the site of Alfred's accident."

"What do you mean, second and third apartments?" Judith shook her head, puzzled.

Our discussion was revealing important gaps in her knowledge. "Nazi Party members, the Germans, and ordinary Viennese pushed Jews from their apartments after the Anschluss. Germany took control of that process, which continued throughout the Holocaust, compressing Jews into a few areas. Jews had to find new apartments but weren't allowed to rent. They moved in with other Jews. Your grandparents were evicted twice."

Judith closed her eyes and shook her head.

I asked for everyone's hopes for our time in Vienna. Micha smiled, his voice businesslike. "I'm ready to begin." He began skimming the chronology. Judith said that the family wanted to visit Alfred's grave and arrange for its repair and care. Celia wanted to attend a concert in the Musikverein, the renowned concert hall where her mother had once performed, and maybe take a day trip on the Danube, as she'd done once with her parents.

Judith stood up. "We're here to learn about our grandparents. Tell us if we can help." She excused herself to phone Herta. Chava rummaged in her satchel and pulled out a large envelope. She explained that she had interviewed Ani for me, and brought the DVD of it and a transcript.

I was deeply moved. This family had done everything they could to contribute to this quest. They'd all been extraordinarily generous and were deeply involved, but for me roles were blurring. Were they story sources, associates, or friends? I felt wary that the multiple roles might collide.

Judith returned and sat down. With a puzzled voice, she said, "Herta didn't answer. Uh...it's early, but maybe she's visiting friends."

I proposed that we begin that morning by reading the chronology, with everyone chiming in with questions and thoughts. Papers rattled. We turned to page 1. The family story began, unfolding with events large and small—births, jobs, marriages, moves, deaths. Everything I had discovered was there, line by line:

> July 2, 1877- Alfred Berger born. Vienna, Austro-Hungarian Empire. Czerningasse 4
> August 5, 1889- Hedwig Grünberger born. Třešt, Moravia, Austro-Hungarian Empire. Now in Czech Rep.
> November 16, 1909- Alfred, Hedwig marry in Jglau. Alfred profession—*privat beamter*
> December 25, 1909- Alfred, Hedwig move to District VI, Schmalzhofgasse 19, 3rd floor, apt 14. Alfred, poor vision early, later legally blind, white cane, macular degeneration....

"Wait," Micha called out. "How do you know he had macular degeneration?"

"I told her," Celia said. "My mother was diagnosed with it, and so was Arnold. It's often genetic."

"But we don't know that's what he had," Micha interjected.

The scientist and storyteller debated, and others jumped in with opinions until we all agreed that we would never *know* what caused Alfred's increasing blindness, but we could make a logical conjecture. We moved on.

Questions, suggestions, laughter, silence. I took a breath and watched, my anxiety about the trip beginning to ease. The room rang with the voices of the Berger family together again in Vienna. The chronology had provided the structure we needed to move forward, triggering memories and emotions, giving depth to one-dimensional facts that so recently had been only shards and shadows.

CHAPTER 12
To Schmalzhofgasse

September 2004

Beneath a clear blue sky Micha, Chava, Judith, Avraham, Celia, Sidney, and I, seven seekers with different goals, set out to find Alfred and Hedwig's Schmalzhofgasse apartment. Strolling along the Mariahilferstrasse, formerly Vienna's most important shopping street, we passed Gerngross, the once-luxurious department store where Martha and Gretl had loved to window shop. Founded by a Jewish textile merchant in the late 1800s, it was one of countless Jewish businesses taken over by opportunistic Austrians after the Anschluss.

"*Strumpf.*" Hosiery. Celia pointed to a small wooden sign with what seemed to be hand-lettering in the window of a small shop. "That could have been one of my grandfather's wholesale customers." I told Micha and Judith that their mother's Jewish youth group had met in a basement room on this street. Judith smiled and said she was picturing the Berger family walking just ahead on the busy sidewalk.

Leaving tourists and shoppers behind, we turned onto a side street, Otto Bauer Gasse. When the Bergers moved into this neighborhood, this street had been called Kasernengasse, Barracks Street, after the Imperial Army barracks that were torn down in the late 1800s to make way for

Emperor Franz Josef's grand modernization plan. His goal was to transform Vienna into a world cultural center while accommodating its mushrooming population. These smaller streets once bustled with lower and middle class businesses—cobblers, tailors, and dry goods stores—that made the district a center for skilled trades. Clerks, craftspeople, and shop owners lived here, typically above their businesses.

Alfred had grown up in Vienna's Second District, across the Danube Canal from the city center. No renovations had disrupted his poor neighborhood, but he witnessed decades of construction, breathed the pervasive dust, and experienced the disruption and the excitement as a new Vienna emerged. Spectacular music halls, elaborate government buildings, museums, monuments, mansions, parks, and plazas rose along the broad new Ring Boulevard, announcing Vienna's preeminent world stature. That bold project still defines the city. Emperor Franz Joseph's rebuilding project remains one of the world's largest, most successful urban renovations, though its costs would prove far greater than even an emperor could afford.

Vienna's freedom, economic opportunity, and flowering culture drew immigrants, legal and illegal, from across the Empire and beyond. Vienna's population quadrupled between 1850 and 1910. Thousands came to work on huge construction projects. Jews never reached three percent of Austria's population as a whole, but waves of Ostjuden, Eastern European Jews from as far as Russia, brought Jews' numbers in the capital to nearly two hundred thousand, almost 10 percent of its two million residents. Those eastern Jews wore traditional garb which set them apart from other people on the streets, and the Hebrew letters on their many prayer houses were a puzzle even to many of Vienna's assimilated Jews—seen by some Viennese as an affront to the city's culture.

Pervasive discrimination and poverty forced most Jews, including Alfred's family, to settle in "Matzohville," where conditions were often squalid, education levels low, and unemployment rampant. Hedwig was among the new residents that flooded into Vienna during that population boom, though she and Alfred counted themselves among the ambitious, assimilated young Jews who "crossed the canal" to find their place in Vienna's vibrant culture.

About three thousand Jews settled in Schmalzhofgasse's District VI neighborhood of approximately sixty thousand in the early 1900s, making them about 5 percent of the district's population. As individuals, Alfred and Hedwig were welcomed there, and they made close friends. As Jews, their presence was an intrusion to some. The large Schmalzhoftempel, a synagogue designed in the style of a neo-Gothic cathedral by noted architect Max Fleischer, had risen in this changing neighborhood about twenty years before the Bergers moved here. Nearby were two smaller synagogues and a number of Jewish prayer rooms, identified by Hebrew script across their front windows. Many Roman Catholic Viennese felt their culture under siege.

As we turned onto narrow, quiet Schmalzhofgasse, the Bergers, too, grew quiet. Since this was before online maps were available, our eyes flitted from one passing address to the next, searching for Number 19. At the next intersection I recognized Stumpergasse as the street where hopeful young art student Adolf Hitler had rented his first cheap, shared room in Vienna. He would move to other nearby addresses three times, and then become homeless. Alfred and Hedwig may have passed him on these sidewalks. A few doors from Hitler's Stumpergasse apartment, the editorial offices of George Schöner's pan-German newspaper *Alldeutsches Tagblatt* churned out angry rants joining Mayor Lüger's antisemitic tirades and urging union with Germany. Hitler probably grabbed free copies of the daily paper from its red box on this sidewalk.

Most structures in the next block appeared to be from the late nineteenth or early twentieth century, five or six stories; but in almost every block, new buildings were sandwiched between the older ones. Only small strips of the old cobblestones remained visible in the street. I worried that Alfred and Hedwig's building might not have survived.

Celia, once again in the role of guide, pulled a photo from her purse and held it up, comparing it to our surroundings. It showed Martha and

Gretl shortly before Gretl's departure for Israel, standing in a quiet street, their faces expressionless. Celia turned suddenly, pointing across the street, and announced that we had arrived. We looked up to see modest, attractive turn-of-the-century Schmalzhofgasse 19, Alfred and Hedwig's home for thirty-one years.

Well-kept, six stories high, the corner building had six windows facing each street. Unlike starker buildings I had seen nearby, its thick plaster walls displayed a few curving "eyebrows" and other plaster ornamentation. With the ground floor painted pale yellow and upper stories the color of heavy cream, the building seemed to glow in the midday sun as the Berger family gathered at its front door.

Looking up at the gleaming structure, I whispered: *Hello. Your family is back.*

★

Finding the front door locked, Judith, Celia, and I peered through two windows where metal vines on decorative grating twined across our view into a small, simple foyer. No doorman waited here to greet visitors; no elevator opened onto the hallway. Instead a plain granite staircase with a wooden banister rose against the far wall.

I stepped back to join Sidney, Micha, Chava, and Avraham. While we discussed what to do next, a woman in a tailored brown suit came out. Seeing us, she paused. In German, Micha explained our purpose. Frau Margit smiled and introduced herself as the building owner. She generously permitted us to explore the building's common areas but requested that we not disturb tenants. She held the door open, and, with thanks, the Berger family passed inside.

Sidney and I lingered out front to talk with her. We stood together in the warm midday sun as Sidney tried out his elementary German. Frau Margit switched smoothly to polished English, telling us that none of the early residents remained, but one elderly tenant had told Frau Margit that her family had owned a butcher shop across the street. She'd told

Frau Margit that several Jewish families had lived in the building before the war, but she'd been a child then and hadn't known them. I noted that, even for children, Jews had been identified and seen as different. Frau Margit did know that Jews who had lived in this building had been evicted and deported. After the war one family, the Chitels, returned to their flat, but they had died some time ago. She spoke knowledgeably about the building's history for ten minutes and offered to send us a floor plan of the Bergers' third-floor apartment. Consulting her watch, she held the door open for us and, with great appreciation, we said goodbye. My concern about encountering resistance to my quest in Vienna had vanished.

Sidney went up the stairs. I heard the Bergers' animated chatter echoing above me, but was engrossed in the lobby, matching what I had learned of this place with the reality today.

The two apartments that open onto this foyer had held a shoemaker's workshop and small grocery in the 1900s. A plumber's and coal merchant's shops in this building had faced the side street. A tailor specializing in fine military uniforms worked a block away. During Hitler's time in this neighborhood, the future dictator would have passed a kosher butcher's shop around the corner.

Before Alfred married he had lived on the Graben, a historic, fashionable street built over the ancient site of a Roman city wall. His apartment, in the bustling core of the city, had been close to music, government, and the business address that I had seen on his stationery. With his own business and high hopes, he had been an up-and-coming young man about town. At a time when Vienna was experiencing a severe housing shortage, he had been fortunate to find this apartment on Schmalzhofgasse—a new one with two bedrooms—to start the couple's life together.

Hedwig, twenty years old when she married, had been a small-town girl from a lively, educated family. Their twelve-year age difference was not uncommon in those years, and their life together was promising. Trained as a seamstress and dressmaker, Hedwig would have found the garment industry all around her on Schmalzhofgasse. If she had wished, she could have found customers or work nearby. And from this apartment she and Alfred could have walked to the world's finest music, theater, and art.

When I later visited Ani and Loli in Israel, they described Hedwig as outgoing. She had enjoyed meeting friends for *jause*—afternoon coffee time. She adored children and sang and danced with her young nieces and nephews. Lively sounds from the elementary school down the street would have delighted her.

Judith would later talk with a woman in Israel who had grown up in this neighborhood and told her that the streets here had been quiet and pleasant, with few cars. Police from the nearby Stumpergasse station were friendly; they carried nightsticks, never guns, and chatted with neighbors.

The Schmalzhofgasse synagogue had been a few minutes from this apartment. Members entered the grounds from the sidewalk through tall ornamental iron gates emblazoned with two Jewish stars. Trees and shrubs landscaped an attractive courtyard. Inside stained glass windows, an organ, and choir welcomed members dressed in their best clothes.

The young bride may have had mixed feelings about moving to a large city, but probably had been pleased when Alfred brought her through these doors.

Schmalzhofgasse 19 had its own stories to tell about a lower middle class woman's life. A plaster sink built into the lobby wall gave tenants a place to dispose of wastewater. The basement laundry room held a faucet but no sink. Hedwig had carried the family laundry from the third floor to the basement to wash it by hand, then climbed to the sixth-floor attic to hang the clothes on lines to dry. Later she returned to the attic to iron and fold the clean laundry before finally carrying it back to her apartment. The courtyard had held waste-bins and a *klopfstange*, a bar over which Hedwig hung rugs to beat the dirt from them. Many Viennese had servants to pick up and deliver laundry, but no one had mentioned a servant for Hedwig. Loli would speak of Hedwig's hard work.

I couldn't help thinking about my own life. We have a laundry room filled with convenient appliances just off our kitchen and clothes that don't need ironing. Sidney shares the housework. Hedwig's life was hard to imagine. How did women manage all of that?

Climbing the stairs that September day, I felt that, in a way, I had finally met Alfred and Hedwig. My previous encounters with remnants of their lives—Peter's Vienna Room, Hedwig's sewing, their grandchildren's stories—had brought them closer, but they had remained strangers to me. Now, they started to come alive.

These halls had rung with their laughter, witnessed their heartaches. I paused where the steps spiraled upwards and imagined the just-settled newlyweds descending, Hedwig's long skirts rustling, Alfred smart in a straw hat, his thick glasses catching the light. Alfred had probably taken his new bride for walks around the city, pointing out sites he loved, describing how Jews had found success in Vienna. Marc Preminger, a Jew, served as the Empire's attorney general and trusted advisor to the emperor. In a previously unimaginable future, his son Otto would later flee Austria and become a leading American film producer and director. Alfred probably explained that so many of the mansions across the broad, busy Ringstrasse belonged to wealthy Jews that Viennese had taken to calling the street "Judenstrasse." Mixed news, to be sure.

The magnificent opera house told of another mixed blessing—the bitterly contested appointment of Gustav Mahler, the first Jewish director of the Royal Opera. Like many ambitious Jews, Mahler had needed to convert to Christianity in order to receive his appointment; even so, his success perhaps helped to lessen the impact of Mayor Lüger's incessant antisemitic blasts. Hedwig's family may have known the Mahler family, who had lived in Jglau in Moravia, close to Hedwig's native village Třešt. Vienna probably seemed to Alfred and Hedwig to be open with promise.

My palm gliding along the handrail burnished satiny by a century's hands, I thought about visiting cousins, aunts, uncles, brothers, sisters who had come up these steps. Their lives had been as tightly interwoven as the textiles the Bergers produced and sold.

Hermann and Mitzi's daughter Lisl had been five years old in 1911 when Martha was born here. Two more family weddings followed, Arnold to "Mitzi Two," and Richard to Hedwig's sister Olga. By 1914, five young cousins knit the young families even closer. I pictured the lively gatherings during those pre-World War I years as Hedwig and Olga shared in the planning of weddings and the joy of babies. I could hear the sisters singing together, see them cooking with each other and meeting in the nearby parks and cafes. Alfred and his brothers had all worked in the textile industry and would have had frequent conversations about people they knew, business prospects, and problems.

Despite challenges, the years before World War I seemed to have been halcyon times for the Bergers and for Vienna. Soaring debt, the influx of immigrants, widespread nationalist agitation, and rising anti-semitism—trouble resounded across the Empire like distant thunder but did not seem to affect gay Imperial Vienna. The Viennese pushed aside those concerns and danced on.

★

In 1914, World War I burst over Europe like a sudden storm, changing everything. Five years after Hedwig had moved to the golden city, its façade crumbled. Poverty, hunger, and disease made a mockery of the city's ornate buildings and grandeur. Contrary to antisemites' later accusations of Jewish disloyalty to the Empire, Austrian Jews threw themselves into its defense. Wealthy Jews underwrote its war debt. Many Jews, including Hermann, Arnold, and Richard, volunteered for military service. Alfred, presumably because of his eyesight, did not serve.

Hermann, thirty-seven in 1914, was wounded and hospitalized in Montenegro. Arnold was stationed in Vienna. Richard served with the War Board for the Cotton Industry in Vienna, then was posted in

Moravia, southeast of Prague. Olga moved to her parents' farm to be near him. Hedwig and Olga's mother saw her three sons, too, go to war. According to family legend, she died from worry.

A sixth Berger cousin, Ernst, was born during the war, and Ani, the seventh, as the Armistice was signed in 1919. Gretl, the youngest of the eight Berger cousins, was born in 1920, at the dawn of the postwar era.

When the war ended and the empire dissolved, Alfred's brother Richard and his wife, Hedwig's sister Olga, chose citizenship in newly created Czechoslovakia—a fortuitous decision that may have saved Olga and Olga's daughters' lives.

A harsh postwar reality confronted the Bergers and other citizens of the former empire. Onerous reparations plunged the newly created republics of Austria and Germany into spirals of poverty and inflation. People cut trees in the parks for fuel as hunger and illness stalked the city. They bartered for goods, rioted in the streets. Ten of the twelve major banks in Vienna, some Jewish owned, fell into bankruptcy as their large loans to the war effort became worthless.

A photo that Gretl had taken offers a view from her bedroom window of the building across the street. Like many pictures of inter-war Vienna, it displays a grimy, neglected neighborhood, not the well-kept blocks we'd passed that morning.

Clarence Berger of Los Angeles had been among America's proud returning soldiers with an optimistic, prosperous world lying open to him. Austria, in contrast was humiliated by the shockingly harsh treaty terms and burdened with debt. Immigrants continued to pour into Vienna, intensifying shortages and inciting increasingly angry, anti-immigrant, anti-Jewish sentiment.

★

Laughter floated down the stairwell. The Bergers seemed to have found cause for humor here too. Some eighty years earlier, Alfred and Hedwig's laughter, Martha's piano practice, and Gretl's whistle

Celia, Sidney, and the author in front of the building at 19 Schmalzhofgasse in Vienna, where Hedwig and Alfred lived for three decades. *Courtesy of the Berger family*

reverberated through these halls. I continued up the steps to join the Bergers at their grandparents' door.

Three apartments opened onto the tight hallway. Dark wooden trim around each entryway rose a foot above eight-foot-tall double doors with a silhouette resembling a country chalet flanked by mountains. Celia grinned at me, waggling her thumb at the apartment facing the stairs. "Number fourteen!"

"Look," Micha pointed to the door frame. "The original number sign. And this keyhole has been filled, but you can see it used a big old-fashioned key. Hmmm...this is the original door, maybe chestnut wood." He ran his finger over scrapes and nicks, coated with aging, thick red-brown varnish. "It's seen a lot over the years."

Frau Margit later emailed me a floor plan showing the layout of the third floor. Alfred and Hedwig's apartment was somewhat larger than the others, on a corner where it could catch summer breezes and good light. The front door opened to an entry hall where the family left coats, hats, wet galoshes. The small kitchen opened off the hallway. Women of those times made shopping rounds almost daily, putting milk and other perishables in the "ice box." Children typically met the iceman daily at a specific location. The ground floor grocery carried staples, but Hedwig ventured farther to the butcher, baker, fishmonger, and produce stalls. The sole kitchen window opened onto the hallway, allowing cooking smells to waft down these stairs, probably quickening the steps of family coming home.

Ani and Loli remembered that the central living-dining area, about thirteen feet square, had contained a small dining table, a couch, and Martha's piano. Her music books were everywhere. Alfred stacked boxes of socks for his business in the entry hall. The family canary's birdcage sat on the deep windowsill. Martha and Gretl may have sat at these windows watching for Alfred or calling to friends. An elderly Viennese woman told me that in those days, before television and computers, sitting by windows, watching the street below had been a Viennese pastime. People sat by their windows, watching their neighbors, watching everything.

The Bergers had been proud to mount a telephone on the wall near the hallway. Privacy? Personal phones? Not in those times. All the Berger families had owned radios, the boy cousins building their own. A record player with a "big ear," a large, funnel-shaped speaker, let the family listen to the music they adored. Older family members loved waltzes. As Martha and Gretl grew older, they listened to jazz. They had practiced the Charleston and talked about movies in the main room. Different times, but not so different from today.

Hallways were considered a waste of space in lower-class homes. A door in the common room opened onto Alfred and Hedwig's bedroom, the biggest room in the apartment. Hedwig kept her prized sewing machine there, and bedrooms commonly held a commode—a dresser with a pitcher and basin for washing up. Residents of each floor shared the lavatory in the hallway. The family brought all water from the hall-way but, like many Viennese, bathed weekly in public bath houses.

Another door off the common room brought Martha and Gretl to the *kabinette*, their tiny bedroom. Seven by thirteen, it could barely contain two small beds. Martha and Gretl, though nine years apart, were close, according to Celia and Judith. In that small bedroom they had whispered into the night until one fell asleep or Alfred shushed them. Each night at bedtime, they said the *Shema*, the Jewish prayer, with their mother.

Berger cousins visited each other often, slept at each other's apart-ments, attended concerts together, swam in the large public pools with each other, walked in the Vienna woods. Loli said that Martha, Gretl, Trudi, Loli, and Ani had been "closer than sisters."

Alfred and Hedwig frequently loaded their daughters onto the train to spend weekends with Olga and Richard's family in their expansive apartment in nearby, more rural Baden. Sometimes they all squeezed into a *fiaker*, a horse-drawn carriage for hire, and rode though the coun-tryside. Other times, while their parents talked, the girls danced in the garden, walked by the river, or bought sandwiches and cake at a local shop where the owner called the girls *lachtauben*, laughing doves.

About 1930, Olga and Richard moved to a similarly elegant apart-ment in Vienna so their daughters could attend schools there. Visits back and forth continued more easily.

Loli told me that growing up "it was like we had four parents. If one shopped for shoes or found special fabric, they bought for five. Aunt Hedi was good with children. She was very sensitive. She cried easily but was good with everyone. It was only love you got from her." Alfred was kind, too, she remembered, and had a soft voice. They remembered that he traveled often during their younger years and worked hard.

"Their apartment was much smaller and simpler than ours," Ani said, "but we never thought about that. They had an 'open' house. They had many friends, and we could bring girlfriends there too. There was always love around their table."

✦

The time we spent at the apartment had been invaluable, but we needed to move on. We agreed to meet for dinner and said goodbye in the hallway. Celia, Judith, Micha, and Chava wanted to meet Herta at her hotel. Sidney and Avraham left to find lunch and explore the city. I had an appointment at the City Archives.

Walking slowly down the steps, I thought that Micha had been correct; this building had seen much history. Throughout the 1920s, unrest had seethed throughout postwar Austria. Hitler was the main speaker at the Nazis' first major Vienna rally in 1922. Fractious *Alldeutsches Tagblatt* editor Schöner, a hero of the young Hitler, continued to promote a racially pure, aryan, Austrian-German nation. The Sixth District became a hotbed of pan-German agitation. Neighborhood taverns provided hangouts for the movement's noisy, often drunken meetings. Alfred had navigated the city's hazards all his life, but in those postwar years he and Hedwig, like most Jews, tread a cautious, narrowing path between extremist factions.

Thinking of those ominous changes, my mood darkened. As I descended the stairs, the echo I heard was the clack clacking of jackboots.

CHAPTER 13

Turnings

September 2004

After leaving the Bergers' apartment building, I rode the U-Bahn to the Vienna Archives office, where I surprised the archivist by asking for back issues of the *Wiener Adressbuch*, the annual city directory from before there were phone books. "They aren't often used," he explained, leading me to a back room where they lay in uneven, dusty stacks.

I sought the books to confirm family locations during the Nazi occupation. Searching for the changing addresses, I noticed that Berger had been a common Austrian surname. In 1938, there were four pages of Bergers. The Bergers' first names were also common—eight Alfreds, two Arnolds, thirteen Hermanns, four Mathildes, and seven Richards—reaffirming that for generations the family had felt themselves a part of Austrian culture.

The directories for 1936 and 1937 included phone numbers of government offices, forgettable descriptions and stock photos of city attractions, and a wide variety of advertisements—Jupiter brand typewriters, women's clothing, central heating, a mortgage broker on Stumpergasse. In one full-page ad Marie Lang's laundry included photos of workers hanging wash on "light and airy" outdoor lines, the underpinnings of

Viennese life waving in the breeze. I thought of Hedwig, hauling her family's laundry up and down five flights of stairs.

The 1938 directory, emblazoned with the Empire's double-headed eagle, had been published before the Nazi invasion and proved another placid compendium of city information.

I searched for the 1939 directory, but it was missing. The archivist explained that it might have been stolen, or else never printed, or perhaps pulled from distribution. I wasn't surprised. In 1938, the year the 1939 directory would have been printed, the Anschluss had severely disrupted life in Vienna. Bedlam prevailed for months as the Nazis scrambled to establish order. Berlin officials named and renamed, organized and reorganized Austrian government departments and fired all workers who were not loyal Nazis.

The 1940 directory boasted about the city's new order. Nazi flags flew over public buildings in new photos. Nazi officials made lofty promises. A newly drawn map displayed the city's enlarged boundaries, ordered by Berlin to bring suburban infrastructure, industry, and population under centralized control.

The 1941 directory turned out to be a research jewel. Skipping over flowery messages from Nazi officials, I discovered a seven-page timeline, *Wiener Chronik Seit der Herimkehr*, 1938–1941, "Vienna Chronicle after Coming Home to the Reich." The title itself of this devious Nazi history was a pan-German racist lie. Neither Vienna nor any part of Austria had ever been part of Germany. To the contrary, iconic Prussian leader Otto Von Bismarck, who unified independent German states in the late 1800s, had devastated Austrian pan-Germans' hopes by forcefully rejecting a union. The Anschluss was no "homecoming."

The chronicle began on March 11, 1938, with another deception— "The demise of the Schuschnigg Government." As history has long shown, March 11 had seen not a "demise" of the Austrian government but a military invasion and armed coup. It did not simply replace one chancellor or elected government with another, but replaced the Austrian Republic with a fascist state.

The chronicle laid out a record, day by day, of the pacification and Nazification of Vienna: torchlight parades, celebratory visits from Hitler and General Field Marshal Göring, new antisemitic laws; antisemitic art exhibits in public spaces, required classes promoting large families and explaining racial marriage laws. Hitler Youth events appeared, as did dates of mandatory practices for air raids and citywide blackouts. This was a fascinating record of indoctrination and preparation for war.

I felt lucky to have discovered this illuminating resource but even more strongly, horrified. An inescapable campaign of Nazi deception and propaganda had pervaded city life, confronting Jews with an over-powering new reality. It had employed common, easily recognized per-suasion and promotional techniques—and it had worked. I realized that such a campaign could happen anywhere, and it could be effective.

I was exhausted. I made copies, thanked the archivist, and headed for the U-Bahn. This second day in Vienna had been intense and seemed to stretch for weeks. I looked forward to regrouping over dinner at Servus Café with Sidney and the Bergers, perhaps including Herta. I climbed the narrow hotel stairs and headed down the hallway, looking for Sidney and the Bergers. I froze at the entrance to the reception area.

Sidney and Chava were talking quietly on the sofa. The others, heads bent, clustered around a nearby table speaking in muted tones. Micha stood up and said, "Herta is in the hospital. Come, sit with us." I exchanged glances with Sidney and sank down next to Celia at a table.

Micha explained that when he'd first arrived in Vienna, he had phoned Herta. "She didn't feel well, but still planned to visit friends. We couldn't reach her by phone, and so after you left us this morning, we went to Herta's hotel. The manager informed us that she collapsed in her room sometime last night. She was taken to a hospital on Stumpergasse, near Alfred and Hedwig's apartment."

Judith broke in, her face pale. "It could have been a stroke or heart attack. They'll know more soon. I've been talking with the doctors." With her nursing background, Judith was the natural family point of contact. She continued in a rush, "She has emphysema. We went to the hospital. She recognized us, but…" Her voice broke. "She's in and out of a coma."

"The doctors aren't optimistic," Celia added.

"I'm sorry," I said, feeling awkward and uncertain of my role. "Can I help?" All the Bergers knew Herta well. She was the widow of Ernst Berger, the son of Alfred's younger brother Arnold, connected to the family since she was a teenager in Vienna.

The Bergers had looked forward to this trip as a time of reunion and renewal. They had leapt at the chance to be together and learn more about their grandparents. For them, the Holocaust was not just history. It was a haunting family event. Now instead of connecting with their past, they were losing another piece of it.

I was shocked and saddened. Selfishly, I also regretted the loss to my quest. I had hoped that Herta could tell me more about Alfred and Hedwig and the entire family's experiences during the Anschluss. I ached to ask her why Alfred and Hedwig had not immediately thrust aside every obstacle to emigration, like others in their family. Had they, like too many Jews, believed they could ride out just another antisemitic storm? Had anyone—friends, colleagues—tried to help them?

✱

The next day, our third in Vienna, the family conferred over breakfast. Micha, who had spent the night at the hospital, reported that Herta's condition had worsened. "She's comatose most of the time now." He ran his fingers through his short grey hair, his voice low and raspy. Judith said she'd spoken to Amnon, Herta's son, in Rio de Janeiro. He would arrive that evening. "He's a wonderful person," she told Sidney and me. "Very kind. You will like him." She accepted Sidney's offer to accompany the family to the hospital, in case, as a physician, he could answer questions.

I conferred with Celia about whether she still wanted to go with me to see her parents' first apartment, a ten-minute walk from the hotel and a few blocks from the hospital. I felt that this family site would have its own stories to tell. She decided to join me, and we set out an hour later, chilled by an autumn breeze and overcast sky. We talked about Martha and Leo's marriage in 1936, a hope-filled occasion despite the dangerous times. By that point, two years before the Anschluss, Germany was already actively exporting terror, destabilizing Austria's fissile mix of conservatives, communists, socialists, and Nazis. Acts of sabotage—bombings, slashed telephone cables, vandalism—had become almost daily occurrences, and the Austrian government was struggling to maintain order.

Two years earlier Austrian Nazis, with German support, had smashed into Vienna's government buildings and assassinated Chancellor Dollfuss. In fact at that time the Nazis briefly took control of the country in a poorly organized uprising. Hundreds died in the resulting violence, but the military, police, conservative militias, and supportive Italian troops together quashed the attempted coup. A reconstituted Austrian government under the authoritarian rule of Chancellor Kurt Schuschnigg executed revolt leaders, banned both the Nazi and Communist Parties and detained thousands of suspected subversives without trial. The Viennese settled into an uneasy calm. Martha and Leo, who were courting during that time of upheaval, dreamed of a safe and happy life.

The Bergers, like many Jews in the interwar era, clung to assimilation as their survival technique, and they remained scrupulously apolitical. Ani remembered hearing gunfire during the 1934 street battles, but she never heard any Berger adult discuss them or other political events. Her father subscribed to three newspapers but didn't allow his daughters to read them.

The end of open fighting in 1935 gave the Bergers and other Viennese a reprieve. Hermann retired in 1936, receiving generous pensions from Honig and the city, along with public honors for his service on city commissions. After floundering in several textile jobs, Arnold, along with his wife Mitzi and with support from his brother Hermann, had started a business making stuffed animals that were soon in demand around

Europe. Their brother Richard directed a prosperous textile factory south of Vienna. And their widowed sister Mathilde continued to visit her four brothers' families each week; Loli recalled her as beloved, "a good aunt."

Alfred had struggled, coping with increasing blindness. Loli said that Hedwig's life then was difficult; Celia thought that Richard had helped her grandfather financially. Despite their problems, Alfred and Hedwig's family seemed to have been happy. They still enjoyed evening concerts, summer trips to the mountains, and close family and friends. In many ways those were good times for the Bergers. Like other Jews, they seemed inured to the looming Nazi threat.

Two blocks after Celia and I passed Alfred and Hedwig's apartment, Schmalzhofgasse ended and we found Mittelgasse, Middle Street, a cobbled lane that began under a stone archway. That was a charming entry to the three-block-long street that stopped at the Gurtel, the Girdle, a hectic commercial ring road. We easily found Number 35, Martha and Leo's building.

Several bikes were chained to the lampposts here. A young woman pushed a baby stroller along the sidewalk. Near the West Bahnhoff, a rail station, and beautiful Schönbrunn Castle with its parklike grounds, this quiet street seemed now, as in the past, ideal for students and young families.

Martha's professional life in the mid-1930s had revolved around music. At age twenty-three, she had graduated from the prestigious Institute of Music and Fine Arts and earned the state certification essential for performing and teaching. She'd built a following of students, worked as an accompanist, and sometimes performed with Loli, who had earned an equally respected dance degree.

At age twenty-two, Leo had left his parents, sister, and—he had believed—violent pogroms and antisemitic repression behind in Poland. He had found his way across forests, towns, and national borders to reach Vienna. With a twinkle in his blue eyes, he was known in the family as multi-talented—a skilled tailor, salesman, leather worker, electrician, artist, and soccer player. When he first reached Vienna he sold wallets, vests, and belts, probably from his family's leather shop in Trembowla, and he joined Hakoah-Vienna, the famed Jewish soccer club. Later he also sold wholesale jewelry from the shop of Adolph Berger, Alfred's cousin. The family knew Leo as a hard worker, but even more for his resourcefulness and impish humor. If something was possible, everyone agreed that Leo could do it.

Leo's city registration showed that he and Martha had moved to the apartment on Mittelgasse on their wedding day. I was amazed to see that the law requiring wives to take their husband's citizenship had revoked Martha's own Austrian citizenship. On this form she had become "stateless" like Leo.

Martha and Leo Cizes's wedding, 1936. *Courtesy of Celia Cizes*

When I later met with Ani in Israel, she'd whispered to me that she thought Martha and Leo had met through a matchmaker, but Celia said that her parents met at a social event of a Zionist group whose outings they enjoyed.

They had especially loved musical evenings with friends, when Martha sang and played the piano, favoring classical music—especially Schubert, Beethoven, Chopin, and Mahler—and lively contemporary American songs. Leo played Polish and Slavic folk music on an old violin—the sentimental, "My Yiddishe Momma" and "Dumka" with its happy and mournful strains.

Celia laughed, recalling that her mother had loved to dance—and that Leo mostly just jumped alongside her. However, she said, her father could dance a mean kazatsky, the thrilling Russian-Cossack folk dance climaxing as the whirling, leaping dancer folds his arms across his chest, squats low, and kicks one leg after the other.

Celia and I tried the door to her parents' former building, but it was locked. Peeking through a window in the door, we saw a simple foyer just big enough for residents to walk past the bicycle there. In one of Celia's photos of her parents' apartment on the third floor, Martha's grand piano sat on a parquet wooden floor in a sparsely furnished, spacious sunlit room. In another Leo, hair rumpled, sat at his easel intent on painting. Like Martha's parents Alfred and Hedwig two decades before, they had been lucky as young newlyweds to find comfortable space in apartment-starved Vienna.

As Celia and I turned and strolled around the corner, she nodded across the street to the Raimund Theater, Vienna's historic center of musical theater and light opera. Her parents had had little money to spend on performances, but on sultry summer evenings, in a time before air conditioning, the staff threw open the theater's windows, allowing breezes to cool the audience and strains of music to filter into the neighborhood. Looking up, I envisioned the young couple opening their own windows, leaning on the sill, and relishing their life in Vienna.

I remembered Sidney's and my first apartment and our attachment to it despite its leaking pipes. I tried to imagine how it would have felt for the life we had planned and were working so hard toward to be suddenly swept away.

Celia pulled out her phone. No messages, but she was anxious to check on Herta. "I should get to the hospital. Maybe they've heard from Amnon. His first name is Alfred, you know. He's named for my grandfather. Somehow, Ernst and Herta knew before my folks did...that's how my parents found out after the war that my grandfather had died. Jews don't name their children after living people."

CHAPTER 14

Alarm

September 2004

I watched Celia slowly walk away from her parents' Mittelgasse home, take one last glance, then stride briskly toward the hospital. I had an hour before my appointment at Austria's State Archive, just enough time to walk there, and to think. The years preceding the Anschluss in Vienna troubled me. The widespread denial among Austrians—especially among Austrian Jews—about the threat that Hitler posed made no sense. That denial seemed to require vision as blurred as Alfred's.

I crossed the street and strolled past the historic Raimund Theater, which sprawled over most of a triangular block. It interested me because a piece of its history was linked to the Bergers. One of the most successful works of musical theater ever, a sentimental fictional tale titled "Drei Maederlhaus," House of Three Maidens, played here for over a decade, closing in 1927 after more than 650 performances. The show went on to enjoy huge success in Germany and other countries, but ironically the concept for this popular operetta and its libretto had been the work of a Jew, Heinz Reichert, who later fled Vienna.

Reichert and Richard Berger had been close friends. They met after World War I, when they were recovering from illnesses in the same Czech sanitarium. They had joked about Richard's own house of three maidens, his home with three daughters, and after they both recuperated Reichert sometimes joined the Bergers' musical family evenings.

The mid-1930s was a confusing time for Jews. Austrians were aware that Nazi Germany was an increasingly aggressive neighbor, but it seems that most Jews didn't see the peril. Globalization was not a familiar term then, but it should have been. By assassinating Austria's aging heir to the Emperor's throne in 1914, a single nineteen-year-old Serbian nationalist, Gavrilo Princip, had dragged the world into its first world war. And then in the 1930s shattered economies around the globe struggled to recover from the impact of America's Great Depression. Corporate business was increasingly international. But despite growing evidence to the contrary, world leaders and average citizens—including, tragically, Austria's Jews—continued to believe that borders could be impenetrable walls.

One in four people walking along the Mittelgasse, the street where Martha and Leo lived, had been jobless. The Nazi party capitalized on the chaos of Vienna's uncontrolled poverty and hunger. At riots staged by the Nazis, Viennese shouted, "We want bread and work." The Nazis blamed capitalism, democracy, and Jews for Austria's raging inflation and unemployment. Their ideology resonated with disaffected office workers, teachers, police, and working-class citizens who were unhappy with their lives and resented Jews' perceived prosperity. Gangs of Nazi university students beat their Jewish classmates within sight of professors and police. Hitler Youth in their trademark brown shirts and white stockings rampaged through Vienna's heavily Jewish Second District, smashing shops and throwing torches into prayer rooms. Driven underground by Schuschnigg's government, Nazis still met and organized, relying on direction and funding from Berlin.

The thousands of Jews streaming out of Germany in the 1930s set off anti-refugee reactions in Europe, the United States, China, and South America, but immigration to the United States and other nations was still possible before the Anschluss. It's tragic but understandable that many Viennese Jews, including the Bergers, didn't take advantage of that early opportunity to flee the horrors to come. They experienced the 1930s as good times. Herta and Loli, in particular, loved the city. Jews had entered the ranks of Vienna's leading scientists, economists, artists, writers, and musicians. They didn't want to believe that the cataclysm next door could move across the border. In the turbulent year before the Anschluss, the Austrian quota for immigration to the United States went unfilled.

✦

Walking on, I tried to make sense of the conflicting information. I thought about Celia's photo of Hedwig lighting Hanukkah candles in December 1937, three months before the Nazi invasion. The Bergers and Hedwig's brothers often celebrated holidays together, and I thought Herta might have been at that gathering. I was reminded how deeply Ernst's widow was still woven into the Berger family's life.

Her collapse had shaken us all. The Bergers' hopes for this trip were shattered, my plans suspended. As had happened for me often during this quest, time seemed broken, pieces moving in different directions and at different speeds. The family had come here to revisit the past, but now they needed to stay involved in the present. I worried that they would lose heart and simply leave if Herta died. I wouldn't blame them. This was an awful situation; I said a silent prayer for her recovery.

Turning down Stumpergasse, I pictured a family celebration—a photo Celia had showed me with nineteen family members gathered at the home of Richard and Olga Berger—Trudi, Loli, and Ani's parents—in Baden for Hannukah. Their fourth-floor apartment in Vienna, overlooking the Swiss Gardens on one side and Belvedere Palace on the other, was also spacious, including quarters for their live-in maid. Their extensive art collection decorated its walls. I thought that the family may have gathered there for their last Hanukkah together in December 1937, barely three months before the Anschluss.

That winter of 1937 was exceptionally cold. Snow lay thick and sparkling in Vienna's parks and plazas. Loli told me that their antisemitic door attendant had grown rude then, hissing "*Sau Jude*," Dirty Jew, at them. He had begun to insist that they use the building's stairs, not the elevator. Instead, they stamped the snow from their boots and brushed past him.

Alfred, at sixty, would have been the oldest family member at the gathering that night, as his older brother Hermann typically spent holidays with his wife's large family. Martha was twenty-six, Gretl, seventeen and the youngest. Hedwig, at forty-eight the eldest woman, would have lighted the Hanukkah candles and led the prayers of gratitude.

Barukh atah Adonai…shehecheyanu…
Blessed are you, our God…who keeps us alive…

Loli and Ani said that clear soup started many Berger family dinners, followed on Hanukkah by a feast of favorites—potato latkes, chicken roasted with vegetables, steamed carp, noodle *kugel*. For dessert linzer torte, its butter-rich hazelnut crust filled with red currant preserves, and Hedwig's apple strudel.

Ani said that at family dinners, typically everybody laughed and talked, "parents more than children, but we had our talk too. The sisters, Hedwig and Olga, always had to talk together."

As they hung up their heavy coats and exchanged news that portentous evening, the Bergers would have had to work hard to avoid worrisome topics. To explain his limp, Leo may have told the story of his accident when riding on the back of a friend's motorcycle—a friend who was both a policeman and a Nazi, stationed around the corner from Alfred and Hedwig's apartment. By December 1937, three months before the Anschluss, many Vienna police were already Nazis—even those who kept friendly relationships with Jews.

Martha may have told how her Jewish friend and colleague Felix Galimir, a violinist with the Vienna Philharmonic, had been humiliated at a recent concert. As the lights dimmed, the principal clarinetist shouted, "Mr. Galimir, have you eaten your matzohs today?"

Alfred, too, may have shared distressing news. The Honig Shoe Store, a division of the Jewish-owned textile company where Alfred and Hermann worked, had just been vandalized. The week before Hanukkah the shop's owner had become incensed about Germany's persecution of Jews and impulsively kicked in the windows of the ostentatious German

Travel Bureau, which was adorned with a huge portrait of Hitler. In quick reprisal a Nazi gang had destroyed Honig's shop. The Nazi intrusion into Vienna's life was moving closer to the Berger family. What did they think about those changing times?

Both Ani and Loli would speak to me with still smoldering anger about their father's refusal to acknowledge the Nazi threat. Richard had made numerous business trips to Germany, but he heatedly discounted stories about radical persecution there. He didn't approve of political talk at dinner. Perhaps he chalked up the Honig episode to a few hotheads. Hadn't he lived most of his life in Vienna and prospered despite the *gesindel,* ignorant lower-class thugs? The Nazi Party had been outlawed; its leaders were in jail. Looking around the table he could reasonably ask, *Who among us has been harmed by the Nazis?*

Some members of the family might have argued back. Hedwig and Olga's Czech brothers were keenly aware that Hitler was fomenting terrorism where they lived. And Jack, the husband of Richard's eldest daughter Trudi, was a Zionist leader. All the cousins except Ani belonged to Jewish youth groups that rejected the assimilationist lifestyle their parents had chosen and urged Jewish pride in the face of mounting antisemitism.

Ani found herself increasingly at odds with her father. A top student, she had deferred her prestigious university admission in chemistry that fall to enroll in a one-year business program. If she had to flee, she reasoned, she would need job skills. Richard had been exasperated. She seemed to him to be throwing away everything he had worked his entire life to give her.

Loli, twenty-four, also felt frustrated with her father. Richard had dismissed her distress when schoolmates flashed the forbidden swastika pins hidden under their collars and hissed that Jews would soon "get what they deserved." She and Otto, her fiancé, had asked her father for permission to be married that winter. Like Ani, they dreaded a political crisis that could disrupt their plans. Richard—who would be working in Istanbul for six months in the new year, consulting with Turkey's government about modernizing its textile industry—dismissed their fears. He said that their wedding could wait. Nazis did not run his family.

Record showing Ernst Berger's military service in the Austrian infantry before and during the Anschluss. *Courtesy of the Berger family*

Arnold and Mitzi's son Ernst had made a radical decision that fall. Instead of following in the footsteps of his older brother Willi, their father, and three uncles to work in the textile industry, he had joined the Austrian army. It seems that the younger Bergers, at a time of life when change is more feasible, recognized the Nazi challenge and were preparing to face it when their parents simply weren't.

Hedwig and Alfred's life differed significantly from their siblings' lives. They weren't affluent like Richard and Olga, Herman and Mitzi. They lived in a working-class neighborhood where they could see more clearly how times were changing. Fighting insurrection from Nazis, Communists, and Socialists, Austria's chancellor had become a dictator—and still the Nazi tide was rising. People were angry. Many didn't have enough food. Their hardships made them vulnerable to the Nazis' propaganda.

Unlike Richard, Alfred and Hedwig strongly supported their daughters' political activities and took their worries about the approaching menace seriously. Martha and Leo had been involved in a Jewish youth group, and Gretl wholeheartedly embraced the Zionist tenets of building a strong Jewish identity, fleeing Europe, and creating a safe haven, a homeland for Jews. She was a leader in the Betar Zionist youth group, one of a number of Zionist youth organizations that sprang from the infamous 1894–1906 Dreyfus Affair. A Jewish officer in the French Army's General Staff headquarters, Dreyfus had been falsely imprisoned for treason and tortured on French Guiana's Devil's Island. He was eventually exonerated, but Europe's deeply rooted antisemitism had been on full display, and some Jewish leaders predicted that disaster lay ahead for Europe's Jews. They revived Jews' long-dormant dream of returning to their ancient homeland, Palestine. Where else could they go?

By 1937, Gretl was conducting Betar meetings for children, attending weekly teen meetings, and volunteering in Betar's downtown office. She attended Betar camps where, like Hitler Youth in their pre-military activities, she drilled like a soldier and sang ardent hymns. She also learned farming skills, deemed crucial for a young nation. Her Uncle Richard, like many Jews, thought Zionism was nonsense, and worse—dangerous for Jews in Gentile cultures.

I imagined the outspoken Gretl, that last holiday when the family was together, telling about a recent Vienna Betar assembly. City officials had sat on the Vienna Concert Hall stage with Ze'ev Jabotinsky, Betar's founder. Jabotinsky took the microphone to describe the urgency for Jews to leave Europe and form their own nation. He detailed Britain's increasingly harsh Palestine immigration policies, including the fighter planes and warships sent to intercept Jewish refugees. Jabotinsky implored Europe's Jews to brave all obstacles and flee. Terrible times loomed in Europe, he shouted. Concluding his oration, he grabbed a suitcase and waved it wildly, shouting, "Run, Jews, Run!"

America's response to Germany's antisemitic persecution and British anti-immigration policies was lukewarm at best. Overt, institutionalized antisemitism and racism were embedded in America's culture. The largest immigrant group in United States from the mid-1800s to 1930 was German, like Clarence Berger's family in Los Angeles; many Americans, even those without German roots, found Hitler and the Nazi Party intriguing. In 1938, unemployment in the United States neared a crippling 20 percent. American Jews' attempts to boycott German goods and stage a mock trial of Hitler so infuriated Hitler that Germany threatened to halt its $2 billion World War I loan payments to American investors. One mock trial went forward, but the U.S. government successfully pressured the Jews to cancel their public anti-Nazi programs.

To young Zionists, Jabotinsky's speech had been galvanizing. To their parents, the notion of leaving civilized Europe for the hostile, backward deserts of Palestine seemed a fantasy. Besides being dangerous and impractical, fleeing meant losing everything they loved, including each other.

Thinking over the crosscurrents pulling on the Berger family, I came to understand that if Sidney and I had lived in Vienna then, with professional careers, friends, and generations of family holding us, we might not have left our home and family either. Life for Jews in Austria was threatened, but still manageable. Jews like Richard asked, *Was it so different from other times?* Life had always been perilous for Jews.

Part III

CHAPTER 15
Anschluss

March 1938

T he next morning at breakfast, the Bergers were in a solemn mood. Herta was failing. Judith joined Sidney and me, telling us that Amnon had arrived and spent the night at Herta's bedside. The family would spend the day at the hospital, but we could meet for dinner.

Since we had arrived in Vienna, Sidney had spent time with the Bergers and explored the city with Avraham. This day, he asked if he could be helpful with my research. He set off for the Technisches Museum to seek train information relating to Hedwig's deportation. Appreciative of this support, I headed downtown to District I, the oldest part of the city, for my appointment at the DÖW (Archive of Austrian Resistance), whose mission is to explore the experience of Austrian victims and resisters under the Reich.

DÖW's mission is complicated. Supported by private donors, the city of Vienna, and the national government, and located in Vienna's historic city hall, the organization must confront the fact that many Austrians were, and some remain, enthusiastic Nazis. Even some eventual resisters initially welcomed the occupation or supported Germany's antisemitic policies—in other words, some victims and resisters have also been perpetrators and enablers. Many Austrians believed, at least at the beginning, that resisting the Reich during wartime was treason. So many groups were in the Nazis' crosshairs that identifying victims is also a tangled issue. Was the Anschluss a foreign military occupation? A welcome revolution? Both? Neither? These issues may never be resolved, but the DÖW has made significant strides in educating young Austrians about Nazi crimes.

The Archive's research director, Dr. Elisabeth Klamper, spent several hours answering my questions, then directed me to their library. Alone there, browsing the shelves in that windowless room, reading personal accounts of the Anschluss, my unease from the previous day returned. *Why?* I asked myself. *Snap out of this moodiness. This is past history, isn't it?*

The history of the Anschluss centers on one violence-charged day and night, March 11–12, 1938. I had read much of this information before. But in that library, deep in Vienna's Inner City, the epicenter of these events, I could imagine more clearly how it might have been for Jews to find themselves suddenly beyond the reach of law, seeing their fellow citizens turn against them and jungle rules replace the civilization they loved. Reviewing numerous accounts, I tried to imagine the event as it was for the Bergers.

The catalyst for the Anschluss, Germany's invasion of Austria, was Chancellor Schuschnigg's surprise announcement on the evening of Wednesday, March 9, that a national referendum would be held in four days. "I want to know," he intoned into radio microphones. "I must know whether the Austrian people want a free independent...and united country...."

The one-question ballot required a one word answer, "Yes," or "No." The referendum was a tool with which Schuschnigg hoped to refute Nazi propaganda claiming that Austrians wanted outside troops to restore order. A national vote was a daring maneuver, intended to catch Hitler by surprise, unprepared to respond. Polls indicated that the referendum would go Schuschnigg's way.

But Schuschnigg misjudged his enemy. Hitler had spent months preparing to invade Austria. German troops had been massed at the border for weeks. Within hours of learning about the referendum, an enraged Hitler probed potential international responses to an invasion. Determining that any reaction would be insignificant, he ordered his surprised generals to invade in two days. As Austrians prepared to vote, Germans raced toward war. In a flurry of campaigning, Schuschnigg's supporters, including the Jewish community, donated large amounts of money to the yes campaign, while Nazi trucks with loudspeakers blared in the streets urging citizens to vote no.

Schuschnigg's plan backfired. On Saturday, March 11, by phone and special envoy, Hitler demanded that Schuschnigg cancel the plebiscite. When Schuschnigg eventually complied, Hitler issued a second ultimatum, that Schuschnigg resign. Armed Nazi Party leaders in Vienna rushed to the chancellery.

Austria's army, with its resplendent plumes and dashing capes, was known as one of Europe's best dressed, but Schuschnigg knew that in battle it would be no match for Germany's large modern military. To prevent a hopeless war, he capitulated. He announced his resignation in a radio speech, and the Republic collapsed like a house of cards, plunging Austria into bedlam. In response, as Hitler had predicted, the world yawned. I wondered whether Alfred and Hedwig had tuned their radio to the late-night address, or been in the crowds supporting the Republic. And where were Martha, Leo, and Gretl?

As Hitler pressed his demands, open trucks loaded with armed, disciplined, brown-shirted, German-trained Austrian Nazis assembled in a Vienna plaza, prepared for either combat or celebration. When Schuschnigg resigned, Berlin issued its orders, and the trucks roared across Vienna.

March in Vienna is still winter, nights often dropping below freezing. Fragrant linden trees on the Ring had not yet bloomed that night, nor had the chestnuts. Traces of snow lay in the shadows, but the cold was no deterrent to the shouting, cheering citizens who poured out of their apartments, joining confused throngs already on the streets.

Violence spread across the country even before German troops had crossed the border. Celebrants attacked supporters of the Republic who were still gathered in plazas and reeling from the radio news. Joyful Viennese swarmed along the Ring toward elegant Kärntnerstrasse. Spontaneously, thousands rallied there in front of the German Tourist Bureau office bedecked with its immense flower-draped portrait of Hitler. Shouts resounded through the city.

> *Ein Volk, Ein Reich, Ein Fuhrer!* One People, One Nation,
>   One Fuhrer!
> *Juda Verrecke!* Death to Judaism!

Viennese who raised voices in disagreement—and there were some that night—were bludgeoned by roaming bands of Nazi thugs, or sometimes by their own neighbors. Nazi flags appeared in windows. Long blood-red banners emblazoned with swastikas were unfurled from rooftops. Smiling women tied Nazi armbands on police, who joined citizens in beating Jews and opponents of the Nazis. Nazis bent on torment or murder attacked Jews on sight and rampaged through apartment buildings, pulling Jews to the streets.

The next day, March 12, violence intensified. Overnight, Nazis had occupied government offices and installed an interim government. Viennese listening to Schubert's *Unfinished Symphony* on the state radio that morning found their program interrupted by bulletins reporting that German troops had crossed into Austrian territory. Under orders to ruthlessly suppress opposition, German tanks, artillery, and armored caravans instead encountered cheering crowds throwing blizzards of flowers as they advanced slowly through heavy spring mud toward Vienna. Hitler crossed the border that same day in his open car and began a triumphant journey across Austria.

British journalist G.E.R. Gedye raced across Vienna in the wake of the Anschluss, witnessing theft and violence in which Jews were assaulted by bands of Nazis, by Hitler Youth, by other Viennese citizens, police, and Gestapo. Thousands of Jews and suspected anti-Nazis were arrested. Gedye reported waves of German planes flying low over the city, on and on for days. Some dropped little pink leaflets: "The German Air Force greets German Vienna." Masters of drama and spectacle, the Nazis staged a torchlight parade along the Ring. In his 1939 book, *Fallen Bastions*, Gedye described the scene:

> ...the Brown flood was sweeping through the streets. It was an indescribable witches' Sabbath—storm troopers, lots of them barely out of the schoolroom, with cartridge-belts and carbines, the only other evidence of authority being Swastika brassards...marching side by side with police turncoats, men and women shrieking or crying hysterically the name of their leader, embracing the police and dragging them along in the swirling stream of humanity, motor-lorries filled with storm troopers clutching their long-concealed weapons, hooting furiously.... men and women dancing.... the air filled with a pandemonium of sounds...Down with the Jews! Heil Hitler! Sieg Heil...Today we have all Germany, tomorrow we have the world.

Three Days after the Anschluss, the Gestapo deported Gedye.

Hitler reached Vienna on Sunday, March 13. Standing in his car in the motorcade, holding a fixed Nazi salute, he rode through streets lined with cheering crowds. Herbert Toch, then four, son of the Bergers' close friends, remembers his father lifting him onto his shoulders to see the amazing, deafening pageantry of military vehicles, motorcycles, and shiny-booted, goose-stepping troops. Later a policeman patted the blond, blue-eyed child's head and complimented Bernard Toch on his fine aryan son.

That night Hitler addressed a delirious crowd of three hundred thousand in Heldenplatz, Heroes' Plaza. He proclaimed Austria and Germany's union, the Anschluss, his life's dream, as the crowd roared its approval. He promised jobs and witnessed the oath of loyalty to himself and the Reich sworn by Vienna's police. Hitler did not explain that what he offered was not unity, equality, or freedom, but annexation. He demanded loyalty oaths. He promised jobs. A great nation once again. It was age-old political manipulation.

I knew almost nothing of Alfred and Hedwig's experience during those early days of the Nazi takeover. Martha and Gretl had never spoken of it to their children. I could imagine the trauma had they been on the streets that night—pushing through crowds, holding onto each other, seeking quiet back streets as they made their way home. Sensitive Hedwig frightened by the vicious mobs. Alfred, watching misty shapes appear and disappear from his peripheral vision.

A few months after our trip to Vienna, when Sidney and I visited Ani in Israel, she told us about that time, for her, in Vienna. Speaking sometimes haltingly, sometimes in a furious rush, she said that during the invasion, her mother Olga and her sister Loli were visiting her older sister Trudi and her husband Jack in Graz, several hours from Vienna by train. Their father Richard had been in Turkey for several months. Ani, then age nineteen, had been at home alone in Vienna. "When Hitler came, I saw the flags out in a moment. All the people had swastikas on their arms. People were so very, very happy they were crying."

Her voice rose. "Nobody can tell me that the nation of Austria was Hitler's first victim. Austrians were the first and biggest murderers of all. It was immediate. They were prepared. They had been waiting for that moment.

"I saw terrible, terrible things all over Vienna. Downstairs, they were pushing people against a wall, and they shot them. They pushed girls and women into cellars, in the storage room under our house, and raped them. They ran from floor to floor and took people out—Jews. They knew exactly where Jews lived."

I asked Ani who had done these things. There were family photos spread on the table before us. She looked down, pushing the photos around in front of her, and didn't look up. "I don't know. People off the streets. Ordinary people. Afterward they could take Jews' flats. That started immediately too. It went on and on."

Ani's memories were accurate. It was a lawless time of wanton violence and theft. The crimes were hidden behind the mask of "aryanization," the taking of Jewish property by so-called "aryans." German racists had appropriated that term from its correct usage related to peoples in India and Persia and applied it to ethnic Nordic and Germanic peoples. Berlin was astonished when Austrians' rampant violence and plunder by "aryanization" burst out of control. The Germans had prepared to suppress their victims, not their supporters, but now they scrambled to install a functioning government.

The more I read that morning in the archive, the darker those spring days of 1938 seemed to me; it was a low point in human history, when ordinary people turned on their friends and neighbors. It was not the only such time in history, but it was shameless and extreme. Like a pistol shot at the beginning of a race, the Anschluss marked the Reich's early movement toward the Holocaust.

Years of detailed Nazi planning had gone into the occupation. The constant thunder overhead was more than intimidation; German planes carried weapons and high-ranking Nazi officials to control the newly invaded country. Troops surged off trains like ants at a picnic. When Germans crossed the border into Austria and Nazis emerged from Vienna's prisons and underground cells, they carried lists of enemies and victims. As Ani said, they knew where the Jews lived—and who was influential, who had money. Sometimes the Gestapo held one family member hostage until the family signed over even their foreign assets to the Reich. Within a week a Reichsbank headquarters had replaced the liquidated Austrian National Bank. Chancellor Schuschnigg was arrested immediately after his resignation and spent years in solitary confinement in a series of concentration camps. Austria's foreign reserves and the Hapsburg jewels were on their way to Germany just as quickly.

The day of the invasion, Germany closed all Austrian borders. They took over Vienna's airport, distributed German uniforms to border personnel and Nazi armbands to Vienna's police. Jews and others scrambling to leave the country crammed trains bound for the borders, but before the trains could pull out German SS troops had boarded, robbed the passengers, and arrested some. They confiscated Austrian passports and declared that all travel would henceforth require Reich-issued passports and proof of exit tax payments.

That first night, two SS men pounded on Ani's door. "They were looking through all the flats, taking people away," she said. They demanded that she give them the two watercolor paintings by Hitler that they believed her family owned. "They told me Jews couldn't own anything by Hitler."

"The pictures were nothing special," she told me with a dismissive shake of her head. "My parents might have gotten them as a wedding present. One showed a small house beside a street. The other was of a cathedral. It had plaster tablets with the Ten Commandments on the wall. Hitler painted those Hebrew letters."

Ani held out her hands to indicate that the paintings were small, about eight inches wide. She recalled stamps on the back from the Jewish-owned gallery on Taborstrasse where her father had been a frequent customer. He told her Hitler often visited the shop. I was amazed that the Nazis knew where to look for Hitler's paintings—but then remembered his obsession with his work and his history.

Ani continued with her story, "The pictures had been hanging in the corridor in our flat, but hadn't been there for a couple years. I didn't know where they were. I never thought about the paintings then. I was busy with my friends and school.

"It was not a good situation." As the two Nazis confronted her," she said, "they softened. They liked me. They said they would give me time to find the pictures, but before they came back we had fled Vienna." Her mother Olga later told Ani that several years before the Anschluss her father had shipped Hitler's paintings to a dealer in Germany, hoping to sell them, but they had been stolen.

Ani had been lucky in her encounter with the SS. Within a few days of the invasion the Germans had arrested thousands of Viennese. They maintained long and growing lists of political enemies, which included even Nazis whose politics didn't align with the party's increasingly radical vision.

Jews were arrested and sent to Dachau, where many perished. In those first months distraught families could ransom their loved ones if they had enough money and could prove the prisoner would emigrate. Other families received a box of ashes and a bill for cremation. Jewish suicides soared to two hundred a day. Newspapers published a daily count. In the articles, Nazi leaders gloated; Reich Minister Hermann Göring warned all Jews to leave Austria.

Because Hedwig's sister Olga had been born in the Czech region of the Austrian Empire, she and her husband Richard were able to claim Czech citizenship when the Empire was dismantled, a lifesaving decision for their family. With her blond hair and foreign passport, their daughter Ani was safer than other Jews, and she took on the task of searching for youth group friends who's been arrested or detained. "At eight o'clock every morning, I went to the Zionist organization in the Inner City and got a list of the people who were missing. I came to terrible, terrible things, all over Vienna.

"One day, I came to the Zionist office, and it was closed. I didn't understand that it was dangerous. I knocked and called for someone to open the door. An SS man opened it and pulled me in. Threw me in. All my friends were there." She said that the SS kicked and punched her. "It was painful. I didn't cry. I was too proud. Those were terrible hours."

Her friends urged her to show the Germans her passport and get out. "You can help from outside," they told her. Finally she agreed and was released. She reported what she'd seen to the Jewish Agency, but neither Ani nor the Agency could help the detained Jews.

Richard, in Turkey, was frantic. Ani said he called frequently, told her to pack up the flat and leave with her sisters and Olga. Go to Czechoslovakia, he insisted. He called Hedwig and Olga's three brothers—Hugo and the twins Julius and Otto—and asked them to come to Vienna to help his family move. The uncles came every weekend for some time, also visiting Alfred and Hedwig. They brought packages of food. Bringing heartening family news, Hugo showed off photos of his new infant daughter.

After the Anschluss, Ani said, the family never gathered again. "It was too dangerous to go out on the streets." Richard and Olga's family pressed her brothers for information. What had they witnessed at the border? Did the world know what was happening?

"No help came from anywhere," Ani said. "My uncles should have fled when they could. They all stayed. They wouldn't leave until their sisters were safe." She couldn't help sighing. "None of the Czech Jews left then, and it was a time when Czechoslovakia was free."

Ani said that she and her father Richard had "a big fight" over the phone about their future. She refused to go to Prague, told him he didn't understand. Hitler would grab Czechoslovakia next. The family would be running again. They must join Richard in Turkey, she insisted. "He said I was making up fairy tales. He didn't believe me."

Ani proved to be more farsighted than her father—and the world leaders who gathered in Munich six months later, in September 1938, to consider Hitler's demand to control western Czechoslovakia. Without consulting Czechoslovakia, they acquiesced. "Peace in our time," the British Prime Minister infamously announced after his return home. Within days German troops occupied the region and six months later— one year after Ani's prediction—Hitler swallowed the rest of Czechoslovakia, trapping Hedwig and Olga's three brothers.

For Alfred and Hedwig, holding defunct Austrian passports, immigrating to Czechoslovakia had never been a possibility. They had nowhere to run.

★

Across Vienna, signs had appeared in shop windows immediately after the Anschluss: NO JEWS ALLOWED. Looking through DÖW's photos from the era, I found myself staring into faces contorted in hate-filled grimaces or frozen in silence—ordinary people on the streets observing and carrying out acts of intimidation and humiliation against Jews; jeering crowds surrounding Jews on their knees scrubbing side-walks; groups of well-dressed citizens in suits and ties intimidating a lone, elderly Jew; young people and a man in a Nazi armband forcing a boy to paint the word *Jude* on a Jewish apartment.

Uniforms appear in some pictures, but just as common is the everyday clothing of men, women, and youth, who are watching, chatting, some-times laughing—seeming to enjoy the torment. Did the grocer on the ground floor of Alfred and Hedwig's building, the butcher across the street, or their neighbors of thirty years find ways to help them? Where was the majority who had planned to vote "yes" for a free country?

When I visited Loli in Israel, she told me a story that said a lot about Gretl during the Anschluss. Deeply involved in the Zionist movement, Gretl had been vulnerable to harassment and arrest. When she walked home from class one day that spring, German soldiers forced her to stop and wash their car. She did sloppy work, then threw the basin of dirty water on the car and ran away.

Talking about those days, sometimes Loli spoke easily; other times she paused, looked away, or closed her eyes. "What I saw, what I suf-fered, I thought it was the end of the world. We lived across from a train station, and I saw the soldiers coming in. I saw them take dresses from girls. They made them clean the streets with the dresses, and beat them and…" She paused. "They used them. They didn't hurt me, but they often beat people. All the time.

"We couldn't go out. It was dangerous. I don't know myself how I overcame it. Every day we saw horrible things. I think every stone in Vienna remembers."

CHAPTER 16
The Violence Worsens

Sidney, who was still at the railroad museum, called me at the archive to check in. The museum was fascinating, he said, but not helpful for finding information about Hedwig's deportation. "That's research," I laughed. "Many steps in place. No progress until you open the right door." Unamused, he said he would leave soon to meet Avraham (the husband of Gretl's daughter Judith). They would walk through the city and have *jause* together, good Viennese coffee and a pastry. We agreed to meet at the hotel at dinner time and said goodbye. I began searching through more resources, adding to my understanding of the event. The Anschluss closed in around me again. The Anschluss would become even more personal, more incredible when Loli and Ani later talked about it in Israel.

"Europe doesn't smell good." Loli told me that the only Jews she knew who emigrated before the Anschluss had explained their departure that way. They had owned a travel agency but moved to South America in 1937. That family was the exception, she said. "After the invasion, all Jews regretted not leaving earlier."

Shaking her head, she said that before the Anschluss her family had believed that even if Hitler took over, Austrians would never enforce

Germany's draconian racial laws excluding Jews from society. For one thing, there were too many Jews in Austria—almost three percent of the population, about three times the percentage in Germany. Many Jews thought that if a takeover happened, it would be gradual. There would be time to react. Others judged Hitler a passing phenomenon.

Those had been wishful, out-of-touch fantasies.

After Chancellor Schuschnigg's referendum vanished along with the Republic, Hitler ordered a different referendum—to approve or reject "unification." Germans promptly set up soup kitchens in city plazas and took photographs of grateful citizens for use in newspapers in Austria—and around the world. Coaxing, courting, and threatening Austrians to vote for the Anschluss, the Nazis laid out an aggressive schedule of events, exhibitions, parades, and official visits. "High point of election, Führer speaks in Vienna," the *Vienna Address Book* exulted. Officials from Hitler and Göring to members of the Reich Women and Hitler Youth touted the benefits and moral responsibilities unfolding for the Viennese, as if the Nazi takeover was a gift to children rather than the death of Austrians' freedom. Jews were excluded from voting. Suspected resisters were intimidated, arrested, or murdered. The referendum passed with hardly a *"nein."*

By April, street level brutality and the fleecing of Jews had evolved from frenzied to systematic. Neighborhood garbage collectors, local railroad workers, and longtime employees of Jewish businesses joined roughnecks and mobs terrorizing Jews to exact their demands—a weekly cash payment; an apartment convenient to their workplace; a business. Jews had no recourse to law, friendship, or morality—any familiar touch point of justice. The world had spun off its axis.

Fear spread beyond Austria's Jews and invaded the lives of many citizens. Vienna's Nazi offices complained to Berlin that they could not keep up with requests for documentation of aryan ancestry. Businesses sprang up providing fake *Ahnenpass* identification booklets that displayed one's purported genealogy.

The new Reich regulation that most decisively shattered the rule of law in Vienna was the permission for the Gestapo, SS, and police—with no oversight—to arrest any *unliebsame*, a disliked person. Anyone, old or young, rich or poor, friend or foe, could denounce anyone else for violating Nazi norms or being an "enemy of the state." Everyone became a de facto state agent empowered to accuse a neighbor, business associate, or stranger for infractions so numerous that even police could not keep up with them. Non-Jewish Viennese worried about whether they seemed adequately pro-Nazi and antisemitic. Families protecting their patriotic reputations and their jobs insisted that their children join Hitler Youth.

Herbert Toch, the child of the Bergers' family friends, remembered standing in his kitchen as a child yelling and waving a spoon in the air, "ranting and raving and imitating Hitler's speeches. My mother hushed me. She was afraid the neighbors might hear. You couldn't make fun of Hitler."

Austria had become a nation of informers, snitches, and spies, where everyone—Jews, resisters, even uninvolved apolitical citizens—had reason to fear their neighbors.

✱

The lightning speed of the German takeover stunned Jews, and it would not be long before they learned that they stood alone in the world. Leading Austrian public figures—Karl Renner, who had been the Republic's first Chancellor, followed by Vienna's Archbishop Cardinal Innitzer and other Austrian religious leaders—promptly announced their support for the Anschluss. Newly elected Pope Pius XII canceled Pius XI's in-process encyclical condemning antisemitism. Britain and the United States recognized the new German-Austrian government even before the rigged Nazi referendum blessed it.

Austrian Jews might not yet have learned that some high-ranking U.S. State Department officials were antisemites who complained openly that the department was "infested" with Jews. But they did know during that summer of 1938 of the failure of the Evian Conference. The goal of the conference, initiated by the United States, was to relieve Americans of bearing too heavy an immigration burden by enlisting the international community to accept more refugees. Thirty-two nations attended, but only Costa Rica and the Dominican Republic offered to ease immigration restrictions, and only for a high price. Murray Burnett, a young American schoolteacher who traveled to Vienna in 1938 to help his Jewish relatives, returned home to write a play that became the iconic anti-Nazi film *Casablanca*. The hit movie aroused anti-Nazi sentiment, but it did not affect rigid U.S. immigration policies.

Loli and Ani told me that news and gossip about who was leaving, when, and for what country dominated Jews' lives. Lisl's future husband Fritz was emigrating to Kenya. Cuba offered transit visas for a price. Shanghai was exorbitant. The magic word on many lips was *bürgschaft,* affidavit—the life-saving key that opened the door to U.S. immigration.

Olga and Richard's daughters described waiting for hours or sometimes days in lines at consulates and government offices across the city. Ani said, "Everybody was trying to understand how to come out. We ran from one legation to another. We all had our own experience. I went at four in the morning to stand in line to get one paper. Sometimes, we didn't eat all day. We tried every place. We went to the English. We went to the French. Loli went one place, I went another. Trudi and Jack were underground because of his Zionist work. We went everywhere. Every family went. Everyone wanted to go."

Older Jews like Alfred and Hedwig, and younger ones like Martha, Leo, and the Berger cousins flooded consulates and embassies. In line, Loli said, sometimes they met or made friends. Standing for long periods people chatted and even joked but were nervous. Sometimes trucks loaded with SS descended on the lines and beat or arrested Jews.

Collecting necessary immigration documents for the United States could be like running blindfolded through a labyrinth. U.S. immigration regulations changed constantly; the State Department issued frequent guideline updates that different American consuls interpreted differently. Required papers included, for example, birth and marriage records; a statement of good character from the police, many of whom were openly hostile to Jews; valid reservations for travel; an affidavit of support from a United States citizen; and a final medical exam and interview at the consulate. Each document had an expiration date. If one expired, the applicant reapplied and hoped it would arrive before others expired. A deficiency in one? Start over, at the back of the line.

Ani pointed out that Jews' situations varied. "Every family and even every person in a family had to find their own way." Within two weeks of the occupation Martha's husband Leo had contacted his aunt Anna Weinrib in New York, then in her seventies, who had emigrated from Poland thirty years earlier, and her son, Jack, an engineer. Without hesitation they offered to immediately apply with an affidavit for Martha and Leo.

In May of 1938 Martha and Leo obtained copies of their birth and marriage certificates and joined the lines waiting at the United States consulate for a visa application. It was a forty-minute walk from Mittelgasse, but using public transportation, not yet formally prohibited, was risky; anyone might demand that Jews get off.

Later that month, Martha and Leo finally reached the head of the line of people waiting at the consulate to add their names to the list of Austrians wanting to apply for visas. Their registration number meant that 28,545 others had stood in line before them. The consulate told them that the wait for their interviews might take months—a gross underestimate. It would take more than a year.

May 1938 was a crazy collage of change. According to the *Vienna Address Book*, a Nazi May Day celebration on Heldenplatz, Heroes' Plaza, attracted "hundreds of thousands of citizens." The State Opera, heavily supported by Jews, found its attendance plummeting. The Gestapo fired 153 of 197 University of Vienna Medical School Jewish or "unpatriotic" professors and forced a Jewish Nobel Laureate to transfer his prize money to the Reich. Sigmund Freud was among the very few Viennese Jewish intellectuals who resisted Reich pressure to leave. He relented when the Gestapo detained his daughter, but the

Reich then demanded extraordinary exit taxes, which were paid by an American millionaire.

As Martha and Leo stood in lines to secure their stacks of documents, Alfred, Hedwig, and Gretl worked to arrange Gretl's escape, which did not require multiple papers and long lines—because it was illegal.

As an eighteen-year-old group leader in Betar, Gretl was perfectly positioned for an astonishing loophole developing in the German emigration scheme. Anticipating the looming catastrophe for Europe's Jews, a small cadre of Zionist leaders had worked for years developing a plan to bring young Jews to Palestine. After the Anschluss they pushed ahead with furious energy. At great personal risk throughout April and May they negotiated with, persuaded, hoodwinked, and paid off Reich officials. Officials could arrest any Jew on a whim. But needing foreign capital and eager to rid themselves of radical young Jews, Reich leaders including Adolf Eichmann agreed to allow small numbers of young Jews to leave Vienna for Palestine. Jews from around the world donated to Betar's effort.

That May, Gretl attended a one-week Betar camp to prepare for her escape. There, the Zionist youth wore uniforms and practiced group discipline, camping, and outdoor survival skills. They drilled on precisely what they must do at the Vienna rail station, on the train, and aboard the ships that would carry them across the Mediterranean. They learned what they could take—a small rucksack of personal items—and what their lives might be like in Palestine—impoverished, but driven by a deep sense of purpose. The flurry of preparations involved educating parents as well as the young people who would make the eighteen-hundred-mile illegal trip without valid passports across three countries and a dangerous sea to a hostile land.

I could not imagine Alfred and Hedwig's burden of grief and worry as they helped plan and pay for both daughters' departures. Their fear must have been somewhat lightened by the expectation that Martha and Leo would be together, and that Gretl's cousin Ernst, fresh from the army, and his girlfriend Herta would make the trip too. They could watch over each other and then, everyone hoped, they would try to find a way for Alfred and Hedwig to follow.

Almost immediately after the Anschluss Alfred's prosperous brother Hermann and their sister Mathilde had sought ways to escape. In March 1938 Hermann asked New York relatives of his wife "Mitzi One" to apply for an affidavit for them and their daughter Lisl (Peter's mother); in May, Hermann appeared at the U.S. consulate in Vienna and registered for a visa. Not knowing whether they would receive affidavits, Lisl applied for work in London with her father's business colleagues. In the Vienna Room Peter showed me letters his mother had written describing her impressive background. A graduate of Vienna's School of Fashion and Design, she had run her own design house, Marlene's, specializing in jersey knit women's clothes for local customers and international exporters. She made her own patterns and collections, was a journeyman dressmaker and master in needlework, fluent in English and French. In desperation, she added that she was a master cook, able to do housework. But Britain was already flooded with refugees. Her letters brought no offers.

Alfred's sister Mathilde applied for immigration in South America, but there was almost no possibility that any country would take a sixty-four-year-old widow. His brother Arnold and Arnold's wife "Mitzi Two" considered following their younger son Ernst to Palestine but delayed, waiting while their older son Willi developed his plans.

During those dark days, some Viennese sympathized with Jews and helped as they could, despite the mounting German repression that impacted everyone. The antisemitic door attendant at Ani and Loli's building had a change of heart and made efforts to be kind. The director at the Wiener Handel Akademie, Vienna Business School, where Ani had completed three-quarters of her business degree, understood that she must leave and awarded Ani's diploma early—a few hopeful moments of human kindness in a relentlessly cruel time.

*

Trudi—the eldest daughter of Hedwig's sister Olga and Alfred's brother Richard—and her husband Jack were the first in the family to leave. At high risk because of his leadership in the Zionist movement, Jack had slept in different places every night, Loli said. "If they found him, they would take him." Richard helped arrange their escape— through Italy, and then on a quick flight to Turkey, where he had secured a construction job for Jack.

June of 1938 felt calamitous to Loli. She and Otto were forced to cancel plans for their early summer wedding. Richard was able to bring his family to Turkey but could not help Otto, who eventually escaped illegally to London. The lovers promised to wait forever and to find each other, but no one then could imagine the long world war that lay ahead.

In Vienna's charged atmosphere that June, sorrowful goodbyes echoed across the city. Jews understood that despite the *"Auf Wieder-sehen"* they spoke, they were not likely to "meet again." Shops ran out of trunks and suitcases; lines stretched for blocks around every consulate. All of Vienna had to have understood what was happening. An exodus of epic proportions was underway.

As Gretl's anticipated departure approached and Ani's family made frenetic plans to leave, the two girls agreed to walk together one last time. "Jews weren't allowed in parks or coffee houses," Ani said. *"Jews Not Allowed*. The signs were everywhere. That happened very, very, very quickly.

"Jews also weren't allowed to walk in the Vienna Woods, but we wanted to say goodbye. We walked and talked. Jews weren't allowed to sing in German. We sang Hebrew songs instead. It was not very clever, but we did it."

In spite of all my research, I found no information about Alfred and Hedwig's early efforts to leave Vienna. Celia believes they followed the common strategy of first using the family resources to help their children to safety and then evaluating their own situation—which child they would try to follow with what money remained. Wealthy Jews like Hermann, with prosperous international connections and money for the skyrocketing costs of escape, were more fortunate. Even so, I didn't understand why Alfred and Hedwig had not registered for an American quota number that spring or summer, a fateful delay.

★

The day—immersed in the Anschluss and its terrible aftermath—had been filled with emotion for me. I walked through the old city towards our hotel still feeling anxious, thinking again how quickly and completely Alfred and Hedwig's lives had turned upside down. It seemed that nothing they had done before that time—their hard work, their deep ties in Vienna, or their professional and neighborhood friends—counted for anything. I was disturbed, too, thinking about how Herta, who had barely escaped Vienna as a young girl and now was back, this time by her own choice, was once again fighting for her life.

I found Sidney and the Bergers in the hotel lobby talking in low voices. Herta had remained unresponsive. Judith introduced me to Herta's son Amnon, who was surprisingly warm and gracious for a person in his unhappy situation. Walking to the Servus Café for dinner, Amnon lagged behind the others, talking with Sidney and me. He carried his left arm, debilitated by childhood polio, close to his body, but his eyes twinkled, and his voice was soft and thoughtful. He asked about my progress and handed me a folder containing copies of documents for his father Ernst (Alfred's nephew), which Amnon had brought to Vienna—Ernst's birth certificate, records of his yearlong post-gymnasium study in textiles, his military record.

We slid into our usual corner booth. As we ordered dinner, I perused Amnon's papers. Military records he had brought documented his father's Austrian Army service from September 30, 1937, two months before his twenty-first birthday, until March 30, 1938, two weeks after the Anschluss. Ernst had served during six pivotal months of Austrian history. I asked Amnon if his father had talked to him about that experience. He wagged his head side to side. Yes, and no.

Hitler's welcome into Vienna has been heavily reported. Filmed footage, photos, reporting, and a wealth of historic analysis testify to the celebration that greeted Hitler's return. The streets, draped with Nazi banners and German and Austrian flags and lined with thousands of ecstatic Viennese, reverberated with the tumult of his motorcade, the ringing of church bells, and crowds shouting, "*Sieg Heil. Sieg Heil.*" Hail Victory.

Not as often discussed is the Austrian military's mind-boggling role reversal. Amnon explained that on one night the military were loyal defenders of the Republic. The next morning, they owed allegiance to Hitler and Nazi Germany. I waited, absorbed, to hear what Amnon could tell us.

I knew that in advance of Hitler's arrival in Austria, Reich security chief Heinrich Himmler had ordered thousands of potential enemies arrested, but without sufficient German troops yet in Vienna, he had been forced to call on Austrian units to protect the Führer.

Amnon told us that Ernst had spoken very little about those times but had described one event that stayed with him all his life. "Ernst's unit had served near the German border but at some point, withdrew to Vienna. As Hitler's schedule for invasion became clear, Austrian soldiers spread out along Hitler's motorcade route. My father was posted to a building overlooking the procession. He was a sniper, ordered to stand watch at a window."

Impossible, I thought. Who would permit a Jew to point a gun at Hitler's motorcade?

Ernst trained his rifle on the scene below, but as Hitler's big open Mercedes approached, an odd thing happened. The officer who had been in the room left, and Ernst was alone, pointing his rifle at Hitler.

Amnon said that his father debated what to do. He was a Zionist, fully aware of Hitler's treatment of Jews.

I was frozen, astonished. Sidney, next to me, reached out and held my hand. Of course, we knew what had happened. No shot had been fired. Hitler was not killed.

Amnon said that at that last, drawn-out moment, Ernst could not do it. "My father wanted to kill Hitler. He was tempted to pull the trigger and end everyone's nightmare. But he feared that when his role was discovered, repercussions for Jews would be horrendous. And so...he allowed Hitler to pass."

What a thought! Ernst had held not only Hitler's life but also millions of other lives in his hands. But he had been young and raised in a gentle family that did not deal in murder.

Amnon continued with his tale, explaining that his father came to believe later that the officer had intentionally left him alone, hoping Ernst would solve the army's problem.

Around the table we went silent, staring at Amnon, the restaurant clatter rising around us. Then we began asking questions, proposing possibilities. What if...? Had this really happened? It was a wisp of a story, handed from father to son, a jarring, tantalizing tale. That morning I had been reading British journalist G. E. R. Gedye's account of post-invasion Vienna, which revealed an Austrian military in disarray, unsure about their duty. I had read about the conflicting emotions and confused impulses in the proud, loyal Austrian military. Many resented their new, foreign commander in chief.

Amnon's story was possible, and it contained a horrible truth. Like the nineteen-year-old Serbian assassin who had triggered World War I and the demise of the Hapsburg Empire, this one young Jewish soldier could have transformed world history.

I gathered my thoughts to ask Amnon why he had brought these documents to Vienna. His answer, too, amazed me. This descendant of a family who had risked their lives to flee Austria, or were trapped and murdered here, said that he intended to apply for Austrian citizenship. Responding to my startled silence, he explained. "Life in Brazil is good now, but one never knows. A second passport could prove useful."

Again during this quest, I was startled to see my own life from a different perspective. My father had returned home safe from World War II. I had led a privileged, secure life and never imagined being forced to leave my home. Now, with a partly Jewish family, should I be thinking differently?

Around the table, heads were nodding approval of Amnon's plan. Sidney was nodding too.

CHAPTER 17
Escape

June 1938

A lfred and Hedwig's family had no time to waste. Gretl was a target, as were other Jewish youth leaders. To many Jews, these young people embodied the future, but to the Reich, they presented a radical opposition which was trained to fight antisemitism, not endure it. Unknown to most of Vienna, even as the Nazis beat and arrested Jewish youth on the streets and sent them to concentration camps, they were also finalizing plans to permit some young Jews to depart for Palestine.

Secrecy was critical to that sensitive planning. In 1938 there was mounting anger over Jewish refugees among Arabs. A trickle of Jewish immigrants returning to their ancient homeland in the early twentieth century had raised some alarm, but a flood was altogether different. As Nazi terror intensified and Jewish immigration mushroomed, Arabs—already rebellious under British control—resisted this further European incursion into their land and culture.

To appease Arab rebels in Palestine, Britain slashed Jewish immigration and blockaded the coast just as Gretl and other Jews were attempting to flee. The British military bombed, strafed, and boarded ships suspected of carrying illegal refugees, imprisoning captured Jews in Palestine and British territories around the world. Britain's anti-immigration enforcement enabled it to retain faltering control of Palestine, but bottled up terrified Jews in Nazi Europe.

This convergence of deadly enemies and complex politics made the escape uncertain until the day Gretl, Ernst, and Herta departed. Loli said that before they left no one in the extended family knew their plans. "We knew they were going to leave, but Gretl had to keep it from all her friends. It was a secret from everyone but close family. I already knew that I would go, too, so we talked a little. We hoped we would meet in Palestine. About the hope, we talked."

Families had been told that they would not receive news or updates. There was no time line for their journey. Indeed, there was no clarity about anything during the Jews' harrowing negotiations with the Reich, with shipping companies that would smuggle the illegal human cargo, with suppliers of an uncertain quantity of rations, and with countries the youth would pass through. Alfred and Hedwig waited and worried, hoping plans would come together and Gretl could flee.

I had found only skeletal information about her escape until Sidney and I visited the Jabotinsky Institute in Haifa several months after our Vienna trip. The Institute maintains extensive records about Betar efforts to rescue European Jews, but its most helpful assistance was putting me in touch with two survivors of Gretl's journey.

One of them, Hani, lived in Israel and spoke no English, but talked with Judith, mostly about the pre-departure organizing. "We knew Jews must leave Europe," she said. Betar, anticipating trouble for European Jews, had organized three "trial" departures before Germany invaded, but after the Anschluss the organization needed to move quickly. "We weren't afraid. In Betar, we got such a spirit, we were not afraid of the Gestapo. We were not afraid at all. Our parents were. They knew what could happen.

"Each family paid $250, a high price. Some people didn't have this much, so others, including my parents, donated money. We didn't leave anyone because of money—that was Galili."

Hani was referring to the young Russian-born Jew Moshe Galili, devoted to helping endangered European Jews establish a homeland. A shadowy figure whose efforts resulted in a British bounty on his head, he accompanied the youth on their trips to Palestine. "He was like a messiah to us, taking us to the Holy Land."

The second of Gretl's fellow travelers the Jabotinsky Institute connected us with was Marta Trefusis-Paynter, a retired journalist in her eighties who had grown up in Vienna, fled to Palestine, and later lived in Africa and Australia. When I first spoke with her by phone, Marta revealed that she had kept a journal during the escape, but she was hesitant about sharing it, thinking she might someday write her own book. She sent me several emails with broad-stroke details, but as we continued our email correspondence, her penchant for storytelling and her journalist's drive overcame her concerns. She began adding details in answer to my questions. Some days she sent me two emails. Other times ten days would pass with no word, but over a span of eight weeks she generously wrote twenty emails describing the escape, telling the story that she and Gretl had lived through.

As I received Marta's emails I forwarded them to Micha, Judith, and Celia, who received the information as a godsend and shared it with their families. When there were delays, they wrote me, "What happened?" "Will she continue?" She always did.

In her emails, Marta explained that she had first met Gretl in 1933 when she joined District VI Betar, where Gretl was a member. They were both thirteen. Three years later Gretl became a leader of about twenty fourteen-year-old girls.

"Betar was a steady bright flame burning in us...a flame of ideals, enthusiasm, and passion. We were working for our people's salvation.... Nothing else was as important."

William Perl, a young Jewish Viennese lawyer helping to negotiate the exodus, had turned his law office into Vienna's last Betar meeting space. Like all other Jews in the city, Marta had been expelled from high school immediately after the Anschluss—three months before she would have graduated. As Betar's Vienna Girls Leader, she turned her energies to helping coordinate the escape plan.

Gretl was among the more than eight hundred young Vienna Jews who applied for that journey. Three hundred Betar members, age seventeen to about thirty, were selected, plus about eighty other Jews whose situations were especially dangerous. The five hundred who were not chosen received the discouraging consolation that they could apply for the hoped-for next transport.

Marta told me that Gretl had graduated from intermediate school, which she finished at age fourteen, and she believed that Gretl then took secretarial and business courses and did bookkeeping for a small business. Marta was working in the Betar office when Gretl came to pay for her passage and turn in her passport, as was required of all participants.

As a group leader, Gretl received the names of youth in her charge, along with instructions for travel. Everyone would wear their Betar uniform: earth-brown shirts, dark skirts for girls, shorts for boys. Packing instructions read like the list for a Spartan summer camp: one backpack weighing not more than two and a half kilograms (five and a half pounds), one change of clothes including a sweater, slacks or skirt, plus underwear, pajamas, shoes, socks, toothpaste and toothbrush, soap, and a small lunch box with a few sandwiches, hard-boiled eggs, two tins of sardines and cookies. "We filled our backpacks to bursting. Our families helped us pack."

Besides security concerns, difficulties arranging almost every aspect of the escape kept Betar from releasing any travel details to the families until the last moment. The young people waited, backpacks ready, to learn if and when the group would go. Tomorrow? Next week? Perl instructed Marta to organize a communication chain to alert families about the departure.

Early on the afternoon of June 8, 1938, Marta activated the chain: the 386 travelers living across the city, many of them in hiding, needed to arrive at the busy *Ostbahnhof,* East Train Station, in three hours.

A few puffy clouds drifted across the darkening sky that Thursday evening when the Betar group departed. There was turmoil below as hundreds of families crowded the circular drive, bidding their children goodbye. City police, storm troopers, and Gestapo were stationed everywhere. Adolf Eichmann himself directed the potentially explosive process to ensure there would be no disruptive emotional scenes. Ani and Loli remember tears, but the departing youth had been lectured and drilled and their families sternly warned to maintain order. Any incident would result in cancellation of this and possible future departures.

Trip leaders received their itineraries at the station: their sealed train would pass through Austria and Yugoslavia during the night and continue on to Athens over the next several days. From Athens a bus would transport them to a coastal village where they would board a ship bound for Palestine.

It sounded much simpler than it was. Marta sent me her account of the journey's start:

> The station swarmed with uniformed Nazis. Relatives were not allowed in the station. The Nazis did not want any commotion. Taxis had converged in the streets around the station, but inside was quiet. We deposited our backpacks on our assigned seats, then assembled on the platform in formation as we had often drilled.
>
> Perl, flanked by Eichmann and other Nazis, spoke briefly to the assembled group with muted but heartfelt language. He told us we were now going to our true homeland. I was the girl who started the group singing the Hatikvah, the song that became the Israeli national anthem, but I burned with fury at Perl's words. I felt that we were being thrown out of

our homes, and Perl THANKED the Nazis for having been good and kind enough to have given us shelter and for ALLOWING us strangers to breathe their air!

The fervent young Marta did not understand that Eichmann had forced Perl to submit his speech for Nazi approval, and that trip organizers would pay with their lives if trouble broke out.

Gretl, Ernst, Herta, and Marta lined up with their fellow Betar members. On command they strode in formation to their assigned cars and took their seats. As an experienced group leader, Gretl watched over her assigned group of younger teenagers. She would comfort them, instruct them on procedures, and see to their care during the journey. They would sing bracing Betar songs and not look back.

Nazi guards took their places inside each of the six train cars, every door bolted so that no one could enter or leave as the train traveled through countries that did not want the young refugees. From Marta: "We had sixty girls assigned to Coach Four. Saying goodbye to our parents who had no idea what would become of us tore our hearts out.... We wondered whether the uncles and aunts who'd come to our homes to see us off had gone, leaving our parents alone. Were they talking about us? What was happening to us? We fell into a fretful sleep, interrupted only by two uniformed Gestapo women who inspected the compartment."

Outside, some parents may have stayed until the final whistle shrieked, smoke billowed, and the train slowly pulled away, picking up speed and rumbling toward a distant future. It is heartbreaking to think of Hedwig letting go of her youngest, and Alfred, attuned to the last bass notes of the departing train, turning to walk home through streets emptying of friends and family.

My God, I thought. What strength and sacrifice that time demanded!

✦

Marta's emails to me continued:

> At dawn the next morning, we awoke on the Yugoslav border, sticky, thirsty, and feeling bruised; there was no water. In Zagreb and later in Belgrade, a Jewish organization was allowed to distribute brown bread, hard goat's cheese, and hot black coffee to us, making us feel better, knowing somebody cared.
>
> At four in the morning on June 12, four days after they had departed, they reached Athens—stiff, aching, and tired—and spent the night in a dingy hotel.
>
> The following morning big old buses with hard seats and squeaking springs took us an hour from Athens to the peninsula of Oropos.... We stopped on a piece of land between parched desolate fields.... The sand was so hot it burned through the soles of our boots. Eight large grey-white canvas tents under the blistering sun blinded us. Galili told us we would wait here for our ship, two days, "or longer."...
>
> We stayed for a week. We soon found out we couldn't wash with sea water. We were not allowed to jump into the sea before evening because the sun burnt too fiercely. We slept on the ground in our clothes. Our water ration for cleaning or washing was one mug a day.

On June 20, ten days after they had left Vienna, Galili came from Athens with the news that the Greek Government had given him an ultimatum: leave Greece within twelve hours or he would be arrested, and the youth deported back to Vienna.

At noon a ship steamed into the tiny port of Oropos. "What a *shinakl*!" unseaworthy boat, said a girl next to me...a small cattle freighter with a dirty deck and rusty funnel. As she approached, we saw her name in grey letters, *Artemisia*. Three lifeboats, paint peeling, were lowered. A large truck chugged in from Athens. Galili ordered four boys to off-load what he said were provisions.... In the hold, there were no portholes. A little light and air came through an opening with a half-broken ladder leading down; the floor was covered with straw-filled bags, smelling musty and rotten. A thick layer of grime covered the floor and walls.

I had seen films of pirate ships and this reminded me of one. The captain, whose name was Kosta, looked like a mummy, with a yellow face, sharp, jutting cheekbones, and two black stumps in a cavernous mouth. The crew was six sailors and a cook. They might have been escaped galley slaves, with bare, tattooed rumps and thickly muscled arms, glistening daggers in the belts of their tiny shorts.

We had been aboard a few hours when Galili ordered the boys to find a crowbar and open one of the wooden crates from the truck. They did, but there were no provisions—nothing but grey and yellow pebbles. Another crate was opened and another—stones. In two sacks were stale rusks [hard, crisp bread] a quantity of hard, sour lemons, and a few bags of tea.

We had been forced to pay heavily for what we were assured were foodstuffs, but we could not risk turning back. Galili cursed and damned their evil souls. Our rations would be two rusks and a cup of lemon tea a day. Water was rationed to one cup a day.

The first evening, a sharp, cold wind rose and the waves grew. The *Artemisia* rolled violently. Shivering figures hung over the railings; most of us were seasick. Everything reeked.

There was one lavatory for three hundred sixty passengers. We queued up all day and night, and those who could not hold out wetted and stained their pants. We vomited over the railings or where we stood.

On our third night, a gale pounded the *Artemisia*. The deck dipped beneath the foam-streaked cauldron and reared crazily into the air, then crashed into the trough beyond, straining the ancient timbers. I was certain we would not survive....

None of us had known the parching force of burning thirst. Our throats were scorched, our lips cracked, our tongues wooden. The insipid sour tea did not help....

We soon realized that the sailors stole. A gold ring, a coat, a compact, a pair of shoes disappeared. If they wished, the sailors could throw any of us overboard and no court in the world would punish them...this was a ghost ship, and we were the ghosts.

The hours crept. It seemed we had never known another life, only this filthy, rocking, floating coffin. Things became blurred. We were weak.... one night a fat black rat settled on my face. It seemed we had been sailing since the beginning of time.

It is easy to see why Marta felt that the ship and her passengers were phantoms. Officially, they did not exist. Even speaking about Gretl or the departure would have imperiled the transport. Alfred and Hedwig lived in suspense with their fears.

Onboard, time had a strange quality. Life before the journey had ceased to exist. There was no turning back. If they returned to Greece, they would be deported to Vienna, and probably then to Dachau. Memories were painful, the future unknown. There was only the present, forward motion, and hope.

Finally, after eight miserable days at sea, they sighted land. Marta continued:

A loud roar broke from our throats. We embraced and kissed. That night, we saw many lights. One came on and off at regular intervals like from a lighthouse. Galili said that "our men" must have been waiting for days.

Someone was waiting to welcome us, welcome us home.

Galili would not allow section heads to give landing instructions: the swells were too high for the fragile lifeboats and the *Artemisia* could not approach shore without endangering us. We had to avoid the British Navy. The next day was the hottest and longest. Most of us were feverish.

In the evening, Galili divided us into groups of five. Each lifeboat could not take more than one sailor and five passengers; this meant seventy-two trips. He ordered all of us down into the men's hold—360 people in a space for perhaps twenty-four.

The air hit me like a sledgehammer. We stood on each other's toes almost choking.... If someone had fainted, there was no space to collapse, not even to sag.... Galili said we could not board the lifeboats before ten that night. I could not imagine how we'd survive four hours in that pesthole but we could not risk remaining on the deck in case the British spotted us from the air.

After hours, Galili called down that he was going ashore, and we heard oars splash against water. Minutes ticked away. Galili returned and the first few groups stumbled upstairs. I could move my arms, but still had trouble to breathe.

Time dragged to hours before the boats returned and the next groups of five went. Again, oars knocked the water.

This time it seemed much longer before the boats returned. Galili shouted at the sailors in Greek, then called down that it would soon be daylight and he could not risk another trip that night. What could we do but scramble upstairs, gasping for breath? After that night in the boys' hold, even the dank air of the girls' bunker struck me like pure ozone. We fell on our straw bags and slept.

I awoke at midday.... The hours crept, hotly, brightly, with fleas and flies. Another night and again we girls moved into the boy's hold to await orders. That night there were no signals from the coast: the strip of shoreline where signal lights had blinked for the past two nights stayed dark.

Galili tried to work out what had happened. Perhaps the Irgun men [Zionist paramilitaries] had been discovered or arrested.... We had no radio or telephone contact. I was ready to die. It would be simple: close my eyes and let life ebb away.

The memoir of the young lawyer William Perl describes that night, when the *Artemisia*'s landing was imperiled. Unknown to the refugees huddled below deck, Jews watching for their arrival with flashlights lay hidden in the dunes. Others stood beside saddled horses in nearby stables, ready to ride. Those waiting in the dunes sighted a ship and flashed their signal. The same pattern shot back. This had not been the arrangement. The rescuers fled into the hills as a British launch sped toward shore. "The next day," Marta recounted,

on Galili's instructions, we threw half of our belongings overboard because we were no longer strong enough to lift our rucksacks.... As the sun disappeared, we were again sent into the boy's hold and a few tense minutes later Galili said, "*Baruch ha shem*," blessed be His name. Signal lights were flashing.

Anxious minutes ticked away...the rattled breathing of my companions proved we were slowly choking. We waited....

Galili stood on top of the rope ladder, shaking hands. I managed to thank him. Then I stood on the edge of the cattle freighter and far, far down in a black, surging mass of water rocked the tiny lifeboat into which I was expected to jump. A friend gripped me under my arms. He lifted me and for a long moment I was dangling in the air before Willy, already down in the boat, caught me.

"Don't forget my accordion," I shouted at Marcel against the roar of the sea.

One of the Greek sailors told me in English to shut up or the whole shore battery might be alerted. A friend pulled me down on a plank. We were in the lifeboat, blackness engulfing us. The waves shot the boat high on the crests and low in the troughs. The thunder of the sea drowned all sounds. Planks had worked loose and the boat leaked. The sailors rowed blindly through the shrieking wind to an invisible shore, yet the boat did not seem to move.

One of the sailors shouted, "We are here. Get out."

Were they simply going to throw us into the sea and let us drown? Panic clutching me, I jumped. Swirling waters closed over my head, the rucksack, wet and heavy, pulled me down. Then I was caught and pulled up.... I felt dry sand under my feet.

I sat down. The sand seemed to rock. I could not believe it. The chain of hills I saw in the dim starlight were the ancient hills of the land of Israel. I took sand into my hands and buried my face in its coolness.

William Perl described the *Artemisia* as a small craft that broke the British blockade repeatedly over several years and became the most hunted ship in the eastern Mediterranean. He wrote that many in Israel owe their lives to Captain Kosta's skill at handling ship and crew while evading the British.

The crews that Galili and Perl could recruit were indeed similar to what Marta called "pirates." Officers and sailors knew the risks of the illegal trips. Crew could be killed by British guns and, later, by German torpedoes. Refugees, who were frequently ill, overloaded the ships. Sanitation was abysmal. There were almost no lifeboats.

By 1938, the Palestinians had escalated their two-year revolt against British control; in attempts to pacify them, Britain tightened immigration policies. Britain persuaded Greek dictator Ioannis Metaxas to punish seamen involved in smuggling Jews. Many officers on those illegal voyages had already lost their licenses, and the sailors typically were wanted for crimes, including murder. If captured, they would, at best, end up in British prisons. Working with these seafaring renegades, Perl, Galili, and their small group of organizers negotiated ever more uneasily with the Nazis. As the war widened, Arabs increasingly leaned on Nazi support, absorbed the Nazis' virulent antisemitism, and received German training in terror to fight British domination and Jewish immigration. The brief Nazi-Jewish partnership ended in 1941—after saving as many as forty thousand trapped Jews.

Family stories placed Gretl's landing near Binyamina, a small village along a sparsely settled desert shore. The Bergers believed that Gretl and Ernst had not reached shore in a lifeboat, like Marta. The family had been told that Arabs from a coastal village rowed small boats to the ship to take refugees ashore for a price. Since Gretl and Ernst had no money, the family story goes, they stuffed their few possessions into backpacks, tied their shoes together, slung them around their necks, and jumped into the dark water. They swam, losing their shoes and ruining the photos they had packed. Penniless and barefoot, they arrived on the beach of the ancient land that promised—they hoped—a new home.

Celia's story of the landing included a handsome, recently arrived refugee pulling Gretl from the sea, but Micha and Judith chuckled at that. They told me that Gretl met the handsome stranger, their father, weeks later in a refugee camp where she was interned and he worked.

Like most refugees, soon after she arrived Gretl Hebraized her name. She chose Miriam, for the resourceful biblical heroine who

Gretl in Palestine in 1938. *Courtesy of the Berger family*

guarded the floating basket that saved her baby brother Moses from Pharaoh's death order.

The Betar had laid plans upon plans. On some landings, if the British appeared, immigrants ran up the hills to a Jewish settlement where hundreds of townspeople rushed to mill about and hide the refugees. "It was a miracle when anything went smoothly," Perl wrote.

Often things did not go well for fleeing Jews. Illness, hairbreadth escapes, and death awaited later voyagers and refugees in Palestine. On the day that Gretl landed, June 29, 1938, the British hanged a twenty-five-year-old Betar refugee for supposed terrorist activity.

I had wondered why Alfred and Hedwig had not escaped on a Betar journey to Palestine. Marta's account convinced me that Betar had been right to accept only healthy, younger Jews. The elderly and handicapped probably could not have survived such a journey, and might have imperiled it.

After nearly three weeks of imagining the best and the worst, word filtered back to Betar families in Vienna that their children were safe. The relief for Alfred and Hedwig must have been enormous, yet blunted by loss. Their passionate, sometimes awkward teenager, whose lilting whistle had echoed in the stairwell, was gone and would never return.

CHAPTER 18

Roundup

Summer–Fall 1938

In the summer of 1938, Alfred and Hedwig's world was falling apart at a pace unimaginable only a few months before. On June 13, as Gretl and Ernst sweltered on the Oropos peninsula, United States consul John Wiley in Vienna sent a memo to the U.S. secretary of state describing Austria's disintegrating "Jewish Situation":

> Sir,
>   ...In respect of Jewish activities, there seems to be no relaxation whatsoever in the pressure applied by authorities. Wholesale arrests continue on an ever-increasing scale.
>   There is, moreover, a new wave of Jew-baiting....
>   There are innumerable cases where individuals are given the choice of leaving Austria within...two to eight weeks, or of being sent to Dachau. In many cases individuals are supplied with police certificates attesting that there is nothing against them. This innovation is interesting in that German authorities are expelling German citizens and forcing would-be migrants to the United States to leave before a quota number can be made available.

Authorities encourage clandestine emigration. I received what I believe a conservative estimate from an authoritative source that over 1,000 have been obliged to cross the frontier at night into Belgium. A few days ago 350 were sent in sealed cars to Greece whence they will be shipped to Palestine without visas or permits of entry. It was explained to me that competent British authorities are unofficially in the picture and not raising obstacles.

The rampant persecution of Jews had become common knowledge in Vienna and around the world within three months of the Anschluss. Nations including the United States and Britain monitored the severity of the terror as Austria's Jews tried every conceivable means to flee. Before discovering Wiley's memo, I hadn't understood that the British possessed details of Betar's "secret" rescue operation and were tracking Gretl's journey.

Even so, the British may not have been as obliging as they reported to their American counterparts. In fact, if Britain permitted some transports to land in Palestine, its military also strafed, bombed, and impounded refugee ships, killing or imprisoning fleeing Jews. The young refugees were well advised to use all possible caution.

★

Shortly after Ernst's departure, German soldiers pounded on Arnold and Mitzi's door demanding to know where their son, the former soldier, was. And where was his service revolver? Frustrated to discover that Ernst had fled and his weapon was missing, they grabbed Willi, Arnold and Mitzi's older son, and took him away.

That summer, Nazis had orders to harass and arrest Jews on sight or abduct them from their homes or work. Party members and Reich officers forced young and old, healthy and ill Jews to perform demeaning tasks. Leering, jeering crowds surrounded Jews on their knees scrubbing sidewalks and streets. Nazis laced cleaning water with acid, or forced Jews to use their tongues. Jews cleaned public toilets, amid taunts and beatings—whatever humiliating conditions their captors inflicted on them. Willi's wife said that he never spoke about his experience being dragged to the streets; it's not clear where or for how long he was held.

Before that incident, Willi had been reluctant to leave his parents; afterwards, they all agreed he must go. Strong, young Jewish men, most of them by then fired from their jobs, were on Nazi lists of potential troublemakers. I imagined Arnold and Mitzi waiting in terror for Willi to return, and when he did, urging their last child at home to flee.

Willi, twenty-six, was a year younger than Martha. Growing up, they had been especially close; he, too, was an excellent pianist. Even so, he may not have revealed his rushed plan to escape even to her. As Loli said, "A secret that slipped out might cost a life."

Snow was melting in the Austrian Alps in June when Willi made his way to the Swiss border. Drifts could reach waist high and winds might be freezing, but the mountains were passable. Family lore says that Willi was turned back and imprisoned one night near the Swiss border, but the next day a border guard showed him where to cross. This may be true. Several Swiss guards were punished for lax enforcement—but after the war honored for their courage and compassion. One acknowledged saving more than three thousand Jews.

In Zurich, a cousin of Willi's mother found a place for him to live. Through his own or Hermann's contacts in the Honig Corporation, Willi found a job in a Zurich textile company that soon led to emigration and a job in Brazil.

As I heard Willi's story, I was impressed again by the courage and enduring legacy of individuals who risked helping Jews. What had motivated them? Ordinary human kindness? Shame? Why had others failed to help? Bigotry? Fear? Apathy?

★

The day that Gretl swam ashore in Palestine, June 29, was the same date Loli and Otto had planned to be married. Otto had long since fled illegally to London, and that day passed in a blur of tears and packing for Loli, Ani, and Olga as they prepared to depart for Turkey.

Loli said that it was so dangerous for Jews to appear in public then that her mother, her Aunt Hedwig, and her Uncle Alfred rarely braved the streets, instead phoning each other to stay in touch. "Nobody can imagine what it was like then, and if you ask me, I can't tell you because it was so terrible. We wanted to help others, but we couldn't. So many people asked us for help because my family had some money and foreign connections. From Turkey, my father did what he could."

Loli's comment that she couldn't say more about the horror is a classic post-traumatic response, one that speaks volumes about the depth of her emotions. Even so, she also said that in the midst of the overwhelming cruelty, "some people behaved decently to us." By midsummer 1938, several of her non-Jewish friends had dropped out of Bund Deutcher Maedel, BDM, the girls' Hitler Youth organization. "First one, then a second, and a third. So I knew they were against it. When I came back years later for a school reunion, I had no problem contacting them." Ani had no such fond memories, but Celia told me that a number of Herta's friends, too, had stood by her with heartening acts of kindness. Why weren't there more, I wondered? If I'd lived in Austria in those times, would I have joined the small, courageous opposition?

After Olga and her daughters obtained their exit and visa documents, Nazi emigration officers scheduled their appointment in their flat to inspect and tag the belongings they would be allowed to take out of the country—a rigorous process during which Jews lost furniture, cars, art, clothing. Sometimes inspectors stole what they fancied while Jews stood by waiting for the life-saving stamps on their documents.

The relatively early departure of Hedwig's sister Olga and her daughters meant that they were not subject to the far more onerous exit procedures imposed later, when Jews could take nothing but their clothes and about twenty dollars in Reichsmarks [RM], the new currency. Olga was able to take her Persian carpets and clavier-piano, but art was a Nazi obsession. Vienna's museums confiscated some Jewish artwork, and the finest went to Hitler's hometown of Linz for his proposed world-class museum, or to powerful Nazi collectors like Goebbels and Göring. Loli said that officials took a number of her family's paintings. "For one, we had a Pettenkofen, an Austrian painter. Some SS man took it. They took jewelry, too. I had a silver ring with an onyx that wasn't worth anything, but they took it anyway."

The day before their departure, Loli ran headlong into trouble. By late April, the Reich had already restricted when and where Jews could shop and enforced a boycott of Jewish businesses. Storm troopers arrested aryans who shopped in Jewish stores or forced them to parade through the streets wearing signs marking them as traitors to their race.

"My mother had a special diet for her ulcer. I needed to buy things for her to take on the train, but as a Jew, I couldn't shop near our flat. Nobody would have given food to me. In the more Jewish Second District, there were no signs then forbidding Jews, so I walked there.

"When I was inside, no one wanted to give me anything. I didn't know why. Then I noticed an SS man walking up and down, up and down, in front of the shop. It was a Jewish store. Then I realized that because of my blonde hair, he was thinking I was Christian. I hurried out. The man hit me, tried to put a stamp on my forehead that meant I helped Jews. With that, I couldn't have gone anywhere. We couldn't leave. I tried to spring onto a moving tram, but he stopped me. I knew I had to be strong. I pulled free and ran, and so I came away.

Loli was lucky. A mountain guide, an athlete, she must have surprised her larger, stronger attacker with her determined fight for her life.

On July 8, Olga, Loli, and Ani boarded the Orient Express bound for Istanbul. Leaving family, friends, and home, they felt no joy, but when they crossed into Bulgaria, then still free of Nazi control, they breathed more easily. Loli was "very, very sorry to leave." She had loved Vienna. Ani was glad to get out. This was yet another terrible blow to the close-knit family. Olga and Hedwig had been inseparable. Eight family members were now gone from Vienna.

In Istanbul, Richard met his wife and daughters at the station. At dinner, Ani said, he explained that they had permission to remain in Turkey for six months. He told them he wanted to go to Czechoslovakia, where they were citizens, and he urged them to go with him. He said he couldn't live or work permanently in "the Orient." Ani didn't know why—whether because he couldn't extend his permit or simply didn't want to live there, but later that evening she pulled her father aside. She told him about their experiences in Vienna, some that she hadn't told her mother or sisters. "He told me these were *backfischträume*, dreams of an immature girl. He didn't believe me."

Fearlessly outspoken as always, Ani argued back, and her sisters supported her. They told Richard they "wouldn't allow" Olga to go. They would take care of their mother, they said, and they did. Richard left Turkey shortly after his family arrived, and his three daughters became governesses.

Describing that abandonment in low voices some seventy years later, Loli and Ani said they believed that Richard had left to join his mistress, a Romanian actress. They guessed that he believed her non-Jewish status would protect him; he may also have been attempting to save his assets in Austria. Over the next few years Richard wrote several letters from Romania, Budapest, and the Slovakian region of Czechoslovakia to various family members, but no one in the extended family seems to have seen him again. They didn't know what became of him until Hermann found answers after the war.

★

By late June, Leo's situation had become critical. Hitler saw Polish Jews who had entered Germany and Austria illegally—or whose ancestors had done so generations earlier—as easy prey in his race war, and he accelerated their deportation. Poland responded decisively to the large numbers of returning Jews. Facing a potential influx of more than fifty thousand jobless German- and Austrian-Polish Jews stripped of their assets, Poland passed legislation in the fall of 1938 requiring all citizens who had lived outside the country for the preceding five years to return or revalidate their passports by October 30 or be declared stateless; in effect, Poland was disowning its own citizens, the Jews it had pushed out with virulent antisemitism. Now Leo could be grabbed anywhere, anytime. Heeding warnings from his police friend and relying on his wits, he held himself ready to "take a walk," to leave his apartment and disappear into the city.

As Gretl was still sailing toward Palestine in mid-June, Alfred signed the city housing registration card confirming Martha and Leo's move from Mittelgasse to his and Hedwig's apartment. Someone may have aryanized the young couple's apartment, their finances may have forced the move, or the family may have decided they would be safer together. Whatever the reason, moving wasn't easy, physically or emotionally. Martha and Leo probably sold their grand piano and most of the furnishings they had so recently put into their first home at bargain prices. Prohibited from hiring aryans for menial labor, they very likely hauled their most precious and useful possessions themselves, or with help from friends. Jews changing apartments while others carted off their belongings was a common sight on Vienna's streets at the time.

With Martha and Leo moving into Gretl's tiny former bedroom that summer, the closeness of their daughter and son-in-law must surely have eased some of Alfred and Hedwig's grief and fears—cold comfort in those dismal days. Martha and Leo's situation was dangerous, and Alfred and Hedwig, too, were struggling to find a way out as time and the poisonous tide of antisemitism rose around them all.

Reich laws continued to rain down on Austrian Jews throughout that summer. Law after law abrogated their legal contracts, including rental agreements. Jewish physicians, lawyers, teachers, and journalists could practice their professions only for Jewish clientele. Ever more restrictive laws curtailed when and where Jews could shop and dictated what they could purchase and own, which public parks were open to them, which schools, which hospitals. Storm troopers guarded the tramline at the Vienna Woods, where Gretl and Ani had walked, barring Jews.

As the summer of 1938 wore on, new laws required Jews to identify themselves in all business and official encounters. Alfred and Hedwig carried a *Kennkarte*, an identity card, bearing the new middle names mandated for all Jews. He became Alfred Israel Berger; she was Hedwig Sarah Berger. Even their identities had been stolen.

★

At the time of the Anschluss in March, Germany's goal was total aryanization of Jewish assets within four years. Austria blew past those expectations. Within a year, only 6 percent of Vienna's Jews were still employed.

Vienna's daily Nazi newspaper, the *Volkisher Beobachter* (*The People's Observer*), expressed the new government's intentions concisely that summer: "By 1942, the Jewish element in Vienna will have been wiped out.... Viennese wonder at all the trouble [authorities] take.... It is all perfectly simple: The Jew must go, and his cash stays!" Berlin leadership wrung every possible Reichsmark from Austria's Jews. That massive wealth transfer, along with large forced labor programs, buttressed the widely accepted propaganda about Nazi-produced prosperity.

Hitler's persecution of Jews was at bottom a racial war, but he also pursued their assets fanatically. Immediately after the Anschluss, the Reich issued a cluster of laws targeting Jewish property. Jews with a net worth more than 2,000 RM were required to submit forms identifying their assets, including foreign holdings, real estate, businesses, savings, income, pensions, valuables, furniture, jewelry, and art. Reich bankers froze Jewish accounts, replacing them with *sperrkonten*, Reich-controlled savings accounts.

I couldn't find any record of Alfred and Hedwig's registering their assets. It's likely they fell below the level of wealth that required a report. But Peter had given me copies of Hermann's required documents. The first asset he listed was the largest, his National Lottery windfall two weeks before the Anschluss. Peter said that his grandfather hadn't bought the "Lucky Hit" ticket awarding him 133,333.33 RM, about $45,000 in 1938 dollars and the equivalent of over $700,000 today, a fortune at any time but especially in Depression-era Austria. He had received the ticket with his electric bill or as a bank premium. That a Jew won must have infuriated the Nazis—which I admit gives me some irrational pleasure.

In the "Listing of Jews' Assets" that Hermann submitted just before the June 30 deadline, he reported the total market value of his holdings to be 150,973.33 RM, including his pension, stocks, currency, cutlery, furniture, silver, and a carpet—some of which I had probably seen in Peter's Vienna Room. He declared that he was a retired merchant aged sixty-four receiving monthly pensions from M. Honig and the Employee Institute Insurance.

Endless Nazi demands would drain Hermann's assets. In midsummer of that same year, Hermann received a letter from the State Commissioner for the Private Sector informing him of the Reich's Four Year Plan and mandating that he sell all his securities and prepare to pay an unspecified assessment in one week.

Hermann had deposited his lottery winnings in the soon-to-be-nationalized Österreich Creditanstalt-Wiener Bankverein, but was never allowed to touch that money. Peter believes that it sat in a "dead account," not available to Hermann's siblings as he had hoped it would be, and probably at some point was absorbed by the bank.

★

Austrians' euphoria over the Anschluss lingered through the summer. Hitler buttressed his popular support with speeches and visits to Vienna, boasting about the Reich's accomplishments. Viennese waited for hours in the streets to catch sight of his motorcade. Austrians basked in the uplifting feeling that the empire's glory days had returned. They railed against the "lies" Jews and foreign newspapers told about their Führer.

But for some the bubble of euphoria began to deflate as the Viennese experienced the reality of living under an iron-fisted dictator. Berlin appointed their local leaders. Orders from Berlin reorganized their city's districts. City engineers found their work ridiculed by superiors in Berlin. Unemployment was not an option; jobless Viennese received work assignments in Germany and young people not in school were sent to work on German farms and cities. All public correspondence ended with *Heil Hitler.*

The more I delved into those times, the more frightening I found them. With greed and baseless, spiteful propaganda as motivators, the citizens of one of the most cultured civilizations in the world had embraced lawlessness, hatred, theft, and murder as solutions to perceived wrongs. Thinking about those forces, increasingly at work in today's world, made me cringe.

By mid-August Reich typists and presses were clattering out laws aimed at reining in Austrian street violence and property theft. On August 18, the Vienna Nazi Party Headquarters sent a circular to all offices of the Nazi party, SS, SA, Nazi Party Motor Corps, Pilot Corps, Hitler Youth—an amazing array of Nazi groups—forbidding theft or attacks on Jews without direction from superior offices. So many Austrians had stolen from Jews that the Reich began charging thousands of surprised aryans with theft, not from Jews, but from the state; Germany intended to control the Jews' wealth.

The Reich crackdown on Austrian lawlessness gave some Jews a small reprieve. Berger family friend Bernard Toch successfully petitioned Reich offices to recover his apartment and small business in the Naschmarkt. That he was a World War I veteran who had been wounded in action probably made less difference to the success of his appeal than the influence of his wife's high-ranking Nazi relatives.

Bernard's four sisters had no such protection. By September his sister Hilde had made her Second District apartment on Czerningasse a haven for family evicted from their own flats. Alfred and Hedwig were still in their home at that time. Perhaps neighbors helped to shield them from aryanization, or they were among the handicapped Jews who petitioned the government to remain in their homes, or maybe they were simply lucky.

Several non-Jewish groups in Austria tested the Reich's tight-fisted grip that summer and fall. Catholics had not offered Jews the protection of a quick baptism, immigration to predominantly Catholic countries, or charity, but when Hitler closed Catholic religious schools they staged large demonstrations. Swift Nazi reprisals, including arrests and destruction of the Archbishop's palace in Vienna, ended the short-lived resistance.

World leaders, too, misjudged Hitler's fury and aggression. On September 30, 1938, as Great Britain, France, and Italy agreed to Germany's occupation of Western Czechoslovakia, headlines in the *Los Angeles Times* described the appeasement as a "Four Power Peace Pact" and "Compromise Plan," and alluded proudly to American mediation. The adjoining front-page news, "Stocks Continue Upward," may have drawn as much attention from readers like Clarence and Bea Berger who, within a year, would receive Alfred's letter begging for help.

As doors opened for Germany throughout Europe that fall, Alfred and Hedwig watched events closely. Responding to a Swiss request, Germany recalled all Jewish passports and issued replacements stamped with a large "J"—border guards could now instantly recognize Jews and turn them away. Belgium shut its borders to the flow of Jewish refugees. Spain's dictator General Francisco Franco drew up lists of Spanish Jews for Hitler's future use. The Daladier government in France passed laws identifying and monitoring "undesirable aliens," refugees pouring across its border. Watching Germany's militarization with concern, France also mandated that male refugees would be interned in work units during a national mobilization—a law that would soon imprison nearly twenty thousand mostly Jewish refugees, including Leo, and lead to deadly French concentration camps.

In late summer 1938 Adolf Eichmann established Vienna's Office of Jewish Emigration, located in the Metropol Hotel, the site of Betar's former basement headquarters where Ani had been trapped. Eichmann's system was so efficient that his methods were replicated throughout the Reich, and he rose rapidly in Nazi ranks. Leo's application for emigration, and his Polish birth certificate, were among the first papers to pass through Eichmann's new center. The document declaring him stateless was approved there on August 20.

Even as thousands of Jews poured out of Austria and evictions forced others to share apartments, Nazi district leaders continued to clamor for more housing for aryans. Reich Property Offices attempting to rein in unauthorized aryan appropriations of Jewish property were helpless to stop Nazi party loyalists demanding Jewish property as payback for their service. Citizens coveting apartments protested the "health hazard" and annoyance of multiple families crowding into small spaces and the disturbance of SS or police storming up their stairs and demanded that the government oust Jews from their districts.

In late summer Viennese authorities explored solutions to the persistent housing shortage. Their solutions didn't include building new apartments for their citizens. Instead, city councilors tallied the numbers: Before the Anschluss, Jews had occupied about 10 percent of total Vienna housing stock, consistent with their percentage of the city's population. Evicting all Jews could release seventy thousand dwellings. Drawn by the irresistible vision of that large housing supply, the city council began construction of a barracks-like camp for interning Jews in a Vienna suburb—an imminent threat to Alfred and Hedwig.

The plan failed largely because of citizen complaints—not about the injustice or cruelty of the policy, but about potential disease outbreaks and the undesirability of a nearby concentration camp. City councilors soon found that they needn't have rushed into a quick solution; harsh repression was already doing their work for them. By late summer, 1938, about fifty thousand of Vienna's two hundred thousand Jews had emigrated.

By late September, all that had been stable in Alfred and Hedwig's lives was in motion. Their family was breaking apart. Gretl was gone. Willi, Ernst, Olga, Richard, Trudi, Loli, and Ani were gone. Hermann, Mitzi, and Lisl nervously awaited the affidavits that would allow them to immigrate to the United States. Mathilde explored immigration to

Paraguay. Arnold and Mitzi weighed their alternatives—follow one son to Brazil or join the other in Palestine? Hedwig's three brothers, living an anxious existence in what remained of Czechoslovakia, had applied for work outside Europe. Martha and Leo would flee as soon as their American paperwork permitted, but they continued to search for a safe place to wait.

Friends talked about leaving. Friends left. Friends disappeared. The city that Alfred and Hedwig had loved no longer wanted them. No cafe, no workplace, no opera or music hall welcomed them. I asked Ani how she imagined Alfred and Hedwig coped with the turmoil and sadness. Would they have given up? Fallen apart emotionally and become passive about their own safety? Without hesitation, she replied: "Alfred would FIGHT. He would have kept fighting... Hedwig was softer. She was too good for this world."

What had Ani meant by "too good?" She was by nature a fighter who had rebelled against her father and argued with antisemites. Her work later in life involved helping Holocaust-era Jews fight for restitution. It seemed she believed that Hedwig had thrived in pre-Nazi Vienna, but dealing with hatred required qualities other than a kind heart.

✦

Researching U.S. immigration laws and regulations, I finally discovered the answer to one of my most intractable, but important questions: Why did Alfred and Hedwig apply for an American immigration quota number only in the late summer of 1938, rather than immediately after the Anschluss in March?

In Hebrew Immigrant Aid Society (HIAS) files in New York, I finally found the answer in an advisory bulletin to Jews that explained significant changes in U.S. immigration policies in September 1938. For the first time potential immigrants could apply for a visa before an affidavit for them was received. Regulations were revised partly to better organize immigration procedures, but also in part to help Jews suffering in Reich camps and prisons to win release; a quota number could serve as evidence that the prisoner would soon immigrate.

At summer's end Alfred and Hedwig stood in lines, paid money, and obtained new passports with the required middle names that were not their own. On September 7, 1938, they received quota numbers for immigration to the United States: 45,868 and 45,869.

Those numbers were daunting. The U.S. quota for immigrants from the German Reich was 27,370 per year. By the end of October, the United States Consulate in Vienna estimated they held 70,000 applications, and lines still snaked for blocks.

More discouraging news followed. Leo's aunt in America wrote that her family's application to sponsor Alfred and Hedwig had been rejected for insufficient income. With that, their chances of fleeing to the United States shrank to the hope that Martha and Leo could immigrate soon and find a sponsor for them there.

Perhaps the story that Bernard Toch's daughter Trudy told me about Alfred and Hedwig's attempt to flee illegally came from around this time. She remembers going to Alfred and Hedwig's apartment with her parents as a child of eight. Listening to the adults talk, she became upset. Alfred tried to joke about evading arrest when he and Hedwig had attempted to escape to Belgium. As U.S. consul Wiley had reported, for a brief time Belgium permitted Jews to enter without visas, though German guards tried to prevent those tolerated, illegal entries. Trudy recalled Alfred's nervous laughter as he described Reich border guards stopping them, and his talking his way out of arrest; possibly, he'd relied on his poor vision as an excuse. Hedwig admitted to being so frightened that she'd wet her clothes. Even a child understood that a brush with German officials was no laughing matter. I was heartened to learn that despite the danger, that summer Alfred and Hedwig had tried every possible avenue of escape and their spirits remained strong.

For Germans to impede the exodus that they had created seemed inexplicable to me until I read German historian Hans-Peter Ullman's analysis. Confiscated Jewish wealth paid for roughly one-third of the German war effort; Jews fleeing illegally had not paid all their taxes.

Although Jews continued to flood out of the Reich, in October 1938 Hitler grew impatient. Facing Poland's deadline for expatriate citizens to return legally, he ordered the expulsion of all Polish Jews from the Reich. Despite Martha and Leo's progress toward immigration and their efforts to evade arrest, they were not safe, caught between the need to hide and the necessity of filling out emigration forms. For them, the danger was not peril at sea or British warships—as for Gretl—but the equally deadly bureaucracy. For months they stood in lines, wrote their address, and signed their names on endless German forms, each contact making them more visible and vulnerable. They had been identified as stateless, and at the end of October they were arrested.

★

Celia's parents told her countless stories about their lives in Vienna but said only a few sentences about their deportation. She didn't know when they were deported, how, or what they experienced. They did tell her they were taken first to the notorious Rossauer prison.

An imposing, fortress-like compound with soaring towers and turret-style battlements, the dank, aging structure on the Danube Canal had been built after the 1848 Revolutions as a deterrent to internal unrest. It could hold four thousand prisoners or troops. Under German rule, Rossauer became a police prison and detention center where Jews and other "enemies" were terrorized and beaten before being deported to concentration camps. Martha and Leo may have been imprisoned there during the weeks that Germany seized—with considerable violence— nearly seventeen thousand Jews suspected of illegally entering Germany and Austria from Poland.

This roundup was a shocking event for many Reich citizens. For the first time forces grabbed entire families in broad daylight, giving them moments to pack or no time at all and allowing them to bring only ten Reichsmarks. In this frenzied operation, authorities had cast a wide net. Nearly forty percent of those taken had been born in Germany or Austria; some of their families had lived there for generations but never received citizenship. Many were well known to their neighbors.

The SS herded the Jews like doomed cattle through the streets to holding areas and prisons, or pushed them into trucks, then loaded them onto freight trains. Scenes of terror erupted, mothers holding children or hiding them, families separated, the aged and ill beaten as Jews were taken en masse. Deportees recall riding toward rail stations in police trucks, hearing bystanders shout *"Juden raus! Aus nach Palaestina!"*— "Jews leave! Go to Palestine!"

Some horrified Reich citizens protested and tried to hide Jews but were themselves intimidated, brutalized, or arrested. SS guards easily quelled the unorganized, vastly outnumbered opposition.

Alfred and Hedwig must have been panic stricken. After their months of striving to protect their children, Martha and Leo were gone in a moment. The battle must have seemed lost. They were probably among the frantic relatives who gathered outside the prison's bolted iron doors to bring warm clothes and food for their loved ones and beg for their release.

★

On the fifth night of our trip, Herta passed away. The family grieved, supporting each other and helping Amnon arrange to fly Herta's body home.

Amnon had spent his time in Vienna caring for his mother, but before he left he pressed his case with the Austrian government to grant him an Austrian passport, a second citizenship. Many Jews value such a resource, remembering times when there has been nowhere for Jews to run. Austria refused his petition on the grounds that Amnon had "chosen" to become a citizen of another country.

CHAPTER 19

Kristallnacht

October–November 1938

On a cold October morning, guards forced Martha and Leo from their cells and onto a waiting train crowded with hundreds of other imprisoned Polish immigrants. Racing west and then north, these trains from Vienna were joined by a phalanx of other trains sweeping across the Reich, carrying an estimated seventeen thousand Jews with Polish heritage back to Poland in advance of the October 30 deadline for return.

Just as the Austrian chancellor Schuschnigg's plebiscite had triggered the Anschluss, Polish leaders' legal maneuvers had triggered Hitler's fury and made Poland even more vulnerable. Responding with brute force, the Nazi dictator ordered the long-planned mass deportation of Polish Jews living in the Reich. The roundup began with no warning, and the Polish immigrants, many of whom had lived in Germany and Austria for generations, were permitted to leave with only one hastily packed suitcase.

German trains began reaching the Polish border around October 29—about nine thousand Jews at the border town of Zbaszyn, six thousand at Bytom, and the rest at Chojnice and Gdynia. At some crossing points German guards pushed refugees from the trains, beat, and herded them with guns and dogs past unprepared Polish border guards. The largest number of deportees, at Zbaszyn, were driven on foot, dragging their suitcases two miles into a no man's land between borders, and left stranded in filthy conditions without food, shelter, or permission to enter Poland.

The Jews suffered appalling conditions. A contest of national wills trapped them for weeks in the deepening cold in makeshift camps. Jews traded their possessions to local farmers for food. Jewish and Polish aid groups mobilized to provide meals and clothing, but many of the Jews fell ill, some died.

Nine or ten days into the standoff, seventeen-year-old Herschel Grynszpan, a distraught, stateless Polish refugee who had been born in Germany but was living in France, and whose family was among the deportees, strode into the German embassy in Paris and shot a German diplomat.

The assassination offered Reich leaders the incident they had been hoping for, the excuse to unleash a pogrom, immense in scale, throughout the Reich. The Nazis' Vienna newspaper *Völkisher Beobachter* had already published the locations of the city's synagogues in preparation for their destruction. On November 9, when the diplomat died, Propaganda Minister Joseph Goebbels was ready to act. He ordered Gestapo chief Heinrich Müller to dispatch storm troopers, Nazi officials, Hitler Youth, and other Nazi groups on their long-planned rampage. He instructed firefighters and police to protect aryan structures but otherwise refrain from interfering in the event that would be known as Kristallnacht, Night of the Broken Glass.

Destructive riots targeting Jews erupted across the Reich. For the second time that year, citizens of all ages poured into Vienna's streets, but this time not in celebration. Wielding axes, hurling incendiary bombs, laying dynamite fuses, they smashed and burned Jewish stores, prayer houses, synagogues, and homes; vandalized the Jewish cemetery; raced through apartment buildings destroying Jews' belongings, pulling families to the streets, herding them into nearby public places to surround, taunt, and batter them, then take over their apartments. Jewish men were beaten, women abused. It was a free-for-all fueled by the lethal union of racism and greed.

On Wednesday, November 9, temperatures held in the low forties; the evening's heavy cloud cover turned to fog and a cold drizzling rain. Fallen leaves still crunched underfoot on sidewalks. Alfred and Hedwig may have been asleep that deeply dark night, grief-stricken by the calamity that had befallen Martha and Leo, when shouting and explosions rose from the street, brilliant flashes reflecting through their corner windows. If they had opened a window to look down the street, heavy billowing smoke and ash would have assaulted them. A half block from their building, their synagogue had erupted in flames.

The last service held in the synagogue had been a month before the Anschluss, a lively Purim celebration full of laughter and singing, commemorating the rescue of the Jews from a fifth century BCE Persian plot to kill them. After the Anschluss, no one went to the synagogue for fear of harassment. A caretaker, a *shamash,* lived on the property, but no one else dared enter. What happened to the caretaker during the violence?

If Alfred and Hedwig rushed to the street for fear that their own building would catch fire, they would have encountered a rowdy crowd that included neighbors cheering the falling synagogue timbers as leaping flames climbed higher. They'd have seen police mixing with the crowd, watching the spectacle. The synagogue's rabbi committed suicide that night.

Caught unaware by fast-moving events, Reich security police chief Reinhard Heydrich acted with dispatch. He sent urgent instructions to storm troopers and state police headquarters and stations that rioters should wear civilian clothes to maintain the façade of a civilian uprising. He urged severe treatment of Jews, ordering local police to arrest as many as possible, especially successful businessmen who could be held for ransom and young men who might pose a threat. He directed the deportation of as many Jews as Dachau, Buchenwald, Sachsenhausen, the new Austrian camp Mauthausen, and other concentration camps would hold. Orders included rare permission to search foreigners' apartments for Jews in hiding.

An Israeli survivor of Kristallnacht who spoke with Judith said that her father was arrested that November night. At that time family members could rescue imprisoned relatives by bartering with Nazi officials and providing evidence of pending emigration. The woman traded her home for her father's freedom.

Gretl's shipmate Marta told me that her twenty-four-year-old brother was arrested during Kristallnacht. Immediately after the arrest, her mother located the young lawyer William Perl and secured a promise that he would reserve space for her son on the next Zionist transport. The resourceful mother then managed to find and approach Eichmann in his office. She knelt before him, begging for her son's release from Dachau. The amused Eichmann agreed. Perl hid the badly beaten young man in his cellar until Betar members carried him to the departing transport. A few years later, he joined the British forces' Jewish unit, one of the first to enter and occupy Vienna.

During Kristallnacht the Bergers' Jewish friend Bernard Toch left his aryan wife and children at home and escaped trouble by hiding in a railroad station, an unlikely, clever haven. Toch's less fortunate brother-in-law, living on Czerningasse Street, was deported.

Lisl, too, had trouble that night. Thugs broke into her Kärntner-strasse design shop and stole her expensive professional sewing machine. She actually went to SS headquarters to demand its return and spoke to a Nazi who was sympathetic and told her he would try to help her. He located the stolen machine and returned it to her—in stark contrast to the cruel acts of so many Viennese in those pervasively merciless times.

After two days of riots, on November 11, Reich leaders called a halt to the chaos. Gauleiter Josef Bürckel, Vienna's district governor, ordered the secretary for public security to secure the city. Goebbels demanded immediate damage reports.

★

It's likely that the evening of November 11 was the night when Martha and Leo returned home after making a miraculous escape from their deportation to Poland. They told Celia only that their train had stopped at some border, where guards would not accept the deportees' jumble of passports and documentation. Celia didn't know how her parents managed to break free; Martha and Leo told her that when the locked train doors were opened, they and others ran and later found a train back to Vienna. As they approached Vienna, the sight of smoke shrouding the city and dozens of fires burning shocked them. What could it mean?

The family's reunion must have been joyous—flowing with tears of relief, disbelief, and new levels of terror. The world had gone mad. Where was the Vienna of symphony and dance, science and philosophy, and friendly police? Perhaps the Bergers recalled the 1934 street battles between impoverished socialists and the government, the decades of groups chafing for unity with Germany, and many groups, including Communists, Nazis, and others, imprisoned for their discontent. There had been warning signs of deep dissatisfaction, angry divisions, and a nation searching for its identity.

As harrowing as Martha and Leo's deportation was, it probably saved them from far worse. Across Germany and Austria during Kristallnacht, Nazis destroyed, looted, ransacked, or burned more than a thousand synagogues—all but one of the twenty-four in Vienna—along with seventy prayer and study houses, and four thousand Jewish shops. Nearly two thousand Jewish apartments in Vienna's First District alone were aryanized. Nazis arrested sixty-five hundred Viennese Jews and deported nearly half to camps. At least twenty-seven Jews were murdered and another eighty-eight seriously injured. Six hundred eighty Viennese Jews committed suicide.

✦

The Berger family, Sidney, and I and set out one stormy afternoon to find the site of the Schmalzhofgasse synagogue and its memorial plaque. Our umbrellas blowing in the wind, we passed the memorial once, retraced our steps, and discovered it tucked in a corner under the overhang of a 1950s apartment building.

The plaque consisted of two polished granite rectangles, about eighteen inches high, affixed to the wall. The synagogue's silhouette was etched on one above these words in German: "Here stood the temple designed by architect Max Fleischer, erected in 1884, destroyed by National Socialists during the Reich Kristallnacht on November 10, 1938." On the adjoining granite rectangle, a Jewish star floated above the same message in Hebrew.

The Jewish community and Mariahilf District Cultural Forum had jointly placed the simple memorial. As we huddled around the plaque, its existence and the efforts of the two groups moved us, but the memorial had been easier to miss than to find. The Bergers seemed satisfied, but for both Sidney and me the words and sequestered plaques balanced on a line between giving witness to an atrocity and avoiding offense to anyone—a double reminder of the synagogue's brief existence and the German Reich's destructive power. If a people is defined by its shared memory, these plaques made a dubious statement for Vienna and for the Jews.

★

Responses to Kristallnacht in the Reich and around the world were swift—but more complicated than the event itself. After the pogrom, Reich officials doubled down on their repression, issuing a firestorm of Draconian antisemitic laws and ordinances, at least two hundred fifty decrees. They barred Jews from even more areas of the city and from appearing in public on certain days. They confiscated telephones and wireless sets—radios—further isolating Jews, putting them out of touch with their friends, the city, and the world, denying them news, weather reports, the joys of music. The cruelty was unremitting. New laws excluded Jews from attending even Jewish schools and from most sections of trains. Repressive laws kept coming, squeezing Jews, punishing them for existing.

The deportation of Polish Jews had garnered some world sympathy, but Kristallnacht, which was splashed across front pages in the United

States and Europe for days, overshadowed it. The wanton government-directed riots and violence shocked the world. The *New York Times* described Kristallnacht and the antisemitic laws that followed in its wake as the "Nazis' final phase in their war on Jews"—as it seemed to be at the time. More accurately, that first indiscriminate roundup of German-Polish Jews and Kristallnacht's attack on Jews marked the early stages of a genocide that the world could not yet imagine.

One U.S. labor leader described the German government as a "mad bloodthirsty wolf"—a reference to Hitler's nickname "Wolf." He pledged the backing of twenty million union members and their families for a strong American response. Another union leader proposed "a moral ring" around Germany. President Roosevelt recalled America's ambassador to Germany. Behind the scenes FDR began work on the first budget proposal in a decade to prioritize military over domestic spending, a major and enduring shift in U.S. government priorities.

Britain responded guardedly, increasing the quota of Jewish refugees fleeing from the Reich to Palestine for three years, but then shutting down that immigration completely. This weak gesture solved nothing. Instead the prospective closure motivated Zionist groups to lead more clandestine transports and the British to then redouble their blockade. But immediately after Kristallnacht, British citizens worked with their government to initiate Kindertransports, rescue missions for Jewish children in the Reich that would bring nearly ten thousand children to Great Britain. A few other countries, including the Netherlands and Belgium, cracked open their doors for a short time.

The United States, Britain, France, the Netherlands, and other nations began discussions about the mass relocation of Jews. U.S. secretary of the interior Harold Ickes declared his outrage and urged the U.S. government to consider large-scale Jewish settlement in Alaska's undeveloped spaces. The preposterous suggestion reeked of insincerity, like the Polish and Nazi proposals to resettle Jews in Madagascar. In committee, the U.S. Congress killed a bill to establish a program like Britain's Kindertransport. Still collecting World War I reparations from Austria and Germany, the United States constrained its criticism and kept pressure on Germany to meet Austria's "financial obligations."

Hitler responded angrily to the international criticism, lambasting the foreign press and President Roosevelt as tools of the Jews. Mocking the world's refusal to accept the deluge of Jewish refugees, Hitler escalated his rhetoric and launched the next phase of his war on the Jews. He boasted to the press that Reich Jews would be starved and "liquidated with fire and sword." Goebbels urged Nazis to "hammer [Jews] while the iron is hot."

Hitler's extreme rhetoric provided cover for his efforts to patch cracks emerging in domestic support for the Nazi program. The rampage had unnerved many citizens; most had never expected or witnessed such brutality. The actions against Jews had been so ferocious and lawless that even members of the Gestapo expressed disgust at "the unleashing of the lowest instincts."

But with no second thoughts about Kristallnacht on their part, Reich leaders stifled those signs of dissent and churned out a steady flow of propaganda. They insisted that the Jews themselves were to blame. And they launched accusations against another of the Reich's favorite scapegoats, the *lügenpresse*, lying foreign press, for slandering Germany. Resurrecting Europe's long history of antisemitism, they pointed out that Britain, too, had once expelled its Jews.

Intending to keep Jewish property in government hands, Vienna's Gauleiter Bürckel lied shamelessly about bringing rioters to justice, threatening "to put looters against the wall." In reality, he arrested citizens who spoke against Reich policies.

Assembling the *1941 Vienna Address Book* chronicle of Austrian Nazi history, the Nazis omitted Kristallnacht. Why? It had signaled a major intensification of racial warfare. Was there a lingering sense of shame? Were they concerned about mixed feelings that could fuel resistance?

Nazi leaders were concerned about the economic fallout. Reports detailing enormous destruction of property and businesses poured into

Reich offices. Reich business leaders criticized the vicious pogrom as *financially* counterproductive and warned that German insurance companies could be bankrupted and confidence in the country's economy shattered.

But Reich leaders had never intended Kristallnacht to be simply a terrifying destructive riot. One day after the violence subsided, the government decreed that Jews must transfer their retail businesses to aryans within several months. The Reich imposed a punitive levy of one billion Reichsmarks, RM "to cover Kristallnacht damage." That Jewish Atonement Tax assessed Jews with assets of more than 5,000 RM, 20 percent of their wealth, payable in four installments. That breathtaking windfall for the Nazi government, estimated to reach about 27 million RM, was equivalent to some $400 million at a time when U.S. annual wages averaged $1,730, equal to over $7 billion today.

Reich officials promised to turn over that bounty to insurance companies to keep them solvent, but instead kept the bonanza and ordered Jews also to pay for repairs to their own destroyed property. That scheme failed when the business community convinced the government that no one could raise that much cash. More decrees followed, forcing Jews to transfer their stock, retail businesses, and real estate to aryans at prices set by a Reich office. On November 24, the *New York Times* reported, "The joker in this provision appears to be that changes in property values after November 12 will be disregarded [for tax purposes].... Jews now forced to sell their enterprises and real estate for a song must still pay [tax] on the original value—if they have enough left with which to pay."

The collusion of businesses and ordinary citizens in this enormous theft is a horror story in itself. It seems that when enough citizens enjoy a piece of the spoils, persecution can become widely acceptable.

Alfred and Hedwig's assets fell below the levy's threshold, but Hermann was forced to pay. The day after the violence subsided, anticipating onerous new decrees, he rushed to the Österreich Creditanstalt Bank and filed a Change of Asset form reporting that he had sold most of his securities. He withdrew 1,515 RM so that his remaining assets, mostly lottery winnings, totaled 129,060 RM. Since the first required report on April 27, his stocks had plummeted from 151,000 RM to 14,000 RM, and his bank balance was down from 912 RM to 108 RM. Because Germany canceled Jews' pensions, Hermann's income had dropped from 59,000 RM to zero. He valued his jewelry at the same level as before, 1,800 RM. At sixty-five years old and retired, Hermann's lifetime of hard work and contributions to labor relations and the textile industry were practically worthless.

After Kristallnacht, the Reich required Jews to keep their money in *sperrkonten*, frozen accounts, permitting only approved withdrawals to cover immigration expenses and minimal necessities. In less than a year, an astonishingly short time, Nazis had grabbed control of the wealth and lives of the once-thriving Jewish community.

★

As the Bergers lived with the intensifying persecution in Vienna, international bluster about helping Jews fizzled. A week after Kristallnacht, U.S. secretary of labor Frances Perkins emerged from an urgent White House conference on the Jews' plight to announce, "The problem is so serious that a cautious approach is necessary to be certain we are doing the right thing and the American people will cooperate." Employing deft political doublespeak, she admitted that United States leaders had taken no action to revise quota restrictions because "there has been no crystallization of sentiment among the American people." To translate into plainer language, Secretary Perkins was saying that Americans did not care enough to help the Jews.

That day *The New York Times* reported President Roosevelt's comments: "In the face of rigid quota...filled for months to come, there apparently is little hope that this country at present could do other than help finance a movement in London proposed by Joseph P. Kennedy." What Kennedy, U.S. ambassador to Great Britain and an outspoken antisemite, had proposed involved resettling all German Jews in Northern Rhodesia or Tanganyika, British colonies in Africa.

The *Times* reported that the quota for German and Austrian immigrants was filled for fourteen months, and the State Department would not assign more numbers for at least seven months.

The article spelled out yet another hurdle. "Fines imposed on Jews and confiscation of their property combine to make it difficult for them to obtain visas. Before a US consul can grant a visa, they must show that they will not become public charges." Refugees seeking to immigrate encountered increasingly rigid barriers; they needed both a strong affidavit of support and a low quota number. Even those requirements offered only the opportunity to apply, not a guarantee of a visa. Eight months after Germany's invasion, the window for Vienna's Jews to apply for a U.S. visa had effectively closed.

On November 22, with stories about Germany's persecution of Jews still blazed across the front page of the *Times*, a brief news item on page fourteen reported, "Negro Youth Lynched by Mississippi Mob." The ongoing racial violence in the United States drew scant national attention, but Hitler was keenly aware of it—scornfully referring to America's racism to rebuke his critics and defend the Reich's cruelty to Jews.

During those turbulent November days Hermann and Mitzi's daughter Lisl was poised to leave for New York. Lisl's uncles in New York had provided her an affidavit, and she waited anxiously, hoping that the riots would not derail her departure. As she worked to close her damaged design shop and pack all her belongings one step at a time, she acquired the Reich stamps on her documents. Her parents and Mathilde gave her their jewelry to take safely out of the country.

Alfred, Hedwig, Martha, and Leo came to Hermann's apartment to bid her a sad goodbye. She was the seventh cousin to depart, leaving Martha the last Berger cousin remaining in Vienna.

Lisl left Vienna on November 19, a week after Kristallnacht, traveling by train to the German port of Hamburg, then by ship, traveling through Le Havre, France, to London, and on to New York. She sailed on the *SS Washington*, the largest steamer yet built in the United States, dining on iced beluga caviar and paupiette of sole, relaxing to the strains of an orchestra playing European and American music, and visiting with fellow passengers, many of whom she had known in Vienna.

I wondered what she felt. Relief? Guilt? A biting fear for those still in Vienna? The contrast between the destroyed life she had left behind and her luxurious trip must have been jarring, her voyage a surreal interlude as she journeyed toward an uncertain future.

The nine Bergers who were still in Vienna—Alfred, Hedwig, Martha, Leo, Hermann, Mitzi, Arnold, Mitzi Two, and Mathilde—both rejoiced and mourned the departure of their family who were gone. They met and talked often, together facing the charred and broken remains of their world.

CHAPTER 20
Exit

November 1938–April 1939

A fter Kristallnacht, the Bergers' lives continued to unravel. With smoke still clinging to domes and spires across the Reich, Nazi leaders followed up the pogroms with an avalanche of laws stripping Jews of their wealth and freedoms. During the next four tempestuous months, Hermann and Mitzi wrote forty careful letters to Lisl in the United States, painting a picture of the family's fight to survive in Vienna and to escape. In stories half-told through hints and innuendoes designed to slip past censors, information about the family's plans and safety is woven through the letters, which were an attempt to hold the family together even as they scattered around the world. News of friends leaving Austria appears in almost every letter—a sad testimony to the emerging Jewish diaspora.

In his first letter, on November 26, Hermann refers obliquely to an astonishing trip he made to Germany. At that time the Reich still allowed Jews limited travel, with official permission, for immigration purposes. Hermann and Mitzi took advantage of the chaotic changing laws to travel into the jaws of the beast—to Berlin. They went because they were worried about Mitzi's threatened family there. Perhaps they took cash to relatives worse off than themselves. Reeling from waves of confiscation, they also went to confirm the shipping of their belongings to America.

As thousands of Jews fled the Reich—around seventy-nine thousand of Austria's nearly two hundred thousand Jews had departed by early 1939—Germany's shipping industry flourished. Much of the freight moved through Berlin, and as Jews lost legal standing and were unable to bring lawsuits, their property increasingly just disappeared. Hermann needed to make secure, personal arrangements. He wrote Lisl several letters—about viewing a cousin's wrecked apartment, about joyful reunions with other relatives, about shipping, and about his uneventful journey home. Back in Vienna, he was again immersed in plans. "I saw to Aunt Mathilde.... When you receive this, all will be settled. I wish you a good trip and good start in your new home. Good bye, Good bye." Mitzi's first letter tried to ease Lisl's pain at the separation. "Now you are already far away.... We hope you will be happy and forget all the bad things."

In fact Lisl was not as far away as Mitzi envisioned. Flaring international conflict caused frequent worldwide shipping delays, including for Lisl. German U-boats prowled the North Atlantic, a Communist-fomented general strike in France disrupted European commerce, and Britain and France sparred with Italy over North Africa. Slovakia fought Czechoslovakia for independence and fierce fighting between Japan and China embroiled Britain and threatened American shipping. The wary peace of winter 1938 and 1939 was neither certain nor safe, and Lisl's ship waited in a British port for days watching for clear passage.

Again, a few days later, Mitzi was still seeking to soothe Lisl's distress: "My Dear Child.... Here everything is in order. We were worried about nothing because nothing happened [in Berlin]. All went according to plan without disturbance. Hans [Mitzi's New York brother] wrote that he will provide us an affidavit. We appreciate this more than I can say."

Mathilde wrote plaintively, "I miss you so much, but don't worry. I will be brave. I visit Uncle Alfred often. Uncle Arnold and Mitzi visit in the evening.... Aunt Tilde."

Lisl must have opened letters from family with trepidation clouding her eagerness. Hermann wrote in early December, conveying his own sense of urgency while advising Lisl to remain calm: "I am preparing everything. I am sure that new laws are coming, and you never know what surprises can happen. Don't worry, and don't be impatient." He included news that surprised me—Alfred and Arnold had applied for an illegal voyage to Palestine. The Berger grandchildren weren't aware that Alfred and Hedwig had attempted to flee to Palestine like Arnold and Mitzi. Alfred's age at that time, sixty-one, and his near blindness, would have kept him off the list of thousands of Central European Jews competing for that limited transit space. Despite their poor chances, the Bergers were exploring every possible opening for escape.

Later in December, Leo added a note to a letter from Hermann to Lisl, saying that his aunt and cousin in New York were trying to send him money to help him to travel, but they didn't know how to get it to him. He asked Lisl to assure them that they could send it in care of their trusted friend Renée Galimir, in transit in Paris. Leo explained that he and Martha were trying to reach Palestine and that Gretl was helping in their effort. Lisl had been in Vienna during Martha and Leo's deportation and would have understood the urgency in his closing words: "Delay is not an option."

Family news and love flowed across the distance. Hermann wrote, "Uncle Arnold telephoned that he had news from Willi. . . Ernst is in the hospital with malaria.... You know, Lisl, you must try to forget all the past. You will have a new life."

Try to forget. Don't worry. Take care of yourself. Hermann could not follow his own advice. His letters lurch between efforts at a disciplined calm and high anxiety. "Talk to your friend about his mother. He should make plans to get her over as soon as possible."

In mid-December, ten days after Leo wrote Lisl about his and Martha's effort to reach Palestine, Hermann had written, "Leo and Martha have made up their minds and want to get to New York. They hope to leave in January. You should talk to his aunt."

Their Palestine plans had fallen through. Reuniting the family in Palestine had been an optimistic, short-lived dream, but like the Betar Palestine organizers, Martha and Leo were devising plans on top of plans, seeking one that would work to save not only themselves, but also Alfred and Hedwig. They carried train schedules in their pockets, ready to flee with a moment's notice.

Mitzi wrote the innocuous-sounding news that a friend was then living on Rembrandtstrasse, across the canal, in a large, high-rise apartment complex. Goering had just issued orders that evicted Jews must be concentrated in approved buildings. Mitzi was subtly informing Lisl that some of her friends had been forced back across the Danube Canal to Matzohville. By December 1938, nine months after the Anschluss, Nazis had seized forty-four thousand Jewish apartments in Vienna.

"December 15. My Dear Lisl, Yesterday I received Uncle Hans' letter in which he names the QUEEN MARY as bearer of important documents, a true Christmas message, which could not have been more happily transmitted by President Roosevelt himself." Hermann's affidavit had been approved! The news must have been both wonderful and bitter, visions of reaching safety contrasting with the reality of family and friends still struggling. More upbeat than in previous letters, Hermann pressed forward with another of his careful plans: "You can pick up your newspaper at Paramount Novelty Company, Broadway, New York." I suspected that Hermann had withdrawn cash from his accounts shortly after the Anschluss, and that his problem was how to take it out of the country. He had probably devised a subterfuge, directing his lawyer—perhaps an aryan—to send Lisl a weekly newspaper with currency stashed between the pages through a New York colleague. He couldn't send large amounts that way, but as the family, destitute, prepared to start their lives in the United States, anything would help.

Several days after Hermann and Mitzi learned about their affidavit, the U.S. consul in Vienna notified them that it had received documents for Magda and Hermann Guth. The names on the affidavit had been mistyped; it gave Mitzi's maiden name Guth as the couple's last name, instead of Berger. The mistake was a technicality, but correcting it would cost precious time, during which other documents might expire. They feared the simple clerical error could spell disaster.

Hermann's next letter did not mention his worries. Instead, he told Lisl that he had been reading old family letters and come across a poem he thought she would find "interesting," composed by a young nephew in January 1919, as the empire negotiated its World War I surrender and Hermann lay recovering from war wounds. Hermann's letters, piled in boxes in Peter's Vienna Room, were a wellspring of European Jewish history. The poem expressed an Austrian Jewish boy's distress at the empire's defeat and reflected the family's patriotism, typical of Austrian Jews. It offered a sharp rebuttal to the Nazi accusation that Jews' lack of patriotism had led to Germany and Austria's World War I defeat. Hermann's ironic observation delivered the perfect commentary: "Beautiful, isn't it. But now we are not in the world of poetry."

As the disastrous year 1938 came to an end, he updated Lisl: "All the Palestine people are fine .... Leo and Martha were here yesterday. Leo has taken care of the most important things and will leave in mid-January.... Willi is still in Zurich.... We live very quietly now. This year we will not celebrate. Winter is here. The snow made everything look beautiful before it dissolved into dirt and schmutz [mud]."

★

In the New Year, 1939, Hermann began to look ahead with some enthusiasm, sounding almost as if he is about to start a vacation trip: "Please write. Should I bring a vacuum cleaner and carpet brush?... "Also, should I bring a radio?...Mutti worries about the furniture, especially the three couches.... I ordered a dark brown lounge suit. Should I also order a nice light grey suit for the hot summer days, English flannel for the hot days in New York? I have my lovely linen suit. I don't know if it will still be in fashion in America so please write about what people wear, the fashion for an older gentleman.... I think we would like our Biederman chairs. I'm very sorry to sell the beautiful desk. I insured thirteen crates."

Thus the year began for Hermann and Mitzi, the terrifying juxtaposed with the mundane.

Pondering the vulnerability of his family, he wrote more pragmatically, "January 1. Dearest Lisl, Happy New Year. We don't know yet how we will travel, when we have to go to the consulate, then I can try to figure out when we will finish...when we can book our ship. An open ticket is not possible. We are in good spirits, as long as we can get out without more damage." Eight days later he wrote, "My Dear Lisl, Mother is learning English, but she is frustrated.... Ernst is with the Palestinian police. It might take another three months before he can get his parents over."

Ernst's service in the Austrian Army had enabled him to join the British police force in Palestine; his work with the Zionist underground had given Arnold and Mitzi priority for the illegal voyages. Gretl had no such lifesaving influence to help her parents win coveted space on the crowded ships to Palestine.

On January 11 Hermann wrote, "Aunt Mathilde is very worried about her future. Me too. She is really not well and doesn't have much hope."

Mitzi, near sixty years old, also wrote her daughter nervously about the future: "Dear Lisl.... It would be good to know how we will make a living. I'm talking here with a bakery about how I could work as a *zuckerbäcker* [confectioner]."

In mid-January, Hermann wrote that Martha had called to say that Leo would leave "soon," and that she would join him later. "I didn't want to believe it. Nothing will come of the thing." Was Leo's abrupt plan to travel to South America? Africa? Many perilous plans probably seemed unreal and crazy to Hermann, who had never been hunted on Vienna's streets or deported. Whatever the plan was, Mitzi wrote the next day that Leo's paperwork was not ready; he had had to cancel his ticket, a blow made worse because Hapag, the German shipping line, kept his deposit.

With every failed escape that Leo attempted, his situation grew more critical. If he was arrested and sent to a camp, with no plan to immigrate to show, no one could save him. Hermann wrote on January 26, "My Dear Lisl.... Martha and Leo now have different plans.... Martha called right now. They also tried to get to Shanghai but there are absolutely no tickets available. Leo will write his aunt to ask if she can get two tickets to America at $440 per person. It is very important that they get help very soon." And four days later: "Martha and Leo, no success. Illegal actions with Palestine not possible any more." On February 8: "Dear Lisl.... Leo and Martha received a telegram but the English Consul did not see them. Leo will try to get a visa to St. Domingo.... perhaps they will go via Newfoundland. Whether immigrants can work in Newfoundland is the question."

As Martha and Leo battled for survival, Hermann reported that "nothing is new with Alfred." Again, his language is coded. He meant that Alfred and Hedwig hadn't found a way out. They too were working feverishly, spreading their finances thin, trying to find passage anywhere for Martha, Leo, and themselves, while coping with the changing situation in Vienna.

"Martha says their apartment is a big mess because two ladies will move in on January 15." When Alfred and Hedwig had believed Leo would depart, they had rented their tiny second bedroom to two evicted Jewish women. Would Martha sleep on the couch? When Leo's departure fell through, what happened to the two women? Hermann doesn't mention them again.

On January 12, 1939, Mitzi wrote, "Dear Lisl. Big news. We received a letter from the Consul that we have to be there on February 20. Vati [Father]...Yesterday the furniture was assessed. Your Mutti [Mother]." Events whirled forward again. Their chances for safety revolved around that long-awaited appointment.

Hermann and Mitzi's letter to their daughter radiates new energy. "January 16. I hope everything will be all right. We have to think very carefully." Then on January 21: "My Dear Lislkind.... the new tax law

[*Reichsfluchtsteuer*] has started. The expeditor with the transport cannot do anything.... Let us hope it can be ready.... You cannot force these things."

Their anticipation is tempered with worry. Family news is disjointed, and mostly bad. Richard had written Hermann from Budapest that he had been offered a job as director of a new Beirut knitwear plant. He would go soon to either Beirut or Istanbul—very different choices. For unknown reasons, Richard didn't go to either, but remained in Central Europe, his worst option. Hermann reported that he rarely heard from Olga, Trudi, Loli, and Ani."

In numerous letters, Hermann worried about his sister Mathilde, who hadn't found a way out. He wrote that his nephew Ernst had reported that the possibility for his parents Arnold and "Mitzi Two" to come to Palestine was "nil" and that Gretl wasn't well but was looking for work. I wondered if Gretl was racked with fear for her family and guilt over leaving them all behind. "Hugo [Hedwig's and Olga's brother in Prague] should have a permit to immigrate to Australia very soon and will try to bring them there.... Willi has arrived in Brazil.... Uncle Arnold had many pictures from Ernstl [Ernst's affectionate nickname] in a police uniform with a cap and gun. Ernst now has a room with permission to use the bathroom and thinks he is king of Jerusalem."

Several more letters reached Lisl at the end of the January with news of damage to the shipped crates. As Jews, her parents couldn't make a claim for reimbursement.

On February 3, Hermann wrote a nostalgic message: "Yesterday with Mr. U, we went to the Philharmonic for Furtwangler conducting the 2nd and 3rd of Beethoven's Coriolan Overture. It was a sentimental, beautiful farewell from such a sweet place that gave us so many things."

I was taken aback by the risk Hermann and Mitzi had taken. Forbidden from attending all public events, they had gone with a friend to a concert and "passed" as aryans. I recalled a much younger Hermann's letter to Mathilde, warning his sister about dangerously antisemitic Vienna. For the next three decades, his family had enjoyed the best of the golden city—and now, in a situation of much greater danger, he was ignoring his own advice.

In February, Hermann discussed possible ports of departure for himself and Mitzi—Le Havre, Cherbourg, Rotterdam, Genoa—and details of the challenging immigration process. "February 17 I cannot book our cabin on the ship before I have the visa. We can only get the visa after we have permission from the doctor. Then it will take another four weeks.... I have questions. Where will we live? What kind of work could we do?" Four days later, he wrote, "You cannot imagine the work.... Mr. Herbeck, wants our library furniture. We will start selling March 1." Events were so complex and moving so fast that he wrote a second, four-page letter the same day. To avoid more "surprises," he said, they would have to depart as soon as possible.

Then, on March 2, 1939, Hermann wrote, "We have made progress. Tomorrow morning I will take our papers to Prinz Eugen-strasse [Eichmann's Jewish Emigration Office].... We think we could leave the beginning of April. The *Queen Mary* leaves the first of April from Cherbourg, April 5 the *Washington* from Hamburg, April 12 the *Isle de France* from Le Havre.... We count the days."

Just as Leo and Martha monitored train timetables, Hermann and Mitzi tracked changing ship schedules—lifelines for escape and for mail: an ill-timed letter could mean a fateful missed deadline.

"March 5. Finally, something positive. If everything goes well, we will be swimming a month from today. Mutti."

Herman's letter from the next day contained an uncharacteristic flash of impatience and irritation: "The rest of the family seems to believe that we don't want to come as soon as possible. That is not the case. When I received the letter from the Consul, I went there immediately. It can take four to five weeks.... I am pretty sure that there should not be any new regulations before July 31, and they will honor the old quota numbers." America's quirky, changing immigration procedures had instilled terror; any small error could derail nearly a year of his efforts. Hermann added a note so hurriedly that he left it unsigned. "I can tell you happy news. Today the taxes are almost all taken care of. I hope to pay the exit tax tomorrow."

★

Among the glaring omissions in all Berger family letters was any local or world news. The *Vienna Address Book*, in contrast, described some monumentally important history of that time—with more hubris than accuracy:

> March 14- Czechoslovakia puts its destiny in the hands of the Reich.
> March 16- Creation of the Protectorate Bohemia-Moravia.

Czechoslovakia had not "put" itself in German hands. Germany had invaded the unoccupied area of Czechoslovakia and declared it a "protectorate." Hedwig's three Czech brothers had secured jobs in New York, South Africa, and Australia, but a heartbreaking few days before they finalized their exits, German forces drove into Czechoslovakia, took control of the country, and closed its borders. Slovakia and Poland received small eastern portions of Czechoslovakia in return for not objecting to the dismemberment of their neighbor, and they collaborated in making transit impossible. The world watched and did nothing. Hedwig's brothers were trapped.

The *Address Book* continued its March 1939 "history" by reporting the Führer's celebratory visit to Vienna on the anniversary of the Anschluss. For Jews under German rule the need to escape was becoming ever more urgent, but Hermann and Mitzi's letters that month were about weather, gossip, and packing. They held their breath, wrote about neutral topics, and hoped that nothing would impede their departure. "March 21. After so many difficulties, I hope everything will work out…." Two days later: "It is not necessary to write long letters anymore. We are supposed to get our passports in two to three days. Then comes the medical examination. We do not have the visa. We have to have it by April 2, otherwise we cannot leave. The ship is completely booked. What will happen if I cannot book our cabin by March 28?"

The tension was enormous. Would they pass their physical exams? Would their papers be approved? Or would everything fall apart at the last minute, as it had for Leo? On March 29, Mitzi wrote Lisl that Hedwig and Olga's Czech brothers were "all right in Brunn. Mutti." Herman wrote, "My Dear Lislkind, We received your telegram today. I have the feeling that you have forgotten a lot.... The transport crates could not leave before us. You can only get permission to leave the country when you have a passport. Now we have to wait. Vati."

For months family members had toiled on Martha and Leo's behalf from New York, Vienna, and Palestine, but the young couple still hadn't found anywhere they could go. As Hermann counted the days before his and Mitzi's departure, he despaired of their chances. "Concerning Leo and Martha, I wrote you about his Polish quota. We are all worried. His aunt will do what she can, but she must wait until she can send them the affidavit."

The sheer number of countries Martha, Leo, Alfred, and Hedwig were exploring was staggering. Hermann wrote, "... and the matter with Sweden—possibly.... We heard it is easiest to go to San Domingo, Haiti. They would take 100,000 Jews, if they can afford to pay. Everything is costing more and has to be paid in the U.S.... Other possibilities. Newfoundland, Uruguay, Brazil, Paraguay, Argentina. You have to inquire at all those different consuls but only in NY.... It looks as if the two will never be able to leave."

The following week he added, "... the professor will come back from his journey tomorrow. He is trying to get Leo a visa for Cuba. I sent you a telegram that this is his only possibility, via Cuba. If nothing has happened by the time I arrive in NY, I will go with you and try to take care of it." The mysterious professor seems to have been a "fixer," someone who could make the impossible happen. Hermann appears to have helped Leo obtain a Cuban visa.

"Alfred and Hedwig want to go to Paris," Mitzi wrote in one brief sentence in March. What did that mean? I had found no other reference anywhere to this idea. It seems to have been one more of their frustrated efforts to escape.

Thinking over his brothers' and sister's situations as he prepared to leave, Hermann wrote that Mathilde would soon move into Alfred and Hedwig's spare room but that Alfred and Hedwig, too, would have to move in May. Leaving precious family in precarious situations, he eased his agony at their plight by reminding himself that Mathilde still had helpful family in Vienna.

Alfred seems to have appealed his May eviction—most likely on the grounds of his poor vision. The building owner and neighbors may have supported his efforts. However he managed it in the complicated, confused world of Vienna 1939, Alfred did not have to move that May.

On March 30, Hermann wrote: "Yesterday we received the number of our cabin on the Queen Mary. The cabins are very fancy. Main Deck #M4." Finally, five days later, he allowed himself to express his pent-up anticipation. "We can only get the visa on Wednesday. We will fly on Thursday the 13th. I hope everything works. We are not patient anymore.... Vati."

Mitzi added, "The people are here to pack. Happy *Weidersehen* [reunion]."

On April 6, 1939, the U.S. Consulate in Vienna stamped Hermann and Mitzi's passports. His quota number was 14,239; hers was not listed. A few hours later he registered for the last time at his local police station, stating that he and Mitzi would depart that day for New York.

❋

Ani and Loli told me that Hermann was a "snob person," and that the cousins felt some distance from their uncle. When Celia first read his translated letters, his superficiality made her angry. She thought he sounded "foppish." The lounge suits and manicure sets, carpet brush, and elegant desk...while her parents, grandparents, Arnold, Mitzi Two, and Mathilde fought for survival. At first, that contrast was too much for her.

"My G–d,"she wrote me, using the respectful Jewish way of spelling God. "What contrasting preoccupations came into play! That hurts. The money and contacts put him so far above the misery of most. His concerns seemed in large measure to deal with what finery to pack.... the proper GALOSHES! He expressed concern for his sister, but little else."

As Celia read Hermann's letters more deeply, she began to understand the pressures he had faced. He didn't know how to support his family in New York. He hoped that his lottery winnings, unavailable to him, would help his family in their fight to survive in Vienna and to flee. Discussions of suits and galoshes were interspersed with mentions of ongoing support for Richard and concern for dozens of friends and family leaving or trying to leave. He hid vital information next to the trivia—sandwiching news about Leo between questions about furniture in just the same way as he was slipping cash to Lisl between pages of a newspaper. He had risked traveling to Berlin in part to help Mitzi's family. While he had started out in a better situation than most Vienna Jews, he had also been dogged and stalwart. When Celia learned of Hermann's attempts to assist his family and friends, both in Vienna and from New York, she remained guarded in her feelings, but her opinion softened.

Hermann's records documented his hurried November 12, post-Kristallnacht sale of stocks, converting them to cash, and laid out his expenses from September through November. He had given monthly stipends of 200 RM to Alfred, Arnold, and Mathilde; perhaps the Kristallnacht laws ended that outflow from his account. He had also given to friends in need: 3,000 RM to Paula Hammerschlag for her emigration expenses; 1,000 RM to Lazar Weisz for his Jewish asset tax; and 3,600 RM to Max Lassner, making possible both his release from Buchenwald and his emigration. Hermann noted discretely in a letter to Lisl that his friend Lassner "has returned, reduced to about one-third."

I read Peter's lawyer's summary of Hermann's situation: "Your grandfather wrote in the property statement of April 27, 1938, that he had securities worth 150,973.33 RM on deposit in [a Vienna bank]....
According to his statement of November 12, 1938, your grandfather had sold most of the securities and put the money in several accounts. Within the next year, he had to spend most of the money on special taxes for Jews and expenses concerning his and his family's emigration."

Hermann's own Kristallnacht "Atonement Tax" amounted to 25,800 RM, equivalent to about $10,340 in U.S. dollars at a time when the average US income was $1,731. Hermann paid yet more taxes in January, and in early February 1939, the Reich Finance Ministry assessed a Reich Flight Tax, a new exit tax, equaling 25 percent of taxable property, which stalled Hermann's departure. He had hoped his last remaining asset, his lottery prize, would be available to family left in Vienna. However, the Reich bank, the Oesterreichische Creditanstalt-Wiener Bankverein, later Bank Austria, maintained ferocious control of that bonanza until, decades after Germany unconditionally surrendered after total defeat in World War II, Peter's group claim finally forced it to relinquish what remained of Hermann's assets.

Hermann paid smaller taxes in February and then again in March. That month he also gave Arnold 2,000 RM, perhaps to pay for Arnold's proposed illegal trip to Palestine. Having read the evidence of Germany's thefts in Hermann's financial records, I wasn't totally surprised to later read German historian Hans-Peter Ullmann's estimate that confiscated Jewish wealth paid for about one-third of Germany's World War II effort. The Reich permitted Hermann to take ten RM out of the country.

★

After Hermann reached New York, Reich Asset offices in Vienna and Berlin continued to hound him. They found his address and sent him notices of taxes due, implying repercussions for relatives still trapped in

Vienna. Hermann ignored those demands; he was finished paying Nazi extortion.

In New York, teeming streets and rising skyscrapers seemed to proclaim a promising future for Hermann's family, but he was no longer wealthy or influential. At age sixty-six, he had become one more impoverished, heavily accented immigrant. He continued trying to help his trapped family, but watched in anguish as his three brothers, his sister, and their families struggled to flee the darkening world of Europe 1939.

CHAPTER 21

"Dear Madam"

May–August 1939

A s Nazi tentacles tightened around Austrians' daily lives, 1939 was
a time of loss and despair for Alfred and Hedwig, still trapped in
Vienna. Jews were fleeing Austria in epic numbers. Nearly seventy-nine
thousand of the country's two hundred thousand Jews had emigrated
within nine months of the Anschluss. By April 1939, seven of the eight
young Berger cousins had scattered to three continents, Hedwig's three
brothers were trapped in Germany's Czech "Protectorate," and Richard
was moving through Central Europe, unsure which way to turn. Alfred
and Hedwig, Martha and Leo, Arnold and Mitzi, and Mathilde
remained in Vienna, urgently seeking a way out.

Four months of Hermann's letters to Lisl in the United States after
Kristallnacht reveal the family in disarray, fighting to preserve their
close ties, to survive under the Nazis, and to flee. Richard's work in
Turkey had saved his family. Hermann's wealth in Vienna and Mitzi's
flourishing New York relatives had offered his family a lifeline, but
possibilities for the others were limited. Hermann wrote that Mathilde
was sad, "crazy nervous," pinning her hopes on Paraguay, and that

Arnold and Mitzi Two were relying on Ernst to help them reach Palestine. He described Alfred and Hedwig's strategizing with Martha and Leo, exploring places as disparate as Palestine, Canada, Central America, China, Paris, and the United States, pounding on doors, hoping that one would open.

★

The international reaction to the tightening noose threatening Reich Jews never became the "moral ring" around Germany that U.S. leaders had called for after Kristallnacht. Instead, the United States made immigration more difficult, and then went further, obstructing fleeing Jews: American business interests complained to the government about competition from Jewish refugees in Shanghai. And as the Bergers frantically searched worldwide for sanctuary in early 1939, U.S. secretary of state Cordell Hull responded to business demands to obstruct Jewish immigration, instructing American ambassadors to discuss with Germany and Britain the "desirability" of preventing Reich Jews from reaching Shanghai on German or British vessels. That collusion caused passenger liners to be booked for many months in advance but didn't completely cut off the immigration. Needing capital for its military aggression, Japan ignored Western machinations and required refugees to settle in its section of Shanghai, for high fees.

An advisory from HIAS (the New York–based Hebrew Immigrant Aid Society) described the obstacles the Bergers were facing in March 1939. It warned that admission requirements around the world had grown ever more stringent and complicated. Britain was overwhelmed, Belgium and Holland were saturated, steamers departing Europe in all directions were booked for months, German nationals applying that March for entry to the United States would have to wait four years for their number to be called.

How did Alfred and Hedwig, Martha and Leo manage their lives, trapped in Vienna's deadly environment? Ani had described them all as having many friends, but Jews were leaving in droves. Nearly half of their friends were gone. Cafes and groceries turned them away. They couldn't travel. Newspapers regularly mocked and threatened Jews. Neither Alfred nor Leo could work; they had no income. In the United States Leo would be considered Polish, but in Austria he was "stateless," hunted, sleeping in parks. He and Martha had an affidavit, but their quota numbers wouldn't be called for many months.

The family had been shaken to its core. Where, I wondered, were their aryan friends? Were non-Jewish Viennese so satisfied with their plunder that no crime was too great? Were they terrified of repercussions to themselves for befriending Jews? Despite the intense persecution, I saw the Bergers as resourceful, determined, and loyal to each other. When I had begun researching Alfred's letter, one force driving me was my desire to understand how the Holocaust had happened to the Bergers, how they had been caught in its grip. Given their situation, I couldn't think of anything I would have done differently to escape—and that thought was frightening.

In Celia's mementos, I had seen evidence of Leo's dogged resolve during that time. In February 1939, as his hope for departing with Martha dimmed and his life in Vienna grew more precarious, Leo renewed his membership in the well-known Makkabi Jewish sports club, founded when German clubs excluded Jews. Celia kept that membership card, which Leo had carried across Europe despite its dangerous, prominent Jewish star. She had also shown me the scorched prayer book that Leo had rescued from a smoldering pile of burned books. At a time when Jews were threatened and arrested at every turn, Leo inscribed an undaunted message in that book to Martha: "Pray well and luck be with you. Times are difficult for us now, but always be proud that you are a Jew. February 26, 1939."

HIAS offered one possibility for desperate Jews in the spring of 1939. The organization had secured a limited number of temporary visas for Cuba, available through steamship operators or travel agencies for $300 plus a $500 cash bond. Despite the large fee, companies sold those visas with "no assurances" because, in fact, they were illegal, obtained through bribes. Even so, the byword for Vienna's Jews that spring was "Cuba."

Needing a safe place to wait for his U.S. visa, Leo had investigated the Dominican Republic to the south, and Iceland and Newfoundland to the north. Finally, through Hermann's mysterious "professor," he obtained passage to Cuba.

✶

In New York, Leo's aunt Anna and cousin Jack had submitted an affidavit of support for Alfred and Hedwig, but by spring, prospects for that avenue of escape seemed poor. As the family plotted and planned together, hope for their safety centered on Leo and Martha's reaching the United States and there seeking a sponsor for her parents.

By the end of March, Leo's plans for Cuba seemed firm. Martha, Leo, Alfred, and Hedwig marshaled their savings to ship eleven hundred pounds of their belongings—two trunks and three crates—to Jack's home on Long Island. The packing list ran long: rugs, oil paintings, silverware, watches, jewelry, two sewing machines, down comforters, table linens, cooking scale, pans, lace curtains, books, Leo's stamp collection, photos, and a violin. Hermann may have helped with this expense before he departed. But the shipment surely depleted Alfred and Hedwig's finances and their household, making life even more uncomfortable. Still, it was an investment in a new life. Those goods would ease Martha and Leo's jarring relocation, and carry the family's hopes, dreams, and sense of home to America.

✶

Shaping a master race into a master nation demanded invasive control, and German intimidation of all citizens intensified that spring.

Private life, free thought—any deviation from Nazi norms—vanished. Street-corner book burnings incinerated a wide range of free thought. The Reich restricted its citizens' work, finances, food, marriage partners, child-rearing, culture—the totality of German life. An endless array of events working to reshape Viennese culture are chronicled in the *Vienna Address Book*: Nazi parades and speeches, Nazi history exhibitions, mandatory trainings for Nazi women, events for Hitler Youth, and "window darkening" practices (covering windows during citywide blackouts) and "protection from air raids" (air raid drills), preparing the Viennese for war.

From white-stockinged Hitler Youth to brown-shirted storm troopers, the party continually coerced citizens into supporting even minor Nazi causes. Party members knocked on neighbors' doors or barged into beer halls every few weeks, announcing meetings or rattling red donation cans for fund drives like "One Pot Meals." In that project, families were told to cook inexpensive meals, such as soup, and give the saved grocery money to the party. Those who didn't participate were named in newspapers or beaten. Door by door, event by event, Nazis recorded party loyalty and punished dissent.

In a crushing blow to Austria's last vestige of freedom that spring, Hitler dismissed Vienna's highest Justice Court, declaring that all Reich law would be subject to the Führer's review. The Fuehrer had placed himself above the law; his totalitarian dictatorship was firmly in place. Chilled, I wondered when the German people had lost the will to fight for their freedom.

The Viennese were not yet finished with their love affair with Germany. The *Vienna Address Book* documents a full-throated propaganda blitz, lockstep with the Reich's tightening control: blaring military parades, antisemitic art exhibits, Hitler's inspection of military recruits, and his swearing-in ceremony of thousands of political and civic leaders. Viennese lined up for hours to catch a glimpse of their Führer, while the Bergers stood in other long lines—to buy groceries, obtain documents, and pay taxes.

★

On May 6, 1939, an overcast Saturday, the day after Leo's thirty-fifth birthday, he gathered his suitcase, tucked his ship's ticket, Cuban visa, and identity papers into a large canvas wallet, and joined the exodus. Trusting to luck that his travel through the Reich would not trigger arrest, he left Martha, Alfred, and Hedwig in a heart-rending separation.

A week later Martha wrote Leo the first of many letters the young couple would exchange and preserve during their odyssey to America. She addressed her letter to the Hotel de la Paix, the Hotel of Peace, in Paris, Leo's first stop before proceeding to St. Nazaire, France's northwest port.

> Dearest Leole,
>
> Your dear card just arrived. I'm happy everything is going so well.... I wish so much I could know more.... Before anything, dear Putzi, pick up two important letters at the Hotel du Commerce and the main Post Office. One is crucial. [documents? proof of the affidavit?] Jack wrote here very kindly. Yesterday I was at P——'s. You said that would be the easiest. It was not. Now, I am standing here with a washed throat. [She had cried.] In the end, everything was all right. You predicted that. Hopefully, the easiest is yet to come. I wrote to Sabine [Leo's sister in Poland].
>
> With a heavy heart...many thousand kisses, your Mädi
> [your girl]

Martha's carefully composed, heavy-hearted letter also provided Leo with important information about mail from his American cousin Jack; one letter contained promised money. Like all emigrants from Germany at that time, Leo was setting out for his world travel with ten Reichsmarks, the amount then permitted Reich emigrants, hardly enough to last a week.

I couldn't decode Martha's oblique reference to a difficult experience: "Yesterday I was at P—'s." Eventually Celia told me that her mother had revealed on her deathbed that she had had an abortion before leaving Vienna. The United States would not admit pregnant women.

That revelation had been traumatic for Celia, who grew up shadowed by her lost family and her longing for siblings. The abortion was surely a terrible blow for Martha and Leo. It must have been a secretive procedure in heavily Catholic Vienna. Had they turned to a shady backstreet practitioner? How well did Martha recover? Hedwig and Alfred must have suffered, too, if they knew about the loss of their first grandchild and Martha and Leo's heartache. To me, the heartless, rigid immigration regulations meant another life lost to the Holocaust.

Martha wrote Leo again the next day, more emotionally collected, c/o the ship, *Flandre*, third class, St. Nazaire.

> My Dear One
>
> Today we received your dear letter and postcard. I am very happy with your news.... Today, we finally received mail from Gretl. The poor thing is, again, without money and has to travel to Tel Aviv every week where she needs money for the hotel, the doctor, and medication. For my dear Putzi [Leo, for his birthday], she sent a pretty, satiny handkerchief. I'll send it to you with the documents. Tomorrow I'll inquire where I can write to you on the ship and when it will dock....
>
> My Putzi writes that he is yearning.... In my thoughts, I am always with you. Everyone sends you greetings.
>
> Thousand kisses and everything good, Your Martha

Martha's letter reached Leo as he and 103 other passengers set sail for Havana. Then, weeks passed with no news. To us today, it seems that that must have been a nearly unbearable silence for the young lovers, and for Alfred and Hedwig, who thought of Leo as their son. But perhaps in those dangerous, chaotic times, it was easier not to know.

★

The first record I had found of Leo's journey aboard the *Flandre* was his "Transit Identification" card issued May 28 by Republica de Cuba, Departamento de Inmigración, and stamped—not "Jew" in large red print as on Reich documents—but Transeunt, Transient, someone passing through. The overcrowded aging steamer had sailed uneventfully for twelve days across the Atlantic, but in Havana's harbor Leo's luck ran out. Cuba summarily refused landing permits for the *Flandre* and two other refugee ships. The three liners, filled with fleeing refugees, had no choice but to remain at anchor and wait for the resolution of a dispute not of their making and beyond their control.

The *Flandre*'s passengers hadn't known that a few days before their departure, another, larger steamer, the *St. Louis*, loaded with 938 mostly Jewish passengers, had sailed from Hamburg, Germany, for Havana. The Hamburg-America shipping line Hapag had urged the *St. Louis* to make haste because two other refugee ships, the French *Flandre* and British *Orduna*, were following closely. Their concern was not business competition, but politics, and they had good reason to worry. Just before the three ships sailed from their home ports, Cuba's President Federico Laredo Bru declared all recently issued landing permits invalid. Most refugees' transit visas had been issued illegally by Cuba's Immigration Department for large bribes. Eager to participate in the windfall, Bru had proposed another layer of extortion. He ordered the Jewish Joint Distribution Committee (JDC), an American aid organization, to pay him an additional $500 per passenger.

Bru's demand was fueled by greed but also by growing anti-immigration, antisemitic sentiment on the island. Goebbels's global Nazi propaganda, including claims that Jewish refugees were Communists, had brought anti-refugee sentiment in Cuba to the boiling point. Influential Cuban newspaper owners with family in Fascist

Spain and Italy published Goebbels's diatribes and fomented large angry demonstrations. When the JDC could not meet Bru's demands, he supported the protests. I had to wonder about the United States' deep ties to Cuba in those years; had the U.S. State Department played a role in the refused landing?

Five days after the *Flandre* arrived, Cuba ordered the first arrival, the *St. Louis*, to depart without unloading its passengers. It sailed north, stopping at cities along the United States seaboard from Florida to Canada as frenzied international negotiations and humanitarian pleas failed to find any country in North or South America willing to accept the refugees. The *St. Louis* returned its passengers to Europe, where nearly a quarter would die. Its story became the subject of a book and movie, *Voyage of the Damned.*

From the *Flandre*, still waiting in Havana Harbor, Leo sent frantic cables to his cousin Jack in New York. Jack replied:

> My dear Leo,
>
> We received your two letters today. We have been constantly in touch with conditions and have been trying to help in every way we can. So far, we do not know definitely whether you can land or not in Cuba.
>
> We have informed Dr. Sass [the "professor"?], also the French Line, if a bond of $500 will be required for deposit with the Cuban Government, we shall pay it.
>
> You may feel sure that we shall do everything possible for you.
>
> Jack Weinrib
>
> We have been in touch with your uncle Hermann Berger.

On June 8, Cuban Immigration issued Leo a second Transient card extending his stay, a hopeful sign. The small steamship had languished eleven days in the harbor. Celia showed me photos that other passengers took of Leo aboard the *Flandre*. One captures him sketching a fellow passenger. In another, which probably dates from early in the journey, he stands

Leo's sketch of Madame Goretsky, a fellow passenger aboard the *Flandre*. As Celia notes, Leo's sketches of women were starting to look like Martha, he missed her so much. *Courtesy of Celia Cizes*

with a ship's officer and twenty other passengers from about age five to sixty, relaxed and smiling. In later pictures, laundry hangs limply from railings and clotheslines on deck behind bedraggled travelers. Sketches Leo made aboard ship testify to a sense of community and camaraderie among those despairing refugees.

Negotiations failed again. Ordered to leave Cuba, the *Flandre* crossed directly back to France. Leo disembarked in St. Nazaire, where he had boarded thirty-seven days before. The French newspaper *Ce soir*'s front-page story of the ship's saga includes a photo of the ship docking in France, with Leo leaning heavily on the ship's rail, looking down.

The following day, French authorities conveyed the *Flandre*'s passengers to Nantes, a northern French port forty miles up the Loire River from France's Atlantic Coast. There the refugees were lodged in boarding houses, supported by HIAS. Again, Leo waited while another government, this time French, debated his fate.

✶

Either Jack or Leo cabled Martha with the shocking news of his return, but I had no letters that described their emotions. Leo had lost precious time, and once again Hapag kept his money. Cuba had been his last possible refuge while waiting for his visa. He had escaped from Germany, but now he had no place to run.

ENFIN UN HAVRE DE PAIX... *Ce soir*

Photograph of the front page of *Ce soir* newspaper showing Leo on the *Flandre*, which had transported him to Cuba but then back to France. *Courtesy of Celia Cizes*

As he sailed back to France, on June 25, Martha wrote him c/o Nantes, Poste Restante [general delivery], with surprising news.

> Dearest Burli,
> I haven't heard from you in so long. Write soon. Let me know how are you! Today I received the letter for my examination on August 8.... Stay well.
> Greetings and Kisses from your M

A harrowing eighteen months had passed since Martha and Leo had applied for their visas, just a few weeks after the German invasion, and at last she could report wonderful news. The American Consul in Vienna had notified her that her quota number was called and her all-important visa interview would take place in one month. Her tone was extraordinarily constrained, as if nothing eventful had occurred; she may have worried about censors, or else she was concerned that something could go wrong, again. In fact, this was thrilling news, though the consul's factual, impersonal letter committed to nothing.

> Mr/Mrs/Miss Martha CIZES,
>
> We received your application for an immigration visa for the U.S., and we are informing you that the general consul will review your application. You have an appointment on August 8, 1939 at 9 in the morning and must bring your personal identification and everything with you. We also want to bring to your attention that if you do not appear on the above date and time it will take much longer to have another appointment.
>
> People who do not belong to the German immigration quota, people who were not born in Germany, have to wait for their visa until the quota number of their country of birth comes up. Making reservations for the train, plane or ship before you receive your visa is at your own risk. You must bring all your documentation.
>
> Yours Sincerely,
> A. O. Hammond, Jr.
> United States Vice Consul

It seems that Martha didn't write Leo again for three weeks. Perhaps she was simply too exhausted to write. She had been working hard. She had obtained a copy of their marriage certificate from the Jewish Community Office, under the watchful eyes of the Gestapo stationed there. Martha had also secured travel reservations, made yet another down payment for an anticipated departure, and begun to pack. Knowing that a music career in America depended on her diploma, she had repeatedly tried to obtain it from the Vienna Music Conservatory, but they had refused her requests. Again, that calculated cruelty is difficult to comprehend. Where, over the years, had those office workers lost their own humanity?

✦

On July 6, Hermann wrote Leo at "Hotel Restaurant Santeuil" in Nantes. He didn't speak French and misunderstood that "Poste Restante" in Leo's address meant general delivery, not a restaurant. The letter is missing, but the envelope is another testimony to the family's continuing close bonds and efforts to help each other. Two weeks later, Martha wrote Leo,

> Dearest Leole!
> I've had no mail from you since Saturday. Hopefully everything is still going well for you. Yesterday we received news from Uncle Jula and from Uncle Otto [in Prague]. They are grateful that you are attempting to help them.
> What do you do all day? Do you need anything? You'll soon receive something to nibble on.... We were registered with the American Consulate on May 2, 1938, but that number applies just to me since I am on the German quota. I am hoping that you, G-d willing, will also soon be on it.
> There was an attached clause...that Rhineland people registered by May 25 will be called up by February 1940. Even though I hope to be on the preferred quota, it could be sooner.... Rosa left last Thursday. Although we were together every week, she didn't once inform me that she was leaving....
> Love and kisses, Your M

Immigration, theirs and others', occupies the entire letter. Even with the flattened prose, the Bergers' worry is palpable. All the family, including Gretl in Palestine, Ani in Istanbul, and Hermann in New York, were trying to help Hedwig's Czech brothers find a way out. Why wouldn't the Reich let the talented, educated Grünberger brothers out of the country? At this point the racial war seems to have been less about "purifying" German lands, than about abusing Jews. A contagion of hatred was sweeping across the Reich.

July came and went, with Alfred's sixty-second birthday at the beginning of the month and Martha's twenty-eighth at the end. Hedwig celebrated her fiftieth birthday on August 5. That Saturday morning was warm, sixty-six degrees. By afternoon it was eighty-eight and humid. Vienna traditionally empties in August, as residents trade oppressive city heat for cool mountain lakes and resorts, but in August 1939, Alfred and Hedwig were not vacationing in the countryside they loved. The family probably observed Hedwig's birthday quietly at home.

The date on the letter Alfred wrote to the Bergers in California either that day or two days later is blurred, either August 5th or 7th, just before Martha's appointment at the U.S. Consulate.

As loneliness and desperation crept through their lives, Alfred and Hedwig may have walked to one of the travel companies that helped Jews write letters to the United States seeking immigration assistance. Their friend Bernard Toch may have gone with them, explaining how he had written to strangers in America and received an offer to take in his two children.

But I envision that day differently, with Alfred and Hedwig at home alone, closing their windows against the sudden wind that rose midday to twenty miles per hour, causing people on the streets to grab their hats and shield their eyes from blowing dust. I picture them turning from the neighborhood they loved, where they had raised their children and enjoyed long friendships, then placing blackout cardboard, piece by piece, against the glass, as the Viennese had been instructed to practice. For Alfred and Hedwig, that would block the intrusive gaze of the neighbor who sewed Nazi uniforms or the butcher across the street, curious about what Jews still in Vienna might be up to with a typewriter, illegal for them even to own.

Sitting at their dining table, they begin writing a letter to strangers in America. They discussed what to say, what words to use. Should we address it to the wife? What will move them to help us?

Dear Madam,
  You are surely informed about the situation of all Jews...

Part IV

CHAPTER 22
Hope

August 1939

T uesday, August 8, the day on which so much depended, finally
dawned, but Martha's visa appointment held equal parts hope
and terror. A forgotten document, a wrong answer, or a poor medical
exam could bring rejection. For Martha that would mean nowhere
left to run, no way to help her parents. She could make no mistakes
that morning.

She walked the forty minutes through her district, probably past
Richard and Olga's elegant former apartment, then occupied by aryans.
As she neared the American consulate, she may have been buoyed by the
bucolic Swiss Gardens still blooming in southeast Vienna.

Martha carried a sheaf of papers—her appointment letter, visa
application (five copies), birth certificate (two copies), proof of her quota
number (22548-A, May 2, 1938), certificate of good conduct (police
dossier), and the crucial, precious affidavit of support provided by Leo's
relatives in New York.

Her case had been complicated by the contradictory views of her
nationality. In the German Reich she shared Leo's status as a stateless

illegal Polish Jew, but America placed her under the Austrian-German quota.

Making her way across the consulate plaza, past blocks-long lines of Jews who had come before dawn to register, Martha appeared at the general consul's office at the assigned time, 9:00 a.m.

After presenting her papers she proceeded to the medical area. When the examining officer, F. J. Krueger, handed her a carbon copy of his report, she was horrified to discover that he'd stamped it "Class B." Class B conditions included heart disease, senility, pregnancy, and other "chronic conditions that might render an applicant likely to become a public charge." The one-page form was a model of concision. It declared that Martha was a music teacher, of Hebrew race, with a stateless passport but applying under the German quota. It specified that she had "defective vision, right corrected with glasses to 10/200, left corrected to 20/70"—and was stamped with the frightening dangling phrase: "may affect ability to earn a living." Class B conditions could be grounds for immediate rejection or, on arrival in the United States, for sending an immigrant back home.

Perhaps Martha's strong affidavit helped her case, or the official that day felt generous. Whatever the reason, Martha was lucky. The consul approved her visa, Number 1095307.

The long-sought visa did not bring complete relief but instead plunged Martha, Alfred, and Hedwig into a frenzy of emotion and preparation. Many deadlines and conditions were attached to the opportunity to leave the Reich and enter the United States. Martha's visa was good for three months, not a long time to travel thousands of miles across international borders in those fraught times. Proof of tickets to America was not required by the consulate, but a reservation, fully paid or held with twenty percent deposit, was essential in the cold-blooded, catch-22 transportation gamble. Waiting lists were long. Many Jews' visas or tickets expired while they were waiting for a critical document.

Martha needed to act quickly. She had already paid her deposit to sail on the SS *Hansa* on August 25, two weeks after her visa appointment. Owned by the German Hapag company, the passenger liner would begin its voyage in Hamburg, but she would embark in Cherbourg, in northern France. Ironically, two years earlier, on Hitler's orders, the name of the ship had been changed from the original, SS *Albert Ballin*, honoring Hapag's former Jewish director. Despite its new aryan name, its mission at this time was to carry European Jews to safety.

For the Bergers, the week before Martha's departure was something like a vigil or a wake, their time marked by grieving for great losses as they emptied the apartment of her belongings and prepared for her departure. Together Martha and Hedwig sewed, washed, ironed, packed—and imagined Martha's new life in America. With Alfred, Martha made last-minute luggage purchases and queried the shipping agent Schenker and Company about the delay in their April shipment. Alfred promised to monitor their crates' progress. He completed the sale of Leo's leather goods. Hedwig carefully folded the engagement party suit that she had sewn for Martha. She wrapped two small silver spoons in soft clothing and tucked those, too, into Martha's suitcase. Martha went, perhaps with her parents for support, to Eichmann's Central Immigration Office on Prinz Eugenestrasse to arrange for the inspection of her luggage and to pay her exit taxes. The Bergers devised codes for writing about money and formats for keeping track of the dates letters were sent and received. Over the seventeen months since the Anschluss, Alfred and Hedwig had done everything they could to protect their children and see them to safety. Now it was time for their final good-byes.

A steady stream of friends, including the Tochs, neighbors, and Martha's piano students came to wish her safe travel and good luck in her new life. She said farewell to her dear Uncle Arnold and Aunts Mitzi and Mathilde. Agonizing, she embraced her parents, fifty and sixty-two, from whom she had never lived farther than four blocks. What could they say at such a parting? I could only guess. Everyone understood they might never see each other again.

I will find a sponsor for you.

We will come.

Be careful!

Write.

The day after Martha departed, Alfred walked from their apartment, past the charred rubble of their synagogue, around the corner to the Webgasse police station. At the housing registration desk, he filled in the card declaring that "Martha Sara Cizes," piano teacher, stateless, had left her residence the previous day destined for New York, USA. He signed his name on the leaseholder line, Alfred Israel Berger. At that same station thirty years before, Alfred and Hedwig had registered their move into the apartment with high hopes for their life together. It must have been painful for Alfred to sign away his older daughter and place the record of his loss in Nazi hands. Did the officer smile empathetically? Comment? Sneer?

Martha was the last of the eight young Berger cousins to leave Vienna, but thousands of similar heart-rending scenes had taken place across the city since the Anschluss. By fall 1939, approximately two-thirds of Vienna's Jews were gone, leaving some sixty-five thousand still struggling to get out. Jewish families impoverished themselves to help their children escape over mountains, on Kindertransports, legally, illegally, by land and by sea. The young and the healthy, the well-connected and wealthy, the lucky ones left. Then the unlucky, the elderly, poor, handicapped, or sick Jews remaining in Vienna pursued ever more risky and restricted means of escape, or steeled themselves to survive under Nazi domination.

That emotional week marked an ending for Martha but also a beginning, fragile and unknown. She would make the perilous journey to a new life, crossing borders and entering her new homeland with a large red "J" stamped on her passport.

No doubt Alfred and Hedwig accompanied Martha to the rail station. I didn't know how many friends and family they had seen off, but saying goodbye had become a painfully familiar routine. Martha's train hissed and steamed out of the Vienna station on Tuesday, August 15, at 2:30 p.m., bound for Paris. She crossed into France early in the morning, reaching Paris twenty-four hours later. A person traveling today would reach Paris in less than half that time, texting and phoning, checking arrangements, staying in touch. In 1939, a person traveling alone was truly isolated.

Martha crossed Europe during one of the most volatile times of the twentieth century. That summer Hitler renewed his demands for the return of the formerly German city of Danzig, a port on the Baltic Sea, tucked within Polish territory after World War I as an international city. Poland and its allies, the British and French, again negotiated frenetically with Hitler. But this time they stood firm, vowing no more appeasement.

Tensions built. The British sandbagged buildings in London. France debated evacuating Paris and fortified its vaunted Maginot Line defenses. Soldiers and war equipment filled trains roaring across Europe. Threats resounded across borders. During one hair-trigger standoff, Hitler threatened all-out war, telling Danzig's high commissioner, "If the slightest incident happens now, I shall crush the Poles without warning in such a way that no trace of Poland will be found afterwards." Negotiations lurched on.

In Paris Martha found that she had entered a country overflowing with refugees. Spain's civil war had ended several months before her trip. While Jews fleeing Nazis flowed into France from the east, defeated Spanish Republicans poured across France's southern border to escape bloody retribution from Spain's self-declared head of state, General Franco. France wrestled with the upheaval, clamping restrictions and internment orders on all refugees, while buttressing its defenses, alert for signs of German aggression. During that charged summer of 1939, Hitler strengthened Germany's treaties in Central Europe and with Japan and covertly negotiated with the Soviet Union, a supposed ally of the Western nations. In Paris Martha would have heard Hitler's stunning August 24 announcement of a new Berlin-Moscow "non-aggression" pact. The news astonished the world, but the agreement's darker secret provision remained masked: the two totalitarian nations agreed that they could each act with impunity in their own spheres of influence in Poland, essentially dividing that nation between themselves. With one stroke a masterful German maneuver of double-edged deceit stripped the West of an ally and lulled Russia into collaborating with Hitler's imperial dreams.

Martha had begun writing her parents as her train was leaving Vienna. Three days later, on August 19, Alfred and Hedwig wrote to her in Paris. "We received your four cards, and hope you arrived in Paris." They told that they had had visitors all day after she left. Family and friends had congratulated and comforted them, exchanged news, staying connected in their shrunken and traumatized world. With humor much like Celia's, Hedwig reported that their friends, the Rathsprechers, had come for *jause*—the traditional Viennese afternoon coffee and visit. "I had the honor to serve two noshers, people snacking. I overheard them talking to each other. They will come back next Friday and probably every week!!!" Alfred was more restrained. As he had promised, he had reviewed the status of their shipment; it was still stuck in Hamburg. Alfred and Hedwig both urged Martha, "Please write."

Martha checked into the Hotel Victoria on August 18. The next day she found the Hapag shipping line's office and deposited her heaviest luggage for transfer to the *Hansa* in Cherbourg. She met with Marguerite Galimir, a friend from their conservatory days who had become a celebrated cellist and, like Martha, was running from the Nazis. Marguerite, who had been in Paris for several months, offered her hotel address for Martha and Leo's crucial mail.

More than half of Martha and Leo's two years of marriage had been under Nazi terror, and they had not yet escaped its reach. Bracing for war, France severely restricted foreigners' movements. Since Leo could

Martha and Leo in France, August 1939, snatching a few hours together just days before World War II broke out in Europe. *Courtesy of the Berger family*

not travel to Paris, Martha made the three-hour train trip to Nantes for a fleeting visit.

After four months apart, they had less than a day together before Martha needed to make her way to Cherbourg. It must have been equal parts joy, hope, and misery. When Alfred and Hedwig wrote Martha again a week later, sending family news and love, they mentioned Martha's postcard telling of "beautiful hours spent with Leo."

Martha found no respite in Paris after her whirlwind visit with Leo. She immediately collected her mail from Marguerite's hotel, then located the office of the Jewish Joint Distribution Committee (JJDC), an umbrella refugee aid coalition, where she pleaded for help expediting Leo's visa and ticket to the United States. At Hapag offices she nervously inquired about the suddenly unclear departure date of the *Hansa*.

On August 25, Alfred and Hedwig wrote Martha what they believed would be their final letter to her in Europe. They addressed it to Schiff Hansa, Passenger Martha Cizes, Cabin 336, Cherbourg, France. Hedwig wrote that they had received her much-anticipated letter from Paris, and offered words of comfort: "We are sorry that again, you had to endure things that were quite unpleasant, my dearest Martherl. This seems the same everywhere.... The main thing is that you and dear Leo are well. My thoughts are with you always. When I think that you will move from there tomorrow, I am just as scared as if I would be there myself.... I wish you again a good and beautiful journey. Stay healthy, and recover well. Enjoy the meals and everything to your heart's content as calmly as possible. You are heading to fine relatives, thank goodness, which is far more than many people who move into uncertainty. From your mother, loving you faithfully and deeply and with kisses."

What trouble had Martha endured? Her "unpleasant" experiences are never explained. I couldn't guess what she had encountered, but Hedwig offered love and understanding, verbally hugging her distant daughter, who was adrift in a chaotic world. Alfred's letter was short and loving, again including information about difficulties with the family's shipment to the United States, his way of remaining close and trying to help. Included in their letter were continuing worries about Gretl, who had not been well and had not found work. They also rejoiced over rare good news—Gretl had become engaged and even enclosed a picture of her fiancé Moshe. That Gretl had found happiness in her challenging new life brought comfort to all the family. Arnold, Mitzi, Mathilde, and Hugo, who was visiting from Prague, added their good wishes and three photos of Hugo's year-old daughter Eva Ruth.

Martha's and Leo's letters to each other during that time are filled with longing and worry, but also attempts at optimism. The first of four letters that Martha wrote Leo on one day, August 25, at Hotel Santeuil, Nantes, reported that she had had a "good trip" returning to

Paris, slept a little, and eaten "dutifully." "I think about you all the time, my dearest. I always hope to G-d for a miracle. Maybe Dr. S [the "professor" who'd helped Leo escape Vienna?] can do something so that we can see each other."

She reported that Hapag, the shipping line, was "optimistic." She expected to take the train to Cherbourg later that day and board the *Hansa* the next morning, but her confidence seems thin and unconvincing. Her second letter to Leo that day was so poetic it falls naturally into verse:

> My Dearest,
>> I wrote to you first just a few hours ago.
>> It is the only thing I can do.
>> At least I can chat with my love,
>> So I am writing again.
>
>> I am sitting in the lounge car on the way to Cherbourg.
>> The train will depart soon.
>> When I arrive I will surrender my ticket.
>> How happily I would trade it for you...
>
>> Until now dear G-d has helped us.
>> If only He would help once more.
>> Please write me a lot,
>>> and often, and honestly.
>
>> I will write again later.
>> May all go as well as possible for you.
>> Stay healthy. Be hugged and deeply kissed
>> by your loving Martha.

In her third letter to Leo that day, she wrote that she had reached Cherbourg, made an effort to eat, but hadn't yet boarded the *Hansa* and didn't know if her luggage was aboard. It seems that Leo had been concerned about her health and emotional state, perhaps because of the abortion. She tried to reassure him.

Leo wrote his first letter to Martha in France that same day, August 25. It, too, is a moving love letter, filled with longing, intended to be opened on board.

Nantes

My Dearest Darling little Martha

I hope that you are having a good journey. I also hope my darling that you were as courageous as you promised. In my thoughts I see a picture—that our dear relatives are picking you up at the boat.... I went to my room to sleep with my roommate. He snored a lot. I was not able to fall asleep, and I see you.... I pressed your hand and in my thoughts, followed your journey. Unfortunately, it was only a fantasy. I am so sorry I was not able to accompany you to Paris, to help you my darling.... How is the ship's journey? I hope the ocean air has done you some good.

Today I learned that the Committee [JDC] gave a friend in Paris 160 francs for a medical examination and he should have his visa in a few days. He said that the Polish quota was especially undersubscribed and the few who registered in spring as we did should definitively be called in three months...the people from the Flandre are privileged. I hope, G-d willing, I will see you in three months, Putzi! What then? Of course we will take care of the dear parents. Do not give up hope...You must recover because when I come to you, you have to look well...Don't worry about me.

About the talk of war you may hear, we do not have to fear any more so don't worry. And now my dear little one, I have to finish because my eyes are closing.

I kiss you a thousand times, your loving Leo.

I will see you very soon.

Reality would not prove so simple or rosy. As Leo, Martha, Alfred, and Hedwig were studding their letters with "hope," Hitler recalled the *Hansa* and hundreds of other German vessels out at sea, stranding thousands of refugees fleeing the Reich, including Martha.

On the back of an envelope, Martha scrawled a draft of her fourth communication to Leo that day, a telegram: "AGAIN PARIS. AGAIN MUST WAIT."

★

Leo wrote back that day, masking his worry, instinctively reaching for calm and trying to prepare Martha for the long haul ahead.

> Nantes, August 26
> My Dearest,
>   While I was writing to the dear parents, I received your telegram. My love, don't lose your head. Handle everything practically. Do you have an exact terminal where you can wait? If not, take a day off. Then go to the Committee and inquire about a train to Nantes, and request that further stipends be directed here. Take some clothes from the suitcase that you might need.... The main thing is that you come here. Don't rush around a lot. You've had enough stress.

Martha responded that day:

> Paris
> August 26
> My Dear,
>   As you know from my telegram, I am in Paris again. We all were prepared to board the boat that was to take us to the

Hansa when they informed us that the ship had been recalled to Hamburg, as the *Bremen* had been earlier.

I waited there hoping that everything would somehow work out. An American steamer will probably come for the American citizens. Hapag will not help us.... Tomorrow I'll beg once more at [the JJDC]

Your loving Martha.

The next day, Leo wrote again, betraying rising concern. "My Dearest One, I'm writing another time because I didn't write everything I wanted to say." He asked if she had discovered whether her luggage was being held in Hamburg, Cherbourg, or Paris. His *Flandre* companions had told him that the Committee would help trapped refugees with a new ticket. He hadn't received some of the letters she said that she had written, and he had no address for her. He would continue to write to her c/o Marguerite's hotel.

Remind the Committee that I was on the *Flandre*.... Don't push. Do everything in a calm, orderly way. I'm only happy that you did not embark in Hamburg. God forbid, that you had to return to Germany. My darling, don't take this too tragically.... We will be together soon.

Do you think my dearest one that you will be able to leave soon? As much as I want to see you, I would prefer, my dearest, to know that you are safe...My dear Lumperl [Rascal], if you think it is not necessary to come here, spend the days pleasantly. Recover. My thoughts are always with you.

In her brief visit to Nantes, Martha had met Leo's *Flandre* companions, who began to add their greetings to Leo's letters. Their movements restricted, the refugees had grown close, isolated and dependent on each other as they were. They hungrily shared tidbits of information, some lifesaving, some misleading. Relaying talk that he had heard, Leo added a striking forecast: "People here are optimistic that no war is coming." Interned refugees didn't understand that the French and English, on high alert, had also suddenly confined all their ships to port. If Alfred and Hedwig were monitoring sailing schedules from Europe, they would have seen their possibilities disappear, too.

Refugees were not alone in their optimism. As August ended, the *New York Times* and other newspapers suggested that continuing diplomacy over the Danzig crisis had successfully averted war. Naively misinterpreting Hitler's continuing negotiations as a positive sign, the Allies exhaled.

Urgent letters flowed between Martha and Leo, perhaps traveling in the same heavy canvas mailbag on the train, back and forth, east to Paris and west to Nantes, across the 250 miles between them. A fleet of French postal workers strove arduously in those years, and heroically in the coming year, to do what electronics later would make archaic—keeping a nation and the world in touch via words written on paper. Sometimes they delivered mail several times a day, but August 1939 was no ordinary time. Some letters never arrived.

> My Dearest Leo,
>   Today I was not home all day. I received your card in the afternoon and was overjoyed. I didn't answer right away because I didn't know what to say. Even now, I don't know.... I don't know whether I will have to wait for a ship here.... The parents will probably not receive our mail. I don't dare to think about that…

As tensions continue to rise in Europe, mail between France and German lands was halted, cutting off Martha from Alfred and Hedwig. I didn't have any letters that they wrote to Martha then, and surely all of the family suffered from the silence that separated them.

Describing her troubles to Leo, Martha said that she had inquired about her stipend from the Committee. It's difficult to make ends meet here, she told him. Could she live on that amount in Nantes? "Please let me hear from you. Be kissed a thousand times."

The next day Martha wrote that she had gone again to the Committee office before 7:00 a.m. but received no help. "They considered my trip to Nantes part of their support." Uncharacteristically, Martha burst out in anguish, writing that she didn't know how to scrape together money for another train ticket to Nantes. "Is it possible to send me the fare? It is at least fifty francs. I don't know how everything goes so crooked for me.... Please let me hear from you."

Again their letters crossed. Leo sent her a registered letter on August 29, his clearest most urgent yet. "My Dearest! I see that you are very sad and having trouble. I told you from the beginning, if you have no way to leave soon on another ship, come immediately to Nantes. Some arrangement will turn up here." He was working to "attach" her to his group, he told her. "When it is settled, I will cable you to come. Then, you must report to the prefecture. If you don't have more important things to do, come right away."

He advised Martha to apply for a refund from Hapag but not to worry if, again, they had lost their money. "There is nothing one can do about that." He had just received two postcards and the registered letter containing fifty francs that she had sent from Cherbourg when she believed she would sail the next day. "Why did you send it? You probably need it more," he wrote and sent it back, plus a hundred francs and a dollar. The U.S. currency was worth forty francs, he explained. "Come to Nantes. Don't wait for the next stipend to save a few francs. Soon, we will all be happy again. Let me know when I shall expect you. It is best to leave Paris at noon. If possible, do not speak German at the depot, rather English. Be glad, my dear, that you did not depart from Hamburg, otherwise you would be in Germany today."

Then, for the fifth time in this letter, he begged Martha, "Come to Nantes." It's hard to think that the advice woven through this letter relieved her fears. All around them, tensions were rising.

Frustrated at the distance separating them, Leo wrote her a second time that day. "Come to Nantes immediately. *Auf wiedersehen*." Until we meet.

Do not appear to be German, Leo counseled, concerned about growing French animosity toward Germans. A day later, on August 30, Martha replied. "I wrote you just yesterday. It is my only pleasure. I didn't accomplish anything," she began, dropping all pretense of energy or progress. She had borrowed nine hundred francs from her friend Marguerite, who had then left Paris. She had missed a visit from Leo's *Flandre* friend Fantl but would await his call "as if for buttered bread." She had moved to another hotel, and then another, she wrote without explanation. Had she left without paying? Had she found cheaper rooms? The mail could not keep up with her deteriorating situation. She had not received Leo's money, or his increasingly urgent pleas to join him in Nantes.

Martha's second letter that day included a new hotel address where she shared a room with two others. She had missed meeting a potentially helpful person Hermann had told her about, she said, and Hapag had advised her to continue waiting in Paris to "see where I stand." Thwarted at every turn, her money gone, her visa running out of time, she felt trapped and confused. With every step, the ground beneath her feet seemed to shift.

Increasingly frustrated, Leo sent Martha a postcard on the last day of August: "Today I received two postcards from you. I am amazed that you don't confirm the two registered letters with 50 and 100 francs and one dollar. The Galimirs have already left? I addressed my letters to Marg. Galimir.... Are you on your way to Nantes? Can you borrow money? I'm very sorry my dearest, but don't worry. That is the way things are. Most important, my dear, come immediately. A beautiful room has been arranged for us, and you are attached to us for a time. All your tasks can be done from here. Come. I expected you yesterday." Leo, too, was groping for solid, current information. Their delayed letters had cost them precious time and excruciating distress.

His second postcard of August 31 offered Martha the Paris address of a Vienna acquaintance and news that he had received a postcard from her parents in Vienna. "They are all right. Come to Nantes."

Reeling from Leo's failed escape through Cuba and Martha's canceled passage, the young couple found themselves caught in France— several hundred miles apart and set on separate paths. They endeavored tirelessly to communicate, to find and help each other. "Come to Nantes." "Send money." "Please write."

Not a single one of the flurry of thirteen letters they wrote that last week of August 1939 ever reached either of them. Leo's cards to her were twice stamped Parti, Departed, and Retour l'Envoyeur, Return to Sender. Martha had moved again, leaving no forwarding address. Ominous black ink obliterated Leo's return address. Leo, too, had moved again.

CHAPTER 23
War

September 1, 1939

B anner headlines and crackling airwaves flashed the news across
America: Germany had invaded Poland, and World War II had
exploded in Europe. The *Vienna Address Book* chronology would
report that on September 1, 1939: "Führer tells the people that the German army began a fight with Poland," an understatement of staggering
proportions. German forces had invaded Poland with a merciless blitzkrieg attack designed to stun and crush all opposition. The juggernaut
slowed only when it reached the new German-Soviet treaty line in
Central Poland.

Two days later, France and Great Britain declared war on Germany,
and the conflict went global. The globe-circling reach of the British
Empire dragged regions from Canada, Australia, and New Zealand to
India, South Africa, Egypt, and Palestine into the war. France and Germany's colonial empires in Africa, Asia, and the Pacific entangled millions more. Britain and France blockaded German shipping as open
maritime warfare spread worldwide. Germany bombed British naval
bases, causing civilian casualties. German U-boats mined the Thames

River. Germany's somewhat surprised new ally, the Soviet Union, rushed to organize its military and, on September 17, overran eastern Poland.

Martha was still in Paris when the war erupted. Stunned and frightened, she pursued reimbursement from the German shipping line Hapag for her unused ticket, sought her lost luggage, and chased rumors about another ship. Her meager funds had run out. She applied again for emergency support from Jewish refugee aid groups but encountered long lines, forms, and delays. Menacing news pushed Martha to work tirelessly. Leo had counseled patience and a level head, but also caution and urgency. Finding a way out of Europe continued to be a lonely, confusing, and terrifying task. On Saturday, September 9, Martha finally boarded a train to Nantes. But by the time she reached Leo's Nantes hotel, he was no longer there.

★

Immediately after the invasion, France had enacted a law authorizing confinement and forced labor for all foreign males ages seventeen to fifty. During war the twenty thousand German refugees and thousands of other foreigners in France were at best a drain on France's strained resources. At worst, they might form a dangerous "fifth column" of spies and provocateurs.

French soldiers had rounded up Leo's group of refugees and transferred them to a holding camp near the Nantes train station. In the camp, they were sequestered, unable to communicate with the outside world except for an emergency postcard as they awaited transport.

It is possible that Leo's group was still in the camp when Martha's train pulled into the station. On that day, Leo hastily scribbled a postcard postmarked from Nantes Gare, Nantes train station, addressed to Martha at Hotel Santeuil, Nantes: "Dear Martha, We are 19 persons here at the train station and are being taken to Sables d'Olonne. The treatment is not bad, even good. People are friendly....We are not going to the military. Do not worry. Greetings and kisses many times, your Leo."

Scrawled on the card are crucial messages from others in Leo's group to wives or friends in Paris and the United States. "Please inform Feuchtwanger that Dr. Heilpern is with us." "Dear Enis, We are fine." "Friendly." "Not to the military." Leo had taken care to distinguish his current situation from his and Martha's nightmare of the previous November. One year earlier they had escaped their harrowing deportation to Poland by a quirk of poor German planning; their fears of a roundup ran raw and deep.

Before he was moved, Leo had succeeded in arranging for Martha to be "attached" to the Flandre refugee group and to join him at the Nantes hotel. They had anticipated a wonderful reunion and time to make plans together, but she had arrived too late. After three days in the detention camp, Leo's group was transferred to an aging French fort in Les Sables d'Olonne, a small Atlantic coastal town seventy miles south of Nantes.

★

A single line in the five-page *Vienna Address Book* chronology pinpoints September 24 as the "End of Polish Campaign." Historians give other, later dates, but the issue is moot. The attack culminated in a ruthless, astonishingly swift victory. The small unadorned *Address Book* listing minimizes its significance. To Hitler, Poland represented more than a "campaign." He risked world war because Poland held the key to his dream of a German empire. He called Poland his "staging area"—a geographic necessity for expanding into Russia. Poland was also central to his obsessive racist dream of eliminating Jews from Germany. If the world would not take Germany's Jews, Hitler needed somewhere to send them.

With the invasion, Hitler's threat to destroy European Jews in the event of war took on an imminent new reality for the Berger family. The advancing German army targeted Jews, rounding up and burning many alive in local buildings. The SS Einsatzgruppen, newly formed German commando units that followed the front lines, terrorized Jews and forced them into ghettos. Germany imposed a deadline of September 23, the Jewish Yom Kippur holiday, for huge payments extorted from Polish Jewish communities to fill German military coffers. In the invasion of Poland, the Germans killed three times as many Jews as other Polish citizens.

Over the Nazis' six years in power in Germany, the Western Allies—Great Britain, France, and Poland—had essentially ignored Germany's military expansion. Hitler had assiduously tracked their tepid responses to his aggression and gambled again on the world's apathy and, especially, the Allies' abhorrence for war. German armed forces chief of staff Alfred Jodl testified during the Nuremberg Trials about the risk Germany had taken. "That we did not collapse in 1939 was due to the fact that the approximately hundred and ten French and British divisions were held completely inactive against twenty-three German divisions." The invasion caught Poland's allies woefully unprepared—militarily and politically, but more crucially, in national will.

Poland's allies resumed their neglected war preparations like old locomotives laboring to gain momentum. After the invasion, a few resolute French troops had marched into Germany but quickly recognized their deficient strength and pulled back. The French military took positions behind the Maginot Line, France's hundreds of miles of border fortifications—concrete fortresses, obstructions, and weapons installations—while across the border German troops monitored the French from the walls and towers of their Siegfried Line.

With no treaty obligation to Poland, the United States was equally unprepared, and resolutely opposed to fighting in Europe. Jolted into awareness of the flaring crisis, Americans rallied in huge numbers to demand that the United States avoid Europe's endless conflicts. Sympathy for Poland and the Jews paled next to their dread of war. Congress responded quickly with yet another Neutrality Act, though President Roosevelt managed to insert an amendment permitting arms sales to Britain and France. Isolation was still the byword for the American voter.

Thus began the so-called "Phony War," "Twilight War," or Sitz-krieg, (Sitting War, a play on the word Blitzkrieg). Over the next seven months the warring European nations improved their combat readiness and maneuvered like boxers, circling, sparring, and seeking advantage—looking for their moment to strike.

The Phony War gave Martha and Leo a reprieve, but their troubles escalated. Among Celia's papers I found Identity Card Number 44, approved September 9, 1939, by Chief of Security, Nantes Commissaire of Police. Martha's picture is affixed to one corner, her fingerprint smudged across the top. I was startled to see the picture was taken in profile, with Martha's dark, wavy hair pulled back and gathered behind her ear, a style I had not seen in her other photos. Nazis favored this pose for Jews, believing they could identify a Jew by jaw angle and head shape. She had probably brought it with her from Vienna.

The commissariat had stamped Card Number 44 three times, and the security chief stamped it again. I could see Martha waiting nervously as French officials pored over her documents, filling in the lines for the Austrian refugee, residing in Nantes, permitted to stay until October 15, then—stamp, stamp, stamping it. The proliferating insignias on the small card testified to the dead seriousness of Martha's situation. This was war, and she was a German-speaking traveler from an enemy nation.

The French coast Martha was encountering in Nantes no longer resembled the holiday destination she had seen just a few weeks before. British Expeditionary Forces arriving in Cherbourg had replaced vacationing cruise line passengers and families strolling on beaches. British troops disembarked a few blocks from Hotel Santeuil. By early October nearly 160,000 British troops had landed in France. From her hotel windows Martha watched trains unloading war matériel at the docks and streets teeming with soldiers. Troop movements, train schedules, rationing, the mood of the country—everything had changed.

Martha had witnessed Vienna's overnight transformation into a police state and had lived under Nazi brutality. Her parents still trapped by German tyranny, her husband imprisoned, she was caught in a war zone with time running out on her lifesaving American visa. She knew how quickly everything could go from bad to much, much worse. Alone in France, she must have been terrified.

Leo's destination in Les Sables was a drafty sixteenth-century stone fortress including a tower, la Tour d'Arundel, an aging lighthouse guiding ships into the harbor. Its thick walls had few windows. Cold winds whistled through its adjoining courtyards in the fall. Atlantic storms pounded the tower during the dark, wet winters.

During that first month of war, Leo wrote nine letters to Martha but received none from her. On September 12 he wrote from the Center for Foreign Workers in Les Sables. He explained that he could not describe his situation but urged her not to worry: "I am well taken care of here. We are a lot of comrades plus all those of the *Flandre*. We have good food, wine too. The work is not very hard. . . The guards are good to us. The Commission will decide our case soon."

With his seemingly bottomless reserve of hope and determination, he advised Martha to write in French, not German, and asked her to send his thick towel, winter coat, and old sweater. In their rushed departure, the refugees had left most of their belongings behind, and they were suffering in the advancing cold weather.

Four days later, Leo wrote again, still looking for a letter. How was she? Had the American consulate helped her? On September 21 Leo wrote her c/o Poste Restante, Châteaubriant, a small town about a hundred miles from Nantes, where a regional government center managed affairs for interned foreigners. He began with an accounting of letters that he had finally received from her. Then he turned to vital news: his cousin Jack in New York had sent Martha a ticket to the United States. "My dearest, you should not think long. Whenever you can go, just go. It is it is better for me in every respect."

For the first time in any letter, in these lines Leo stuttered, repeating words, his emotions in conflict as he urged Martha to leave. I felt the anguish in this true expression of love. As much as he wished Martha could be nearby, he saw the impending grave danger and wanted her safe. He continued resolutely, "I would be happy if you could be there. You would spare me many worries. I feel that it is hard for you to go without me, but one cannot do much about it."

Jack's ticket, like others that Martha and Leo had purchased, failed in some way. I could imagine scenarios—new regulations, a canceled departure, fighting at sea—but I didn't know what happened. It was never mentioned again.

Why had Martha gone to Châteaubriant? I didn't know that either. She may have needed more documents approved and stamped.

The next day Leo wrote Martha in Nantes, acknowledging her recent cards and expressing relief that she had heard from her parents. The contact was a blessing, but those must have been old letters, sent before war was declared and mail between the hostile nations suspended. Leo sent good wishes for the Day of Atonement holiday. While Jews in Poland suffered severely on that important holiday, in France they could observe it openly, without fear of Nazi horror. If Alfred and Hedwig observed it, fasting and praying, then sharing a meal with others, they would have done so in secret, wary of discovery.

Leo's tone turned dark as he addressed rumors that foreign women travelers, too, might be interned: "...my dearest, even if that situation comes for women, be courageous and think of us. Leave your suitcases and my watch with my acquaintances. Take warm things for yourself. Buy yourself a warm blanket and something to put under you. I will send you back the pad. I don't need it any more. Don't have big worries. We are here in transit. We are not German so our case will be treated differently. It cannot last long. Just persist, my dearest.... Hold out."

His fear is palpable. Leo wrote again the next day, his worries barely hidden beneath supportive words. "My Dear Martha.... I will send you the pad. Unfortunately, my dearest, you must have courage and just hold out." He rushed onward, intense, without punctuation, his usual handwriting stretching out as if reaching for Martha. "If you have to go into a camp buy warm things even take wool socks of mine if you have them don't worry. It is not us alone. Unfortunately this affects thousands of people."

Abruptly, then, the ink color changed. Time had passed, and Leo began again, heartened. "I have just heard you will not be interned, only confined as we were in Nantes.... Just wait, my dear, don't despair. I keep myself steadfast only to be with you. Head high."

Gossip and rumors continued to run through the refugee community, arousing fear, hope, and confusion as shreds of information flowed back and forth along the chain of news, shifting as they went. Again, Leo urged patience, but for the first time also unflagging efforts to leave as soon as possible. Martha had avoided confinement for the moment, but the threat to put women in a camp could resurface without warning.

In early October Leo wrote Martha at the Hotel de la Gerbe de Blé in Châteaubriant. The threat of a women's camp had receded, and his letters were buoyant, brightened by relief. "We all live here in comradeship. The opposite from Nantes. We always help each other.... It looks very funny how men wash laundry and do all other housework. Everybody says, my wife must not know I can do all this."

He reported that "much" was "being done" in his immigration case, and that he was working in the military tailor shop, "a beautiful sunny room with two other comrades." Throughout his imprisonment Leo volunteered for tasks even when he wasn't confident that he could do them. He helped other internees—darning socks, mending clothes, checking for lice, and giving shaves, haircuts, and pedicures. Whatever anyone needed, he did it. In those dire times his skills and willingness to work—and joke with the folks he was helping—improved

Leo's sketch of the private room assigned to him by the military commander because of his useful work for the men. *Courtesy of Celia Cizes* his vulnerable situation, giving him easier assignments in better conditions. Later, those same qualities would save his life.

When Celia and I talked about these letters, she reminded me that her father had learned sewing and tailoring in his family's leather business in Poland. She said that his cheerful outlook and hard work were natural to him, but also intentional; he hoped to make himself useful and indispensable. Celia had shown me his sketches from those days. She and I both felt that they expressed a profound care for his fellow prisoners. According to Celia, Leo often gave his sketches to the people he drew. Except for these drawings, her parents had rarely discussed the prison experience and their separation during the time that they were both attempting to flee. When I told Sidney about these sketches and Martha and Leo's reticence about those times, Sidney observed

Leo's sketch of a campmate at Luchon-Bagnères. *Courtesy of Celia Cizes*

that he had no information about his family's situation before or during that war. I had come to understand that I should not be surprised by these silences. Human nature avoids revisiting trauma, even at the cost of forgetting.

★

Martha and Leo continued to search for passage to the United States. Although the war was stalled on land, it had escalated at sea, and passenger service was difficult to find. British warships patrolled shipping channels, stopped or attacked German merchant ships, mined harbors, and escorted some convoys of commercial Allied ships to safe harbors. German U-boats and destroyers scoured the Atlantic, North Sea, English Channel, and Mediterranean for enemy vessels. On September 17, a U-boat sank the British aircraft carrier HMS *Courageous*, with a loss of more than 500. Three weeks later, Britain lost a battleship with 833 men.

The danger wasn't limited to military and merchant shipping. A day after the invasion of Poland, a U-boat mistakenly sank the SS *Athenia*, a British passenger liner carrying hundreds of American and Canadians fleeing the war. Responding to the outcry that followed, Germany's internal investigation determined the sinking to have been a regrettable accident. Publicly, Hitler blasted Britain for sinking its own ship to inflame public opinion. German warships patrolling the Atlantic also threatened to sink the SS *Washington*, an American passenger ship loaded with refugees—the same ship on which Lisl had sailed. After a tense impasse, the Germans signaled, "Sorry. A mistake."

Throughout October, step by incremental step, World War II in Europe escalated. For Martha and Leo, danger hadn't ended when they escaped Germany's borders, or when they secured immigration documents or tickets to the United States. Until they reached the U.S. the peril was as real as a U-boat torpedo.

Weeks rolled by, and Martha persevered in her quest for a ticket while Leo coped with forced labor and pressed his case for a visa. That fall of 1939, their family was endangered and scattered. They were impoverished, and Leo was imprisoned. They had lost everything except each other—and possibly that too. Their hopes for the future hung on letters to shipping companies and government offices. At times in her letters, Martha, always more prone to worry than Leo, seems simply overcome.

★

Alfred and Hedwig, continued to write to Leo in Nantes and Martha in New York for some weeks after their escapes had fallen apart and they were trapped in France. Imagining Martha's arrival in America, Alfred wrote Leo, "She will be afraid, like us, but it is fortunate for her. Don't be too frightened. Beautiful times will come again, G-d willing. Don't worry about us." Hedwig wrote Martha: "In my thoughts, I go with you every day.... *wiedersehen*, we will meet again soon.... Kisses, kisses, stay well and happy!!!!!"

Martha probably noticed the black stamp, like a postmark, on her parents' August 28 letter, another sign of Germany's move to war footing. Beginning with that mail, all of Alfred and Hedwig's nearly one hundred fifty letters to Martha and Leo would pass under Reich censors' vigilant eyes.

By the time Alfred and Hedwig learned that Martha was trapped in France, mail had been halted between hostile France and Germany. Their letter of August 30 to Martha in Paris was returned, as Martha, too, would have been if she had tried to enter France two weeks after she crossed the border.

Within a week after postal service to France was stopped, undeterred by the disrupted mail, Alfred and Hedwig devised a resourceful new system for communicating with Martha. On September 8, Alfred wrote Erwin Zalan in Zurich:

Dear Sir,

My brother Richard Berger, through his friend in Budapest, made your address known to me, and I dare to ask your goodness. My daughter was supposed to embark on 8/25 in Cherbourg, but we have received a note from her in Paris informing us that her ship didn't leave. Her husband is in Nantes, and she will be with him, if she hasn't yet sailed. I have written there repeatedly but there is no answer. I ask you, dear Sir, kindly to write them in Nantes that we are well. They would like to be able to send us a message in the same way. I ask you not to be angry that I take up your goodness and thank you very much.

With deep respect,
Alfred Berger

The system worked. Zalan turned out to be a willing intermediary and enclosed the Bergers' careful letters inside his own envelopes, mailed from neutral Switzerland. In mid-September Alfred and Hedwig wrote Martha a short test letter through "Uncle Zalan." They expressed concern for Leo's father and sister in Eastern Poland, under Soviet control, and reported that all the family still in Vienna was well. They reassured Martha and Leo that they were in touch with Richard in Budapest and Olga in Turkey; the Prague brothers visited often. "Still waiting for your letter."

Leo and Martha continued to write Hermann and Jack in New York about their deteriorating situation. On October 10, Jack cabled Martha:

Dear Martha,

Today I received advice about your inquiry as to whether it is possible to deposit money for Leo so that he may get his visa at once. This is not so. A deposit of money is only of help if the credit on the affidavit is insufficient. This is not the case with Leo. He must wait until he can get his visa from the

Consul in the regular way. He must make frequent inquiries with the Jewish committee. They may help him.

As for you I can only urge that you try to come as quickly as possible. Otherwise, your visa will expire and you will have more trouble. Try in every way possible. The Jewish Committee is in the best position to help you. You must keep asking them until you get help. If there is no other way…. we will pay for the ticket in New York, however bookings cannot be made here now. The United States lines are safest.

Martha's visa would expire on November 8, just weeks away, but on October 15 she sent Leo an unusual letter, a milestone. In it a new sense of calm and authority have replaced panic and dependence. She wrote from Châteaubriant: "Mon Cheri…. This morning I was awakened from sleep because an express letter arrived from the consulate in Nantes. They advised me to telegraph the United States and Bordeaux about tickets because my visa will not be extended. I was still half asleep so I lay down again and acted as if nothing happened, and really, there was nothing. I don't have enough change to telegraph the United States. I will wait for what will happen. Today I wrote to request to write a loyalty certificate for you."

October had brought other burdens besides war to Martha and Leo. The U.S. State Department had added at least three new visa requirements, tagged with expiration dates that made Leo's immigration even more difficult. Martha wrote "the professor" and HIAS to obtain letters attesting that Leo was not a member of the Communist party or of any other group working against American institutions. Besides a loyalty certificate, Leo also needed new proofs of permission to leave Germany and of means of transportation to the Western Hemisphere. Martha asked, "Are you still eating well? Do you have enough warm things? I am busy all day with letters and applications in German and French for others so that I have hardly any time to study [English]…. My Burli, the important thing is always to keep the peace of our household, though banished from table and bed."

In this letter, Martha took over the role of caretaker for Leo and those around her. She wrote again the next day:

> I am sitting here at home with others over fine potatoes with butter. As an hors d'oeuvre I ate stinking-cheese [a French cheese] which I love. Often I eat in the gasthaus [small restaurant] where for three francs, we had soup, meat, noodles, salad, apples, bread, and oranges. Not expensive, isn't that so?
>
> The sun is shining wonderfully in the window and onto the letter. I send it along to you with this letter.... When they tried to send me back to Nantes, I wrote Mrs. Sexer and today I hear that we can probably stay here. Tell the others.... Life here is cheaper, otherwise I don't care where I am if I cannot be with you. Don't worry for my sake. I am courageous. I get upset over nothing. If the dear Lord helps us and lets there be peace, I am satisfied. Just so our dear ones stay healthy.
>
> It is difficult to concentrate now because the others here are always talking to me and moaning and complaining. That's just the way it is now.

Martha said she had heard nothing from America or from Gretl, and she worried about her sister. Then she joked, "You don't have to write them too. It is very egotistical but I would like for you to write me more often instead."

Perhaps the sense of peace and independence that Martha projected came from her acceptance of their situation; in order to help them both, she must leave Leo behind, imprisoned and in a war zone. Surely torn, she faced that reality with renewed resolve.

Leo wrote on October 13, expressing his "enormous" pleasure at reading her letter and one from Alfred and Hedwig. He was shocked that "They have no idea where we are. Did you write them?" Confined in a military prison, he didn't know about the war's impact on mail across

Europe. Alfred and Hedwig, in a different kind of prison, also found themselves disconnected from their family and the world.

In the same way that Martha had once urged Leo to speak honestly, he asked her not to spare him difficult information. "You are concealing something my dearest. I heard that the Committee gives you only ten francs per day and that's all you have to manage on.... How are you? Please write me everything truthfully, otherwise I have no peace." He was correct that she lived on a pittance of financial assistance, but it seems that she had been resourceful and learned to manage at a subsistence level.

In that letter, Leo enclosed a photo of himself with his six roommates. "I am close with them all especially because I cut their hair, shave them, repair things. They stuff me with chocolates, delicatessen, and cigarettes.... We all hope to be with our women in freedom soon."

★

Tensions, threats, and accusations resounded across Europe like tremors before an earthquake, as Martha and Leo fought to stay ahead of disaster. On the morning of October 21, just two weeks before Martha needed to present her visa in the U.S., Jack and Aunt Anna cabled Martha with solid news of a ticket: "I am happy to write that we have bought a ticket for you to come to New York on the first available steamer via the United States Lines. The ticket has been cabled, and we all hope that you will be able to sail soon.... We hope we can make similar arrangements for Leo. Good Luck. Jack Weinrib Anna Weinrib."

Jack's second attempt to send Martha a ticket succeeded. She and Leo surely received that news with delight, gratitude, and broken hearts. They had no other options. Leo was in prison, his visa application mired in bureaucratic red tape, with open warfare imminent; her visa was about to expire. She had barely enough time to reach Bordeaux, papers in hand, claim her ticket, and depart on October 25.

On October 22, Martha obtained a *laissez passer* from the director general of national security, Châteaubriant Office of Police Commissioner, allowing her to travel that day to Nantes. Celia also saved Martha's receipt for a high-speed train ticket that day to Nantes with two suitcases weighing 143 pounds. There she presented herself at the Military General Commandant for approval of her departure. Leo hurriedly applied for a pass to Nantes "on immigration business," so that they could spend one precious, probably tear-stained day together.

A paper trail makes it possible to trace Martha's journey from Nantes, where she was issued a receipt for ten francs for her exit visa from Bordeaux. On the train, the day before her ship's scheduled departure, she sent Leo a postcard showing an idyllic cottage by a lake and the message "Greetings from La Roche-sur-Yon" surrounded by roses. "Mon Cheri, I've been here since ten o'clock, and I'll continue on. I hope I will be on time because I won't arrive until after seven. I telegraphed the shipping company that I am coming because at that time the office will be closed. I won't have much time in Bordeaux, so I am writing from here to make sure this is mailed. I just ate two sardine sandwiches and have two more for the trip. Could you wire the dear parents? Do not say anything about my trip. A thousand sweet kisses, your Martha."

On October 26, Ticket No. 0683 permitted Martha to sail on the United States Lines' SS *Washington*. One year earlier, Lisl had traveled to New York aboard the same ship, then known for its luxury, but it, too, had succumbed to the pressure of war. Martha boarded with more than seventeen hundred passengers, who slept on cots in the Grand Salon, the library, and other public areas. "Tourist Class," the middle service of travel on the *Washington*, was crossed out on her ticket and "Third Class," the least expensive, penned in. After all the different nationalities she had been designated since the Anschluss—Austrian, German, Polish, and stateless—her ticket listed Martha's citizenship as "None."

✦

The Garonne River flowing past Bordeaux is known for its strong tidal bore and for treacherous currents in the estuary. A wave sometimes three feet in height heralds the tidal change, capable of upsetting even large craft. To reach this place, Martha had traversed far more difficult waters. She was lucky to be aboard. After nineteen months of struggle, as the days grew shorter, darker, and colder, she sailed alone on the outgoing tide to America.

CHAPTER 24

France-America-Vienna

Winter 1939

After two often terrifying months in war-torn Europe, Martha landed on November 1 in New York, just a few days before her American visa expired. She had spent most of the stormy eight-day voyage seasick, below deck in her small shared cabin. More than three thousand miles, a war, and countless obstacles now separated her from her parents and her husband. I imagine that sailing past the Liberty Statue holding her torch high in New York harbor must have felt overwhelming. She may have shed tears of gratitude and exhaustion. She probably also felt the cold stab of fear as she thought about her distant family and the German menace.

I had found no letters to Leo describing Martha's experience going through immigration with her Class B health form, or her first meeting with the relatives whom she had never met but who had probably saved her life. Leo's elderly Aunt Anna had generously invited Martha to live with her in Richmond Hill, a small town on Long Island, near Jack and his wife Ruth. Martha was safe. She had a home, but she would be living on handouts—and she had a family to save. Her new life would not be easy.

She cabled news of her safe arrival to Leo and her parents. Still imprisoned an ocean away, Leo took up pen and paper to reply immediately: "Today I received your telegram that you arrived and are well. My joy is indescribable. I am so happy we saw each other before you left. May God will that we are together soon. Amen! All the Flandres acquaintances send greetings. Write me about everything. Take care of yourself. Recuperate from your trials."

Two days later Hedwig wrote Martha, including their pet canary in her exuberant reply. "I couldn't believe it is true that you arrived safely because I wanted it so much.... Hansi, too, is singing his greetings." Alfred added, "We were so happy to receive your telegram, and I wish with my whole heart that you and Leo will soon be together, and to all the dear ones who helped you, we thank you very much." Unlike his usually reserved language, his breathless prose in this letter reflects the enormous relief he felt after eighteen months of unceasing efforts and heavy expenses to send his children to safety. That grinding worry, at least, had been lifted from his and Hedwig's shoulders as they faced growing Nazi terror.

Martha started work in New York soon after her arrival. Jack had found her a job at Gimbel's Department Store until Christmas, then permanent factory work at Hopp Press, a large printing and advertising firm. That job required forty hours a week or more at low wages, but Germany had stripped her of her hard-won music credentials, and she was grateful for any work. She taught piano lessons after work and on weekends and began saving for three tickets to America.

Without a break, Martha shouldered the responsibility of extricating her husband from a war zone and her parents from Nazi Germany. During her scant free time she haunted consulates, government offices, the shipping agent Schenker, and Hapag, the line responsible for her crates and her canceled ticket. She went to an alphabet soup of refugee organizations—HIAS, JJDC, HICEM, and more. She sought a sponsor for her parents and strove to become one herself.

Meanwhile, Gretl was struggling in an explosive Palestine, where Britain's war with the Reich and an Arab revolt had thrown the land into turmoil. The family discussed whether perhaps she, too, should try to immigrate to the United States and reunite with family there. Overnight Martha had become the center of the family's hopes.

She also served as a hub of family communication as distance and warfare held them apart. After the invasion of Poland, Reich mail could not travel to France or British-controlled Palestine. Alfred and Hedwig could not write directly to Palestine but could write to Martha, to Leo's Polish family, to the uncles in occupied Czechoslovakia, and to Olga's family in neutral Turkey. Interned in France, Leo's mail was three-times restricted: French regulators permitted him to write only to close family and immigration authorities, and they had stopped his supportive mail to Alfred and Hedwig in what had become an enemy nation. Soviets and Germans interdicted his anxious letters to his family in eastern Poland.

The United States clung to neutrality, giving only Martha access to all. She kept them together by writing, receiving, and forwarding mail around the world. News zigzagged from her to the next family member, creating a precious network that changed with the political winds but held the family together.

✦

Exhaustive family effort, Martha's wrenching decision to leave Leo, and luck—some combination of all these had brought her safely to the United States in late 1939. But the situation for her family in Europe was critical. Escape routes were closing, immigration regulations tightening. The frightening rumors about France rounding up refugees proved true; new camps for both men and women were under construction. Celia had been amazed to learn that her mother had sailed on one of the last American ships to leave Western Europe. American passenger liners, conforming to the U.S. Neutrality Act, were forced to change their routes to neutral ports. After docking in New York, the *Washington* could not return to Bordeaux, but sailed between New York and Italy—avoiding maritime battles in the North Atlantic but stranding thousands of European Jews.

In Vienna, Alfred and Hedwig continued to survive at the epicenter of Germany's intensifying campaign to rid the Reich of Jews. Martha began to open their letters with as much dread as delight. Their beloved voices had changed. Visiting-nosher jokes had disappeared. Fewer names came up in their news about friends, as twenty months of exodus had reduced Jews' numbers in Vienna. News that "the Rathsprechers received their affidavit," spoke to Martha of her parents' plight. Their questions increased the pressure on her to help them. "What are your plans?" Martha began to see the words, "sorry" and "worry" replacing "hope."

Alfred and Hedwig wrote Martha several times through Richard in Istanbul and later Budapest. Hedwig began one letter to Alfred's brother Richard with cautious lines of concern: "We've had no news from you since August. I'm sorry you were not able to go like Leo." Hedwig acknowledged that Richard couldn't travel through France—where she didn't know Leo was in prison. The lack of information that was available to the family is appalling.

"We wish we could help you," Alfred added. Richard had lived with his older brother until Alfred married. Their close bond rendered Richard's troubles all the more painful. "We worry about you.... Write us.... Your brother, Alfred."

Richard added a note to Martha to Alfred and Hedwig's forwarded letter. Free of censorship, he could describe his grim situation plainly. He said that he fretted "day and night" over Martha and Leo's forced separation, then added, "I also am in a terrible state of mind. The worries get bigger every day.... I am healthy but in a very bad situation! My [work] here is coming to an end and an extension is more difficult.... Where I am supposed to go, I do not know. I will attempt to get to Palestine. It will not be easy." Previously confident and jovial, in denial about Nazi intentions, Richard had grown fearful as his situation deteriorated.

Alfred—negotiating Vienna's censors—wrote Martha in a tone far more restrained than Richard's. "We are very sorry you can't be with dear Leo. We want to know how he is and what he does.... Write us...." Alfred offered Martha news and advice. He had written Hermann "in detail," he said, and urged her to turn to him for help. He told his older daughter that he had forwarded to her the only letter he and Hedwig received from Gretl in months, but the letter from British Palestine had been returned to him; Palestine, as a British mandate, was an enemy land. Arnold, Mitzi, and Mathilde were still trying to "travel," he continued. They visited often. Hedwig treasured her growing collection of pictures of little Eva, Hugo's two-year-old daughter in Prague.

Sandwiched between folksy news about toddlers and visits that told Martha something of each person's situation, Alfred included a coded message. "All people, including those from the Barracks Street, are away." Without comment or names, he was informing Martha who else from the Schmalzhofgasse neighborhood, built on the site of former Imperial Army barracks, had escaped.

In reality not all people from the Barracks neighborhood were "away." Alfred and Hedwig were still there; so was a new boarder, Mrs. Fischer, a friend whom Alfred told Martha had been "a day too late," most likely with travel plans through Britain or France; perhaps she had had a ticket on the *Washington* before it was diverted from France to Italy. She couldn't leave despite having a plane ticket—an amazing luxury. Having given up her apartment, she had been lucky to rent Martha and Gretl's former little bedroom, the *kabinette*. Many property owners objected to Jews' moving and crowding into overstuffed apartments as Germany accelerated its pace of evictions. Apparently—and fortunately—Alfred and Hedwig's building owner and the other tenants did not protest the sublet. I noted, again, that some Viennese actually tried to ease the Jews' pain.

Hedwig describes the new living arrangements: "The *kabinette* looks very nice. We put your couch in it. It fits nicely and we put the chaise in the dining room with the blue bedspread on top. It doesn't look too bad.... We are well, thank G-d."

I realized that I was starting to "know" Hedwig well enough to recognize changes in her tone. Her words here are upbeat, but her tone is flat. At times I had followed her story from a distance. More often, now, I empathized with her. The couch from Martha and Leo's newly-wed apartment had become a bed for a fleeing friend with no home; Alfred and Hedwig's apartment was no longer their own. Like the blue bedspread thrown over rearranged furniture, mundane details covered the hard new reality.

Hedwig and Alfred were uncomplaining, doing their best to make their lives—and Martha—more comfortable. Their situation was not unique; around them, most Jews were now sharing apartments. As emigration slowed, the ramped-up concentration of Jews proved an inexpensive, easily implemented step closer to their deportation. The policy was well received by influential Nazis who coveted the emptying apartments. Alfred reported that, Hugo, Otto, and Julius in Prague had lost their jobs and that they, too, were moving from apartment to apartment.

Alfred's November 3 letter dropped a bombshell: "Today I went to Dr. Max M. at Rothschild Hospital for my eyes. He gave me a certificate that my eyes are not good, and I hope that this certificate will protect us from the deportation to Poland. Dr. Max says I will need a very strong affidavit, and I should tell my sponsor about my very bad nearsighted-ness. The sponsor has to be sure to state that he can guarantee he can be responsible for our livelihood. Of course this is only a formality because dear Mama and I will be able to work."

Ghettos were being formed in Reich-occupied Poland, and depor-tations of Jews from Vienna had begun. In panic Alfred turned to his cousin Max Meissner, an optometrist married to an aryan. Less than six percent of Vienna's Jews were still employed that fall, and Meissner was permitted to see only Jewish patients. Alfred was relying on the double-edged sword of his disability—as he had before. Trying to avoid threatened deportations, he documented his poor vision; pursu-ing immigration, he attempted to minimize it. A "formality," he said breezily about his poor vision not impeding his ability to work in America. He did not fully understand that the U.S. State Department, with its blatant antisemitism and growing fear of German spies, was constructing a wall of "formalities" that hindered Jewish immigration. But he did perceive the new threat of deportation, and he was fighting for his and Hedwig's safety with the few weapons he possessed.

Alfred's worries were well founded. As the war in Europe dominated world attention, it provided cover for Hitler's intensifying racial war against Jews and other "subhuman" enemies of the German *Volk*. That sometimes invisible war, unprecedented in scope and with no viable opposition, was advancing even more steadily than Hitler's territorial war.

Monitoring the slowdown in Jewish emigration in late 1939, Hitler ordered the top echelon of Reich leaders to develop alternatives. They debated the most efficient methods of ridding the Reich of its remaining Jews, including the fifty-five thousand still in Vienna. Mass evacuation to Madagascar, Palestine, or sites in Africa? Dispersal throughout German-occupied western Poland? "Reservations" in Soviet eastern Poland?

Until a more sweeping solution could be devised, Nazis settled on building more and harsher concentration camps. Those would provide forced labor, free up needed apartment space, and decrease Jews' numbers. Ravensbrück, a large camp in Germany for women that later would include a gas chamber, had opened in May, and others were under construction.

Polish Jews in Vienna were among the first casualties of the accelerating pressure. On September 9 and 11, 1939, four months after Leo's departure, Nazis rounded up more than fourteen hundred Polish-Viennese Jewish men, imprisoned them for several days in underground corridors beneath the Vienna Stadium grandstands, then deported them to Buchenwald. The following day, soccer resumed in the stadium. Before long, boxes containing cremated remains of imprisoned Jews arrived at their families' doors. The few families who could document immigration plans were permitted to secure their freedom with bribes.

Several times that fall and winter, Eichmann presented leaders of Vienna's Gestapo-controlled Jewish Community Organization with deadlines for a *Judenfrei* Vienna. Beleaguered Jewish leaders, forced to participate in Reich plans for evictions and deportations, used large infusions of foreign capital from American Jewish aid organizations as leverage to negotiate extensions.

By late September 1939, Germany was eager to exploit its newly acquired *lebensraum*, living space, in central Europe. Plans for eliminating Jews from the Reich began to coalesce and jolt forward—on a track that ran through Poland.

Eichmann hastily commenced organizing deportations of Jewish "workers." Trains bound for Poland began rolling out of Vienna's Aspang Station and central Czechoslovakia, home to many of Hedwig's relatives. As directed, the "workers" carried tools and building supplies for purported camp jobs. Some Jews had even volunteered, believing they would be paid and spared a worse fate. Alfred, perceptive enough not to believe Reich lies about a positive work experience, fought in every way possible to avoid that deportation.

The trains deposited five thousand Jews in an isolated area near Nisko, a small town close to the German-Soviet demarcation line. Like the failed suburban Vienna ghetto plan, the Nisko project was mismanaged. When the trains arrived in eastern Poland, construction of several theoretical camps in the muddy, war-ravaged marshland had barely begun. Guards separated a small number of Jews to build the camp and force-marched others into Soviet-controlled territory. Some Reich planners hoped that the Soviets would form a large Jewish "reservation" there, but the Russians had no such intentions. Frustrated with their German allies, the Soviets sent thousands of the Jews to labor camps in Siberia. Many died there of hunger and cold. Of the nearly sixteen hundred Viennese Jews deported, about two hundred made their way back to Vienna in April 1940, when the project was dismantled.

Nisko had misfired. A mid-project report by cabinet heads in Berlin described Nisko simply as a political tactic, "a means of putting pressure on Western powers...for a world solution to the Jewish Problem." That hadn't worked. German cruelty to Jews across Europe, their deportations, and a 1939 British report on Germany's deadly concentration camps found space in back sections of some large U.S. newspapers and again aroused some sympathy. But the escalation of the war and the fear of spies and Communists posing as refugees riveted America's attention and further entrenched isolationist opinion.

After Nisko, the Nazis understood that the international community would not take Reich Jews, and Germany began building the first of the Auschwitz prison camps near Nisko. Vienna's Jews were not deported en masse again in 1939 or 1940, but Germany had begun to construct its structure of extermination.

Through winter 1939 and into spring 1940, Alfred and Hedwig continued to share news—who was "traveling" and who was still in Vienna— but increasingly, they also pleaded for help. The growing oppression was taking its toll. They veered, at times irrationally, from gossipy news to agitated questions and concerns. Hedwig, in particular, seemed shaken. On December 3, she wrote, "I see you have a pretty good life. Apparently Jack's brother has two boys.... Mrs. Fischer is fine and asks always about you.... The last two days we have had especially cold weather but in our dining room it is nice. Every evening I read to papa. Right now, "Titan," the Beethoven novel and several books I borrowed from Aunt Tilde. I always think how lovely it would be for our children to be with us."

Then, in the margins, she added, "Do you think we should look into Palestine? How long would it take? Will it be difficult with papa's eyes? Please get more information and let us know soon."

Those last lines had been intended for Gretl, who received their forwarded letters months later from Martha. They had not heard from Gretl in three months. Had Hedwig forgotten their rejected applications? Perhaps lingering hope had blinded her to the painful reality. In another letter Hedwig asked, even more fancifully, "You Martha still have here a lot of leather pieces and buckles. Should I save them for you or take them along? Please write me about this."

Alfred expressed his discouragement openly in a postcard to Richard: "We have no news from Gretl.... When will we see the children again? It is already much too long. It is terrible. Perhaps we will always be here. I hope Martha will be able to help us soon."

His letters to Martha grew terse and short. He devoted much of the space to the only remaining assistance he could give Martha and Leo—his attempts to have their crates, still stuck in Germany, delivered to New York. Through summer, then fall, and dragging into winter 1940, letter after letter carried explanations of his efforts and directions to Martha for prodding the agent in New York. Martha and Hermann took up the effort. At the New York Schenker office they explained repeatedly everything they had done to insure, pay for, and move the shipment forward. They were polite, they badgered, they complied with Schenker's requests for money. The Bergers had initially paid two thousand Reichsmarks...then they paid forty-five dollars...then one hundred seventeen Reichsmarks...and more.

The young couple had counted on the rugs and blankets, cooking pots and dishes. They would need the clothes and Martha's sheet music. The paintings and photos would help them remember better times and hold their loved ones close.

Months after the crates should have been delivered, Schenker told them that the war had complicated shipping, that a neutral port must be found, more forms completed, and a deposit paid for transport to Amsterdam or Rotterdam. In December the agent reported that the shipment weighed less in Hamburg than it had in Vienna. The thieving had begun.

Hapag also refused to refund Martha's unused Hansa ticket or credit it toward shipping charges. The requests for money and paperwork, the stonewalling continued shamelessly, endlessly. The family pushed their case, unwilling to accept that their property would never arrive and that no one would reimburse them for their losses. Their trapped belongings were too clear a sign of the chilling truth; the Reich had taken things from them far more precious than luggage.

CHAPTER 25
Distance

Fall 1939–Spring 1940

From New York, Martha watched with deepening fear as her family faced epic challenges in Europe. A thicket of French and American regulations held Leo prisoner in a nation at war. In Vienna, Alfred and Hedwig faced an onslaught of new immigration policies while living under harsh and racist laws, persecution, and increasing brutality. As dangerous as their situation already was, it was deteriorating.

The October 1939 appointment of a Vienna propaganda minister, another milepost proudly touted in the *Vienna Address Book*, meant more crushing regulations and increased suffering for Jews. In one letter to Martha that winter, Hedwig mentioned for the first time the loss of music, a painful deprivation for the musical Bergers. Jews could not own radios or play recordings. "We only hear music now when the party above us plays the piano," she said, careful not to name a neighbor who may have been Jewish. Music had always infused the Bergers' daily lives, but that, too, had been taken away. I wondered whether neighbors would have protested if Hedwig had sung—and whether she had had any songs left in her heart.

That winter Nazi party leaders assigned Jews fewer air raid shelters than their neighbors. During air raid drills, aryans complained about sitting near Jews and forced them to huddle in the darkest corners. Viennese also complained about Jews in parks and stores. Wartime curfews were earlier for Jews than for other Viennese. Even daylight and fresh air had been restricted.

Alfred and Hedwig never wrote about the hardships of the rationing system, but their new ration cards represented a major change. In October, responding to the shortages caused by Germany's wars, Berlin ordered ration cards for all citizens, but only Jews were forced to travel outside their districts to a central office to receive their cards, stamped "*Jude.*"

Some historians believe that the centralized ration system was as ominous for Jews as the Nisko transports had been. The change marked a shift in German priorities—from emigration to deportation, from terrorizing Jews and stealing everything possible from them to collecting them in ghettos awaiting deportation to life-threatening camps. The new ration cards provided an accurate census of Jews, tracking their numbers and their moves from one apartment to the next, enabling evictions and planned deportations to run smoothly. The food Alfred and Hedwig were allowed to buy and the hours they could shop were even more limited, but Hedwig wrote Martha that she shouldn't worry: Hugo sent "wonderful treats" from Prague every week. The new rationing practices were implemented without a ripple of concern from the citizenry.

★

In the darkening winter of 1939–40, a few sparks of hope brightened the Bergers' world. In January Gretl sent Alfred and Hedwig a twenty-five-word telegram through the Red Cross in Geneva. She had tried to write, she said, but her letters had been returned. She'd been ill, but was better. Moshe, her fiancé, was well. Gretl never explained her illness, and the cable didn't contain much news. It may have brought more worry than reassurance, but after five months of silence, Alfred and Hedwig treasured the contact with their dear "Minkel." It also marked the start of somewhat more frequent letters from Gretl, since at that point she could forward mail through Martha. The Bergers' younger daughter began sending news about her fiancé and her efforts to find work in Palestine, and she requested favorite recipes—*schokchinde wurst*, sausage and dumplings, and bishop's bread.

Martha's letters offered her parents constant love and words of hope, but it was Leo who provided the balance that steadied the family. That winter, after months of no mail from him, Alfred and Hedwig received a few forwarded letters from Les Sables d'Olonne. Filled with information, stories, and Leo's teasing manner, the letters gave Alfred and Hedwig sorely needed moments of fun. Their son-in-law wrote to Hedwig that he wished for her *servietten knoedeln*, napkin dumplings, the Czech specialty she prepared by tucking delights like plums, hard-boiled eggs, or chocolate into soft dough, then wrapping the dumplings in a cloth and suspending them in simmering water. She happily mentioned his request several times to Martha, and probably others. When Leo told Alfred about his barbering in the internment camps, Alfred wrote back that he too was waiting to come under Leo's razor. As important as any news, Leo's irrepressible humor and unquenchable determination helped the family relax and be themselves again.

In late January 1940 Alfred and Hedwig wrote Martha with more good news: they had received copies of the affidavits and supplemental documents that had been submitted for them. I was confused. Had they known these were coming? No one had mentioned them in any previous letters.

"You can imagine how enormously joyously surprised we were, for which I thank you from the bottom of my heart," Hedwig wrote effusively. More guarded, Alfred said: "Hopefully it will turn out well for once."

The documents had probably been a joint effort of Hermann and Lisl, his daughter, with his in-laws and Martha providing extra statements of support. Martha asked for her parents' visa registration numbers and the date they had applied. They promptly sent the information—September

7, 1938, Numbers 45,868 and 45,869—along with Alfred's wish: "Hope for good news from you."

They also spoke of a few visiting friends, of their progress learning English, and about how much they enjoyed the company of their boarder, Mrs. Fisher. They reported, again, that Arnold and Mitzi believed they would "travel" that spring. Hedwig and Alfred's news could have been part of any family letter in ordinary times. But those were not ordinary times. Each line, subtly crafted to avoid censors' redaction, paints a picture of a family in severe distress.

January had been colder than usual, Alfred concluded, and the Danube was icebound. That would delay shipping of the crates, he said, floundering for news to write. Like the river that winter, he and Hedwig were stuck, frozen in place.

★

During Martha's first three months in the United States, she and Jack worked tirelessly with the American consulate to help Leo. Leo himself petitioned U.S., French, German, and Polish offices to renew expired documents and obtain others newly required. And in late January 1940, their combined efforts paid off. The Nantes consulate informed Leo that his papers were in order. Elated, Martha wrote Alfred and Hedwig that Leo might already be on his way to America. "Has he arrived yet?" they wrote back. The Bergers' situation seemed to have changed. Perhaps, finally, spring was coming, and relief was within reach.

Martha and Leo's letters to each other were less sanguine. She wrote on January 28, 1940, that she was happy they had been successful in collecting his documents, but worried that she hadn't heard from her parents in two months.

Leo replied, "I am surprised that you said I would soon be in America. I wish it were true.... The consul says that my papers are in order. Now I have to be patient.... I am sorry, my dear, that you worry so much. I always ask you to do so much for me.... I have to try everything."

While Leo toiled to complete the labyrinthine immigration process, the French government organized and reorganized refugees in preparation for the looming battle with Germany. Leo's interned group was transferred further inland to a large camp for foreigners, mostly Jews, at Meslay-du-Main. He described the other prisoners working "like cattle," while he became "indispensable" for less grueling jobs. After a few weeks his group returned to Sables, only to move again, this time to a camp near La Roche-sur-Yon. Leo remained in Sables, practically alone, but the group came back, and on February 18 he wrote that they had all been reassigned to La Roche: "When I came, first I took a good bath.... I am working as a tailor. After work, we are free to go wherever we want but are far from town, and there is no electric light.... We must go to bed at nine o'clock, so I am not in bad habits, like you are. You go to bed so late. Why do you do this? It won't be good for you. I see that I must write the police of the U.S.A. to take care of you."

Leo explained that, once again, he must wait months for his visa. He also reported another setback. Newly implemented French laws had forced internees to "take service as *prestateur*," meaning that Leo had been formally impressed into military service and was no longer governed by civilian authority.

In New York, Martha continued her efforts to help Leo, but the time between letters from her family lengthened; sometimes she didn't hear from any of them for months. In early March, she filed for citizenship, a step toward sponsoring her parents. But she reported unhappily to Leo that she had failed to find anyone willing to join her in sponsoring her parents. "I really don't know what to do to help them. It is so sad." She had had an upsetting dream that Gretl was sick, she said, discouraged.

Martha told Leo that Aunt Anna had fallen and needed nursing care. Martha had moved to live with Jack, Ruth, and Ruth's brother—a livelier household. She had five piano students, including Jack, she reported, and she joked that in her new home she slept with the family dog. Leo shouldn't worry, she was taking good care of herself. "Too good. I am a little chubby."

On March 27, Martha told Leo that she hadn't received mail from him since his February 1 letter, over a month before. "What is happening?" She tried to remain upbeat, but that seemed to require increasing effort.

In late March, Leo sent his first letter by "clipper ship," the seaplanes that were revolutionizing mail service between the United States and Europe. It was more expensive than regular mail, but it could arrive from Europe in an unbelievable two or three days. Leo wrote that he had visited the American consul, who again told him to be patient—but this time with a difference. "The consul is waiting for new quota numbers, and I will probably be one of the first. I think I can take the next ship, *De Gras*, which is supposed to leave by the middle of May."

The good news continued. Leo reported that he was glad to be in La Roche. "I have a very nice life here. In one word, it's like a sanitarium. We don't have any guards.... It doesn't matter if you gained a few pounds. I know you, Lumper. You exaggerated. If Jack puts you on the scale, tell him he should guess in advance how much you will weigh, perhaps 310 kilo [683 pounds]?"

A week later, Leo wrote that a fellow prisoner would soon receive a visa. "You were amazed that the other friend was able to go before me. That is simply his good luck, namely that his papers were in Paris, and no longer in Nantes. I think things are not kosher in Nantes. There is a new consul there. If it is possible for you to intercede in Paris with the general consulate, write that you are puzzled that your husband was registered on May 2, 1938 as a Pole, but isn't it your husband's turn while others who registered on May 25 have their visa. But all of this in a very polite manner!"

With rising anticipation, Leo's thoughts turned to finding work in New York. He had heard discouraging stories, he said, but "when I come, I will be able to help toward the affidavit. I would be happy to help the dear parents. I love them as much as my own."

Martha permitted herself a long-constrained surge of optimism. "I was so excited to get news about you that I got hives.... Sunday I went with Schmucklers to beautiful Radio City. I can hardly wait until you are here and we can go together. We will celebrate your birthday."

She added the good news that Gretl planned to be married soon, but she had other, more mixed news, too. Alfred and Hedwig's long-awaited letter had triggered new worries. Mrs. Fischer's visa had come through. She had left for New York, and Aunt Mathilde had moved into the *kabinette*.

Martha fretted that Mathilde's presence would become too heavy a burden for her mother. "She cooks and takes care of everything," she wrote. But Martha may not have fully understood the significance of Mathilde's move. Ominously, as a single, elderly Jewish woman, Mathilde was among the most vulnerable Jews in the evolving German deportation scheme. A few months earlier, Alfred had believed that his poor vision might protect him from a labor camp. Since that time, older, dependent Jews had risen to the top of the Reich's list of expendables. Mathilde's move from her own apartment may not have been her own choice.

While Leo's prospects were improving, Alfred and Hedwig's situation was falling apart. They told Martha that the American consul had informed them that their affidavit was too weak. Martha had already seen the rejection and resumed her endless quest to enlist sponsors. The harrowing reality of alternating hope and despair that Alfred, Hedwig, and Martha endured is hard to imagine. The word "whipsaw" came to my mind, but I didn't really know what that was. It turns out that it's a saw with a narrow blade and handles at both ends; pushed and pulled, the blade cuts in both directions. For the Bergers, good news, bad news...both had cut deeply.

✦

Martha and Leo's prospects tumbled again. He wrote that he was sorry, but he wouldn't be with her for Passover as they had envisaged: "My suitcase still stands in the Nantes hotel, ready. Some day we will all celebrate together. Dear Jack has been so nice. It is all very well that he thought I would come on April 1st at 6:30. His chosen date turned into an April fool's joke, but I understand that he is thinking of me. He could just as well put *hamantaschen* [holiday pastry] in the envelope since you baked so many. Next year, I will eat them all myself."

Leo's humor in this letter has an uncharacteristically sharp edge; he seems jealous of his cousin. In his next letter he told Martha that he had made a "liberation request" to the French War Ministry asking to be released from Army service in advance of his departure; a lengthy release process might cause him to miss a ship. He had received a day's leave to visit the American consul in Nantes. Everything seemed in place for him to finish his long run escaping the Germans. He concluded with long-awaited news: "Today, I can report something joyous. I received the appointment to come to the consul on May 9, 1940. I will now write to HICEM concerning the boat ticket. Am very excited. Two others have their appointment too. We will go together."

Leo's exhilarating letter had not yet reached Martha when she wrote him on April 27. She hadn't heard from him in a long time, she said. Had he received his visa? She was searching for a small apartment for them. "Single rooms with kitchenette and sink, sometimes a bath, are $6.50 a week.... While I am writing you, I am listening to the radio, to Liszt's Rhapsody...lovely. The poor parents have not had a radio for many months."

On May 5 Martha wrote again, saying that she and Jack had toasted Leo that day, his birthday. Jack had asked his congressman to write the Paris consulate. They had sent Leo a telegram about ship tickets. If Leo needed money for the ticket, he should cable Jack immediately. He and Martha had suffered a terrifying year of separation, but Leo's arrival now seemed imminent.

But Martha reported distressing news from her parents. "They are sorry Uncle Arnold and Aunt Mitzi will leave soon. Perhaps they are gone already.... I am so sorry too. I don't know why I cannot do anything to help them. They are writing in English already."

Before mailing her letter, Martha added a few wistful lines: "I still don't have any letters from you. I am sending you the telephone number of Jack's house Vigilant 4-7943. I hope we will get the date of your arrival soon and can meet you at the ship. I had a piano lesson today after work. Now I am alone, writing my dear Burli."

★

To avoid censorship, Martha and Leo never wrote about the war. On April 9, the *Vienna Address Book* chronology boasted, "German armed forces take Denmark and Norway into protection of the Reich." That spring the Soviet Union pushed north and west; British, Indian, and Canadian troops reinforced their units in France as Hitler finalized plans to invade France, Belgium, Luxembourg, and the Netherlands. By spring 1940 no one was calling the situation a "phony" war.

Mail to and from France was delayed that spring amid the enormous uncertainties. Martha and Leo proceeded blindly with their plans. On May 5 Jack deposited funds with the New York office of HICEM, a Jewish refugee support agency, for Leo's travel expenses. On May 9, the U.S. consulate in Nantes approved Leo's visa.

On May 10, Vienna officials ordered an unscheduled citywide blackout. That day, in a surprise attack, massed German forces pushed through the mountainous, forested terrain of the Ardennes Woods on France's northeastern border, avoiding predictable attack routes and the French Maginot Line. The gigantic ground and air offensive was multipronged; it simultaneously pierced into Belgium, Luxembourg, the Netherlands, and France. In Britain, Winston Churchill replaced Neville Chamberlain as prime minister.

Like Germany's blitz in Poland eight months before, this attack caught the Allies off guard. On May 15, Churchill made an emergency fact-finding flight to Paris and learned that the French military had all but collapsed. Within a few weeks Reich forces trapped outnumbered Allied armies against the English Channel, then raced west toward the

Atlantic and south to Paris. The fighting was ferocious, the carnage overwhelming. By month's end Dutch and Belgian armies had capitulated, and the Allies were in full retreat. On June 3, Germany bombed Paris. The Reich had bested the Allies, leaving them reeling. Germany had achieved almost total domination of Europe.

In America, isolationists mounted a major campaign: "Keep the United States out of the War." Germany secretly funded the campaign's full-page ad in the *New York Times*. Later, the movement's celebrity spokesperson, American aviation hero Charles Lindbergh, was discovered to have a second family in Germany. Germany's reach into American politics had contributed to America's costly delay in strongly opposing German aggression.

Within days of the invasion, the French government evacuated first to Tours, then to Bordeaux, and then to Vichy in south central France. Panicked French citizens fled the north of France in a human deluge streaming away from the German advance. While all of France seemed to be moving south, Leo was marching with the French Army against the flow of panicked citizens, toward the front lines.

★

Martha hadn't received news from Leo since mid-April. There had been no cable to let her know that he hadn't boarded the ship to the United States as expected. Among Celia's collection of family documents, we found a shadowy photograph of Martha that Jack had snapped on the docks of New York Harbor and two passes issued by the U.S. Customs Service, stamped May 27, authorizing admittance to the customs area on the pier of "the next French Line Steamer."

Martha, a small figure in a heavy coat and hat, stands on the pier with her back to the camera, facing a large, seemingly empty ocean liner. But as she and Jack waited at water's edge to welcome Leo to America, he was running for his life with a remnant of the French army.

The picture Jack took of Martha on the dock in New York, waiting, that time in vain, for Leo to arrive from war-torn Europe. *Courtesy of the Berger family*

CHAPTER 26
War Fever

May–September 1940

As war in Europe shook the world in the spring of 1940, the web of communication holding the Berger family together was cut to ribbons. Martha saw gaps between letters from her parents and Gretl stretching for months, but the biggest change was the terrifying silence from Leo. The family on three continents listened to the news and watched their mailboxes in anguish, waiting to hear that he was safe.

Leo rejoiced for one day after receiving his long-sought American visa. He had already purchased his ship ticket to New York when word reached Les Sables: Germany had invaded France, Belgium, Luxembourg, and the Netherlands, and he would be ordered toward the front with French Army Unit 313, *Compagnie T.E.*, [*Travailleurs Étrangers*, foreign workers]. Leo had been caught in the fiercest fighting anywhere in the world.

Compagnie T.E. paused at Le Mans, headquarters of the French Army Corp's Fourth Region, where Leo built roads, strung electric wire, dug ditches—everything he was commanded to do and more. One evening, noting his captain's ripped uniform, he volunteered to repair it. Working through the night, he scavenged material, took the garment apart at the seams, cut new pieces to match the old, and stitched two new uniforms to present to the officer in the morning.

On May 15, as Churchill was in Paris learning that French defenses had all but collapsed, Leo wrote Martha from Le Mans. Careful to avoid any mention of the war, he said that he had done a lot of "running around," but couldn't talk about it. Surprisingly, he also said that he was then under English command, but again couldn't explain. "I hope I will be free soon.... Sorry this letter is not long. I'm very tired and exhausted. A little *meschugge* [crazy]."

English command? On May 15, the English were retreating and in a catastrophic situation, just days away from evacuating across the English Channel. Leo's unit was supporting that frenzied retreat to the coast.

Twelve days later, on May 27, Leo wrote Martha from Meslay du Maine. Again he avoided mentioning the war: "Our liberation now depends on the War Minister. But they have other worries now. You can imagine how upset we are. My dear Martha, we have to be brave and hope the dear Lord will help us. Don't be sad. There are so many terrible things happening, let us hope we can live in peace soon.... They have called us again. We have to march and will work in factories or in agriculture."

Leo apologized for telegraphing Jack for more money and explained that he could obtain a ship ticket and send a copy to Paris HICEM, the European arm of New York-based HIAS. He lacked only an exit visa from France. "If I know more, I will send you another telegram." Escape seemed at his fingertips.

The two organizations Leo mentions, HIAS and its European arm HICEM, had become bankers, information resources, document processors, communication links, and support for immigrants in a new land and for those fleeing Europe. Leo apparently didn't know how dire the situation across France had become. Allied defenses had collapsed so quickly, and the French people had abandoned their homes, farms, and cities so abruptly, that perhaps no one had a grip on reality. But as Leo was writing Martha, the HICEM staff, along with most other agencies, government offices, and citizens, had already evacuated Paris. There was no HICEM left in France to receive anything.

The peace that Leo wished for would not come "soon." Fighting intensified as Germany unleashed the second phase of its offensive and pushed deeper into France. Days passed, then weeks. Leo's letters to Martha took months to reach her, or never arrived. Hundreds of French postal service workers died in the German attack. News reports from Europe turned grim as German troops outmaneuvered, outflanked, and outnumbered the Allies. In Vienna, Alfred and Hedwig heard constant news reports trumpeting Reich victories. They wrote Martha, trying to sound calm, but asking, "Where is Leo?" "Have you heard from Leo?"

By May 26, Allied troops were retreating en masse across the English Channel. On June 3, German planes dropped eleven hundred bombs on Paris. A week later the French government resigned, naming a small spa town, Vichy, France's new capital, and the antisemitic, eighty-four-year-old World War I hero Philippe Pétain absolute head of a new government.

★

As fighting penetrated deeper into France, the entire nation seemed to be fleeing south, barely staying ahead of the German offensive. The massive exodus drained Paris of two-thirds of its three million citizens. German fighter planes strafed clogged lines of cars, trains, buses, and bikes, miles of people walking, pushing baby carriages, riding in horse-drawn carts. An estimated eight million people, including citizens from invaded countries to the north, ran in a confusion of terror, and Leo was among them. Facing overwhelming German force, Leo's unit had turned south. He was permitted to run with the soldiers, joining the millions of people on the roads. Leo was fortunate. Most Jewish refugees in intern-ment camps were not released so that they could evade the Germans, and many of them were later murdered.

Leo never wrote about his experiences fleeing south, but he spoke briefly about it. Celia said that he referred to his time in the labor battalion as "slave labor." In fact he had lost his freedom and had no rights. He was subject to military authority. Disobedience could mean instant death. For two weeks his unit raced south, nine hundred miles to Marseille on the French Mediterranean coast.

Celia had little information about how he had traveled. Did the military commander commandeer space on trains or other vehicles? Possibly. Leo told Celia that they ran. He said that they ran until they could not move. He also said that he nearly starved. At the edge of one village, local women met the soldiers on a bridge with jugs of milk, but Leo was so weak that the milk made him sick. At one point, too weak and hungry to continue, he intentionally fell face down on a patch of wild strawberries. He heard an officer run back to find him, turned his head to see the officer aim his pistol, and heard the order to get up. Leo, beyond caring, did not move. After a pause, the officer said, "Thanks for the uniform," and left Leo behind. Leo rested, ate berries, and as evening fell, found his unit by the light shining from a barn.

When he rejoined them he discovered that the French officers had made space for the Jews to light candles and conduct a belated Passover service—perhaps the most meaningful of their lives as they recalled the Jews' race for freedom thousands of years before.

Belgium, the Netherlands, and Luxembourg surrendered to the Germans in May. Hostilities in France halted on June 25. France signed the Armistice agreement in a railroad car in Compiègne in northeast France, the site of Germany's humiliating capitulation that ended World War I in Europe. That June 1940 cease-fire agreement was the first of several treaties defining boundaries and conditions for the Vichy government, operating under German control in an "unoccupied" southern zone of the former nation of France. In six weeks, French losses had risen to eighty-five thousand killed and nearly a million and a half prisoners of war. France had lost much of its territory, and all of its freedom.

June was devastating for Jews in France and throughout the Reich. Escape routes through France, Belgium, and Northern Europe were gone. Vienna decked itself out with flags and banners celebrating the return of its victorious troops from the Norwegian campaign as the thirst for more conquests spread across the Reich. In southern France the collaborationist Vichy government promptly rescinded a French law banning public hate speech; antisemitic brochures and diatribes flourished immediately. By the end of June, French police had begun arresting foreign Jews and confining them in seven Vichy-run camps.

Leo's army unit stopped running when it reached the Mediterranean. He was demobilized from his labor battalion in Marseille on July 6. The French Republic, which had promised to pay him one thousand francs for his ten months of forced service, no longer existed. The Vichy government allowed him to remain free only because he held a valid U.S. visa. Without it he would have joined the thousands of Jews arrested and imprisoned in French concentration camps.

On July 9, Leo wrote Martha, "I tried to send a telegram to you through [friends] on July 8. We heard later that they don't permit telegrams any more. That's why I'm writing you today. We are in Marseille, and I am well.... Your loving Leo."

The same day, Martha wrote Leo ecstatically, in English.

> My sweet little Leoboy,
>
> I was so happy when Mrs. Weiss [the wife of a fellow refugee] called yesterday. I went to see her right after work and was very glad to read a few lines from you. I was so worrying all the time and broke my head how to come in connection with you. I asked HICEM and the Red Cross without success. Now we all break our heads how to send money to you. Jack, Mrs. Weiss, Uncle Herman, everybody tries to find out. Till now, I could only get information what we could not do. HICEM in Marseille does not exist anymore. We shall find a way...Write me about everything, truly, please. I close with much love.

Leo wasn't "well." He was surviving in southern France with almost no resources, sleeping in haystacks. He had grown thin and weak from the exhausting run. A hundred-year-old farm woman brought him food as he hid from Vichy collaborationist roundups of foreign Jews. Leo sketched two portraits of the woman, gave her one in gratitude, and kept one to remember her by.

Martha wrote Leo three more letters in July. "Have courage, everything will work out well. If only I would have you here already. I have no patience anymore," she wrote, but did not hear back.

On July 27 she penned, "My sweet little Leoboy, I am writing and writing and never get any answer. I wait for that, like for water, and that means something in this heat.... Do you have any clothes to change? Where are your suitcases? Don't worry about anything, just come." Those letters would not reach Leo for several months.

Leo's sketch of an elderly French woman who let him sleep in her haystack. "I'm 101," she told him. "What are they going to do if they catch me? Kill me?" *Courtesy of Celia Cizes*

Bone-weary, Leo seems not to have had the heart to write—not about his terrible eight weeks of flight from the Germans, and not about his uncertain future. As he had done for two years, he spent July rushing from office to office. He waited in long lines of frightened evacuees in the turmoil of Marseille, swollen with French military, displaced French, and refugees grappling with broken communications and disorganized authorities. The ship for which Leo held a ticket had long since sailed.

★

Martha and Leo lived for letters from their loved ones. Celia had none by Alfred and Hedwig from the months of the war in France; I could only imagine the difficulties they faced, ardently hoping for peace but living in war-crazed Vienna. Throughout Leo's imprisonment and race through France, he had carried Martha's letters. On July 22 in Marseille he wrote her two letters that he saved and never mailed. He wrote a third the next week that he did send—his normal careful, thoughtful style overtaken by a rush of stressed words: "This is my third letter but for some reason I could not mail them because everything changes from day to day. The possibilities are not good for foreigners.... new regulations—we tried everything but haven't been successful. Still, I hope...."

In the unmailed versions of this letter, Leo had asked Martha to send money, the sooner the better. At that time he believed that he had to reserve his own ticket in Marseille, but a week later HICEM workers who had fled Paris reorganized in Marseille and reestablished their connections with New York. With this reversal, Leo urged Martha to acquire a refund for his unused ticket as soon as possible and apply it immediately to a ticket from Lisbon. He reminded her that his visa would expire soon.

He went on more conversationally, "I wrote the parents yesterday because now we can write there. I don't have my suitcases yet, but bought a grey suit for 120 francs. I still need a pair of shoes because the army boots are too heavy.... Why is Gretl not yet married? I hope she is well...I'm sorry I am so much trouble for you.... We have to hope and have will power."

Germany now controlled the territory from France north to the Netherlands, as well as Norway, Austria, Czechoslovakia, and Poland. Leo took advantage of France's new connection to the German Reich to write family there. Alfred and Hedwig were elated to hear from him after months of worry, but Leo was unable to write Gretl in British Palestine.

His options for reaching the United States had narrowed considerably. That summer Britain and Germany unleashed ferocious aerial warfare: The Battle of Britain was the first major combat ever fought entirely by air. German bombers crossed the English Channel, pounding British harbors, factories, shipping convoys, and population centers as a precursor to a possible invasion. Britain retaliated by bombing the German homeland and occupied French harbors. Two-thirds of France remained an active war zone. British bombers sank most of the French navy sheltered in Algerian ports to prevent its confiscation by Germany. German, Italian, and British planes skirmished over the Mediterranean and Northern Africa, ending most passenger travel there also.

Martha had been correct: the time for patience had passed. Competition for tickets was fierce. Leo needed to secure passage to America from Lisbon, the only European port still sending passenger liners to the United States—and he needed to reach the United States before his visa expired in a few weeks. He applied for an exit visa from France and transit visas through Spain and Portugal. He kept his copy of a July 10 letter from the U.S. vice consul in Marseille to the Portuguese consul general, noting that Leo possessed an American visa and requesting that his "dear colleague" grant Leo a Portuguese transit visa.

In early August, Leo wrote Martha with another plan and new optimism—"I hope to be in Lisbon in fourteen days." He had acquired the Spanish transit visa that permitted him to apply for a French exit visa, which would take another fourteen days. "I paid 1000 francs for another ticket at Cooks." He had purchased his third ticket to America. Had she bought one also? Or a train ticket to Lisbon?

There seems to have been some confusion in his plans. He could not be in Lisbon in fourteen days because of the wait for an exit visa from France. Coordination between Martha and Leo was crucial, but in that letter Leo—the plotter, the planner—seems scrambled and disjointed. The events of the past six months had exacted their toll.

On August 12, the U.S. Export Line in Marseille wrote Leo that their New York office had received a $270 deposit for passage from Lisbon to New York. He should come to their office to clarify "questions." Wheels were turning, but Martha and Leo's plans were out of sync, causing confusion and costly delay.

The tagline on the Export Line's letterhead declared: United States Mail Steamers to Mediterranean and Black Sea Ports. Theirs was a risky business. German U-boats patrolled Europe's coastlines, threatening any ship they considered an enemy.

Martha wrote on August 15, hopeful and looking ahead. But having received no mail from Leo in weeks, she was unaware of his fragile situation. She urged him not to worry about work in New York. He wouldn't need his master painter's license in America. He should bring all his drawings. Perhaps he could do commercial art. "There are always new possibilities here.... You bad *putzel*, you don't write anymore."

She wrote again two days later with no energy behind her rambling words. She was alone in the house while Jack and Ruth were on vacation. She had splurged on a movie that cost fifteen cents but hadn't enjoyed it. She hadn't received mail from him in weeks. What was happening? She talked about chores and a few visits with friends and Uncle Hermann, but the tone of her letter was, she conceded, sad. In closing, she rallied for a sardonic joke. "Waiting eagerly for good news. I hope you don't make a fool of me again." Her memory of waiting at the docks was achingly fresh.

Two weeks later, on August 27, Leo sent a letter that would not lift Martha's spirits: "Finally I have time to write you. I wrote last on July 28 and August 7 but did not mail them.... It is not really my fault, my dear. It seems that I am always one day too late. I had all my Spanish and

Portuguese visas, and finally also the exit visa. We five were at the border,
Luis, Kohn, Baumgarten, Rosenzweig, and me. There we learned that
Spain has a new regulation. Men under forty cannot enter Spain."

Spanish border guards had turned away thirty-six-year-old Leo and
three of his friends. Maintaining its pseudo-neutrality, Spain had kept
good relations with Germany but allowed fleeing foreigners to travel
through its territory to reach Portugal. Now, with the fall of France,
Spain had changed its border policies to prohibit entry by men under
forty—fearing that young rebel fighters would return home. Leo had
been one day too late—again.

In his letter, Leo admitted to Martha that he had considered "going
dark," crossing the border illegally through the Pyrenees as Willi had
done in Switzerland. But memories of being halted in the Havana harbor
for his illegal entry there, and visions of Spanish prisons had made him
reconsider. He and three refugee companions made their way to Luchon-
de-Bagnères, a small French village in the Pyrenees at the end of a train
line, near the Spanish border.

He reviewed his situation: "The four of us live in a hotel. Luchon is
a very nice little town, a resort at the edge of the Pyrenees.... The room
for each of us is only two to four francs daily and is very nice and clean.
Food is inexpensive too. Sorry that I used more of the money for visas....
Too bad my mail is forwarded to Lisbon. Now you should write to
Luchon-Bagnères, *poste restante*.... I will write the American consul and
ask to extend my visa. I have to be patient. Please do the same, my dear.
On my march, I was with you all the time and that helped...."

Leo used the word hope six times in that letter, but for the first time
it sounded hollow. He had suffered a major defeat.

Martha's next letter, written on September 5, shows how badly out
of touch she was. "Your letter of July 30 is my last mail from you. You
seem to have forgotten me. I don't receive any letters." Then she put down
her pen and stopped writing. By the next day mail from France had suddenly resumed, and she had received his terrible news: "As happy as I
was to receive news from you it made me very sad that things did not

work out.... We were hoping you would be able to come.... I am so glad that you are very brave.... One day, this has to change."

Martha wrote again the next week, tracing a string of worries. She admitted to feeling downhearted. She asked Leo if he had warm clothes and food. Had he received the money she sent? She reported that Jack had written to the Spanish consul and Washington, D.C.—probably to the State Department—trying to help him. Then, for the first time, she admitted that her fears for her parents were mounting—and complained that Hermann was not helping enough: "I only know that if it would be the other way around, my dear papa would do everything possible. Please don't mention this in your letters to him or the parents.... Papa says if he can come soon, he will speak better English than his grandchildren. Where are the grandchildren? Of course, children would be difficult now but at least I would have something from you....You should write me more often."

Martha was disconsolate. Leo's news was a major disappointment, and she worried constantly about her parents. Pressure to achieve the impossible and guilt over leaving her trapped loved ones without being able to help them from America weighed on her. Martha hoped that her Uncle Hermann could accomplish what she could not, but the truth was, he was no longer wealthy.

Celia believes that her mother and Hermann both ached for their family in Vienna. And yet she had heard that Hermann sponsored an in-law before trying to help his own brother. Was that true? The choices that Jews faced as they tried to save loved ones would have tested Solomon.

It seemed that Martha was losing hope. She pulled herself together to share family news in her letter—the Prague brothers were working in Jewish support organizations instead of their professions, she had not heard from Gretl in three months, Hugo's toddler was sweet, Leo's sister was well. "Stay *fesch* [in strong spirits]," she concluded, "and be brave my Putzig."

As she said, Leo had not written often. But the same day that Martha wrote, September 12, so did he—also in a mood of uncertainty and despair. He admitted that he hadn't mailed letters that he had written in late July and early August. "I sent my last letter on September 27 [he meant August 27], but I don't want to wait for your answer because I want to talk to you. The last letter I received from you is from July 22." Nearly two months had passed without word from Martha. The distance that separated the two lovers had grown in time as well as geography. "I am very sorry but everything is mixed up here.... Until about fourteen days ago, I always hoped that I could leave soon. I have tried everything, and nothing has come of it. Why don't I have more luck?. . . I don't want to be pessimistic, but I am really upset. I spent a lot of money for visas and travel expenses, and now my visa expired. I have to start all over again."

Leo listed the steps they must take, again. A new affidavit, notarized by "a senator or somebody," sent to the American consul in Marseille, a special affidavit guaranteeing that he was not politically radical or ever worked for any political party. Leo believed that time was key to survival. The word *soon* appeared in almost all of his letters. Here he wrote mechanically of the efforts that he felt would never end.

Leo began another letter around that time, an undated fragment that he saved but never mailed, repeating the same information in briefer form, flailing for answers in a world that offered him none—and expressing a new, frightening thought. "I hope I will not end up in another camp. I will probably come after the war."

Leo's fears of being interned in a French concentration camp were justified. Among peace terms imposed by Germany was the condition that unoccupied France give up anyone that Germany demanded. This was Nazi code for French resisters—and Jews.

Leo ended that unmailed letter with an attempt at optimism, however unrealistic: "I will try everything to get out soon.... to Casablanca and from there to Portugal. It is better to wait there than here. There is another possibility, to get out via Switzerland, Belgrade, Russia, and China.... Don't worry, my dear. If I hear of anything, I will try it."

As a young man fleeing Poland's oppression and prejudice, Leo had sought the freedom epitomized by Vienna. Nazis had stolen that from him; now they had also crushed his hopes for reaching the United States. In his latest skirmish with fate, he had seen the face of war. He had been matched against some of the cruelest people on the planet, and he felt that they had won.

CHAPTER 27
Precarious

Summer 1940

With the Spanish border closed to young men in late August 1940, Leo could not reach Lisbon. He hid in the Pyrenees, his optimism waning, but his determination fierce. He needed new immigration papers, a ship, a safe port...a change in his luck. He saw options disappearing as Germany, Italy, and the Soviet Union occupied nations throughout central, northern, and then southern Europe. He watched with foreboding as Germany tightened its grip on France's "Free Zone," Vichy France.

While Leo clung to his crumbling ledge of safety, fighting between Germany and Britain intensified. British bombing raids extended deep inside the German homeland, along the French Atlantic coast, and into the Mediterranean. Combat erupted in North Africa as Italy occupied Ethiopia, closing more escape routes.

The Nazis' ruthless attacks on Jews also advanced at a furious pace, but that "race hygiene" war was harder for the world to follow. Nazis kept long lists of ethnic, national, and religious groups they planned to eliminate or enslave. Gypsies, dissidents, homosexuals, and Communists all suffered persecution and murder under the Germans. Between 1939 and 1941, the Reich's "T4" program of "euthanizing" the handicapped, mentally ill, and others killed over seventy thousand Germans and thousands more in occupied countries, attracting little mention in the world press.

But Hitler's driving obsession and long-proclaimed *Kampf*, his struggle, was to eliminate Jews from German lands, a growing swath of Europe. Germany fought that war with weapons as deadly as bombs and torpedoes, but with less familiar weapons as well. Germany stole Jews' property and pushed them to the margins of society. They promoted hatred of Jews in film, books, art, and politics. German diplomats carried antisemitism abroad, local police enforced it in neighborhoods, and citizens tolerated and enabled it. The focus of Hitler's race war never wavered, but in the fall of 1940 it intensified, and Alfred and Hedwig were on the front lines.

Their letters that year reflect their unflagging efforts to survive. Their resources were resilience; support from family, friends, and some neighbors; and the burning drive to flee. Their twenty-eight letters to Martha between May and December 1940 all probed for an opening that would permit their escape.

Hedwig filled her letters with questions, trying to imagine Martha's new life in America. Had Jack's wife recovered from her illness? Did Martha have enough students? She offered advice, urging her older daughter to relax and have fun. She helped Martha with a sewing problem. "About the blouse, from the first piece take out 2 cm. For the sleeve, you don't cut it in half but connect it with the waist...." Mathilde, living in Alfred and Hedwig's tiny extra bedroom, and Arnold and Mitzi, who visited frequently, often squeezed their warm greetings into the edges of the one-page letters.

Alfred's handwriting was mostly clear and legible that summer, his humor bubbling through mundane and serious news. He wrote several times using some English and reporting that he and Hedwig were making progress with the language. "Only Hansi [the canary] is not learning. He still makes a racket, so we always put him in the bedroom."

Their days centered on mail. Letters brought loved ones closer, but they were a mixed blessing. A letter could bring joy and sustain hopes, or plunge them into despair. Alfred and Hedwig replied joyfully when in the course of one week they received three letters from Martha, one from Hermann, a package from Olga, and the thrilling news forwarded by Martha that Gretl would marry soon. But the small details of daily life that they wrote about in return had a dark edge. Alfred, Hedwig, and Mathilde described with pleasure their routine of visiting a public bathhouse—something that had previously been an unremarkable detail of ordinary life. "Every Friday we go to a bathhouse in Ottakring," Alfred wrote, which had "a little yard" where they could sit in the sun. They had been forced to travel across the city to a "Jewish" facility, but in their restricted lives the weekly bath had become an anticipated outing.

Alfred and Hedwig wrote that they had received a photo of Martha—seated at a piano, smiling, with a basket of fruit nearby. That must have looked like the land of plenty. In December 1939 the Minister of Food had reduced Jews' rations of meat and butter and eliminated their cocoa and rice. In January, he cut their meat, fruit, and legumes even further; later rations were cut again, and then again. Their truncated shopping hours shrank to 11:00 a.m.–1:00 p.m. and 4:00–5:00 p.m. Jews could not buy shoes, clothing, or material to repair shoes or to sew.

When Vienna's cold rainy weather cleared, Alfred and Hedwig wrote that they had gone for a walk. They didn't mention that there were few places for them to do so. The Jewish Community Organization had petitioned Eichmann to open two parks to Jews, but he denied the request. Alfred and Hedwig passed lightly over their troubles. They were well, they said. They needed nothing. They hoped to see Martha soon.

Inevitably, all their letters turned to the subject of emigration. Alfred declared himself optimistic that Martha would find more sponsors to strengthen the weak affidavit. He said—with what must have been deeply mixed feelings—that Arnold and Mitzi expected to leave for Palestine in early April, and he added that he and Hedwig also might "travel" soon. Hedwig wrote that their friends the Tochs had received an affidavit for their children from "a rich man in California"—a sad reminder that they had not yet found any sponsor.

That affidavit was only for the Tochs' children. Trudy, nine, and Herbert, six, left in January 1941, on a train to Lisbon arranged through a Catholic relief organization. The organization had made arrangements for Catholic volunteers to meet the children at transfer points and in Lisbon escort them to their ship to the United States, where they would live with the strangers who had supplied the affidavits. The Tochs comforted their children, "Be brave and don't cry. We will join you soon in America." I wondered why the worldwide Catholic organization hadn't helped the whole family escape together. Bernard and Pauline never found a sponsor for themselves; they survived in Vienna because Pauline was aryan and—perhaps as crucially—because her uncle was an influential Nazi party member.

Vienna's Jews studied immigration regulations of countries around the world like holy writ, but those policies rarely worked as written. In a 1940 report the U.S. State Department's Visa Division reported that Polish, German, and Czech consuls had no more space even to file affidavit material and advised HIAS not to send any more. The U.S. Department of Labor was in arrears by thirty-one thousand requests for information. HIAS warned applicants under the German quota that new regulations might require American sponsors to establish an escrow account demonstrating that they could support the immigrant for a year. That would be a new, prohibitively high barrier—another anti-refugee, antisemitic State Department strategy for circumventing immigration law. Synchronizing documents and transportation had become so complex that applicants without help from a refugee organization had almost no chance of success, HIAS advised. Martha, Leo, Jack, and Hermann joined the more than thirteen thousand people consulting HIAS that year.

After the burst of emigration from the Reich in 1938 and 1939, the numbers of emigrants began to decline in 1940. Those who could most easily obtain visas and had money for the large expenses had already departed. Many of the refugees who could tolerate the hardships of the illegal transports to Palestine or treks over mountains were also gone. By summer 1940, 40 percent of the Jews in Vienna were over sixty years old, and women outnumbered men two to one. The penniless aging Jews who remained were not welcomed by any nation.

Alfred and Hedwig could not know much about what controlled their fate, but Leo had sensed the truth when he wrote Martha that the American consul in Nantes "didn't smell right." In June 1940, U.S. assistant secretary of state Breckenridge Long had written a memo describing the State Department's options for controlling immigration during emergencies: "We can delay and effectively stop for a temporary period of indefinite length the number of immigrants into the U.S. We could do this by simply advising our consuls to put every obstacle in the way which would postpone and postpone and postpone the granting of visas." Indeed, immigration fell from 1940 to 1941, in part because of State Department foot-dragging, as well as difficulties arising from the war—like Leo's lapsed visa.

Assistant Secretary Long also misled Congress about immigration numbers and processes and in summer 1940 helped to formulate State Department rules that cancelled all existing visas, requiring legitimate applicants to reapply from the beginning.

Long's actions seem to have been motivated partly by fears about supposed economic stress of a hypothetical mass immigration. Public hysteria over potential German spies may have moved him, too, but the restrictions also satisfied Long's avowed and ingrained antisemitism. Supported by his extensive bureaucracy, he delayed thousands of applications, most likely including Leo's, Alfred's, and Hedwig's.

In summer 1940, Alfred asked Martha, "Do you think we will be able to come to you soon?" He dropped the important question casually into the flow of conversation, just like jokes about their canary—easing the impact on Martha and the censors. The word "soon" appeared in Alfred and Hedwig's letters like a reverberating echo. Alfred and Hedwig were letting their daughter know that their situation was becoming critical, and that time was running out.

In July Hedwig expressed her delight at the news that Gretl was working in a children's home. "You know how much she loves children." She encouraged Martha not to worry, to have fun. She teased Martha that the best present she could receive for her upcoming twenty-ninth birthday would be Leo. "The way I know him, I am sure he will try everything to make this possible!...My dear Martherl, buy yourself a very fine *torte* and pretend that it is from me."

Their disciplined words allowed Alfred and Hedwig's letters to get past the censors and help maintain the family's spirits, but that summer's tension and longing hovered close to the surface. Hedwig wrote, "We hope Gretl is okay. Tomorrow it will be two years since she left." "It's always a celebration when I receive a letter from you. You know how much I like to *plauder* [chat] with you.... I'm not enjoying my English lessons any more. I think I am too old."

In July, Alfred wrote again that Uncle Arnold might leave in a couple days. He had been saying goodbye to his brother, his closest friend, for more than a year. Reliving that separation over and over must have been heart-wrenching.

The scattered family continued to stay in touch, but much of their news was not good. Alfred and Hedwig wrote Martha of their pleasure at Hugo's pictures of "little Eva" but included the news that Hugo had moved to his third apartment. Otto, no longer employed as a chemist, had sent chocolates and a photo of himself in his white coat surrounded by his students from the re-training course he taught for other Jews who, like himself, were seeking to emigrate.

Hedwig had heard from Olga that her Turkish visa was expiring; she would need to leave soon. Martha must have poured her heart out to Olga, who wrote back to Martha, "I too can't cry anymore."

On August 5, 1940, Hedwig's fifty-second birthday, she found happier news to share. At last she and Alfred had heard from "Dear Burli" in Marseille. Perhaps Leo hadn't wanted to write without good news, she surmised, because now he expected to leave for New York soon. She had been hearing similar words from Leo for nearly two years, but even so she declared herself hopeful. In fact, the reason that Leo hadn't written was that he'd been in the war zone in France, unable to write to his family in an enemy nation.

Hedwig added that her friends the Polens had agreed to make her a new suit from Martha's gray English coat. She couldn't buy fabric or new clothes, so Martha's abandoned wardrobe had turned into unexpected treasure. I loved reading this. Despite all her deprivations, Hedwig still cared how she appeared and found happiness in old clothes. Her ability to rebound from misery was extraordinary.

Alfred added a note that he couldn't write much because, "It is time for vegetables. I am canning green beans for winter." At that time in Vienna men rarely cooked or did housework, which was considered strictly women's work, but Alfred's unemployment and the crowded apartment had made a modern househusband of him, as he seemed amused to relate. But who had given them a harvest of beans? A caring neighbor? The grocer downstairs? In the midst of the Reich's rigid repression, some Viennese showed kindness to their Jewish neighbors.

In late August Alfred wrote that he wished he could hear from Gretl—that they had written her through Olga in Turkey, but heard nothing back. Ironically, that very day, Gretl was married, but the news wouldn't reach Alfred and Hedwig for six weeks. Alfred also reported, for perhaps the fifth time, that Arnold and Mitzi's transport to Palestine hadn't departed.

★

Alfred's handwriting, often a bellwether of his circumstances, tilted across the paper of his September 3 letter, running past blotches and words that were over-written. His usual signature, Papa, is illegible. "Today Uncle Arnold and Aunt Mitzi left. I was with them the whole morning at the collection place. We are scared for them, but hope they will be lucky and arrive safely."

Hedwig added, "This is a sad week because Arnold and Mitzi left today. We hope Gretl will see them soon, but know she will be sorry we can't come with them.... Tomorrow the Rathsprechers [close friends] leave for Shanghai. Almost every day we must say good-bye to dear friends. Now we will be very lonesome." These great losses had finally moved Hedwig to admit the pain she felt.

Life for Vienna's Jews continued its downward slide that fall. In September Alfred and Hedwig took in two new tenants, elderly siblings who had roomed with Arnold and Mitzi. Hedwig explained, "It's not about the money. The important thing is that they are decent people." In fact they had had no choice about accepting renters. The Reich program of concentrating Jews in shared apartments convenient for later deportation—*wohnung zuwachs*—had begun in rural Austria. Jews evicted from their small towns were forced into shared apartments in large cities, then forced again into more central, more crowded apartments.

By mid-1940 the "relocation" was running seamlessly. Waves of evictions typically began with Eichmann forcing the Jewish Community Organization to move a specified number of people from an area by a certain date; the organization identified and notified Jews of their eviction and helped them to find rooms in an approved location. Eichmann's office then dispensed the vacated apartments as political favors.

I wondered what room Alfred and Hedwig gave to the elderly siblings. Mathilde already occupied the small *kabinette*, leaving only two possibilities: the corner bedroom or the central living-dining area. Either way, privacy and a sound night's sleep must have become rare luxuries.

Once more Martha expressed concern about the work the roomers would cause Hedwig, but Hedwig deflected her daughter's worry with joking irony: "I cannot complain about too much space in our apartment. You can imagine what it looks like. I wish I had more time to learn English, but it's not only time I need, but also that my brain should work better."

Alfred explained their new situation more clearly: "The new tenants, a man of circa 72 and lady of 77 will stay with us. You are probably very curious how it looks in our apartment. On the wall where your couch was is now as follows. The wardrobe is next to the door, then a night table, the two beds in the middle of the room. In the corner is one night table. By the window, the desk. We gave the wash stand to Aunt Tilde.... Now, to your letter, we are not allowed to send pictures."

Their next letter again attempted cheer, but it, too, faltered. They spoke of their Rosh Hashanah [Jewish New Year] gathering with friends. The brothers in Prague had sent a box of apples. There was no news from Gretl. Alfred complained, "I hope she is all right. Is she married? Did you give her Uncle Zalan's address [the Swiss mail connection]? We have not had news from her for so long. We will try to have nice holidays and think of you. We had a card from the Rathsprechers from Moscow. Maybe they are in Shanghai. No news from Uncle Arnold. We were told that now we can send just one page of stationery in one envelope, otherwise I would write more."

Alfred and Hedwig had become increasingly isolated. Six weeks after Gretl's August 28 wedding, they finally received her forwarded letter telling them that she was married. Alfred wrote to Martha, "You cannot imagine how happy we were about Gretl's wedding. If we know you both are happy, we are too, and we hope the time will come when we are all together. Richard is in a small town near Budapest. Still no news from Uncle Arnold. Our friends are all very helpful, especially on the left side where you often used to practice your piano. We can visit our former greengrocer.... Winter is here."

Alfred mentioned that he and Hedwig had received help from friends and neighbors—including probably the grocer in their building, a bright note that surely offered comfort to Martha and Gretl, who must have known those unnamed people. On her half page Hedwig wrote to both Martha and Gretl in a confusion of pronouns: "Now I understand the dream I had on Rosh Hashanah. I stood in front of the temple and you [Gretl?] came out with a young man and quite a few people. I kissed Gretl and cried so hard I woke up. How much I would like to visit her even for a few hours. The same for you [Martha?], so far away."

Loneliness and longing pervaded these letters. As a mother, I felt Hedwig's anguish and the cruelty of her situation. At the end of October Alfred wrote again. Hedwig's sewing project, repurposing Martha's coat, had turned out well, he said: "Dear mama wore her new suit from your coat for the first time for Yom Kippur, and I can tell you it is beautiful. We received a long letter from Richard, with another new address in Teplice [a small Czech health resort town]. Excuse me if I do not write clearly. The days are dark and gloomy.... The dull days are not pleasant. We now have a *hausfreund* [house friend]. Aunt Tilde has one too."

To me, Hedwig's new suit and Alfred's "beautiful," meant that the spark of life still flamed brightly in them on that holiday. So much had been taken away, yet their love for each other, and their resilience in the grimmest of times, were moving.

The "house-friend" was a small perforated tin box to fill with coal and set on a metal surface to serve as a makeshift heater and stove. Military demands for coal and severe rationing for Jews had caused shortages. Hedwig elaborated, trying to remain cheerful: "We have a new friend in the house. It gets warm very fast. Water boils in a few minutes.... Please tell Leo to hurry to be with you. I would love to cook his favorite food, the *serviette knödel*, before I forget how to do it."

New patterns were emerging in Alfred and Hedwig's letters. They were now sending more greetings to friends who had reached the United States than news about friends who were still trapped in Vienna. The departure of so many friends was a significant loss—and a reminder of their own peril.

They had also begun to speak more plainly. Hedwig sometimes ended her letters with a plea: "Dear Martherl, try everything to get us over. I hope, with God's help, it will be very soon. Then we will have lots of time to chat." As hoped-for avenues of escape disappeared, their cour-age seemed to be faltering.

With war shortages pinching all Viennese, the Reich's propaganda machine operated at full tilt that fall to keep public morale high. Recall-ing Austria's former glory days as a world empire, the Viennese celebrated Axis victories across Europe and welcomed visits from Hitler, Goering, victorious troops, and world leaders—foreign ministers from Italy, Japan, Hungary, and Romania.

Goebbels released an emotional antisemitic propaganda film, *Jud Süss*, portraying Jews as an international threat. Required viewing for all Reich officials and their families, it inflamed antisemitic hysteria across Nazi Europe. In that contrived atmosphere, deportation rumors terrorized Vienna's Jews but seemed not to raise concern among other Viennese. The scope and subtlety of Germany's preparations for mass deportations of Vienna's Jews astonished me; Sidney was less surprised at the layers of insidious planning and the exportation of hatred.

Despite the trauma she and Alfred were undergoing, Hedwig's mask was back in place in her November 1 letter. She described her new routine mechanically: "We are well, thank God. I get up at six in the morning, prepare something for the midday meal, fix breakfast for all our tenants. At nine, I tidy up until about ten-thirty. At eleven I shop because it's not possible earlier. I'm usually home by noon, then I prepare the meal.... I'm still trying to learn a little English."

Alfred spoke with recovering spirits, his humor having found a new subject: "We have everything we need. We have potatoes! We have to be inventive to find places for them. They are in good little boxes near the front door, new decoration for the front hall. In the kitchen, the towers are surely to the ceiling. We have enough space because the *kabinette* desk now stands where the kitchen sideboard was. We conducted electric-ity there so mama can see to work. Besides my English studying, I am quite busy. The stove is completely my province, as well as drying the dishes, helping carry groceries home.... Please write the American con-sulate providing testimonials."

Little boxes. Potatoes. Alfred inserted a few English words, showing off. After two years without work and now devoting his time to house-keeping tasks, he seemed focused and determined and full of purpose, not crushed. Martha may have wondered, where had the potatoes come from? Had they sold their sideboard for potatoes? Were there exposed wires looping across their kitchen walls?

Two weeks later, Hedwig, too, seemed to have recovered some strength: "English lessons are more interesting now. The teacher said we've made progress, and I think so too. Otherwise I am very busy, not bored. It's good that we don't have much time to think.... the consul tells us that they cannot send the documents."

I didn't know what documents Alfred and Hedwig requested, but reading that letter I recalled the State Department's deliberate obstructions and delays. In New York, Martha continued her quest for more support for the weak affidavit. She asked everyone she knew—and some she didn't.

On November 26, Alfred wrote, "We received a cable that all three ships with Arnold and Mitzi reached their destination. They will see Gretl!! We would like to do the same.... I have new tasks. Yesterday I rolled out many rolls and *lebkuchen* [gingerbread] cookies.... Congratulations on your raise."

Hedwig added, "Apparently Gretl's letter with pictures was lost again. I would have loved to read it. I am jealous about Uncle and Aunt. They will soon be able to see her."

Alfred and Hedwig had tried to reach Palestine, but they had been low on the list of hundreds of thousands of European Jews vying for limited space. Imagining the family together there without them must have been another painful blow.

But Arnold and Mitzi had sent their cable too soon. They had not landed in Palestine—and their journey had been terrifying. They had written while they were still anchored in Haifa's harbor, interdicted by the British and forbidden entry, as Leo had been in Havana Harbor.

Two years later, from Mauritius, Arnold wrote a short account of their journey down the Danube with eighteen hundred other Jews escaping on

a ship meant for five hundred. In the Black Sea those passengers, along
with other escaping Jews, transferred to three leaky old ships with minimal
food, water, and sanitation. Some weeks later they docked in Crete, where
the bodies of the first dead from typhus were unloaded. After a two-month
journey of missteps and mistakes, the three ships reached Haifa's harbor,
only to be intercepted by the British. There, shortly after Arnold sent his
joyful cable, radical underground Zionists, intending to lightly damage
one ship and force the British to allow the hobbled ship to dock, bombed
it too heavily. It sank, drowning 254 refugees, as Arnold and Mitzi watched
in horror. The British transferred all surviving refugees to a transport that
sailed to a prison camp on Mauritius in the Indian Ocean, a fever-stricken
island east of Madagascar. They were to wait out the war there.

After her parents' mid-November letter, Martha heard nothing more
from them for six weeks. Finally, on December 23, 1940, Hedwig sent
an unusual, disjointed narration: "We are well, but we had a big change
here. Dear Aunt Tilde lives with a very nice couple in one room. We could
only keep our bedroom furniture, sewing machine, and a little table
because the tenants also brought a few pieces of furniture with them. We
moved last Monday, just a week ago today."

The news was scrambled. Hedwig could not bring herself to begin
with or clearly relate the shocking news. She avoided explaining that she
and Alfred been evicted from their apartment of thirty-one years, instead
rambling on about the brothers in Prague and a food box from an American aid organization: "We supposed it was from you. We thank you a
thousand times but I ask you, do not do it again.... I don't have much
work here cooking. I make simple meals."

Alfred and Hedwig had found shelter with long-time family friends,
the Russos, the aunt and uncle of Martha's musical friends the Galimirs.
Hedwig stuck to light topics, except for one note of sorrow that escaped
her self-control: "How are all of you? I wish I could see you and Gretl....
While I am writing, papa is in the next room with Russos.... Usually we
have breakfast with them because we have little space in our room. We
live in the last room. You will probably remember what it looked like.

Aunt Tilde and the couple are in the third room.... We are not doing well with our English. We cannot take lessons here. We do not have the space or the peace for it."

Alfred added a short message, scattered, and evasive: "We did not write because we didn't have time. Now everything is in order again.... Tomorrow is your anniversary. Fortunately, we could move in with the Russos. It's better to be with good friends than with strangers. We will try to keep in touch with all our other friends.... We miss our neighbors."

The Russos, their friends and landlords, added a few lines: "We are very happy that we have your dear parents with us. The room is very small but you can be assured we will do everything to make it cozy and comfortable for them. Michel Russo." "Please do not worry about your parents. We hope they will be happy in our home. Angela Russo."

Alfred, Hedwig, and Mathilde had been caught in the Nazis' ghettoization machine. The Russos lived at Aegidigasse 5, Entry II, 4th floor, Number 27. Their quiet street was a few minutes' walk from Schmalzhofgasse and Martha and Leo's former Mittelgasse apartment, but their building was larger and had wood-paneled elevators—which Jews were not allowed to use. Sidney and I saw it when we were in Vienna.

Martha must have wondered what had happened to the rest of her parents' furniture. Did they give it to friends? Sell it? Had they trudged down the familiar apartment stairs clutching photos and Leo's paintings? Walked neighborhood sidewalks carrying suitcases or boxes of dishes? Where in their new apartment could they put Alfred's canned beans? And Hansi?

Their forced move was a shock to the whole family. It had been tempting to believe that Alfred's blindness would protect them, as it had for more than two years—that what had happened to others would not happen to them. But Vienna was marching to the German drumbeat that winter, and Alfred and Hedwig's situation rapidly grew more precarious.

More important than the words Alfred and Hedwig wrote that December was what they could not say. Their overcrowded situation was not sustainable, and the Germans did not intend for Jews to remain caged in ghettoized apartments. Orders were already trickling down through the bureaucracy for five transports to depart Vienna that spring, each carrying a thousand Jews to Poland.

CHAPTER 28

Bitter

December 1940–June 1941

Winter 1940 blew into Europe early. It was a pivotal, turbulent, chaotic, and unpredictable time throughout the world. In January, after painstaking negotiations, the Soviet Union and Germany renewed their nonaggression pact—at the same time that German generals were fine-tuning plans for Operation Barbarossa, the code name for a massive German invasion of the Soviet Union.

Preparing for combat in the east, Germany labored to stabilize its Western European conquests and bring Britain to its knees. Instead, Germany encountered widening war across the British Empire and fierce resistance in Britain itself. Few merchant marine vessels from any country escaped attack that winter. Areas once distant from the conflict—from Greece to the Canary Islands, from Libya to New Zealand—were sucked into war.

The United States was drifting into danger. Daily headlines across the country featured news about battles in Europe, North Africa, and China. Although the United States continued to espouse neutrality, Congress had instituted the nation's first peacetime draft that September. The compromise measure restricted service to one year, only within the western hemisphere. An inadequate budget meant that soldiers trained with wooden sticks instead of guns. Yet the U.S. Army doubled in size from a small peacekeeping force the size of New York City's police department to 270,000 soldiers.

Recognizing the need for a firm hand to steer America's course in troubling times, President Roosevelt took to the airwaves on December 29, 1940, to deliver a major national address. Dramatically describing the horrors of Nazi aggression and its growing threat to America, he framed the decision to provide arms to the Allies through the Lend-Lease Act in terms of the financial benefit to America, the defense of democracy, and American national security.

Isolationists and xenophobic conservatives staged mass rallies and radio campaigns protesting the United States' slide toward war. They railed against Communists, socialists, atheists, a multi-ethnic world, and immigration, which, they warned, threatened America's white, Christian, democratic culture. "The people of Europe don't ask us to do their fighting," Roosevelt argued over their voices. "We must be the great arsenal of democracy."

American Jewish groups' response to Nazi persecution was hobbled by their own fear of antisemitic reprisals and of accusations that they were pushing the United States into war. Bills framed by a Jewish Congressman proposing increased immigration were met with threats in Congress to cut off all immigration. Roosevelt privately called on Jewish leaders to minimize publicity that could upset America's delicate balance between neutrality and war.

American Jews donated generously to a large rescue effort, contributing millions to Jewish communities in Germany and Austria to help Jews pay exorbitant German exit taxes, fees, penalties, and immigration costs, but they agreed to mute their public protests.

Stymied in their effort to mobilize public opinion, some American Jews turned to alter egos—artistic creations that demonstrated their patriotism and excoriated Nazis. That tumultuous winter two young Jews, Joe Simon and Jack Kirby, invented "Captain America," the nation's newest cartoon superhero, who fought Nazis and socked Hitler in the jaw. Martha may have seen *Casablanca*, the 1942 anti-Nazi film inspired by events in Vienna and written by three American Jews, Howard and Julius Epstein and Howard Koch. At the 1940 San Francisco World's Fair, an audience of fifteen hundred rose to their feet to join Jewish songwriter Irving Berlin in an emotional rendition of his song "God Bless America." The Ku Klux Klan reacted vehemently, urging Americans never to sing that "Jew song."

★

As the world careened toward war, the Berger family remained trapped—Leo in the Pyrenees, Alfred and Hedwig in Vienna. In Palestine, Gretl agonized over her imperiled family and worried for her own security as Arabs garnered German support for their fight against Jews. In New York, Martha was increasingly discouraged. She told Leo of her fears for her parents and admitted that she no longer had the heart to play the piano.

That winter, for the first time, Martha began to write weary complaints and impatient criticisms of Leo. She said that he should write only in English and with greater care. Had he tried to find a flight to Lisbon or asked his friend in Spain for help crossing the border? Couldn't he find a ship from Marseille to Lisbon? She said she had little time for friends or relaxation and always felt tired: "You said that I don't write often.... When I told that to Ruth, she laughed and said 'If only he would know, you write every free minute.' When you will be with me, [God willing] you will complain because I have to write so much."

At that time Martha was corresponding with nearly twenty family members plus friends and recent immigrants who knew Leo from France. She worked forty hours, taught five piano lessons a week, and contacted agencies in New York, Washington, D.C., France, and Vienna. Her patience, emotions, and physical strength were all fraying as she strove to bring her family together. "I am losing all my courage," she wrote Leo.

When guards had stopped Leo at the Spanish border the previous fall, Martha had offered steadfast, loving support. During this tumultuous winter it was Leo's turn to give comfort. From a distance and across the black hole of time between letters, he tried to shore up her spirits:

> My dear Girlie. Happy is the person who has some entertainment. I am glad when you are able to have some fun. When I come to my Mädi [girl] I can catch up on all the wonderful things....You wrote me about two new dresses from Ruth. Use them in happiness.... I will be able to buy you everything soon.
>
> You write that this torture is hard on you. My dear, don't despair. Pull yourself together and see things from the good side. Do it for us. Be courageous and patient. Everything will be ok soon. I pull myself together simply because of you.... I understand how much trouble you go to for me. It seems without end. I hope you understand your Burli. I don't like it either. I thank you dear Jack too for so much trouble.

At Martha's prodding, Leo began, sometimes, to write in English: "It is very needful to have all prepared, in order to don't hesitate the matters. It is also needful in order to forget so many troubles.... Do not be so sorrowful.... We must hope. It is the best we can do."

He worried about her. "Till what a clock are you working?" "Are you eating enough?" "I would be very glad to be with you now and I could more care for you." He responded gently to her suggestions. "No, to answer you, it isn't possible for my Spanish friend to invite me there." It was no longer possible to travel to Palestine, Shanghai, or Lisbon, he told her. "That occasion is passed.... I have to wait." Then he joked,

> Enis wrote and knowledged me he have visited you, and I should be glad you are very good looking.... I am wondering that you don't mention it. Now I know why you are coming so late home my little bad girlie.... Nevertheless I would like

to see you soon. I will pay out you for all. I don't fear there would be many kisses. Excuse many mistakes. I have written in haste. You suppose I will complain about your big correspondence. On the contrary, I will help you....

Much love, your bad boy, Leo

Martha wrote, in English, that she was lonely and "breaking my head why no letters come from you, my dear one."

By late February 1941 she had begun to recover from her lowest, most dejected mood: "Don't worry about whether I am sick, it is warm in the house and I am able to stand much, only the worries...make me sad. I know that my little husband has a good nature and courage. I try to do the same, even when it is hard to hope the best after so many disappointings."

★

In Vienna, Alfred and Hedwig were fighting a vastly different battle from Leo. While Leo strove to remain free of German control, the Reich already held Alfred and Hedwig in its grasp. Their letters about their forced move did not reach Martha until seven weeks after they had been evicted from their apartment; three more letters they wrote that January never arrived at all. By intercepting Jews' mail during evictions and deportations, Germany diminished unfavorable world attention and defused the fury of American Jews and the horror of the American public—which might disrupt the flow of Jewish aid money into the Reich or propel the United States into war. German leaders also worried about shocking their own citizens, who might be repulsed by the cruelty around them. Even so, Germany pushed ahead; collection of Jews in a central area had become a high priority.

Alfred and Hedwig wrote again in early February, describing their changed situation almost casually and expressing relief that they, along with Mathilde and two other Jews, had been able to move in with dear friends rather than strangers. There was no common space left in their new home, they explained, but at least each family had a bedroom.

Hedwig wrote with her familiar ironic humor that they had recently attended their first "concert" since the Anschluss. They had reveled in Mendelssohn's violin concerti and the Sarasate gypsy songs, she enthused, and then explained: what they had so enjoyed was a recording of the celebrated Galimir string quartet—Martha's friends, the niece and nephew of the Russos, with whom they were now living.

Hedwig reported, too, that she spent several days each week helping in a food kitchen, but teased that her favorite "work" was chatting with Martha. "If only we could talk face to face." Sidney and I noted that, despite the intense persecution, Hedwig had again found ways to maintain her self-respect, making her miserable situation bearable.

Alfred added only that months had passed since they had heard from Arnold and Mitzi. Though he and Hedwig had tried to conceal their emotions, Martha knew very well the strength required to write a chatty letter from hell.

★

Despite their ceaseless efforts, the family's escape plans were not working. As the Nazi war on Jews advanced relentlessly, two years of attempts to get Alfred and Hedwig out of Austria had failed. Instead of Leo reaching New York in spring 1939, finding work, and helping Martha and Jack to bring Alfred and Hedwig to America, he was trapped and in peril. The family's limited resources were diverted to help him escape. Hermann and Lisl had not established successful businesses as they had envisioned, and though impoverished, they were besieged by pleas for affidavits from Mathilde, Richard, the Grünberger brothers in Czechoslovakia, and Hermann's in-laws.

Vienna's Jews, forbidden access to any media, lived with rumors—some true, some born of fear and isolation, still others planted by Nazi disinformation and propaganda. Deportation rumors flew through the

Jewish community again that winter, but this gossip originated in the truth: debate was raging in the German hierarchy over what would be next stage in the Nazi solution to "the Jewish problem."

The slowdown in Jewish emigration had come as no surprise to Nazi leaders; exporting virulent antisemitism and stealing Jewish assets, they had engineered the problem themselves. A January 1939 German foreign ministry circular described the Nazi "revolution" as "an earthquake with distinct tremors" that would destroy Germany's enemy, the Jews, even in distant countries.

A flood tide of impoverished Jews forced out of Germany would cause an international reaction, the circular continued. Borders around the world would close. "The poorer the Jewish immigrant, the greater burden he constitutes, the stronger the reaction, and the more receptive to German anti-Semitic propaganda."

The circular described the "tremors" caused by Germany's international antisemitism. "Germany has an important interest in seeing the splintering of Jews," who might work against German interests abroad. "It must be an aim of German foreign policy to strengthen the wave of anti-Semitism."

But by early 1941 German planners promoting the worldwide campaign against Jews still hadn't decided what to do with the hundreds of thousands of Jews remaining under Reich control. As reports, memos, and heated arguments circulated among Germany's leaders—not about whether the Reich should expel Jews, but about how—Hitler lost patience and summarily ordered deportations to the East. On January 30 the Viennese celebrated the "German Revolution's eighth anniversary" of Hitler's appointment as chancellor. Two days later, Eichmann confirmed the rumors by summoning the Jewish Community Organization's president and informing him that deportations would begin immediately. The first train, carrying nearly a thousand Jews, left Vienna for Poland on February 16, 1941. Four more trains followed within a month.

With no sponsor or visa, no viable way to emigrate, Alfred and Hedwig were vulnerable. In Vienna's shrinking Jewish community, they would have understood their imminent danger, yet their letter of February 25 to Martha does not mention it. Instead, they wrote about a crocheted blanket Hedwig was planning to make for Gretl, and about Alfred's gratitude for the Russos' help. "We would prefer to visit you rather than going elsewhere," Hedwig said casually. "Do you hear from the rabbi who promised to help us? We hope we will have more good news from you. Maybe someone will help you with the affidavit."

The reference to a blanket was surprising. Had Hedwig heard good news about Gretl? If so, this was the first hint of it in her letters, which continued to be full of the news of friends leaving. Alfred and Hedwig's English teacher would depart for Shanghai in April, she said. There was some undescribed bad news from Steinhardt. Their close friends the Tochs wanted to follow their children to the United States. "We would like to travel with them," Hedwig wrote forlornly. The Russos had an affidavit and ticket from their niece in America, she added, and they expected to leave by April. It may have seemed to Alfred and Hedwig that they were the only Jews who had not found a way out. They didn't mention that if the Russos departed they would be forced to move again. "In the evening we usually sit and talk about you and all the relatives who are not here anymore.... Do you see our old friends? We have fewer and fewer to visit."

Martha, still lagging six weeks or longer in receiving the mail from Vienna, wrote to Leo in March that she had received a second letter from her parents about their move. "No one is better off now. I can't tell you how bad I feel."

That winter Alfred had adopted a newly gentle, supportive tone with Martha, his daughter with whom he had been strict, sometimes authoritarian, as she grew up. "It would be so wonderful if we could all be together, but do not worry too much if things do not always work the way we think they should.... Dear Martherl, keep your hope up."

The family had more unhappy news to deal with that winter. Hedwig wrote, "I wish you much luck my dearest Martha and to dearest Gretl. Tell her how much I think about her and keep her in my thoughts...."

Please pass on my whole-hearted condolences for the loss of the dear child." Two months after it had occurred, Alfred and Hedwig learned that Gretl had suffered a miscarriage. They were growing ever more distant from their daughters, and their loving letters had begun to sound like farewells.

The winter deportations to Poland proved disastrous for all involved. As in the Nisko fiasco of the previous year, the Germans had organized only transportation. Thousands of Jews sent to Opole and other Polish towns encountered scarce food, water, and sanitation. Disease and death tore through wretched, overcrowded camps and makeshift housing. International news reports resulted in an outpouring of aid to victims. But the most effective protests came from German military in Poland, warning that the typhus epidemic among the deportees threatened troops in the region. Military readiness in advance of the top-secret Operation Barbarossa, not international pressure or humanitarian concern, persuaded Hitler to suspend the deportations.

Germany's winter of indecision had passed. On March 1, 1941, anticipating an influx of Jews and Soviet prisoners of war, Reich Security Chief Himmler directed the expansion of Auschwitz to accommodate at least a hundred thousand more inmates. Himmler also ordered mandatory reporting of all apartments occupied by Jews in aryan buildings.

Although Alfred and Hedwig muted their growing desperation and presented a brave front to Martha, she anguished over their situation. In late February, she wrote Leo that "I have trouble about my dear ones and am often afraid.... The dear parents are in terrible fear."

In March Martha fought melancholy with redoubled efforts and a new plan. Unable to bear her parents' plight, she wrote Leo, "You see I made out an affidavit for my dear parents. I know it is not strong enough, but I want to do my best. I always hope to get a strong one. Until now, I have not been so lucky, but I do not give up."

Her desperate strategy of combining letters of support from different sponsors was not promising. She reported her earnings at Hopp Press, $13.20 a week, plus $13.80 from piano lessons. She pressured Hermann again. Jack wrote a letter, as did Hermann's brother-in-law. "Friendship" letters were not equivalent to sponsorship, but Martha pressed on and found others who were willing to add their names.

She had also attempted to raise money for her parents' ship tickets. "I ran around from one bank to another, to committees and all kinds of places. I finally borrowed $100, only an eighth of what tickets to America cost but I could not get more. I will try to cable it to [the Vienna Jewish Community] and hope that the parents get at least some more from the organization there. If I should get an affidavit, then, I'll see what I can do next. It is hard everywhere, especially with money.... If only I would have you here. Everything would be easier. I can't imagine it. It would be too beautiful."

She admitted to some impatience with Leo: "What I wrote concerning your letters was to punish you a little, because you never write carefully. I am a little hurt if you do not take time to write without forgetting several words. But I am not angry. I know it is hard. I personally would prefer to speak to you and even give you a kiss, if you are good."

★

Martha cabled her parents about the affidavit, omitting the identity of the sponsor: herself. With the news of the affidavit, Alfred and Hedwig's spirits soared. They wrote Martha five letters in March, more than in any month since she had left. "We hope, with G-d's help, we will be able to come soon, dear Martha." The Russos wrote to their niece in America who had provided their affidavit, and the niece offered to add her support for Alfred and Hedwig.

"We thank you for the stronger affidavit. We thank you with all our heart," Alfred replied. "We hope you will tell us more about it. An affidavit from whom? I believe it should work out now. I can't put into words how much we appreciate it."

Hedwig responded, "We were happy to receive your cable and hope we have made a big step forward. I am excited about our affidavit. We hope to hear more about it soon. It probably is a very good person to whom we will be thankful all our lives. Please tell him this. We hope we will not have another disappointment."

At the end of March, Hedwig was still exuberant. "It's a special day when we receive a letter from you, especially when you tell us about your future plans for us." She and Alfred wrote Martha about several Seder meals with friends, celebrating Passover, the Jewish holiday of escape and freedom.

Martha had hidden the truth about the affidavit's weakness. Had she persuaded herself of its strength? Even as their hopes brightened, Alfred and Hedwig's real prospects were dimming. Hedwig wrote at the end of March that—as Leo had already explained to Martha—it was no longer possible to immigrate to Shanghai. Alfred and Hedwig's English teacher, Mr. Schreier, had planned to travel there but instead would continue to give them lessons. A few weeks later, Hedwig wrote that Palestine, too, was no longer feasible from Vienna.

What Hedwig wrote was true. That spring Britain and the United States declared Shanghai's international area indefensible and abandoned the city. Japanese troops quickly occupied the entire city, where there were twenty thousand Jews and thousands of other unprotected foreign nationals. The Rathsprechers, the Bergers' friends, were alive, but the Japanese—at Hitler's urging—restricted Shanghai Jews to a ghetto rife with disease.

Signs of worsening trouble for Vienna's Jews were everywhere. The Jewish Community Organization's charity food kitchen had closed for lack of money, Hedwig wrote, and the Community no longer offered financial help for emigration. Mathilde complained to Hermann that another renter now shared her bedroom, which was so small that they took the extra mattress up during the day so that they could move about. Nazis began deducting the value of food sent to Jews from their rations.

Martha poured out her worries to Leo: "Dearest…. When I come home and ask if there is mail and it is only from New York, Ruth will answer NO. When I hunger for mail, this is always the rule about letters from all my dear ones. No mail this week.... I hope, God willing, next week will bring a larger affidavit from a friend of Uncle Hermann's. Now the big question is where to get the money for the ship tickets. What to take from. Both of them together cost $800."

Two days later, she wrote, "Thank God, the parents are in good health, as far as they will tell us. They only wish they could stay where they are. The Russos even read for my father. My dear parents beg me to book passage for them. My heart hurts because I don't know what I shall do. I will try to get one part from the [Vienna Jewish Community], and then try to borrow the rest from a bank.... It is easy to say that I should not worry. I can't enjoy anything as long as I am alone. Remain in good health and be lucky."

Alfred's letter of April 7 is splotched and smeared. He makes no statement indicating the cause of his distress, but a change is obvious. He may have heard news about the affidavit from the consulate. He wrote, "If everything remains the same, we will have to have patience until we will be together. In the meantime, you should not worry about us anymore. It is spring here, and we can walk on the avenue in the afternoon."

Hedwig's spirits, too, had collapsed. She reported that the earliest passage the Russos' daughter could book for her parents was a year away. Other friends—the Neukrafters, Tochs, and Jedlinskis—had arranged tickets for January and February 1942. "Now you can imagine how long it will be until we can leave. Yesterday, we found out that everything is booked until then." She said that they had received a cable from Arnold and Mitzi with the news that they had not reached Palestine. "Everybody thought that leaving would be much easier. Now, I know it's the opposite."

Again, Hedwig's information was accurate. In June 1939, 123 ships had reached New York harbor from Europe. By June 1941 that number had fallen to 12, most of them from Lisbon.

Martha's letters—carrying reassurance, but also important and time-sensitive plans for the future—continued to take six weeks from the time she mailed them to be delivered. Alfred and Hedwig clung to their remaining shreds of hope. They would try to get their passport renewed, they told her, and hoped to use them before they expired again, in a year. "Perhaps we will find somebody who will help us. Here we can't hope for this."

★

As Alfred and Hedwig's chances for immigration diminished, Leo— still in France—was seeing signs that his three years of effort might finally bear fruit. Claiming caution over spies entering the United States, the State Department had added new regulations and required documents to the immigration process. But in February Leo received the new document that had taken him, Martha, Jack, and Aunt Anna months to acquire. His "Morality Guarantee" attested that Leo had never been found guilty of a crime or involved in subversive or political activities deemed unfriendly to America. The requirement was intended to bar Communists, atheists, criminals, and hordes of other "undesirables"; the guarantee was as crucial as an affidavit.

By early March Leo's situation was changing with the speed of a runaway train; he redoubled his efforts to keep pace. The month had begun with his formal, meticulously crafted letter handwritten in German to "Honorable Sirs"—probably at HICEM in Marseille: "May I permit myself to pose a request and several questions regarding important opportunities to arrange some things?" Leo had explained that his American visa had expired in Nantes six months before. He had completed the forms required to extend it. His affidavit and morality certificate had recently been sent to Marseille. Had his dossier been forwarded from Nantes? When his papers were in order, would they recommend that he come to Marseille? Would he need a safe conduct voucher? A ship's passage had been purchased for him in New York, he concluded—without mentioning that he had already missed its departure.

Leo wrote Martha in English that HICEM had informed him they would work with the consulate about his case. This was a major step forward. He told her that he had applied again for a visa de sortie—his exit visa—and he was waiting, waiting for any news from the consul in Marseille. He dared to hope that this time would be different: "The secretary from the Comité here and his family are our good friends who can cause some speeding.... every day [wasted] could be very costly. I have enough experience of that. I hope it will come to an end now.... It is a pity for every lost day. You can imagine how I am anzious [sic] to see you again."

Leo's assessment of lost days as costly and dangerous was no exaggeration. A few miles from his Pyrenees refuge, the French government had interned four thousand refugees at the infamous Gurs camp; another seventy-five thousand prisoners, most of them Jewish, would arrive soon. Hundreds of inmates would die there of disease—and thousands would be deported to their deaths.

Martha, too, felt change in the air. Hope at last seemed more than an empty word. She sent a quick note: "Last night I dreamt that you wrote that you would leave in the middle of the month. Allwei! [Let it be so]"

In mid-March, the mountain moved. The first sign of solid progress that Leo had seen in nine months was a copy of his letter to HICEM returned to him with the word "CONVOCATION" scrawled across the top. That single word meant that his case would be considered; sometime soon he would receive an invitation to appear at the consulate on a designated day with all of his documents in hand for a face-to-face meeting with the official on duty. That meeting would decide the next turn of his fate—whether his visa would be approved, allowing him to immigrate to the United States, or rejected, probably condemning him to internment by the Vichy national police.

In late March more documents arrived in Luchon. An exit visa. A letter from the consul that had traveled first to HICEM in Marseille, then to the Luchon Comité, and finally, to Leo: "We have the honor to call for the presence of Mr. Leib Cizes, protégé. It was decided to hold convocation in Marseille. Please tell M Cizes to present himself in April...."

Papers. Words. It was impossible to know whether, in the end, the documents would be worth the money they had cost, the stamps and signatures that covered the pages, and the time and tears expended to acquire them. This was the appointment he had striven so long to attain. But Leo had learned that documents spoke a language of their own. They promised action, but he wouldn't know their value until he boarded a ship, crossed a border, and landed in America.

★

Leo was on the move. On March 16, Martha wrote him in Luchon, but he was not there to receive her letter. He had obtained a safe conduct pass from the French National Police valid for one six-day trip to Marseille beginning April 1. He had left his mountain niche abruptly, and Martha's letter was forwarded to Marseille, *poste restante*, where it was stamped with a Nazi swastika and "*Oberkommando der Wehrmacht*"—the German military censor operating in Marseille.

How Leo spent his time in Marseille, where he stayed, and how he lived, can be established only sketchily through documents, but it is clear that the harrowing thirty-nine-day experience pushed him to near collapse. What is known:

April 4- In Marseille, Leo received a letter from HICEM informing him that the consulate would be closed until April 8, two days after his safe conduct pass expired.

April 7- Jack and Martha sent Leo a telegram: "Lisbon. Offer Leo Cizes Tourist Second. Siboney. Option May Fifth." They had obtained passage for him from Lisbon, but he had no way to get there.

April 9- French police extended his safe conduct pass to April 18.

April 11- French police requested that Leo return to the Prefecture.

April 29- After weeks of not writing, Leo sent an airmail letter
in English, to Martha. It is smeared, scribbled first in faint
almost invisible lines, then in dark ink with rushed words,
mistakes, and cross outs: "I received your letters.... Excuse
that I didn't answer at once. I wanted to write some decisions
at last. After many troubles and time, I can tell you about
my case now, that I can obtain passage via Martinique...."

The Caribbean again? All conversation had been about Lisbon,
where hotels overflowed with Europe's refugees and once-quiet neighborhoods rang like the Tower of Babel with the voices of anxious travelers
from around the world. "By the United States Export Line," Leo wrote,
"I would have to wait until 1942, and HICEM likewise. For this ticket
[by way of the Caribbean island of Martinique] I am grateful to my friend
Dr. Feuer who forwarded money to pay for passage. Otherwise I was at
a loss how to pay.... Now my dear you can annihilate the United States
Export Line [sailing out of Lisbon in neutral Portugal] because till now
didn't come an answer. I hope to set out in early May...."

Leo's ticket was a gamble. While the ship he had borrowed money
to sail on would leave "in early May," his appointment at the U.S. consulate was on May 3.

Leo wrote that the voyage to Martinique would take three weeks;
he would wait there for a steamer to New York. Feuer would travel with
him. His four other companions in Luchon were still waiting for their
papers. "With HICEM, I had very hard to fight till they helped me a
little. They couldn't get an answer from HIAS. You can hardly imagine
how I was at a loss. There are so many expenses. Excuse that I am not
much writing.... I am got quite tired."

On April 30, unaware of these new developments, Martha wrote
to "My sweet little Leo" to explain that the United States Export Line
had told her they could not manage a ticket sooner than midsummer.
"I was there and begged, but could not change it. What do you think?
Will you be able to come to Lisbon?" She told him not to worry about

his suitcases or his clothes. "You just try to come out however you are, in pajamas if you want."

Jack also wrote to him: "My dear Leo, I have written you so often hoping that by the time the letter arrived you would be on your way.... I hesitate to express that hope again.... You may be assured that when you do come, you will be very welcome, and we shall do everything possible."

On May 3, the American consulate filled out Leo's Alien Registration Form, two brief pages, with surprisingly few words. "*Name*: Leo Cizes. *Proposed U.S. address*: [Jack's home address on Long Island.] *Birthplace*: Trembowla, Poland. *Citizenship*: Without nationality. *Whether alien expects to remain permanently*: Permanently."

The all-important morality guarantee attesting that he was not a threat to the U.S. government required just one word on that form: No—and the form was complete. It was signed Leib Cizes, and below that was the signature of Vice Consul of the United States of America Hiram Bingham Jr.

The document lacked the stamps and flurry of writing that accompanied French documents of far lesser importance, but it was all that Leo needed to enter the United States.

As unlucky as Leo had been during the previous three years, the final signature on his visa registration was a lightning bolt of good fortune. Hiram Bingham was a young diplomat who swam against the tide of State Department's practices of delay, deception, and subterfuge. During Bingham's truncated tenure in Marseille, less than a year, he legally and expeditiously saved as many as twenty-five hundred refugees. When grateful praise from rescued immigrants and news of the increased activity in the Marseille Consulate reached higher levels of the State Department, Bingham was transferred to Argentina, his career effectively at an end. Leo had been one of his last cases—the form finalized, in fact, after Bingham's own scheduled departure date.

Leo had understood the dangers closing in on him when he had written Martha that he had no time for delay. Increased State Department scrutiny and the upheavals of the war had caused immigration to the United States from German-occupied and collaborationist countries to plummet 38 percent between 1940 and 1941. Immigration would stop completely in July, as the State Department's newest regulations forced thousands of refugees to re-apply with an entirely new set of documents. Later that month the United States would close its consulates in occupied countries, making the issuance of visas for Jews still trapped in German-controlled lands practically impossible.

By July, twenty-six thousand Jews had been imprisoned in camps in unoccupied Vichy France and French North Africa. Of those twenty-six thousand, only thirteen refugees would emigrate during the next three months. Just months after Leo departed, the Germans—with French assistance—began deporting Jews from all parts of France to Auschwitz.

But Leo was heading west, not east. On May 9, aboard ship, Leo wrote Martha in English, "Excuse that I could not write much. I was too tired and couldn't gather my thoughts. On May 6 we set out from Marseille with the *Winnipeg*. The ship is like the *Flandre* [which had taken Leo to Cuba but then returned him to Europe] and the food isn't half so bad. The journey was rather calm today. We stopped at Oran [Algeria] for two or three hours.... I must confess that my feeling is always that I am on the *Flandre*. Let us hope for better fortune now. We will sail through Gibraltar to Casablanca and Martinique.... If you can, reserve for me please a ship to New York.... What difficulties I had in Marseille."

Two days later he wrote again: "Yesterday I didn't write for we were excited. Two hours out of Oran we had to return. You can imagine how it was.... I thought of the same experience on the *Flandre*. Then we set out in company of a [British] ship of war....there was a terrible storm and all were seasick. I lay on the bed and couldn't eat.... Today the sea is calm. Good bye."

On this voyage luck traveled with Leo. That week German planes sank an Egyptian steamer in the Atlantic, killing more than three hundred passengers. British, Italian, French, and German planes, ships, and armies

Leo's sketch of a fellow passenger aboard the *Winnipeg*. *Courtesy of Celia Cizes*

continued to fight fiercely that week around Greece, Sicily, and Crete and maneuvered by land across North Africa, but Germany's greatest focus was Operation Barbarossa. Two weeks after Leo sailed along the African coastline, French naval boats under German control ordered two liners bound for Martinique to return to Casablanca, where the fleeing passengers were imprisoned. Leo had sailed safely through the narrowest of open pathways in extreme and treacherous times.

Lonely and out of touch, Martha continued to write Leo faithfully. "May 15 My dear little *Manschuli*. I feel bad not to have any news from you. Where do you stay?...Are you by yourself?"

On May 30, twenty-four days after Leo had departed Marseille, Martha was teaching a piano lesson when Ruth phoned to tell her that Leo had cabled from Martinique.

"He is there! He is coming!"

Martha wrote Leo immediately, possibly to General Delivery in Trinidad. "Well, my little husband, now I really hope it will be not so long! I can hardly wait to get a letter, telling me what chances you have. We are all sitting around the kitchen, doing nothing." She seems stunned, caught in war's tangle of hope and uncertainty. Like the rest of the family, she had learned not to trust good news.

Leo would later write about his voyage to America in two sentences remarkable for their brevity. "Left France aboard the SS *Winnipeg* for Martinique, but the boat was captured by the Dutch and the British and taken to Trinidad. Left Trinidad June 11, 1941 and arrived in New York June 16, 1941."

I don't doubt that Martha and Leo's longed-for reunion at New York's harbor was filled with a torrent of tears, vise-like embraces, smiles, laughter, and words tumbling together fast and slow in happiness. Their joy must have been overwhelming, as their two years of separation, fears, doubt, and longing finally came to an end. Leo's long journey—and Martha's anguished wait—were over. He was safe. They were home in America.

✦

Martha had not heard from Alfred and Hedwig in months. In early June they probably received the American consul's response to their application. It comprised two dense single-spaced typewritten pages with sixteen numbered points, plus subcategories, large checkmarks, and highlighted sections enumerating the reasons why it had been rejected. For one thing, Hermann had been listed as the primary sponsor but his income, including his daughter Lisl's contribution, was insufficient.

On June 21, five days after Leo had arrived in America, Alfred wrote a long postcard—in his worst handwriting yet. Censors might have given up deciphering it no matter the contents, but Alfred had been careful to camouflage his message. As he had done for two years—whatever his message—he began with pleasantries. "My Dear Martha and Leo!... how happy we are to know that you are finally together and will now set up house together.... You have to excuse dear Mama today. We have moved."

This was the only letter Martha had received with no message from her mother. Alfred wrote that they were now sharing the apartment of Hilde and Rudolf Bergmann, sister and brother-in-law of Bernard Toch. "Aunt Tilde cannot come with us. She has an apartment to herself close by. Do not worry. We will write again soon."

Do not worry? The times were increasingly treacherous. Martha and Leo must have understood that the parents' lives were precarious. Alfred scribbled down his and Hedwig's new address and Mathilde's, both in the second district, Matzohville, the Jewish section that he knew well. Their new apartment was on the block where he had been born. "Our next street," he joked, "should be with you."

✦

The next day, June 22, Germany unleashed an attack on the nation that Hitler had long considered the aryans' mortal enemy and greatest prize: the Soviet Union, home to despised Communists and about three million Jews, and rich in natural resources and agriculture. Leaving a wake of scorched-earth destruction, Reich air and ground forces and their allies slashed a great arc through Eastern Europe from the Baltic Sea, through Soviet-occupied eastern Poland, Ukraine, and into Russia. The massive invasion, on an unparalleled scale, appeared unstoppable.

CHAPTER 29
A Lifeline Severed

June–December 1941

O n June 22, 1941, commanding the largest invasion force ever assembled—nearly four million troops—the German Wehrmacht and its allies smashed through Poland, veered south to the Black Sea and north to the Baltic, then drove east into the Soviet Union. On some days the fighting advanced at the unheard-of rate of fifty miles a day. Italians, Romanians, Bulgarians, pro-Fascist Spanish partisans, anti-Communist volunteers, and Finnish soldiers avenging Soviet occupation all joined Germans fighting along a nearly two-thousand-mile front.

Caught unprepared and on the ground, a quarter of the Soviet air force was destroyed on the first day. German tanks sped across Soviet territory surrounding, capturing, or killing hundreds of thousands of Soviet troops. Auschwitz was operating at full capacity, imprisoning and murdering Soviet prisoners of war. Within weeks German forces had reached striking distance of Moscow and surrounded Leningrad [St. Petersburg] in a suffocating "Iron Ring."

By late summer the swastika flew over European capitals from Paris to Oslo and east to Minsk, deep inside the Soviet Union. Conquests not even Napoleon had dreamed possible seemed within reach of the German

Third Reich. Confident German generals, satisfied with the war's progress, projected that the invasion would effectively succeed by fall—and in that optimistic belief did not order winter uniforms for most troops.

Historians still debate the reasons for Russia's confused response to the invasion. Some believe that Stalin had been plotting to invade German territory and hadn't focused on defense. For whatever reason, the Soviet dictator refused to heed months of warning from the United States, his own spies, and regional newspapers reporting German troops massing along Soviet borders. Instead he ordered messengers who delivered invasion reports to be shot and the Soviet military to stand down, then—when it was impossible to deny the German invasion—fell into what has been described as a mental breakdown. The Russian Bear, nickname for the largest nation on earth at that time, seemed to be slumbering as Germany continued its march.

On the Western Front, Britain continued to inflict damage on Germany that summer, ferociously bombing its homeland, blockading its ports, and attacking its military in North Africa. But Britain itself was enduring unsustainable losses. Germany had sunk more than half the British navy and merchant shipping and was pummeling British forces across northern Europe and the Mediterranean. Hitler anticipated turning from a successful Eastern campaign the following spring to finish off Britain and subdue the United States, Britain's undeclared ally. In the summer of 1941, the tide of war was running strongly with Germany.

Churchill sent urgent letters to Roosevelt pleading for help. On May 27, Roosevelt made his strongest radio broadcast yet to the American public. The three-term president proclaimed Germany's war for world domination an "unlimited national emergency." For the first time publicly and forcefully, he castigated isolationists as appeasers who were sabotaging freedom and abetting the spread of tyranny.

Seventy percent of the American listening audience, an all-time record, tuned in to Roosevelt's speech, causing power usage across the nation to surge. Declaring the world divided between human slavery and human freedom, the president proclaimed, "We choose human freedom."

As his message reverberated through the media, Roosevelt asked Congress for unlimited authority to requisition private property for war industry and national defense.

American public opinion at last began to favor war preparation at home and aid for Britain. Labor unions backed the president, promising to halt strikes that delayed war production. Newspapers ran sensational coverage of "the War," as the Selective Service drafted increasing numbers of young Americans. Political leaders called for unity in public discourse, warning that Hitler was listening.

German leaders sneered at Britain and the United States. That summer Minister of Propaganda Goebbels crowed to the world in a radio broadcast that resistance to the Nazis was useless: "We have the entire economic capacity of Europe at our disposal."

✶

As war intensified, so did the Bergers' suffering. The Reich's war on Jews did not slide out of Germany's top priorities. If anything, the momentum of that war increased. Martha, Leo, Gretl, and Hermann waited in anguish for news of Alfred, Hedwig, and Mathilde, but the German censorship operation had been especially careful. An envelope addressed to Leo in New York from Alfred Israel Berger on Czerningasse and postmarked June 11, 1941, arrived at Martha and Leo's door empty. On June 12, Hermann mailed a letter to Mathilde, *"Meine Liebe Schwester,"* My Dear Sister. Two months later it was returned unopened.

Three weeks passed with no word from the Bergers in Vienna.

The next communication the family received was an airmail postcard dated July 14, which Alfred had written to Hermann. It arrived looking like a weary traveler, bearing the stamps of two censors, an *Oberkommando* insignia, a censor's handwritten number, and three postmarks. The card began with Alfred's careful, unfailing courtesy: "My dear ones, I hope you are all well. I want to congratulate you dear Hermann on your birthday and we wish you all the best and lots of luck! I wanted to write you sooner but I was waiting for the arrival of Hedwig so I could tell you everything at the same time. Meanwhile, I had news from her from Nordhausen...."

Hidden among innocuous greetings and good wishes was a shocking, barely coded message: Hedwig had been deported to a notorious forced-labor camp.

Germany's immense two-front war had created severe labor shortages throughout the Reich. In response, a mass conscription effort raised fifty thousand slave laborers—men, women, and children—in Germany alone. Hedwig, age fifty-one, was among the Viennese Jews sent to Nordhausen, a small manufacturing town and rail hub in central Germany more than four hundred miles from Vienna. Workers received a low wage, from which their bosses deducted various charges, including room and board.

By August, the Reich had reduced workers' daily rations to a few slices of bread. Disease spread through the factory before protests from the local community and concerns over a depleted workforce temporarily improved conditions. Over several years the area would grow to hold sixty thousand forced workers supporting the development of the V-1 and V-2 rockets. Thousands of Jews would die there from illness and overwork. At its worst, the camp could have been a scene from Dante's *Inferno*.

Alfred's postcard said, "She is working in a factory in the department for packing merchandise.... I have been able to get a certificate from the doctor. I hope it will help. I hope that I will have success. Toch and Schreier helped me a lot.

"Mathilde is...[illegible] another apartment. I am with her at noon and afternoons. I take English. I don't enjoy visiting friends any more. If only Hedwig would be home again. Your brother Alfred."

Alfred had reached a level of misery he could not hide, and he chose his brother to share it with, shielding his children from the news.

At that time blindness was a legal exemption from the German forced labor program. Alfred's petition documenting his need for assistance may have extricated Hedwig from the camp. Ten days after his postcard to Hermann, Alfred and Hedwig both wrote to Martha and Leo—Hedwig's first letter in three months. In a tone that belies their trauma, she said, "My dear good children.... We were very happy with your letters because you, dear Leo, are with Martha. As you mentioned you have a nice room and you are happy.... I wish you luck with your new job and a good boss and good money.... How I would love to be with you and Gretl and her husband."

Alfred wrote in his most animated tone since he and Hedwig had been evicted from Schmalzhofgasse nine months earlier. He declared that he liked their current apartment better than the last. "We have one large, beautiful room which we can divide with a wardrobe." He enjoyed visiting their former housemates, the Russos, the Tochs, and others. He saw Aunt Tilde every day; sometimes they walked in the Jewish cemetery—possibly because it was one of the few open spaces where they were allowed to go.

Alfred's wry humor was threaded through his letters. He noted, with irony, that the elderly siblings who had lived with them through two apartments complained that he and Hedwig had moved. "You would have to laugh."

Neither he nor Hedwig mentioned her deportation to the Nordhausen camp. His postcard explaining it remained in Hermann's, and then Peter's, collection of family letters. They never showed it to Martha.

✱

Thankful to be together again, Alfred and Hedwig seemed to have felt some relief, blue sky in the eye of a storm. They wrote Martha and Leo five letters in August and four more in September. Surprisingly, Hedwig's letters expressed her enjoyment of the new job she had been assigned in Vienna. At her most vulnerable under Nazi rule, she seemed to have gathered strength, returning from Germany with new confidence.

> Now I have to tell you some news. I have a very good job fill-
> ing little bags. My hours are from 6:30 in the morning until

3. It is not far from home and I have time to do my own work at home. I like my job. It's very easy, and I'm happy that I can make a little money. I'm very proud of that. You will probably think that Mutti is crazy.

Everything is OK at my workplace. We two people always work together and have to fill two thousand little sacks [with medicine]... per week. After all the deductions I earn RM 17.05, and at the end of the week I have saved RM 2.

She was surprised and glad to make new Jewish friends at this work. Missing so many people she loved, the ghetto and her forced labor ironically provided her the chance to chat and be social with other Jews. She was proud that she had an income, and her supervisor liked her work. In an unexpected twist of fate, she had drawn strength from all that she had been through. Ani and Loli, who had escaped soon after the Anschluss, remembered Hedwig as sensitive, her feelings easily hurt. That seems a different person from the woman who returned from Nordhausen.

On August 2, Hedwig delighted in a photo that Martha sent. "You look very fetch [charming]. I'm happy you're well and that you and Leo have settled into a house. I can imagine you introducing everyone to your new husband.... You cooked tongue for your picnic?" "Your last picture is very nice, but I do not like your hat," Alfred added in jest.

He, too, communicated new energy and direction: "As you know, Mama and I changed roles. She is busy working, and I am at home. I try very hard. I move the furniture every day." Alfred wrote facetiously, yet even the routine household chore of cleaning under the furniture seemed to infuse a sense of dignity into his life. Their belongings were meager, everything in the "one large beautiful room," that they shared with others, but he, too, had found strength in dark times.

Alfred then turned serious, injecting a discordant pessimistic note into his cheerful banter. "I read English a little every day. I don't want to forget what I've learned [but] for us, right now there is little hope."

What did that mean? They had accepted the reality that they could not emigrate? He had given up hope for life itself? Again, I struggled for words to describe Alfred and Hedwig's misery and Martha and Gretl's heartbreak, but I failed to find them.

On August 13 Alfred and Hedwig wrote a calm, pleasant letter. He said, "We are well here. The Bergmanns are very nice to us, and Tochs also try hard to make our lives as comfortable as possible.... Dear Mama is usually home by 4:30 and we can still visit our friends.... Uncle Richard feels well."

Hedwig wrote, "After the evening meal, I like to chat with you, which is a labor of love. We are very happy that you are both well, and are satisfied with your life.... Yesterday we were invited by a very nice family. She worked with me for 10 days and invited us for *jause*.... We still visit our friends.... received a package with good things to eat from the dear brothers. I still sew a little, just for us."

By August 21, Alfred's vigor again sagged: "I am writing this while your dear Mama is at her workplace. She will be here any minute.... I am very happy that you were able to take a vacation and refresh yourselves. We would very much like to be with you on the beach, but we must wait for that.... Please send us more stationery."

In a similar wistful vein, Hedwig added, "In my dreams, I chat with you often. These last few days, I dreamt so vividly of dear Gretl, and the next day you sent us news that she also sent us greetings.... Stay healthy and happy, the way I always wish for you. Your heartfelt kisser, Mutti."

In every letter, they expressed their happiness at Leo's safe arrival. They were delighted when Martha and Leo settled into their own small apartment near Hermann in Manhattan. HIAS advisors routinely warned immigrants that starting life in America was arduous, especially for those arriving with no money after years of running and hiding or internment. Leo didn't tell Alfred and Hedwig that he was so emaciated when he arrived in America that he had collapsed at the construction job Jack found for him. Alfred and Hedwig expressed concern over Leo's several job changes and declared themselves relieved that he had begun work at a factory stitching men's leather coats, as his family had done for generations in Poland.

Martha continued to relay Gretl's letters, a pathway that took months for the Bergers' younger daughter's news to travel from Palestine to Vienna. Minimizing her poverty and health problems, Gretl wrote about the best parts of her life. She told Alfred and Hedwig that she and Moshe worked long exhausting days harvesting potatoes, cucumbers, carrots, red beets, lettuce, paprika. They had begun growing corn and tomatoes, even carnations, she said, describing a life remote from Alfred and Hedwig's lean rations, restricted movement, and loss of freedom in Vienna's ghetto prison. Alfred wrote Martha and Gretl, "You can't imagine how we enjoy your letters."

★

By September 1941, Alfred and Hedwig were fighting to stay positive. Hedwig reported that her work hours had been reduced. "I'm not working very hard. My wages will be smaller. I get up at 6:30. Dear Papa has breakfast with me before I leave.... If I didn't work, I would be bored.... Our meals aren't too bad. In the evenings I prepare potato flour dumplings and try to have fresh fruit.... Since I don't work much now, I will try to find something in my own profession."

They no longer discussed ships, tickets, or affidavits. Instead they wrote about their meals, work, and cleaning, reported on a few friends, asked for news, and offered advice. They clung to their routines; there was little else they could safely say, or think.

Their circle of friends was still shrinking, they wrote at the end of September, but no one was emigrating. Everyone seemed to be moving, disappearing. "We see Aunt Tilde every day. Mostly, she comes here for dinner but we also go to her place for visits. She has arranged her little room very nicely.... We met Frau Goldapfel a few days ago and she is fine.... We were at the Russos but they seldom hear from Renee.... Uncle Jula is not an engineer any more.... Uncle Hugo has moved.... We think we can't see the Neukrafters much.... Hansi doesn't sing much anymore."

They wrote, with a control enforced by harsh censorship, about a reality that was difficult to comprehend. Terrifying reports surrounded them. On Friday October 3, Alfred and Hedwig might have heard loud-speakers blaring Hitler's triumphant address to the Reich. Jubilant crowds in the Berlin sports stadium cheered his return from Wolf's Lair, his Eastern Front command post, to proclaim the collapse of the Soviet Union. His vision of a thousand-year Reich—a Nazi world without Jews, but with slave nations throughout Europe serving Germany's every need—seemed horribly plausible.

Alfred and Hedwig didn't mention the redoubled onslaught of laws and ordinances that battered their lives. Hedwig talked about dinners of potato flour dumplings, but didn't say that Jews could no longer purchase regular wheat flour. They didn't write that Jews couldn't buy soap or shaving cream and that henceforth Jewish men would be recognized by their beards. The latest regulations in August mandated that any Jewish statement against Germany must be reported to authorities.

How could the Viennese people tolerate this misery passing them on the streets every day? Turn their heads? Perhaps they avoided District II. Friendship with Jews or attempts to help a Jew—"friendly relations"—were crimes. Jews could not leave their district without written police permission.

There were other laws that Alfred and Hedwig didn't mention. Beginning on September 15, Alfred and Hedwig were required to wear a yellow star with the word *Jude* [Jew] written in black whenever they appeared in public. Citizens, urged to report any Jew with no star, made taunting jokes about the required badge.

A week after that law took effect, Bernard Toch wrote to a cousin in America, "As you know, we all received the Order '*Pour le Semite*.'" He was repeating the dark joke that even Goebbels spouted in public addresses—a pun on the name of the German medal "*Pour le Mérite*"

[For Your Service]. Like other Jewish veterans of World War I, Toch was not permitted to wear his war medals.

Toch signaled to his family that he was forced to write cautiously, "Unfortunately, there is nothing to write about, even though there is plenty to say."

★

In late September Alfred and Hedwig reported, with more pleasure than they had expressed for many months, that they would share the High Holidays with Mathilde, the Tochs, and other friends, in addition to those living with them. Alfred had purchased a kidney roast for Rosh Hashanah. "Very special."

The Jewish High Holidays, a ten-day period of celebration and deep introspection, begin with Rosh Hashanah, the Jewish New Year, a time of joy, hope, and thankfulness, and culminate with Yom Kippur, the Day of Atonement. I could imagine the scene in the crowded shared room, with chairs borrowed from neighbors, perhaps some of the ten or more friends sitting on beds, maybe holding plates on their laps, praying, singing quietly to avoid drawing attention to their gathering, the Bergers telling jokes in the holiday candles' flickering light. What did those most important of Jewish holidays mean to them that year? Why did they observe them at all in those worst of times?

In this and three other letters, Hedwig wrestled with raging emotions, carefully expressed. She would fast on Yom Kippur, she said, and think of Martha and Leo observing the holidays with Jack's and Hermann's families. Picturing Gretl and Moshe in Palestine with Ernst, Herta, Arnold, and Mitzi, she longed to be with her torn-apart family. The holidays made her ache for all that she had lost; her two daughters had been gone for three and four wrenching years.

But it's clear that the holidays strengthened Alfred and Hedwig in their airless ghetto life. As they were observing the holidays, their family in America and Palestine, and Jews everywhere were doing so also. Although they were trapped, separated in distance, in freedom, and in safety, at those observances they were, in a meaningful way, with the people they loved. They were holding on to the traditions that marked them as different. I asked the Berger grandchildren what they thought about Alfred and Hedwig observing the holidays from the depths of their persecution.

Celia had been unwell for some time when I asked her that question. She said, "That would be my way of fighting. I'm answering from my perspective, where I am now. I've been fighting pain and illness for a long time. Sometimes I think I should give up and ask someone to help finish me off. This seems hopeless. Maybe that's how my grandparents felt. Maybe the holidays were their way of saying, whatever the consequences, excuse my language, 'Fuck you, Hitler.'"

Micha, too, thought that the holidays were a way to fight back against repression. Those observances offered a time to be with other Jews in an uplifting, restoring way. "Remember, Jews in those days did not need to remember their Judaism. The Nazis reminded them."

Judith thought, "Maybe they didn't believe that the final catastrophe would happen. We know it now, but they may have thought those bad days would end. I'm happy they made a holiday meal with friends. Probably, those minutes helped them feel a little better. Hedwig was fasting—maybe she was also praying for help from God. I am not religious, but my grandparents were. In that situation, maybe even I would have observed the high holidays."

I asked my husband the same question. Sidney had complicated feelings, especially with regard to Yom Kippur. "That holiday is intensely private, a time for reflecting on your misdeeds, about people you may have hurt. You commit to a better life, and forgive those who ask your forgiveness. But you have to ask, why be a Jew when that caused so much misery? Why not reject God? It doesn't make sense—asking the same God that permits their misery, for forgiveness of your transgressions. Morality didn't exist then in Vienna. In war, it's kill or be killed. I might have thought more about fighting than my own transgressions, though I wasn't there, elderly and blind."

I guessed that Alfred and Hedwig's observing the ancient rituals had helped them reclaim their stolen identity, but I also thought that they probably never considered abandoning what had been central and holy to them for as long as their family memory extended. They were Jewish. Why wouldn't they observe the holidays? As Sidney said, "Whoever looks back and says, 'God did this for me, brought us from slavery,' is Jewish. Whatever history you take to your heart defines you, not Hitler's laws."

At the end of Hedwig's September letter, she turned to her one sustaining wish, probably shared by every Jew at that table in Vienna—and by their family members who had fled to points around the world: "I hope your dream will come true that we can send you a cable and tell you when we will arrive."

★

In mid-October Alfred and Hedwig's minuscule chances for immigration were officially foreclosed by a secret Reich order: "In view of the approaching final solution to the Jewish situation, emigration of Jews with German citizenship is forbidden." The term "the final solution" had been used by various Reich leaders for some years, but it was employed increasingly, and with commitment, that summer of 1941—a fact that highlights a shift in German policy from encouraging Jewish emigration to deporting them to camps, and then to exterminating them. That month Germany stopped providing Jews with emigration papers. As America's relations with the Reich had deteriorated, the U.S. had already closed its embassies throughout German-controlled Europe. With few exceptions the only Jews to enter the United States at that time were already waiting for visas in Lisbon, North Africa, or Latin America, outside the territory under Reich and Axis domination. That fall of 1941, Hitler ordered the first tests of Zyklon B gas at Auschwitz and murdered more than six hundred Soviet prisoners of war.

HIAS's 1941 annual report summarized European Jews' dismal situation, describing the still overwhelming numbers of requests for help. The report explained that Germany had blocked all escape routes from the interior of Europe—the Danube, rail lines, and highways. The few passenger ships still sailing were heavily overbooked. Jews with valid papers should leave urgently, the report said. "Failure to act or to succeed, dooms [the refugee]"—but for Jews in German hands, the time to act had already passed.

The extended Berger family throughout Europe endured under evolving German persecution. Richard was ill, residing in a convalescent facility in Teplice, northwest of Prague, and cared for by his non-Jewish mistress. Hedwig's brothers in Prague sent Alfred and Hedwig parcels of food and wrote regularly, including photos of Hugo's three-year-old, golden-haired Evie. They continued to plead with Hermann to help them with tickets to any place outside of Nazi Europe, apparently unaware that they could not reach any port.

In Trembowla, Poland, Leo's sister Sabina was facing Germany's bloody Eastern Campaign as it raged around her and her daughter, Myra. In July, ten days after the German army had smashed into Eastern Poland, German units marched into Trembowla. SS Einsatzgruppen followed, bringing an even more lethal threat; they organized local death squads composed of police and citizens, who murdered thousands of Jews, civic leaders, intellectuals, and enemies.

In late summer Hedwig wrote Martha, "We received a telegram from Aunt Olga that Ani has left Turkey [for Palestine]." Richard's work visa had allowed Olga and her daughters to remain in Turkey for three years, but the Turkish government was then threatening to expel them all.

By August, the process of herding Jews together in designated Vienna neighborhoods neared completion. The Nazis' strategy of keeping their actions as secret as possible, isolating Jews from the general population, and spreading virulent antisemitism had succeeded beyond Hitler's original hopes. He railed against Western journalists and international press for reporting about German brutality toward Jews, but in fact the international reporting on the ghettoization of German Jews was minimal, and no significant outcry arose either in Germany or abroad. Many Viennese applauded the process of ridding the nation of its Jews.

The decision to systematically kill Jews beginning in fall 1941 appears to have been opportunistic. Hitler had planned to commit the mass murders as the Eastern war wound down, but Nazi antisemitism had taken on a life of its own, and pressure from German leaders and citizens accelerated his timeline. Motivations for the push to kill Jews ranged from hygiene—eliminating overcrowded, disease-ridden camps and ghettos—to greed—assuaging the demand for housing in bombed German cities—and antisemitic malice underlay the entire process.

Newly conquered territories provided that opportunity—"killing fields"—militarized war zones where atrocities could be carried out out of sight of the German people. While many Reich citizens enabled or even demanded cruel treatment of Jews, Hitler believed that Germans would not tolerate actually witnessing the consequences of those demands. Perhaps it's human nature to avoid facing the reality of our darker impulses.

In fall 1941, mass deportations began departing Vienna for the newly conquered regions. SS Einsatzgruppen killing squads had routinely followed front-line troops into war zones, and that fall, transports deporting Jews began to follow the special units. The first transport to leave Vienna since the aborted Polish deportations rumbled out of Vienna on October 15.

It delivered about a thousand Jews to Litzmannstadt (Lodz in Polish), a highly productive labor camp with a corresponding high death rate. Four more transports followed within two weeks, each carrying about a thousand captive Jews on a rail system already burdened with war-related traffic.

When Litzmannstadt could hold no more prisoners, weekly transports delivered Jews to occupied Latvia and Lithuania, and to Minsk in the Soviet Union. Transports waited on sidings, engines running sometimes for days, while trains with higher priority pushed through; when the transports reached their destinations, Jews were shot dead and pushed into pits sometimes dug by the prisoners themselves. Throughout the countryside in Poland, Ukraine, Belarus, and other parts of Central and East Europe, SS Einsatzgruppen and local German-organized killing squads massacred thousands of Jews, both local and deported.

To accomplish this task, Reich Security Chief Himmler ordered special training for the SS Einsatzgruppen to desensitize them to the killing of innocent men, women, and children. You are heroes, he told them, and will accomplish what others cannot. He swore them to secrecy. One soldier, though, did write home from Minsk in early September, "We are making short shrift here of Jews and commissars [Communist party officials], and other riffraff. In the last few days several hundred of them have been killed. It is done extremely fast and without concern. Then they are interred like sardines. All this is absolutely necessary in the interest of security, but nobody is tortured, and the local population seems quite happy."

I wondered, what did he mean by "happy"? The local population had experienced devastating losses during the German invasion, and they were living under German domination.

✶

In America during that summer and fall of 1941, the federal government called for munitions workers to work longer hours and pushed industry to its limits. Roosevelt moved beyond preparation and military aid and began provoking Axis nations. He approved construction of an American airbase in western China to support British and Chinese interests and to establish a presence against Japanese aggression. Even more inflammatory, he announced that American ships would transport military aid to Britain, making U.S. ships potential German targets.

In a front-page *New York Times* article that summer, George Gallup described a national poll revealing that the tide had turned in American public opinion: most citizens now agreed it was more important to defeat Hitler than to stay out of the war. With growing support at home and heightened tension abroad, Roosevelt grew bolder, taking over Britain's presence in Iceland, a shipping stopover within Germany's declared combat zone. Incensed German military leaders pressured Hitler to attack America. Hitler may have been tempted, but the Führer had begun to receive worrisome reports from the Eastern front. As fall edged toward winter, rains had turned roads into quagmires; wheeled vehicles sank to their axles. The first snowflakes had fallen unseasonably early. The momentum of the German advance had stalled, forcing Hitler to deny his generals' requests for war with America. But another powerful force—the pressure for an immediate "final solution"—was not so easily controlled.

★

Alfred and Hedwig's letters from that fall betray their growing desperation. On October 19 Hedwig penned this uncharacteristic outburst: "Dear Uncle Hugo sent you a telegram that it is very important to do something soon. Maybe you will find somebody who could give you the money and you tell them we would work very hard to pay off our debts as soon as we could.... Today also Dr. Singer and Kleins moved.... Tell their children about their new address. When we hear anything we will let you know immediately."

Hugo had not understood that nothing more could be done. Hedwig, too, hung onto the hope that one day she and Alfred would be in America, helping to pay off the debts from their escape.

Alfred was wary. He added, "With us everything is ok and we hope it will stay this way. I know you are doing everything possible. It is very important to us that you do not worry about us.... Please do not worry.... We hope that we can hear from each other and stay in contact."

Again, Alfred seemed to accept the reality that they could not escape. His central concern was for his children, that they would bear no guilt for his and Hedwig's fates.

Ten days later, they wrote again. Hedwig has reclaimed her cautious chatty tone: "Did the season begin for your piano lessons?...Now the main meal is in the evenings, after work.... Papa likes me to make the potato *storz* [fried potato flour, probably something like potato pancakes]."

I wondered how Alfred and Hedwig wrote letters in the room they shared with the Bergmanns and a single woman who had also moved into the "large beautiful room divided with a wardrobe." Was there a shared writing table? Trudy Toch, Bernard Toch's daughter and the Bergmanns' niece, remembered being in that apartment; she did not recall the central room as being "large."

By November Alfred's mood had turned grim. Perhaps he had lost friends to the early transports. He wrote, "Now the days are so short and dark, I can only write the most necessary things. Margarite's aunt [Mrs. Russo] is very worried and requests Krasner to do as much as possible." He avoided mentioning the Russos' name.

Alfred had been impeccably groomed in every photo I had seen of him. I wondered whether he managed some way to shave. Were the Bergers' shoes in tatters? Did he and Hedwig look like ghosts shambling through the ghetto? Or were they still poorly but neatly dressed and well-kept, as I imagined? No photos of them from that time exist.

Even then, under extreme duress, Alfred couldn't resist a chance to tease: "How is everything in your new work, Leo? Hopefully, your thumb is healed. You, dear Martha, should not keep any sweets from him he is so good to you. Your dear Mother wouldn't do that to me. She couldn't anyway because we don't have anything worth hiding."

Hedwig added, "I am working more and am happy about it. I have less time to think. At home, I try to prepare everything in case we can leave.... I wish we could get ready for the U.S.A."

That week Mathilde sent Hermann an airmail letter, but the envelope, stamped by censors, arrived empty. She sent three more. Those, too, were empty on arrival.

Just after the three-year anniversary of Kristallnacht, November 11, 1941, Alfred sent an exuberant letter to Gretl, which was forwarded by

Martha and Leo: "Dear Gretl and Moshe! We were surprised and very happy to receive Martha's telegram! The grandpa sends all his best wishes to you and the little boy!!"

Gretl had given birth to a son, Micha, on November 5. She had telegraphed Martha in New York, who in turn had cabled Alfred and Hedwig. Alfred went on, "It doesn't seem so long ago that you were a little child yourself. Sometimes I dream that I still see you in the pastry shop or Schönbrunn Park. I also think of the last few days we were together and did lots of shopping. Now you are a mama.... What is the little boy's name? We hope the dear Lord will be with you. Your loving Papa."

Hedwig wrote with unbridled joy, "My dear good children! You can't imagine how happy we were to receive your telegram. I'm happy that Gretl is well. With greatest pleasure, I call *Mazel Tov*, and we hope dear G-d will always protect all of you. The young Mutti and little baby should always be well.... My little Minkerl is now a young mutti with a beautiful, healthy boy. I can imagine how happy she is. She always loved children so much....

"How happy I would be if we could be with them, but we can only share our happiness from a distance. I am also happy that you are trying to get a Cuban visa for us. I would gladly work all day and night to help with the work and money. Let us hope it will not be too long."

Alfred added words for Martha and Leo: "It is too bad the mail takes much longer now. We are impatient. The telegram was the first letter since October 10. Did you know about Gretl before you sent us the telegram? I repeat how happy we are for Gretl. Perhaps one day we can celebrate our reunion. That is almost too much to ask. I cling to that happiness."

★

Events whirled forward like a storm racing along its path. On November 17, 1941, six days after Alfred and Hedwig received their good news, Germany anxiously proposed a pact with its Axis ally Japan to the effect that neither country would make a separate peace with their common enemies.

The next week, on November 25, a large Japanese fleet set sail for Hawaii.

On December 3, a day of freezing temperatures in Vienna, Mathilde Sara Mose, Alfred's beloved sister and daily companion, was deported. Litzmannstadt labor camp was hellishly overcrowded, so her transport and three more that would follow in coming weeks were diverted to Riga, Latvia. In Riga there was no labor camp or ghetto to hold the thousands of Jews sent there that winter. There was no sympathetic population, as Hitler imagined existed in Germany, to publicize or complicate German plans to murder Jews immediately upon arrival.

Did Alfred walk to Mathilde's apartment to meet her for lunch that day and find her high-rise building deserted? Had she received a deportation notice that gave her time to bid her brother farewell?

Three days after Mathilde was deported, on December 6, Hermann wrote to her. "*Meine Liebe Schwester* [My Dear Sister], I have awaited letters from you and Alfred. It has been so long with no news.... Do you need money? We hope to see you as soon as possible in the New Year." Why had he written that casual remark? Had he sent her an affidavit that Martha, Alfred and Hedwig did not know about? Hermann seems drastically disconnected with reality, like most people in America at the time. Nazi censors returned his letter unopened.

Night had already fallen in Berlin and Vienna when reports reached those cities that the Japanese had bombed Pearl Harbor. Alfred and Hedwig would have awakened the next morning to the sensational news, and learned three days later that the United States and Germany were at war. Henceforth no mail would travel between the enemy nations. All of their once large, loving Vienna family was gone, and they were alone. Their lifeline had been severed. They had written their last letter to America.

Part V

CHAPTER 30
Mean Streets

December 1941–May 20, 1942

By the time the United States entered the war in December 1941, Alfred and Hedwig had already suffered nearly four years of Nazi boots resounding in hallways and streets, police whistles shrieking in the night, the loss of friends and family, theft, arrests, and murders. They had avoided frenzied Nazi rallies and gangs and art shows depicting Jews as vermin, ugly and misshapen. They had read countless articles and heard pronouncements about Germany's glorious victories and its expanding empire and forecasts of their own eradication.

Now whispered rumors of the first major German military defeats— setbacks on the Eastern Front, battles fought in minus forty-nine-degree weather, losses running to half of the Axis troops fighting around Moscow—worked their way into Vienna. Even so, as winter 1942 set in, the German Reich maintained an iron-fisted control over Europe from the English Channel in the west to deep inside the Soviet Union, a hundred miles east of Minsk.

America's entry into the war may have raised Alfred and Hedwig's hopes for an overthrow of the Reich. Perhaps they thought the worst had passed. But if they briefly harbored such optimism, they would have quickly learned that the defeat of the Nazis was a dim and distant dream compared to their hard reality.

Their abruptly severed mail connection must have been almost unbearable for all the family. Alfred, Hedwig, and Martha had managed to remain close, and they had kept Gretl, living in enemy territory, in loving connection as much as possible. That treasured, nurturing contact ended the day America declared war.

Alfred and Hedwig still may have communicated with family in German-occupied lands. If so, those letters brought anguish as well as comfort. Richard was ill and in hiding. Leo's sister Sabina and her young child were in hiding. Hedwig's brother Julius had been deported about the same time as Mathilde that dark December. Hedwig's other brothers, Hugo and Otto, kept moving from one Prague apartment to another and would have been difficult to reach.

Did Hedwig ever wear her holiday suit, made from Martha's old coat, again? Was she still working? Did Alfred go on cleaning under the furniture and inventing wry jokes? We don't know. Their family was gone. Their friends had vanished. The Bergers' movements were fiercely restricted. Their isolation from the outside world was complete.

The family that had escaped continued to write to Martha in New York. Gretl described exhausting days, farming and caring for her baby in Palestine. In all her letters she asked Martha, "Do you have news of the dear parents?"

During that time, Martha developed a tendency to burst into tears unexpectedly. Gretl wrote to Martha that she had trouble sleeping and often dreamt of their parents.

Martha and Leo may have heard the rumors of deportations and murders that were terrifying Jews and filtering through the U.S. government. Could the rumors be true? No one at that time had a framework for understanding genocide, the intentional annihilation of an entire people. The word, "holocaust," did not yet exist as a term relating to humanity.

Martha and Leo expressed their worries continually in their letters to Gretl, but America was at war. Jewish leaders warned Jews not to raise disruptive issues. Antisemitism and anti-immigration sentiment, at high levels before the war, increased as new waves of patriotism and xenophobia swept the nation. Despite widespread American sympathy for the Jews, talk of rescuing them remained controversial even among Jews. Two of the three Jewish U.S. congressmen, who chaired key immigration committees, remained neutral or hostile to rescue during the war—aware that such efforts would trigger a backlash. Henry Fairchild, a prominent sociologist at New York University and president of the American Eugenics Society, declared that the admission of large numbers of Jews to America would cause antisemitism to "burst into violent eruption."

British and American intelligence agencies were aware of the mass deportations and murders in Poland and Russia. In January 1942, Britain announced it would hold war crimes trials after the war. Most American Jewish leaders, unaware of the full extent of the persecution, counseled caution, patience, and patriotism. Even as Hitler was blaming the Jews for the United States' entry into the war, most Americans remained disconnected from their plight.

Fearing imminent Axis attack, the U.S. deployed warships along the Atlantic coast and in the South Pacific and the waters around Alaska. Fear fueled prejudice against German, Italian, and Japanese Americans. By mid-March more than thirty-five thousand Japanese Americans had been moved inland to internment camps guarded by barbed wire and machine guns. America was in no mood to sympathize with minorities.

The American economy rushed to adjust to war footing. Some businesses closed as thousands of workers migrated to areas where war industries flourished. Unemployment, which had hovered around 19 percent in 1938, dropped below 5 percent by 1942.

Clarence Berger, who had received Alfred's letter pleading for help in 1939, had worked hard to build a thriving car repair shop and welding facility, the Ten Grand Garage, at the corner of Tenth and Grand in Los Angeles. It would be one of the early businesses nationalized for war production. Clarence would then find work repossessing cars, mostly in the expanding inner-city African American ghetto near his home. He

The trunk where Clarence Berger stored Alfred Berger's letter to America. *Photograph by the author*

began carrying a gun, and he and his wife made plans to move from their integrating neighborhood. At some point, Berger stashed his German-language books, brought to America by his immigrant grandparents, at the bottom of a trunk, deep under family papers and his World War I army uniform.

Ties to Germany were suspect. With those family books, he also carefully buried the letter from an elderly Jew trapped in Vienna.

★

After communication between warring nations was cut, our information about Alfred and Hedwig's lives comes almost exclusively from a few official documents and general histories. Despite Germany's troubles on the Eastern Front in 1942, its race war accelerated unopposed in newly conquered lands.

Massacres had begun immediately after the June invasion; in Babi Yar, outside Kiev, Ukraine, nearly thirty-four thousand Jews were machine-gunned to death. Jews were slaughtered in Latvia, Lithuania, Poland, and the German-occupied parts of the Soviet Union. Most often, German soldiers and their local collaborators lined Jews up next to pits and shot them, using one rationed bullet per Jew. The pits were then bulldozed, but observers in some places reported seeing the ground moving for days over Jews buried alive.

This image is hard for me to erase from my mind. What scars did these events leave on the perpetrators—hard hearts or inescapable guilt? How many people, soldiers or locals, refused to participate?

Some field commanders complained about their units' morale. In October 1941 Hitler approved the use of gas vans—trucks whose cargo areas could be crammed with victims, then sealed and flooded with carbon monoxide from the truck's running exhaust. But the horrifying task of cleaning the vans, packed with corpses frozen in postures of terror and reeking with vomit and excrement, was so demoralizing that it eventually fell to Jewish prisoners. By 1942 five extermination facilities using Zyklon B gas were under construction in Poland.

In early January 1942 Reich security chief Reinhard Heydrich called a secret meeting of high-level Reich officials in Wannsee, a Berlin suburb, hoping to establish control over the disarray of solutions to "the Jewish problem." Heydrich informed the fourteen carefully selected participants that the conference would clarify central questions and organize processes. He assured them that "practical experience"—bureaucratic code for previous deportations and murders—had been collected.

Heydrich brought with him a tally of the Jews remaining in Europe, those in nations under direct German control listed in one column and those in other countries as remote as Ireland and Portugal listed in another. The total was 11 million Jews. The Germans had trained their gunsights on European Jews, wherever they resided.

Wannsee participants heard Heydrich report that the Reich had already murdered seven hundred thousand Jews and that ghettos were functioning smoothly in most large German-controlled cities. He cited the war and other factors that had brought emigration almost to a standstill and reminded participants of Hitler's secret order forbidding emigration after October 31, 1941. The first phase in solving "the Jewish problem"—expelling Jews from German culture and expropriating their assets—had been successful.

Adolf Eichmann announced with pride that most Austrian cities were now *Judenfrei* and that the next phase—concentrating Jews in defined areas in large cities—was nearing completion. Eichmann, too, had come armed with numbers. Of 537,000 Jews already "caused" to emigrate from Germany and Reich-controlled countries, 147,000 were Austrian. His office had identified 46,000 Jews remaining in Vienna and moved them into approved apartments. In delicate, coded phrases, "the problem" and "the Jewish question" officially and without fanfare become "the final solution," a term with some years of varied unofficial use behind it. German leaders began to bandy the loaded catchphrase glibly; it was clever slang that stripped Jews of their humanity.

Heydrich told the participants they needn't worry about the cost of eradicating the Jews. During emigration they had already given up significant wealth to Germany through taxes, confiscations, and donations from Jews abroad. The nearly $10 million in much-needed foreign currency that the Nazis had received from Jewish aid organizations had been useful. Affluent Reich Jews also had been forced to support Jewish emigration.

He explained that the organizers of the recent deportations had already negotiated a revenue-neutral payment rate with the *Reichsbahn*, the German Railway, of one-half the usual third-class rate for large groups. Deported Jews would pay that cost, four pfennigs a kilometer per passenger.

Conference delegates were satisfied with that arrangement, but it was no small burden for impoverished Jews. The nearly thirteen-hundred-kilometer trip from Vienna to Minsk, about eight hundred miles, would cost fifty-two Reichsmarks. Recall that Hedwig had proudly written Martha that after living expenses she was saving two Reichsmarks, worth about forty cents in America, per week.

Scheduling trains could involve overwhelming difficulties, but Heydrich avoided distracting the gathering with those complications. The *Reichsbahn*, charged with transporting matériel and extraordinary numbers of men to the front in severe weather over the limited Soviet rail capacity, had been severely strained. Soviet tracks were three inches farther apart than standard European rails, causing delays in transferring cargo and changing train undercarriages at the border. The Germans expropriated locomotives, train cars, equipment, and forced laborers from conquered nations as far away as France and replaced hundreds of miles of existing Russian tracks, but the strain on the system was great.

Some historians suggest that diverting trains for deportations may have undermined the German war effort. But Heydrich and other Nazi leaders knew that the burden of moving tens of thousands of soldiers, coal, and matériel dwarfed the relatively minor demands of deportation. For Nazis the cost-benefit ratio of eliminating Jews left no questions.

Heydrich had arrived at Wannsee expecting arguments over the morality of murdering an entire population solely because of their "race" or over the industrial-scale, assembly-line killing that he proposed. But as Eichmann would later report, Heydrich was pleasantly surprised that delegates raised no objections. In fact, when the intimate, congenial group relaxed over cognac, they began to speak more freely. They proposed improvements to Heydrich's plans. "They spoke openly about methods of killing, about liquidation, about extermination," Eichmann said.

The ambitious group of German leaders also took a lively interest in a second step, beyond liquidating Jews: killing *mischling,* people with some Jewish ancestry. Eventually the conferees amiably agreed on the killing, after their anticipated victory in the war with Russia, of everyone who had a "political record that shows he feels and behaves like a Jew"

or bore "a racially undesirable appearance." Wannsee delegates concluded that "Europe is to be combed through from west to east to imple-
ment the final solution." The extent of the proposed cold-blooded murder
is breathtaking.

The only cautionary statement about the "final solution" recorded
in the minutes of the meeting was a warning that "alarm among the
population must be avoided." The watchwords of this program would
be secrecy and deception, even of the Nazis' own supporters. SS men
taking part in liquidations signed a pledge of secrecy.

★

By April 1942 deportation trains were rolling across the Reich on a
mostly regular weekly schedule, each train transporting a thousand Jews.
Thirteen trains had already departed Vienna destined for Poland, Lithuania, Latvia, and Minsk. Some of these thirteen thousand Jews had been
given hoes or other farm implements and told that they would be doing
agricultural work in the East. Some Jews packed professional credentials
in hopes of finding appropriate jobs. Collection center and railway workers took care to maintain the façade and conceal the murder awaiting
them at the end of the journey, minimizing "alarm" for Jews and Reich
citizens alike.

The much-diminished staff of the Jewish Community Organization,
on threat of death to themselves and increasingly brutal treatment of
other Jews, assembled lists of deportees, which were then approved by
Eichmann.

Debates still rage over that organization's forced collaboration with
the Nazis. Hilde Geisen, the survivor of Theresienstadt concentration
camp who translated letters for me, explained why she disagreed with
the critics. "I saw what happened when we didn't assist in the process.
Guards beat people who didn't move fast enough or didn't know where
to go. People who say Jews shouldn't have helped with the deportations
weren't there." Still I couldn't help wondering what would have happened

if the organization had not cooperated. If Germany's brutality had been forced into the open for German citizens—and the world—to witness, as it had been at Baba Yar, would the final result have been different?

The Jewish Community also delivered deportation notices that included the "collection" location and date and a list of acceptable baggage, but no destination. The deportees were instructed to take:

> 1 suitcase or backpack with equipment, namely—
> 1 pair sturdy work boots
> 2 pair socks
> 2 shirts
> 2 underwear
> 1 work outfit
> 2 wool blankets
> 2 sets of bedding (covers and sheets)
> 1 bowl
> 1 cup
> 1 spoon
> 1 sweater
> Provisions for three days
> Approximately 50 RM per person for travel costs
>
> Not allowed to be taken: extra money, valuables, livestock, food ration cards (to be turned in at local economic offices).

One suitcase for all this? Were the wool blankets and work shoes just part of the deception? Or was the packing list a scheme to get Jews to provide German troops with critically needed supplies?

I didn't know what details Alfred and Hedwig's notice may have included, or even whether they received one. Sometimes notices were not sent—deportees were suddenly rounded up from their apartments at night with dogs and guns and driven in vans to Vienna's Aspang Railway

Station. Alfred and Hedwig may or may not have been notified at the end of April of their imminent deportation.

★

No records exist showing where Hedwig was at 10:00 on Thursday morning, April 30, or what she was doing the day of Alfred's accident. She may have been working, filling little sacks with medicines.

Several records of the day exist—weather information, a coroner's report, and Alfred's death certificate. Bernard Toch, who arrived at the accident scene, later told Martha, Leo, and Celia a little about it.

It had been a dark morning on Taborstrasse, a confusing cobbled street with subway and tram stops, rails in the street dividing and turning corners, and pedestrians crossing unpredictably. Taborstrasse was a heavily commercial street about five blocks from the Bergers' final apartment, and was well known to Alfred, who had grown up nearby and crossed it many times. The morning was ashen when he set off from their apartment. A dense fog flowing from the hills surrounding Vienna crept through the streets with a misty drizzle that sometimes froze when it touched the ground.

For years, Jews had met at the Café America on Taborstrasse, most recently to share news about immigration, tickets, costs, and what regulations might be coming next. The art gallery whose Jewish owner sold young Hitler's watercolors to Alfred's brother was on Taborstrasse. We have no information about why Alfred stepped into the street that morning, probably carrying his white cane and wearing his yellow star—when a German Army truck emerged from the mist and struck him down.

Did the driver slam on his brakes? Or did he see the yellow star and deliberately accelerate, aiming his truck at the old Jewish man? Was it coincidence that the vehicle that killed Alfred was German military? Or did a despondent Alfred intentionally walk in front of the truck?

Toch had no answers. He told Martha only that Alfred did not die instantly, and that Nazi police enforced antisemitic laws forbidding

German citizens, on pain of arrest or deportation, from coming to the aid of a Jew. Alfred died on the street that morning with only Toch there to attend him.

We have no information about how Hedwig heard the news of her husband's death, or how she held up afterward. Before that day she may have thought that she'd already heard the worst news possible—their deportation. Their battle to escape, to immigrate to America, to remain invisible in Vienna had been lost. But through it all she and Alfred had been partners. She had married Alfred when she was twenty. Their lives had been joined for thirty-three years. Together they had raised two resourceful daughters, struggled, and suffered under four years of Nazi terror. They had lost their home, their family, and their friends. Hedwig had been deported to Nordhausen and returned. Together, they had fought and held on.

Some Jewish couples separated during the Nazi period to let one partner emigrate first and then help the weaker candidate. But Hedwig and Alfred had faced their troubles together, picked each other up, regrouped, found humor and hope through the dark years. That loving partnership died that day with Alfred. From that time forward, Hedwig would fight her own battle, finding courage to go on alone.

After the accident, Alfred's body was taken to the city morgue, where a routine autopsy report, signed May 7, 1942, one week after his death, stated that Alfred had died of a skull fracture. In case someone reading the certificate missed the added middle name Israel, the word *JUDE* and a Star of David were stamped across the document.

Jewish custom requires that burials take place as soon as possible after death, but Toch reported that neither Hedwig nor their family friends could find Alfred's body for some time. When they finally located it in the morgue, they had difficulty arranging transportation for a Jewish casket, and trouble getting to the cemetery on the far side of town. He said the casket was carried much of the way. Celia didn't know who had borne Alfred's body to the cemetery.

He was buried in the new Jewish section of the Vienna Central Cemetery on May 11. Six decades later his grandchildren—Celia, Judith and Micha—plus Sidney and I, would gather at his grave. His family hugged each other, shed tears, prayed, talked quietly, and fell silent. No one found humor in that day. The service in May 1942 was surely small, somber, and tragic. One week later, on May 18, Hedwig signed the death certificate for Alfred Israel Berger, age sixty-four, with a steady hand.

The longest section on the certificate was devoted to Alfred's estate. His widow, it says, came in person to the district court bringing evidence of their *Sicherungskonto* (controlled bank account) worth 762 RM. It was their life savings, more than I would have estimated, possibly including support from Hermann and Richard. I wondered whether Martha knew what they had, and whether they could have used the money toward a ticket if they had received a visa. Perhaps at some point it was frozen for all use except food, rent, and taxes—and then expropriated. It's unclear whether, after Alfred's death, the bank account belonged to Hedwig or to the state.

According to the form, Alfred had possessed clothing that was old and "defective," therefore "worthless," and other property also worth nothing. Corpse costs of 155 RM would be deducted from the savings account. The court concluded that Alfred lacked an estate. There would be no probate.

Two days later, on May 20, Hedwig was deported to Minsk.

CHAPTER 31

Vienna–Minsk

May 1942

O n May 20, the day of Hedwig's deportation, she was required to report her assets. She had probably thrown away family letters and photos that she had treasured for years. Perhaps she had packed a few of her most precious pictures, believing that this deportation, like the one to Nordhausen, would be survivable. The Nazi deception typically worked; many deportees expected that nothing worse than forced labor awaited them. Who could imagine that an entire race was being exterminated? Bernard Toch told Martha that Hedwig gave her few remaining possessions to friends, the Tochs receiving her sewing machine and Alfred's silver shaving brush. She reported total assets of fifty-three RM, the exact amount required for her deportation. It's unclear what happened to the rest of her bank account; if she couldn't withdraw the money and leave it with friends for safekeeping, the Germans or the bank must have kept it.

Her train, Da 203—"Da" was the *Reichsbahn* symbol for trains originating in the Reich, not an occupied country—was the second of ten transports carrying a thousand Jews from Vienna to Minsk that year. Gestapo records list the deportees, including Bernard Toch's sister and brother-in-law, Hilde and Rudi Bergmann, who were Alfred and Hedwig's last apartment-mates. The transport also carried the sixty-three-year-old woman who had been moved into their apartment following Alfred's death. Those four may have been able to stay close on the journey. A third of the deportees were sixty or older. Twenty victims were ten or younger; the *Reichsbahn* charged children half-price. Hedwig may have taken note of the young mother deported with her four- and six-year-old sons. Or the eleven-month-old with his mother and grandmother, the woman with two teenagers, or the three-year-old and her parents. Hedwig, who loved children, may have drawn solace and strength from comforting them during the journey.

Deportees throughout the Reich were in large measure the elderly. There were more than twice as many women as men in Hedwig's transport. Most had never been affluent; they were among Vienna's most defenseless citizens. The Nazis knew precisely who remained in Vienna. As Eichmann had complained in a recent forced labor report, there were few Jews fit for labor left in Vienna.

The first transport from Vienna destined for Minsk that year left two weeks before Hedwig's departure. In the DÖW archives I had found a description of that earlier deportation by one of the only known survivors of the eight Vienna-Minsk transports. It was a chaotic journey from hell. Deportees brought the only food they would eat on the journey. Sanitation was nonexistent. Some passengers were beaten. Some went mad.

That Wednesday night of Hedwig's deportation, the train she boarded as most Viennese slept was a standard third-class passenger car—used for Reich-based departures to mask the cruelty of the deportation. In the night trucks crammed with deportees and their luggage drove up to Aspang Freight Station's loading dock, adjoining the city's wholesale meat market. As armed officers pushed the Jews towards toward the train, Hedwig may have noticed the stationmaster's children peeking from behind lace curtains in their second-floor apartment; they liked to watch figures moving through the clouds of steam billowing across the platform. Jews seeking escape from the Nazis sometimes ran from bushes along the tracks and leapt onto trains as they pulled out, but they probably avoided these unscheduled trains, crowded with Gestapo and passengers whose coats bore yellow stars.

When Sidney and I made the trip from Vienna to Minsk, our train took about twenty-one hours. Hedwig's journey lasted much longer. She may have watched out the window as her train traveled north toward the Czech countryside where she had grown up. If the moon was shining, she could have seen the green rolling hills she loved, and imagined spring days long gone, when she had awakened on her family's farm to birdsong and the scent of flowers. That morning, the train veered east and roared on to Poland.

Her train probably pulled onto sidings often, waiting for higher-priority trains to pass. Three days into the journey, at Wolkowysk on the Polish-Soviet border, the train stopped. There, in the black of night, with almost no light to guide their steps, guards herded the thousand Jews onto waiting windowless freight cars, beating and kicking those who moved too slowly. Guards flung those who had gone insane into a single locked car, according to the survivor's account.

At the Wolkowysk station, the engineer of transport Da 203 received a memo telegraphed from the Minsk *Sicherheitspolizei* [security police] commander. Commander Georg Heuser requested that Da 203 halt on a railway siding for three days in Koydanov, about twenty-five miles outside of Minsk. That delay would allow the SS *Einsatzgruppen's* team of shooters and their local recruits to enjoy a break from their killing for the Whitsunday holiday. Also known as Pentecost, this holiday was a time of feasting and leaving food at the graves of family and friends in celebration of the Holy Spirit's descent to earth.

As the windowless freight train rumbled on, Hedwig could not have seen the twisted piles of war wreckage strewn across the landscape or the Russian forests, their still-leafless birch trees glinting bone-white in the early light. She heard only the moans and murmurs of fellow Jews in distress, the shriek of the train whistle, and relentless clack-clack of iron wheels on the tracks.

As requested, the train stopped near Koydanov where it held the deportees in the locked cars for three days with no provision of food. On the fourth day, Da 203 lumbered into Minsk in the first morning light, before citizens were awake to gawk. The trip of terror, hunger, and thirst had lasted seven days, one week, the span of creation in some religious stories. In the Jews' story. In Christianity, seven days also comprise the time from Jesus' entry into Jerusalem until his crucifixion. In Minsk, it was just another week. Seven thousand more Jews would be unloaded there that summer.

Minsk did not look or smell like hell. Some guards who handed the Jews small farm tools had a reassuring Viennese accent. Maly Trostenets, the Minsk site listed on Gestapo records as Hedwig's destination, was only a small work site. The nearby Minsk Ghetto was built to house local Soviet Jews. A Jewish man whom Sidney and I would later meet in Minsk had been a ghetto worker at Maly Trostinets and remembered that the aroma of fresh bread from its bakery would have greeted the arrivals. Guards selected only a few Jews from the trains to work at another nearby camp; those chosen rode on the then empty train, unloaded the luggage, and sorted the huge piles before they were murdered. A hierarchy of Germans divided the plunder.

Almost all of the thousand passengers from the transport were loaded directly onto waiting trucks that bumped along rough dirt roads from Minsk to pits prepared for their arrival. There, at gunpoint, guards forced the Jews to strip off their clothes and throw them into a large pile, where workers scavenged or saved the clothes to be sent back to Germany. The scene was so much like the Christian story of soldiers gambling for Jesus' clothing at the foot of the cross that it sent shudders through me.

The captive and humiliated Jews were marched, naked, in a line to stand beside the large ditch. Waiting German soldiers and other men hired locally faced their victims and shot them at close range.

In the moments before Hedwig's death, a man, probably young, would have looked her in the eyes as she walked toward him, naked, beside the newly turned earth. Perhaps she wept for the children near her and for the children she would never see. Possibly even for the man who knew no better than to shoot an old woman.

Hedwig had taught her daughters to say the most basic and central Jewish prayer every night, sometimes in the traditional manner with their right hand covering their eyes. She may have raised her hand too, thinking of her daughters safe in their new lives, and of Alfred suffering no more, and murmured the words, "Hear O Israel...."

★

On July 30, 1942, five weeks after Hedwig's death, Olga wrote Martha from Palestine to relay the last words the family would hear from Alfred and Hedwig. Olga said that she had just received a Red Cross letter sent by Alfred and Hedwig in January: "They say they are well, only dear Aunt Tilde is not with them anymore. I assume she was deported. It is terrible. One cannot think about it."

Part VI

CHAPTER 32
Moments

September 2004

S idney and I made one final journey before returning home. While the
Berger family arranged for the care of Alfred's grave and continued
to explore Vienna, Sidney and I traveled to Minsk—to research Hedwig's
final days, and to visit the village where Sidney's family had lived for
centuries.

The aging Russian train known as the Moscow Express rattled out
of Vienna at 10:00 p.m. on its twice-weekly, twenty-one-hour, seven-
hundred-fifty-mile journey to Minsk and beyond. It was unlike any rail
trip I had ever taken. At times it was frightening, as if we were riding away
from civilization. Because food was not available for purchase until the
following afternoon, Sidney and I had brought sandwiches. During the
night the conductor cooked his meal on an open gas burner in a little nook
in our car, which seemed to have no passengers besides ourselves.

After midnight a Polish border guard awakened us by pounding on
our compartment door. Flashing a light in our eyes, he shouted for us to
present our passports, which he confiscated and did not return until our
train was lurching forward again. The experience was jarring. Why not
speak courteously? Across Poland we roared through countless small

stations where the train whistle blew and a uniformed station master stood on the platform at attention in a small pool of light, saluting the train as we passed.

At Brest, on the Poland-Belarus border, we pulled into a large open hanger and halted for an hour or so while shirtless workers hammered and banged under the train, as a hoist lifted each car, passengers still aboard, to dangle over the tracks. The workers pushed away the wheels of the cars and rolled new undercarriages beneath, then the cars were lowered, complete with wheels that matched the wider-gauge Russian tracks. The trip thrust us into a different world, but it cannot be compared with Hedwig's journey. As she crossed the border, guards ordered the thousand prisoners out of their passenger cars and into a windowless freight train.

As our train rolled into the station in Minsk, we were met by our required state-approved guides Franklin and Galena Schwartz. The husband and wife team had shepherded other Jewish tourists through museums and Minsk sites focusing on the Jewish experience in the Great Patriotic War—World War II—and the Minsk Ghetto. The war still looms large in Russian memory. Belarus was one of World War II's bloodiest theaters in Europe; one in four Belarusians died, a dreadful end to the alliance between Stalin and Hitler that permitted Soviet Russia to occupy neighboring nations but blinded Soviet leaders to Germany's ultimate intentions.

In addition to showing us through museums, Franklin and Galena also took us to a poorly maintained high-rise apartment building to meet Hirsh Mendelvich Cantor, one of the few survivors of the Maly Trostenets labor camp. The elderly Belarusian Jew explained that almost all the workers at the camp had been drawn from the Minsk Ghetto, which held local Jews, not Reich deportees. Mandelvich had been surrounded by death in the ghetto, and he believed that the camp work had saved his life. He described his role in setting fire to the camp bakery in 1944 as Soviet troops were advancing toward Minsk. The Germans were shutting down the facility, he said, and preparing to kill all the workers, as they would also kill all the ghetto Jews. He and other Jewish laborers escaped in the turmoil of the fire.

That visit ended with Sidney and Mandelvich singing an old Yiddish song neither knew the name of, which Sidney had learned from his grandfather. It was a moving moment, with the mingled voices of Sidney and this aging, resourceful Jew who had outwitted his oppressors. Sidney's lost connection to this distant land had sprung to life—surprising, pleasing, and disconcerting him: he had expected to experience what had happened here as a detached observer, holding it intact and unexplored inside himself, the way he had coped with his relatives' murders and the Holocaust all his life.

The next day we drove to the now wooded mass grave site where Hedwig was probably shot and buried. Today the area is squeezed uneasily between bustling Minsk highways.

Hedwig's remains would not have rested here long. By 1944, Soviet forces had pushed German troops to the city's outskirts in fierce fighting. Dreading imminent discovery of their crimes, the Germans began digging up and incinerating thousands of bodies in an attempt to destroy the evidence. But that task proved too large and the time too short; they left ample evidence of their crimes and the cover-up, including human remains, the furnace, and photographs of the killing. In addition, investigators are still unearthing thousands of bullet shells from around the mass graves.

I felt no reverence at the unholy site. It seemed like desecrated ground. What happened there was too deeply sad to evoke a just anger, and too horrifying a crime to inspire only sorrow. I felt agitated, numb.

Sidney seemed agitated, too, and he was ready to leave fairly promptly. I paused long enough to pick a few wildflowers growing at the site and press them between papers in my satchel to give to Judith, Celia, and Micha.

✦

Hedwig was still grieving for her beloved Alfred when guards pushed and shoved her, shouting in German, Russian, and other Eastern European languages, ordering her death. Following her tracks, I felt more starkly how these things could have happened to Sidney and me if we had lived at that time. The feeling became more visceral as Franklin drove us the twenty miles from Minsk to Radoshkovici, the Belarusian village where Sidney's family had lived for countless generations. His mother had warned him against coming here, not knowing how all of her parents' family had died. Perhaps the village had risen up against its Jews. We felt tense, riding through the idyllic-looking countryside.

Sidney carried his grandfather's memoir of growing up in Radoshkovici and referred to it as we wandered the quiet lanes of the old town, past old wooden houses the vibrant blues, greens, and cadmium yellow of a Chagall painting. My husband was thrilled to find his family's small, simple one-story wooden home on a grassy riverbank. It appeared to be the original structure despite the passing decades and several generations of owners since his family's demise. On that street, a white-haired woman watched us and eventually began speaking with Franklin. "Yes," she told him, she had known the Isaacsons—Sidney's family's name. "Good people." Sidney was deeply moved by this human connection to his roots.

Another curious resident, a retired man about sixty watching us explore the neighborhood, impulsively joined us and began to answer our questions. Chatting eagerly as Franklin translated for us, he led us to the town's well-kept memorial to its murdered Jews. Jews had lived in this village for as long as anyone could remember, he said. He had been a child during the war, but his parents had told him about the several times Nazis murdered Jews in the town. In the first and largest massacre, German troops marched into town, rounded up all the Jews they could find, drove them into a barn that belonged to his family, barred its doors, and burned them alive. We were speechless. He pointed between several houses and down a slope to a grassy field. "There," he said. "It was there." A soft wind ruffled the dry grasses. No one spoke for some minutes before he continued. None of the villagers had approached the burned-out remains for "a long time." The field seemed to be a pasture currently.

Sidney at Radoshkovici, Belarus. *Photo by the author*

During other Nazi incursions into Radoshkovici, he said, Germans sought out Jews who had previously hidden, and shot them. He didn't mention the many Belarusians—sometimes outnumbering Russians—who had been involved in the killing operations.

He invited us into his home for a spontaneous snack including potato latkes, pancakes prepared exactly as Sidney's grandmother had made them. He hugged Sidney and called him "a son of the village." At parting we tottered out to our car dizzied by multiple toasts with our host's homemade vodka. The warmth we had experienced was a welcome relief, complicating Sidney's stereotypes of this region, but it could not blunt the barbarity of what had happened here. The trip shook Sidney, as it did me. Alfred and Hedwig's story, which had come to us "by chance" converged with Sidney's own history here, thousands of miles from our home, bringing the Holocaust to our doorstep. Neither of us knew how to make sense of the coincidence. Neither of us had ever claimed any part of the Holocaust, in any way, as our own. We were unnerved to be suddenly cast into its great, dark shadow.

As we rode back to Minsk, thinking about our experience, Sidney's eyes filled with tears. "I knew many terrible things had happened here, but not something like that. It was heartbreaking. I could see in my mind's eye, all those people, my family, being marched down the street to the barn...and at the killing site in Minsk, in the dirt lay all those people who were shot. So many were lost...so many. For me, the Holocaust has gone from something abstract to believable to unbelievable. I'm glad my grandfather never knew what happened here." Still he planned to show our pictures to his mother, cousins, aunts, and uncles when we returned, and tell them what we had learned—a sad final chapter to his grandfather's memoir about growing up in Radoshkovici.

★

Back in Vienna, several days before we all departed, Micha, Chava, Celia, Judith, Avraham, Sidney, and I walked across a Danube Canal bridge to Vienna's Second District, Matzohville, seeking Alfred and Hedwig's last apartment. As we made our way through the old district of small shops, old apartment buildings, and grand churches, we read plaques honoring well-known Jews who had lived there before the Holocaust. We passed the former site of Vienna's largest synagogue, too, burned during Kristallnacht. Alfred had grown up one block away. Gretl was bat mitzvahed in that striking Moorish-style structure. The building where Alfred and Hedwig spent their last days in Vienna overlooked its charred rubble. In 1941, three years after the synagogue burned, they may have watched the bulldozers finally clear the charred remains, leaving only four, four-story stone columns that remain standing today on the partially redeveloped site.

Around the corner, on Czerningasse, Judith pressed the doorbell of her grandparents' final apartment and explained to the woman who answered that her family wished to see their grandparents' last home. The young woman and her husband graciously welcomed us up to the third-floor apartment. We came into a sunlit living room with worn parquet wooden floors—the "one large beautiful room we can divide with a wardrobe" that Alfred had described. Two young children played on the floor as their father sat next to them, all eyes turning to watch us.

Celia entered first, slowly. She looked pale and shrunken inside her coat as she moved silently and alone through the apartment. Micha asked questions of the young couple, speaking haltingly, with long pauses as he took in the room, not so large as I had imagined, which his grandparents had shared with two other families. Avraham, Chava, Sidney, and I made a quick silent tour of the cheerful updated main rooms. When we returned to the front hallway, we found Judith in distress. Her breath was short, her face flushed. The woman who lived there was patting her arm, trying to comfort her. We thanked the family and departed.

Back at the sidewalk, Judith was near tears. "I stood there and I was…I felt like I saw my grandparents in the apartment, hiding in the room. I knew how they were feeling. That someone is frightened even to step out of the house…and they would never see their children again. It's terrible. I was cold…. My mother cried so many, many times. She said it was because she missed her parents and her sister so much. I was very sorry when I saw the mother take their little girl to another room when I was excited. The husband's face was warm. He asked what he could do."

Decades after Alfred and Hedwig had been warehoused there, and after cruelty emptied that place, the young family had provided empathy and caring. Where, I thought, was that human kindness for Alfred and Hedwig? Watching the Berger grandchildren wander woodenly in this sad place where a young family now thrived had been upsetting. Sidney, too, was deeply affected. As we walked back through the historic neighborhood, he said how strange it felt, like being inside a dream, to see happy children with their brightly colored toys in the same room that once was a holding place for murder.

We traversed the few blocks to Taborstrasse 28, the location of Alfred's accident. It was a broad confusing street, with transit vehicles, cars, trucks, and bikes weaving across lanes, pedestrians hurrying to jump on buses or enter stores and cafes, or walking along engrossed in their own lives. As I stood on that street corner, my emotions churning, the very ordinary nature of the scene was disconcerting, collapsing time. I imagined the day when Alfred died here, Bernard Toch running to his aid, and the ordinary people stopping to see what had happened, consider what they should do, and then continue on their way.

Walking toward the canal, we passed historic Leopoldskirche, Leopold's Church, built on the site of an early synagogue. In the sixteen hundreds, too, the Viennese had murdered and expelled Jews from the city and destroyed their synagogue; later, they incorporated its one remaining wall into this church. As I looked up at the impressive façade, Loli's words about the Anschluss rang in my ears, "Every stone in Vienna remembers." But, I thought, did the churchgoers here hold any such memory? What a situation—where rocks remember, and people forget.

✦

Before we all left Vienna, Sidney, Micha, and I walked to an appointment at DÖW [the Archive of Austrian Resistance] to learn more about Alfred's death and Hedwig's deportation. Micha talked about his conflicted emotions surrounding the Holocaust. He reminded us that in his family the subject had been too painful to discuss. Looking at Sidney and Micha walking side by side, I realized that the parallels with Sidney's family were striking. I reflected on the widespread need for people to avoid the Holocaust—and not only Jews. It is a terrible, momentous reality, difficult for anyone to face.

Micha continued to explore his conflicting feelings, explaining that as he had learned about the Holocaust in school, he had felt embarrassed that Jews did not fight back. Why hadn't Vienna's nearly two hundred thousand Jews risen up against the Nazis? It was really a small number of guards that herded the thousand deportees onto each train. And why hadn't his grand-parents found a way to escape? He still sometimes wondered.

I had read of a Jewish sense of shame and self-blame about the Holo-caust, but hadn't expected it from this educated, thoughtful Israeli. Still, there it was, emotional rather than logical. We talked about how power-ful armies and strong nations—France, Belgium, Czechoslovakia, the Soviet Union and others—were prostrated by the German Reich, and I recounted the physical barriers to escape. Alfred's brother Arnold had been fortunate to have Ernst well positioned in Palestine, able to help him secure a place aboard an illegal ship. Alfred and Hedwig had been too old to be accepted onto illegal Palestine transports—or to climb the Alps, like Arnold's son Willi. They couldn't afford Shanghai or Cuba; they had used their resources to help their children leave. They had wit-nessed Leo's failed voyage to Cuba and Mathilde's abortive efforts to immigrate to South America. And none of the family had known about their attempt to escape illegally through Belgium and Paris, so there may have been other attempts we would never know about. If they had tried to leave, to hide, who in Vienna would have helped them? Should they have encouraged their daughters to remain in Vienna and become ter-rorists? And shot their neighbors? Or fought an impossible war against the Gestapo, and almost certainly ended up dead?

We discussed critical roadblocks to their emigration. Alfred and Hedwig had failed to find a sponsor in America, and without one they could not apply for visas immediately after the Anschluss and acquire life-saving low quota numbers. Six months later, when U.S. regulations temporarily eased, they had applied instantly, but by then the quota numbers were too high to save them. When we spoke of Alfred's letter to America, I told Micha that the only Jews I had learned about whose letters found sponsors were young and single, not an older couple; Americans' empathy seems not to have extended to adults who might be burdens.

German pressure, fearmongering propaganda, and laws impoverish-ing Jews all led nations around the world to bar their entry immediately after the Anschluss. Many Christian denominations promoted antisemitism for centuries, something that had been reinforced by Nazi propaganda and pressures. A perfect storm had trapped Alfred and Hedwig in Nazi Vienna.

Were those forces irresistible? Could they have found a way out? Certainly, they didn't make perfect choices. In hindsight, perhaps there was some opening they had missed. But they had weathered all that came at them, helped their family and others as they could, and fought to their last breaths for each other. They had never stopped fighting with the resources they had. As persecution intensified, they had only grown stronger. Their strength was heroic, I told Micha—a portrait of love and courage at a time when those qualities were in short supply.

Sidney, who had been listening, nodded. "I didn't know anything either, so it was easy to forget about the family I never knew. I learned about the Holocaust from a few books and movies. Because my family didn't tear their garments about it all the time, when I read something, I would just shut my eyes, experience something like a silent shudder, and put it away. When questions welled up, I pushed all that down—and I never asked."

Micha shook his head. It had been simpler not to know, he agreed. But now he and Sidney were striving to learn more.

★

For Micha, Celia, and Judith, this trip had been rich with new connections to their family but shot through with pain. Over several weeks we had laughed, cried, and sought answers. When we said farewell, we hugged and promised to stay in touch and meet again, which we have done. Sidney and I boarded our plane, ready to head home. It felt like we'd been gone a lifetime.

CHAPTER 33

The Present

----

*The moments of the past do not remain still. They retain in
our memory the motion which drew them toward the future.
Towards a future which itself has become the past.*

—*Marcel Proust,* In Search of Lost Time, *translated by C. K. Scott
Moncrieff (Penguin Kindle edition, 2016)*

Proust's words about our endlessly changing experience of time, history, and reality proved true for me. My attempts to comprehend Alfred and Hedwig's lives left me with a feeling of dissonance. My undeniable exhilaration at uncovering the lives of this loving, resourceful family clashed with my dejection and confusion as I encountered their hope, horror, and heartache. Was their story in the past, or does it live in the present?

Back in Eugene, my journey into the world of the Holocaust seemed like a dream of shifting fragments that did not fit together. How would I write this story? I had met Viennese who lived during the Holocaust and showed us kindness; some went out of their way to help us. My Jewish husband and I had walked across the plaza where hundreds of thousands of people had rapturously cheered Hitler, embracing a savior they imagined would rescue them from a difficult and changing world. But I also knew that many Viennese, possibly a majority, had opposed Nazism and union with Germany. Some were murdered for resisting Nazi tyranny, but most quickly fell silent. A few kind, brave souls helped Jews in small ways: groceries, a smile when even that was dangerous. But no crowd of helpful onlookers had surrounded Alfred as he lay dying on the street or Hedwig as she was loaded onto a train. I thought how unreal it must have felt to the Bergers when friends and colleagues abandoned them, and malevolence swept across the city they loved.

★

One of my most complicated and memorable interviews during our Vienna trip occurred the day before we departed—adding to my confusion. Sidney and I met with Frau Huber, a woman in her late seventies who had grown up mostly in Vienna; she was the friend of an acquaintance from Eugene and had agreed to speak with us. Eerily, we found her apartment on Taborstrasse, a few minutes' walk from the site of Alfred's fatal accident. With short grey hair and a warm, open smile, Frau Huber spoke earnestly and thoughtfully in excellent English about her experiences growing up under Hitler. Ten years old when Germany annexed Austria and a teenager at the war's end, she had joined Bund Deutscher Mädel (BDM) the girl's section of Hitler Youth, "like everyone," she told us. "It was like your Scouts. We sang. We went on camping trips. We had a drill team. I really liked the marching."

How enticing it had been. As she described it, Hitler Youth sounded healthy, fun, and harmless. Frau Huber did not mention the racist indoctrination at its core, the antisemitic propaganda, or the cultivation of boys as future soldiers and of girls as future mothers of the master race.

When she told us that her father had been supervisor of Aspang Railway Station, from where Hedwig had been deported, I was riveted. Frau Huber described the station and her family's apartment there. From its windows she had watched trains departing and German soldiers and dignitaries arriving. She remembered that Goebbels was concerned about how his uniform looked and wanted to change into a fresh one after his travel. "He was shouting and waving his stick. People [who worked at the station] were laughing at him." She had once seen Hitler. "You know what charisma is? He had it."

She asked about my research, but when I described Hedwig's death and the pits outside Minsk, she was incredulous. Frau Huber blurted out, "That wasn't the German way. They were colder, more technical. They wouldn't do it like that." She began to challenge my information on every point. "How do you know?"

"There were photographs?"

"Why would they take pictures.... Why take the Jews to the ends of the world, to Minsk, to do this thing?"

I realized how much of Holocaust research was not widely circulated and discussed in Austria at that time. Frau Huber still seemed to be living with unexamined Nazi myths. I told her that research had changed the picture that Germany had so meticulously constructed. The strategy had been to hide the mass murders from the German people as much as possible. Perhaps, Reich leaders thought, their citizens—citizens like her—would protest the large-scale murders of Jews, as they had the killing of handicapped Germans. Gestapo records document Hedwig's deportation and her death. She was sent to Minsk, where there was no camp to hold the deportees. Soldiers—against orders—wrote letters home about the murders and even sent pictures, and those letters and pictures are now published in books and on the internet. Frau Huber seemed unconvinced. I felt chilled that Germany had documented its actions, among the worst crimes in human memory, and yet that was insufficient to convince Frau Huber.

Frau Huber's father had been a Nazi party member before the Anschluss, but as the party grew more radical, he objected, and the year after the Anschluss he had been transferred to a small rural station

Around 1941, Frau Huber returned to the city as a student. I asked what she had thought, as a teenager, when she saw how people treated Jews. She looked past me, speaking to Sidney. "I will tell you two things. I have Jewish friends now, not when I was young. We've talked a lot. I was not stupid as a young girl, but I didn't realize what was happening. I had no feeling against Jews."

Sidney remained silent as she spoke, nodding, giving her a quiet space to think and to express herself. She continued, "Normally, I say, 'This is wrong,' if I see something not right. Then, I didn't. It's hard for me to understand why. Maybe because people had their own problems. It was war. I think you start to fear. And there is ignorance. This is all I can say. It was like blindness."

Blindness. There it was, blindness was woven through this story like a thread through cloth. Vienna betrayed the Jews immediately after the Anschluss, well before the Reich's many wars. But I did not argue. I turned to another example of "blindness."

"Perhaps, it was like when Americans kept slaves or stole land from Native Americans."

She nodded. "Yes, I think Americans, too, have some illusions about themselves.

"The second thing I want to say, and no one told me, I saw it myself. There were two kinds of Jews. One was 'our Jews.'"

Her voice trembled. Was she crying?

"The Viennese Jewish people were well liked. Then you had this big Jewish group coming in from the East. You understand?"

Sidney straightened, his voice tight: "They were different?" he suggested.

"Exactly. They didn't try to fit in. They looked different. They didn't care about our ways. And, you know, it's happening again. Now, they're coming in from Russia. They have money and don't try to speak our language. They don't answer when I say good morning."

I understood her concerns about outsiders. Migration is a global phenomenon, currently roiling the United States, Middle East, South America, and Europe. Still her words were alarming. "It's happening again." What was "happening"? Many more Muslims than Jews were immigrating to Austria, but she hadn't mentioned them. Did *they* all speak German? Did they greet her in the apartment hallways? Perhaps

Muslim immigrants were concentrated in a different part of Vienna, and she didn't often encounter large numbers of them. Or perhaps her reaction to them was different from her reaction to Jewish immigrants because Muslims arriving in Vienna were not tainted by two thousand years of Christian antisemitism possibly still deeply embedded in the culture.

We chatted a bit longer about easier topics with Frau Huber, thanked her for the visit and the conversation, and headed back across the canal, grateful that she had spoken from her heart. It had taken courage for her to talk so openly, but even so we were distressed. Sidney couldn't wait to talk. "Did you hear what she said about those 'different' Jews? They could have been my grandfather escaping pogroms.

"I'm different from many Jews. I'm not much interested in organized religion. I'm against tribalism. I can understand why Frau Huber could be upset if she can't read Hebrew writing on her neighborhood shops. Maybe her property lost value. I do understand. I've never felt more like an outsider than in an ultra-orthodox settlement in Israel—but that doesn't mean you can kill.

"It's a problem, how do you react to people who are different. As the only Jewish kid in my town, I know what it is to be different. Maybe I should have had more awareness about the blacks who lived there and were treated terribly." Silence. A sigh. "People can know—and not know."

★

Since receiving Alfred's letter, I had learned more about the Holocaust than I had believed possible. I'd seen many of its faces. But, as Sidney observed, you can know and not know, see and not see. Many more aspects of the Holocaust existed than I had encountered. It was violent and explosive, bloody and boldly designed for world headlines. I thought about Kristallnacht. The Holocaust was also clandestine, hidden by the German government, local governments, private groups, and individuals. I thought of the expulsion of Vienna's Jews from public parks, from their professions, and from their apartments; of the secret murders of the Jews deported to the east. The Holocaust was sometimes invisible, as hostility toward Jews often is today. It hid in the small acts of ordinary people who told antisemitic jokes, voted for racist leaders, ignored Jewish friends' suffering, or benefitted from Jews' desperation. When ordinary Germans, Americans, Spanish, Cubans, Arabs.... people around the world remained silent and hardened their hearts, permitted hatred to infiltrate their cultures, or replaced honesty with greed, those ordinary acts were far-reaching, enabling Hitler to push from hate-filled rhetoric to expulsion, murder, and then genocide.

What had happened to public outrage in the German Reich? In America? The top-level commission that President Roosevelt convened to formulate the United States' response to Kristallnacht faltered, as Secretary of Labor Perkins reported, because there had been "no crystallization of sentiment among the American people." That failure on the part of the American public killed any effective American response, as Hitler hoped it would. I remembered communications research that insists there is no such thing as an innocent bystander; there are only people who cede their authority to more outspoken influencers.

As I discovered more about the Bergers' fate, it seemed that that was how the Holocaust was built, a step at a time, from the highest levels of government to the streets and the homes of ordinary people who knew and didn't know their own power to shape the world.

I was left with as many questions as I had started with at the beginning of this quest. For one, Sidney's question about the family of his patient who had given him Alfred's letter: Why had they saved it? He had puzzled over the question. A friend had suggested that possibly they felt guilty that they hadn't done anything to help. My husband disagreed: "That may have been a small piece, but people save a remembrance for other reasons, because they're not through with it. They haven't finished processing its meaning. When I've given people the letter to read, when they hold that thin paper that Alfred and Hedwig had touched, when they see the typos, sometimes their hands literally shake. Alfred's DNA is on that paper, and then, theirs is part of it too, their own imprint on this story. You're connected. You care. There's something like the essence of a living soul in it."

Eventually Margaret, Sidney's patient, told me that the letter was more than an interesting artifact, as she had insisted at first. She said she hadn't been able to forget Alfred's plea: "Help us. This is our last and only hope." For her, Alfred and Hedwig were real. She believed that people need to remember what happened not so long ago, when neighbor turned against neighbor, because that, too, was real—and could be again.

★

When I first read the letter, it had laid bare the fault lines in my life, where my Christian heritage and Sidney's Jewish world did not fit together easily. The more I had learned about Alfred and Hedwig's lives, the more I wanted to explore that dark space where differences—of religion, race, and culture—turn people against each other. The Holocaust is an obvious failure of civilization and faith. But I did not know what I would write, how I would approach this narrative.

In the end, I decided to tell the story simply. It was difficult to imagine a conclusion. This epic is not confined to one distant location. The Holocaust happened in Vienna and Belarus, where Alfred and Hedwig died, but also in the United States, where wavering public concern for Europe's Jews prevented Congress from even temporarily increasing immigration quotas. And the State Department set policies to deliberately obstruct legal immigrants. While Britain saved many Jewish children through Kindertransports, America actually rejected a similar plan. Churches did not band together to raise their voices in protest. Despite those failures, the United States admitted more Jewish refugees than any other country, a commentary both relieving and miserable. No Middle Eastern nations offered refuge to fleeing Jews. Some courageous people, in Vienna and beyond, had shown the Bergers kindness, but not enough. Some courageous groups in the Reich had operated underground, and many Viennese died opposing Nazi crimes, but again, not enough.

At the YIVO Institute for Jewish Research in New York, I uncovered another letter from Alfred, identical to the first, sent to a "Berger" in Boston. It felt like a stab in the heart to see his plea again, and again find it unanswered. But I was glad to confirm that Alfred and Hedwig had tried in every possible way, following every path, seeking the one way, the one person who would help them. This other Berger, in Boston, was Jewish. That could have made a difference, I thought, but the YIVO archivist showed me the note that the New England Berger's wife had sent: the couple perhaps eased their consciences by forwarding Alfred's letter to the Jewish aid organization, JJDC. Mrs. Berger wrote that they had been overwhelmed with requests for help, and they hoped the organization could do something for this "unfortunate" person. But the JJDC, too, had been overwhelmed, and could only add Alfred's letter to a large file of letters that would remain forever unanswered.

The story, I had learned, has tendrils that reach in many directions. It does not remain locked in the past. Around the world, ethnic, racial, and political groups still fight and hate. Issues of persecution and prejudice, of refugees and closed doors are pressing and painful. Holocaust stories still resonate forcefully, thrusting us into the core of the human condition, and begging us to consider: Who will repair a broken world?

The evening before we left Vienna, as Sidney and I were packing, I asked him how this journey had affected him. He hesitated, then said, "As you know, unlike Celia's family, mine didn't talk about the Holocaust. I was protected from it. When we got to Vienna and learned that the city had once been about ten percent Jewish, that Jews had contributed so much to Austria, and then were chased from this part of town to that... when Frau Huber spoke about current immigrants, how *those* people looked different, dressed different... it got to be ever more real." He took a deep breath. "I don't feel more, or less, Jewish. I've always had a clear identity, but now I know more. I understand more."

How did I feel about Christianity, he asked, after learning about what had happened in Christian countries? I told him I felt less confident in religious people's living up to their ideals. Christian values were decimated by the Nazis. Even in better times, they can get lost in ritual, apathy, tribalism, and self-satisfaction. "But," I said, "religion holds up ideals for humanity to strive for, that give us reason for hope."

We could both picture our own mixed family running or hiding in those times in Vienna—and now, with neo-Nazis marching in America and in Europe. That was frightening. Before our trip I had wondered what the Viennese would think of Sidney, who "looks Jewish." Friends had advised Celia not to wear her Star of David pendant in Austria. So much denial of responsibility had occurred in Austria during and after the war. So much property taken from Jews was never returned—or returned only after bitter legal battles and decades of perpetrators ducking and dodging and denying. But in Vienna we had also encountered frequent, generous, helpful support, and seen the plaques of remembrance that the Viennese have begun installing around the city. "The past is never dead," William Faulkner wrote. "It's not even past." I told Sidney that I felt ordinary people are always remaking the past—even if they don't recognize their own power to do that—for better or for worse.

I had arranged to meet with Israeli–Austrian writer and historian Doron Rabinovici for coffee before leaving Vienna to hear about his work. He asked why I was interested in this story. I told him that I wanted to understand Alfred and Hedwig Berger's Holocaust experience. How could that have happened, I unintentionally blurted out.

He had almost laughed. "How could you possibly answer that?"

I was embarrassed for a moment. He was right. I told him about another question that had driven me to this quest, the one the journalist had asked, "Were Alfred and Hedwig Berger important?" It had shocked me. I told Doron that the letter continued to draw me in because the story of these seemingly unimportant people is not finished. It lives in troubled places around the world where, under repression and hatred, also lives hope—people who believe in their own power to repair a broken world.

I told him the truth: I couldn't explain the Holocaust. People wiser and more knowledgeable than I have tried, yet the questions persist. The Holocaust is endlessly troubling—and it should be. I told him I couldn't answer those questions about how it could have happened. But I could ask them. And I can hope that others will continue to ask, because the letter, in many forms, is still being delivered.

And so I returned home and began writing the story of Alfred and Hedwig Berger, a blind salesman of socks and a homemaker with a song in her heart.

Epilogue

Alfred and Hedwig Berger's family suffered greatly during the Holocaust. With the indomitable spirit of their forbears, their descendants have found paths to recovery. The extended Berger family lives on three continents. Alfred and Hedwig, who loved children, have four grandchildren, ten great-grandchildren, and twenty-six great-great-grandchildren. The Bergers bear the scars of one of the darkest, most vicious times in human history and turn that darkness to light with their own lives.

Martha and Leo lived happily in New York with their daughter, Celia. Martha taught piano; Leo worked in the men's clothing industry and continued with his art. Celia, with three master's degrees, has retired from a long career as a counselor in New York City schools and is an artist and musician.

After landing as a refugee in Palestine in 1938, Gretl married another recent refugee, Moshe, who had arrived three years earlier from Libya. They worked hard on a moshav [farming community]. Their son Micha, whose birth brought joy to Alfred and Hedwig's last days, recently retired as chairman of a university science department and

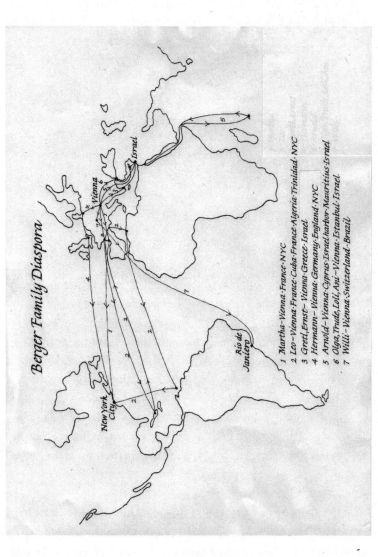

Berger Family Diaspora. *Courtesy of Timothy Hall, calligrapher, Seattle, Washington*

consults internationally. Gretl's first daughter Judith retired as an obstet-
ric nurse and teacher, having helped several thousand babies of all races
and religions into the world. Gretl's younger daughter, Ofra has worked
with her husband on the farm of a different moshav. Together, the three
families have ten children and twenty-three grandchildren—Gretl's
great-grandchildren, Alfred and Hedwig's great-great-grandchildren.

Of Hedwig's four siblings, only Olga, the wife of Alfred's brother
Richard, survived. So did Olga's three daughters—Trudi, Loli, and
Ani—who together have four children and thirteen grandchildren. Hugo,
his wife Hella, and their five-year-old daughter Eva Ruth, and also Julius
and his wife Edith were transported from Theresienstadt to Auschwitz
in 1944, on the last transport before liberation. They perished just before
the war's end. Julius's twin brother Otto died in Austria's Mauthausen
death camp in 1941. Of the 90,000 Jews living in the pre-war Bohemia-
Moravia region of Czechoslovakia, home to the Grünberger family, only
424 survived.

Alfred was one of five siblings; three, including Alfred, perished.
Mathilde Berger Mose, a vibrant widow interested in Vienna's literary
culture, was deported and died in Riga in 1941. She was probably among
the Viennese deportees who were summarily shot and interred in a mass
grave. Richard Berger sought safety in various Central and Eastern
European cities until he became trapped in Czechoslovakia between
retreating Nazis and advancing Soviet forces. He fled with remnants of
the Slovak resistance forces in late 1944 or early 1945. According to a
witness, Richard, suffering from severe illness and unable to run further,
took poison and died in the woods near Teplice, swearing that the Germans would never take him alive.

Hermann Berger escaped to America and lived in Manhattan, with
his wife Magda [Mitzi], daughter Lisl, and her husband Fritz. Lisl and
Fritz had one child, Peter, and one grandchild. After the war, the family
started several businesses and lived comfortably, visiting often with
Martha, Leo, and Celia.

After a harrowing 1940 escape by ship from Vienna, Arnold and
Mitzi Berger did not land in Palestine. Held by the British in a ship

anchored off Palestine's coast, they watched in horror as a sister ship crammed with Jewish refugees burned and sank. They lived out the war in a British internment camp in Mauritius, a tiny Indian Ocean island where many prisoners died of tropical disease. At war's end, the British transported surviving prisoners, including Arnold and Mitzi, to Palestine. Their oldest son Willi trekked through the mountains to Switzerland and emigrated to Brazil, where he worked in textiles, taught piano, and started a successful import business. Their younger son Ernst reached Palestine with Gretl in 1938 and later married Herta, who had sailed with them on the "pirate" ship to Palestine. Willi and Ernst had two children and two grandchildren.

Richard and Olga's daughter Ani, a nanny for the Turkish Foreign Minister in Ankara from 1938 through 1941, begged her employer for travel visas through Turkey for her Czech uncles. But German and Turkey had signed a Non-Aggression Pact in summer 1941, ensuring Turkey's cooperation with Germany in trapping the Jews. The minister only shook his head and said that even he was unable to grant such a request. In New York Martha received a cable from Simmons Tours to come to their office about a ticket for Hugo on a ship to New York, but Hugo had no way to reach that ship.

Leo's sister Sabina and her daughter Myra were trapped in Trembowla, Poland, first by Soviet rule and then by the German invasion. Nazis pulled Sabina's husband from their home, and he was never seen again. Fleeing a ghetto roundup, Sabina escaped with three-year-old Myra out a back window of their home and ran to the countryside, a few gold coins sewn into their multiple layers of clothing. Robbed during their narrow escape, they saved their coins and reached the farm of a Polish family who had done business with Sabina's family's leather shop. The Polish family hid them, at great risk to themselves, for three-and-a-half years—first in an underground pit in a vegetable garden, and then in a secret room above a barn. Myra learned that she must never speak over a whisper. Liberated by the Soviets at war's end, Sabina and Myra made their way across Europe to an American displaced persons' camp. After two years in the camp, they were able to contact Leo in New York.

He was at work when he received the call informing him that his sister had survived, and he fainted at the news. He had been saying the Kaddish prayer for the dead for her for a year. Myra and Sabina lived with Leo, Martha, and Celia for several years until they were able to move into their own apartment. Myra became a clinical social worker, married, and has two daughters and six grandchildren. Some years after the war she was able to help members of the Polish family who'd saved their lives to immigrate to the United States. She nominated the family, and they were named Righteous Among Nations, an honor given by Israel to recognize non-Jews who risked their lives to rescue Jews from the Germans.

Bernard and Paulina Toch survived the war in Vienna as a mixed Jewish-aryan couple. They were able to send their two children to America in 1941 to live with a family who answered the Tochs' random letter begging for help. The children grew up in Los Angeles. Five years after war's end, they reunited with their parents, but by then they were acclimated to American life. They only resided briefly with their parents after their "temporary" separation. Had Germany won the war and the Toch family remained in Vienna, they all would have been exterminated.

The extended Berger family in the United States, Israel, El Salvador, and Brazil remain in close touch. Their wry humor still keeps them laughing.

Acknowledgments

S o many people contributed their thoughts, information, resources, and support to this book that I hesitate to name them for fear of omitting someone. I am immensely grateful to you all. My appreciation and admiration for the Berger family is impossible to overstate. Their stories and documents—including hundreds of letters, newspaper clippings, official documents, and photos—are the foundation of this book. Celia and Mark, Micha and Chava, and Judith and Avraham energetically contributed all the information they possessed with patience and friendship. They have been central to my research. Celia, especially, spent countless hours, despite cranky computers, providing documents, family stories, wisdom, and humor. It was never easy for her, but her dedication to helping me tell this story has been essential. The memories, photos, boundless support, and friendship of Micha and Judith were also crucial to this story. Hermann and Magda Berger's grandson, Peter Wulkan, keeper of the priceless Vienna Room, provided extraordinary hospitality and generous access to his trove of family documents. Alfred and Hedwig's nieces Ani Goldschmidt and Lola Fischbein patiently, intensely, and carefully discussed their family and life in Vienna; sadly, they passed away before this book was finished.

Myra Herbst told me the story of her hair-raising escape with a strong, gentle spirit—and a home-cooked dinner. Amnon Berger, nephew of Alfred and Hedwig, made the effort to provide me with family documents and stories during his difficult visit to Vienna. Willi Berger's widow Judith kindly shared stories of her husband's escape through the Swiss Alps. The family's boundless support has made this book possible.

Gertrude Toch Goldberg and Herbert Toch, descendants of Bernard and Pauline Toch, provided letters, photographs, and stories that were difficult for them to talk about. Deborah Wallach Stauthammer, granddaughter of Bernard Toch's sister, also went out of her way to assist me. Clarence and Beatrice Berger's relatives in California and Canada offered informative stories and documents. Marta Trefusis-Paynter wrote me an extraordinarily detailed account of her and Gretl's escape from Nazi Austria.

I am indebted to Ronald Goldfarb, my brilliant agent, and his associate Gerrie Sturman. Publisher Alex Novak and editor Elizabeth Kantor at Regnery Publishing offered me their steady, intelligent support on many levels, and most important, their belief in this book.

Any errors of fact in this book are my own, but I owe an immeasurable debt to a number of scholars, including Michael Berenbaum, a founder of the U.S. Holocaust Memorial Museum, scholar, professor, rabbi, writer, filmmaker, consultant, and much more. My training is in journalism. He generously offered to review my manuscript for historical accuracy. I'm indebted to him for his generous spirit and guidance. Raul Hilberg, eminent Holocaust scholar, now deceased, offered invaluable advice and helpful documents by mail and during a visit to his home. Judith Baskin, eminent Jewish scholar, offered her support throughout this lengthy writing process.

A number of people at archives and libraries made significant contributions to this work. They include Miriam Intrator who helped find documents during the early stages of my research at the Center for Jewish History and the Leo Baeck Institute in New York; at the Dokumentationsarchiv des Österreichischen Widerstandes, Vienna, Dr. Elisabeth Boeckl-Klamper, who provided sensitive, wide-ranging information to me and the Berger family, and Dr. Ursula Schwarz, who helped me find my way through the archives; the members and resources of Eugene JewishGen, who helped with breakthroughs locating Berger descendants; Valery Bazarov and Estelle Guzick at HIAS, New York, who answered innumerable questions; Heidrun Weiss, Wolf-Erich Eckstein, George Gaugusch, and Alexander Raninger with Israelitschen Kultusgemeinde, Vienna, who provided invaluable names, dates, and places; The Jabotinsky Institute, Tel Aviv, which connected me with survivors; the Jüdisches Museum, Vienna, which shared important information about Jewish life in Vienna.

Drs. Manfred Fink and Hubert Steiner at Österreichisches Staatsarchiv, Vienna eased the way for my research there. Photographs at Österreichische Nationalbibliotek, Vienna, were very helpful for understanding Vienna. YIVO Institute for Jewish Research, New York, provided innumerable resources connected specifically to the Bergers, as well as documents associated with their Otto Frank Exhibition.

The impressive resources of the United States Holocaust Memorial Museum, Washington, D.C., were made infinitely more accessible by the patient, insightful, and generous experts there, who helped to research and provide direction for my detailed questions. They connected me with resources in Germany, Vienna, and Belarus. My heartfelt admiration and gratitude are due to Michlean Amir, Peter Black, Martin Dean, Pat Haberer, Hans Safrian, Paul Shapiro, Anatol Steck, and Megan Lewis for their thoughtful responses to my many emails and phone calls.

Dr. Herbert Koch, senior archivist at Wiener Stadt- und Landesarchiv, Vienna, offered patient and expert personal assistance when less would have been much easier. Gideon Greif and Frumi Shchori helped me navigate archives at Yad Vashem, Jerusalem. Dr. Crista Hammerl at Zentralanstalt fuer Meteorologie und Geodynamik, Vienna, provided clear, precise historical weather information and became a much-appreciated email friend.

In Vienna, Mag Margit Parlow, owner of the Bergers' Schmalzhofgasse apartment building, permitted us to enter the building, emailed us a building floorplan, and answered questions. Her generous help in the early days of our Vienna trip was a reassuring gesture of Viennese generosity. Israeli-Austrian award-winning journalist and historian Doron Rabinovici met with me over coffee in Vienna, trusted me with his research documents, and asked helpful, provocative questions.

I also owe gratitude to Mount Holyoke College for its Alumnae Scholarship, which enabled my travels and work. Patrick Gariepy was essential in helping research specific questions. Librarian Mikki Segall located the obscure newspaper with the story of Leo Cizes's ill-fated Cuban voyage. Leonard Gross and Bob Welch, both authors of Holocaust books, and Debra Gwartney, Duncan McDonald, and Lauren Kessler, outstanding authors and teachers, helped me progress through stages of my work.

I have been hampered by not speaking German. Hilde Geisen (Geisenheimer), dear Hilde, survivor of four years in Thereseinstadt concentration camp, cheerfully translated several hundred pages of documents for me and explained nuances of Viennese culture and life under the Nazis. ("April 20, today? Oh yes, Hitler's birthday. They always had something 'special' planned for us that day. One time, they marched us into an open field. We didn't know what they would do. Maybe shoot us. They made us stand there in the rain and cold all day. I got typhus in the camp.") Hilde and I formed a deep friendship and met regularly until her death in November 2017.

Others also have been crucial to the translating. Carola Balcke in Germany, cheerfully offered her expertise with particularly difficult Berger family letters and with other inexplicable mysteries of language and culture ("hausfreund"). Dieter Manderscheid helped to translate letters and documents and shared a letter from his personal collection written by a German soldier in Minsk. Jim McWilliams, Alice Resseguie, and Barbara Campbell also generously provided important translations. Michaela Grudin generously offered a careful reading.

My ever-supportive writing group, with current members Amalia Gladheart, Elizabeth Lyon, Barbara Pope, Geraldine Moreno-Black, Ellen Todras, and earlier members Mabel Armstrong, Kari Davidson, Carolyn Kortge, and Zanne Miller, gave generously of their time, talent, and fearless criticism. They are wonderful writers all—thank you.

Did I forget my family? I saved the best for last. Sarah, Daniel, Jonathan, Mark, and Samuel have given me faith in this project, their interest, jokes, questions, and support in innumerable ways. And Sidney, my rock, I cannot begin to describe your many, many contributions.

Reader's Guide

ABOUT THIS GUIDE

This reading-group guide for *The Unanswered Letter* includes an introduction, discussion questions, ideas for enhancing your book club, and a Q&A with author Faris Cassell. The questions are intended to help your reading group find new and interesting angles and topics for discussion. We hope that these ideas will enrich your conversation and increase your enjoyment of the book.

INTRODUCTION

In 1939, as the Nazi menace closed in, Alfred Berger mailed a desperate letter to an American stranger with the same last name, begging for help. He and his wife, Hedwig, Viennese Jews, had found escape routes for their daughters, but with funds and connections exhausted, they themselves were unable to flee.

Fifty years later, Alfred's letter ended up in the hands of Faris Cassell, an award-winning journalist who couldn't rest until she had discovered the Bergers' fate. Traveling across the United States as well as to Austria, the Czech Republic, Belarus, and Israel, she uncovered an extraordinary story of heart-wrenching loss and unforgettable love that endures to this day. Called "a poignant and unforgettable journey of determination and discovery" by bestselling author Georgia Hunter, *The Unanswered Letter* is a book you won't soon forget.

TOPICS & QUESTIONS FOR DISCUSSION

1. Describe the letter that leads Cassell to find the descendants of Alfred and Hedwig Berger. Cassell notes that she was "the third 'Madam' to read this letter" (p. xxiii). What effect does it have on each of the women who reads it? Why do you think that each of them chooses to hold onto the letter? How did you feel upon seeing the facsimile of it within the pages of *The Unanswered Letter*? What do you think you would have done if you had received the letter?

2. Michael Berenbaum, the former project director at the United States Holocaust Memorial Museum, called *The Unanswered Letter* "a work of power and passion," saying "it is not the story of six million anonymous victims, but of one person, six million times." Explain the difference. What is the effect of reading the story of how one family was affected by the Holocaust? Were you surprised by anything you read? If so, why?

3. In the foreword to *The Unanswered Letter*, Cassell explains that she uses a "relatively new convention" that she encountered in James Carroll's writing. Like him, she has elected to delegitimize the "pseudo-scientific, racist term 'Semitic' by writing the 's' in lower case and eliminating the hyphen in 'anti-Semitic' and 'anti-Semitism'" (p. xix). She also made the decision to lowercase the term "Aryan" in her writing. Why do you think it was important for Cassell to include this note? What role does language play in legitimizing hate and discrimination? Were there instances when the Nazi Party employed language to give credibility to their claims

and actions? What were they? Can you think of any instances of this happening today?

4. Discuss the structure of *The Unanswered Letter*. As Cassell focuses less on her search for information and reveals more about the Berger family, she focuses on each character's attempts to flee separately. What effect did that structure have on you while you were reading the book? Did you find yourself wondering about the fates of other family members?

5. Ani instructs Celia not to speak with Faris Cassell. Cassell writes "It struck me that Ani's defensiveness had similarities to the Los Angeles Bergers' response to Alfred's letter" (p. 29). What reasons might Ani have had to be wary of Cassell and her questions? Why do you think Celia was open to talking? What would you do if you were in Celia's place?

6. In her letters to Martha and the rest of the family, Gretl "[minimizes] her poverty and health problems," choosing to write only "about the best parts of her life" (p. 372). Why do you think Gretl chooses to gloss over the difficulties in her life? How does each family member attempt to protect the other members in his or her letters?

7. While conducting research to learn more about Hedwig and Alfred Berger, Cassell was able to obtain some of their registration cards. Cassell finds herself "drawn to the sheer physicality of the cards. Unlike today's computer-generated data, the handwriting held its own information" (p. 20). What do the records tell Cassell about Hedwig and Alfred? Think of objects that you and your family have—cards, applications, passports—what clues would the ephemera of your own life give a stranger about you?

8. Celia tells Cassell, "Growing up, I lived with a Holocaust mentality. I think I was born with it" (p. 40). What does she mean by that? How does this mentality show itself in Celia's actions? Do you think that this mentality is passed from one generation to the next? Explain your answer.

9. Who is Frau Huber? Describe her interaction with Cassell. Frau Huber says "The second thing I want to say, and no one told me, I

saw it for myself. There were two kinds of Jews. One was 'our Jews'" (p. 420). What does she mean by this statement? How does she use it to justify her inaction? Why does Cassell find the conversation so unsettling? What do you think of what Frau Huber says?

10. When Cassell brings up the possibility of visiting Minsk and "[Sidney's] family's village, [he] balked at visiting either place" (p. 108). Were you surprised by his reaction or that of Cassell's mother-in-law? Why or why not? Why are they so against the idea? Discuss the effect that visiting Belarus has on Sidney.

11. When Amnon arrives in Vienna, he brings documents with him that verify his father's military records in the Austrian Army service because he intends to apply for Austrian citizenship. He tells Cassell, "Life in Brazil is good now, but one never knows. A second passport could prove useful" (p. 179). Given that Amnon's family risked their lives fleeing Austria, Cassell is amazed by this disclosure. What did you think of it? Why might Amnon feel safety in having a second citizenship? How has he been shaped by his family's history?

12. In the fall of 1941, as Jews in Vienna found themselves facing an "onslaught of laws and ordinances that battered their lives," Alfred and Hedwig report that they would be sharing the High Holidays with Mathilde, the Toch family, and other friends (p. 327). In light of all of the oppression that they faced because they were Jews, why do you think the Bergers chose to observe the holiday? What role do holidays play within a religion or culture? How might observing Rosh Hashana and Yom Kippur have brought Alfred and Hedwig a feeling of community and solace?

13. What effect does being in the "Vienna Room" have on Cassell? Describe the room. Why do you think that Peter decided to set up the "Vienna Room" in his house? Do you have any objects that have been passed down through your family in your home? If so, how do you display them?

14. Sidney tells Cassell, "People can know—and not know" (p. 421). What prompts him to say this? Explain his statement. Do you agree? Why or why not?

15. Ani and Loli described Hermann as a "snob person," and, upon Celia's first reading of his translated letters, "his superficiality made her angry" (p. 234). Explain their initial impressions of Hermann. How do Celia's feelings about Hermann change as she begins to read more deeply into the letters? What pressures were Hermann and other Jewish refugees like him under?

ENHANCE YOUR BOOK CLUB

1. Cassell writes, "Old photos are gifts from the past, opening a frozen moment" (p. 85). Did seeing photos of Hedwig and Alfred Berger and the rest of their family enhance your reading of their story? Take a look at your old family photos and share them with your book club, taking time to tell stories about the events captured on film. Does revisiting the photos help put you back in the experience?

2. When talking about Hedwig, Celia praises her cooking, telling Cassell, "We still use her recipes. Her strudel with lemon peel in the dough is memorable! And I serve cucumbers her way—cold, sliced very thin, sprinkled with salt and pressed under a heavy plate" (p. 37). Have any recipes been passed down in your family? Tell your book club about them—or, better yet, cook them and share them with your book club.

3. While in Vienna, Cassell writes that Alfred and Hedwig's descendants were "realizing that they had their own Exodus story, their own *Night*—Elie Wiesel's story of love, pain, and horror" (p. 104). Read *Night* and discuss it with your book club. In what ways is Wiesel's story like that of the Berger family? How does reading about Wiesel's experiences in the Nazi concentration camps add to your understanding of the experiences of the Berger family?

4. Cassell writes that "stymied in their effort to mobilize public opinion, some America Jews turned to alter egos—artistic creations that demonstrated their patriotism and excoriated Nazis" (p. 344). Examples she cites include "Captain America" and *Casablanca*, which

was inspired by events in Vienna. Read, watch, and listen to some of the art created by American Jews during this historical period, then discuss it with your book club. Was the art successful in promoting an anti-Nazi message? Do you think that art can sway public opinion? If so, can you give recent examples where art has caused you to reconsider a political or philosophical position?

A CONVERSATION WITH FARIS CASSELL

Q: Congratulations on the publication of *The Unanswered Letter*! Is there anything that you have found particularly gratifying about the book's release? If so, what?

A: Every story about the six million Jews lost during the Holocaust is precious. Research for *The Unanswered Letter* uncovered new information and insight about the Holocaust and about the human condition. Alfred Berger's desperate letter was written in 1939, long before I was born. I felt that it came to me for a reason and that I had a responsibility to bring this story into the light of day. I'm grateful I was in a position to do that. The story carries a message that remains crucial for us today.

Q: Pulitzer Prize–winning novelist Larry McMurtry praised *The Unanswered Letter*, calling it "a wonderful book about a terrible subject" and saying, "I found it hard to put down." High praise coming from a novelist! Between your vivid writing and the frenetic pacing of parts of the Berger family's story, *The Unanswered Letter* reads like the best fiction at times. Was this a conscious decision when you began writing? How were you able to strike the balance between the dense history you cover in the story and the more lyrical sections?

A: Thank you for those kind words. Many drafts of this book preceded the final version. I'd been accustomed to writing newspaper features—much, much shorter pieces than this book—but that discipline of discovery, prioritizing, and organizing was crucial for writing the book. Writing draft after draft of *The Unanswered Letter*, learning how to organize the vast amount of information I was discovering, gave me time to ponder how such a disaster could have happened. I read deeply about the Holocaust and was inspired by profound thinkers and great writers.

Q: You tell Sidney that conducting research is "many steps in place. No progress until you open the right door" (p. 169). It was fascinating to read about the instances when you did find the "right door" as you followed the story of Hedwig and Alfred Berger. Were there any particularly thrilling discoveries for you while writing *The Unanswered Letter?* What about the rest of your career? Can you share any instances when you discovered a particularly surprising "right door"?

A: Those doors!!! You have to knock on many doors to find the "right one." Probably the most important door that opened for me belonged to Celia Cizes. I spent months learning how to access public documents like Social Security records of deceased people. Step by step, I finally came to her doorstep—figuratively. Her amazing collection of family records, photos, letters, and her memories were key to this book. Without her trust in me and her help, the book could not have been written. Several other discoveries set my heart racing. The chance meeting with Amnon, the Bergers' great nephew from Brazil, opened the door to discovering the unknown plot to assassinate Hitler. The former Hitler Youth member we met in Vienna was an acquaintance of a good friend of mine. Those connections were lucky, but they couldn't have happened if I hadn't kept knocking on doors.

Q: Early in your quest to learn more about Alfred and Hedwig Berger, you recount that you reached out to a journalist at the *New York Times* whom you "had intended to ask . . . about his research, but he jumped ahead, asking bluntly, 'Were they important?'" (p. 14). *The Unanswered Letter* is a powerful answer to that question. If you could speak to that reporter again, is there anything else you would say in response to that question?

A: Wow, a great question. I understand that the journalist spoke in a professional and rushed way, asking me if the Bergers were well-known, influential news-makers. Even so, ideas about who is news-worthy continue to evolve. I'm interested in a different kind of journalism. Even the most humble, unknown person is important, and stories about ordinary people can change the world. Witness George Floyd.

Q: You write that "Hermann's ledgers, never intended to be read like a memoir, were a surprising communication from the past" (p. 77). As you began conducting research into the Berger family's story, were there any other unexpected sources that provided you with insight?

A: Peter Wulkan's "Vienna Room" still brings a smile to my face. He had not only saved family records but created a space that gave me a feeling of Old Vienna. Walking through that door opened the world of the Austrian Empire for me and made the family's close bonds, their terror, and their desperate efforts to escape feel real to me. Also, of course, I was stunned to discover that the woman who had been a member of Hitler Youth was also the daughter of [the supervisor of the] Aspang train station from which Hedwig was deported. She remembered, as a child, watching Jews being loaded on trains. She remembered watching Göring's train arrive after the Anschluss. He was notoriously vain about his appearance, and she had seen him yell and fuss about changing his uniform before he would leave the train. She said he seemed ridiculous "waving his stick," his military baton, around. I didn't have space in the book for all of her recollections.

Q: After finishing *The Unanswered Letter*, readers are likely to want to learn more about their own family history. Can you offer them any guidance on how to go about learning more based on your own experiences? What resources did you find particularly useful?

A: A number of people have contacted me asking that question. I'm glad to help people with a few shortcuts. For Jewish families, JewishGen.org is a great resource with local chapters that welcome visitors. They offer guidance and maintain collections of resources. Germany and Austria keep amazing records, as does the Arolsen Archives International Center on Nazi Persecution. I found Vienna's city archives and the DÖW and IKG in Vienna to be a treasure trove of guidance and information. In New York, the Center for Jewish History and HIAS are wonderful archives. These are sources for Jewish genealogy and history. A wealth of other helpful genealogy organizations are easy to find online.

Q: You write that the "Holocaust was sometimes invisible" and go on to say, "I remembered communications research that insists there is no such thing as an innocent bystander, there are only people who cede their authority to more outspoken influencers" (p. 422). Having seen the effects of inaction, are there any specific actions that you think your readers can take to combat invisible oppression and discrimination?

A: This is a big question, but the solution is simpler than it might appear. Americans love to organize so it's easy to find groups online or through friends or religious organizations; they work on problems as close as your neighborhood or as distant as international politics. I think the hardest step is the first one. Ask yourself, when I look back on this year, what effort will I be glad I've been part of?

Q: You recount how your mother-in-law forbade you and your husband from going to Belarus and your own parents "remained ambivalent about my quest" (p. 110). In light of their reactions to your pursuit, how did they react to the news that you were publishing *The Unanswered Letter*? What did they think of the finished book?

A: That's difficult for me to answer. My parents and my mother-in-law died before the book was finished which is a sadness for me. Though skeptical in the beginning, they all became supportive as I persevered and made progress. They would have been moved by the story and by the message that we are all important and can make a difference in the world. I learned that from my wise, but very human family.

Q: What would you like your readers to take away from *The Unanswered Letter*?

A: I hope that readers of *The Unanswered Letter* will find the story compelling. An author may have certain wishes, only to discover that the story moves different people in different ways. This is really a book of questions. I believe that the Bergers, an ordinary family caught in extraordinary times, carry a message of love and hope, heartache and courage. I hope people will be inspired by their story and find their own answers to the questions.

Q: Do you have any advice for aspiring writers? Is there anything that you wish you had been told at the start of your writing career?

A: My message to aspiring writers is this: Believe! Believe in yourself, believe in your work, and never give up. I'm very glad no one told me at the beginning how long it would take me to finish this book.

Q: Are you working on anything now? Can you tell us about it?
A: I'm considering a number of options. I'm very interested now in how Americans are coping with the many refugees still pounding at our doors.